The History of the Christmas Card

THE HISTORY OF

THE

CHRISTMAS

CARD

by

GEORGE BUDAY

SPRING BOOKS · LONDON

741.68
B927

Originally published 1954
Copyright 1954 by George Buday
This edition published 1964 by
Spring Books
Westbook House · Fulham Broadway · London
Printed in England by Richard Clay and Company Ltd.
Bungay · Suffolk.

PREFACE

IN my attempt to piece together the story and to rescue the fading colours and vanishing sentiments of the Victorian and Edwardian Christmas card, which was, of course, my main task in this book, it was my good fortune to find many kind helpers. In varying degrees and in various ways, they all contributed to my work on this subject.

First of all I am greatly indebted to Her Majesty the late Queen Mary, who was gracious enough not only to bring her delightful personal collection of old and new Christmas cards to London (from Windsor Castle), but honoured me by the loan of the full eighteen albums in her collection. I am also most grateful to Queen Mary for her characteristic, kind thought in identifying and noting the senders of the cards in her collection, which was a most helpful co-operation. I should also record my grateful thanks for her gracious permission to photograph and reproduce an extensive selection from her cards. This selection was no easy matter for me, since every card in her collection automatically commands great public interest by the fact that it was included in it, in addition to the often historic personalities of the senders. Her Majesty Queen Mary showed a most encouraging and helpful interest throughout my work on this book, and I am deeply grieved that it will not now be possible to dedicate this book to her, as I hoped to do.

I am also greatly indebted to the late Mrs. Lilian Frances Strongitharm, a great collector of Victoriana and a very dear friend, for her manifold interest and help.

I should like to acknowledge my thanks here alphabetically with the same gratitude for the loans or in some cases gifts of examples or selections of old Christmas cards made by Mrs. M. E. Armstrong, F. M. Atkins, Esq., Mrs. D. E. Bell, C. Birnstingl, Esq., Mrs. Marjorie Bowhill Gibson, the Rev. Fr. Daly Briscoe, the Rev. Dr. Rosslyn Bruce, Mrs. F. J. Burnley, Mrs. P. R. Butler, G. E. Camm, Esq., Mrs. R. J. Chaplin, Mrs. Astley Clarke, Gerald Cobb, Esq., F. A. Davey, Esq., Mrs.

v

PREFACE

Cynthia de Alberdi, H. J. Deane, Esq., Lord Doverdale, James A. R. Dryden, Esq., the Rev. Canon Gilbert Elliott, Miss Flanagan, Miss Emily Ford, Miss A. Grasemann, A. P. Green, Esq., Mrs. G. C. L. Griffin, David R. Hardman, Esq., Miss M. F. Hardy, Miss C. M. Harris, the late Mrs. Florence Haxell, Mrs. L. Hopkins, Dr. Bela Ivanyi, Mr. E. Willis Jones, Miss M. Agg Large, the Rev. John H. Layton, Miss W. I. Leonard, the late Guy Little, Esq., The R. Mander and J. Mitcheson Theatre Collection, Mr. and Mrs. Gerald Mann, Miss Joan Marsden, Mrs. G. McPhail, F. H. Melhuish, Esq., Frank Newbould, Esq., Mr. and Mrs. John S. Nichols, Mrs. M. Steppat, Robert Swan, Esq., Major A. G. Wade, and Miss J. M. Winmill.

The Trustees of the British Museum and the Director of the Victoria and Albert Museum, London, were good enough to permit me to study, photograph and reproduce a number of Christmas cards in their respective collections. I should like to express also my thanks to the Keepers and their assistants, who were most helpful during my researches. My sincere thanks are also due to Mr. Clarence S. Brigham, Director of the American Antiquarian Society, Worcester, Mass., and the Directors of the Museum and Art Gallery of Sunderland and the Harris Museum of Preston for information about Christmas cards in their collections. A great deal of useful information reached me as the result of my letter published in *The Times* (in December, 1946), for which I am grateful to the Editor.

I wish also to express my thanks to Miss Charlotte Angel, Miss M. Barker, Douglas C. Bartley, Esq., W. Turner Berry, Esq., and the Technical Library, Saint Bride Institute, London, under his care, John P. Boland, Esq., F. E. Bryant, Esq., Harry G. Carter, Esq., Mr. Ernest Dudley Chase, the Lady Cynthia Colville, Keith Ewart, Esq., F. C. Friend, Esq., Dr. L. Gerevich, J. Gordon Hassell, Esq., Mrs. M. Hellmann, A. M. Hind, Esq., Stanley A. Kisch, Esq., Commander A. D. Lacy, R.N., the Lady Constance Milnes Gaskell, Professor W. Frazer Mitchell, Selwyn Oxley, Esq., Mr. Stephen Q. Shannon, Dr. D. E. Sharp, Desmond Tuck, Esq., Miss F. J. Vinter, Frank J. Ward, Esq., W. F. Wardley, Esq., Mr. Frank Weitenkampf and Major J. L. Wickham for useful information, the loan of otherwise unavailable sources, or for other, much appreciated, personal assistance.

PREFACE

Finally, I should like to express my thanks and gratitude to my friends and close collaborators in the actual production of this book, Miss Pamela Booth, who with her well-known skill and thorough knowledge of modern photography, took most of the necessary photographs for my work, and Miss T. M. C. Bremner, who assisted me in many ways in the preparation of this book.

GEORGE BUDAY

CONTENTS

CONTENTS

ILLUSTRATIONS

(When not otherwise stated the card is reproduced from the author's collection.)

COLOUR PLATES

DUST JACKET 1. Christmas card of the 1870's, size $5\frac{3}{4}$ by $3\frac{1}{2}$ inches. 2. Sixth card from the set " Father Christmas and His Little Friends " of the early 1870's, published by M. Ward. The set was issued also in the form of concertina booklet and at least four varieties of embossed edges are known. Size about 4 by $2\frac{3}{4}$ inches. 3. A modern American French-folder card, printed on a four-colour offset machine. Size, folded, $4\frac{1}{2}$ by $5\frac{1}{2}$ inches. 4. S. Hildesheimer card of the 80's, heavily frosted. Size $3\frac{3}{4}$ by $5\frac{3}{4}$ inches. 5. Chromo with gold background, probably produced by Canton in 1872 or before ($4\frac{1}{2}$ by 3 inches). 6. Gold-embossed and scallop-edged card of the 70's. The four layers of scraps on it can be elevated ($4\frac{1}{2}$ by $3\frac{1}{16}$ inches). 7. One of a set of three designs by R. Dudley, published by Castell Brothers (No. 504). Size $4\frac{1}{2}$ by $3\frac{1}{2}$ inches. Brief greeting texts on the backs. 8. Lithograph in colours with stuck on chromo of Father Christmas. 1870's, size $3\frac{1}{4}$ by $4\frac{3}{4}$ inches. 9. Two cards from a concertina type Christmas card, " Father Christmas, His Procession " by Moyr Smith, published by M. Ward probably in 1875. Size of each section $4\frac{1}{4}$ by 3 inches. 10. Embossed scrap, *c.* 1877-8. 11. A rare, scallop-edged card of the 1860's ($2\frac{1}{2}$ by $3\frac{3}{4}$ inches). 12. Early shaped card produced by Joseph Mansell ($2\frac{5}{8}$ by 4 inches). 13. One of a set of two designs of the 1870's, with sentiments by L.N. on the reverse of each ($2\frac{5}{8}$ by $4\frac{5}{8}$ inches). *Agg Large collection.* 14. Early De La Rue card (No. 95). Probably of 1875, size $3\frac{1}{4}$ by $2\frac{3}{8}$ inches. 15. " Apollo and Daphne " (1880's), designed by R. Dudley. Castell Brothers, No. 505. Gold bevelled card of $4\frac{1}{2}$ by $3\frac{1}{2}$ inches. 16. From Louis Prang's booklet (1864, $2\frac{1}{2}$ by 4 inches) of C. C. Moore's " A Visit from St. Nicholas " designed by F. O. C. Darley or T. Nast (?). *E. Willis Jones collection.* 17. Scrap of 1880. 18. Back page of a triptych card (S. Hildesheimer, 1884 or 5) containing five gold edged pictures. $4\frac{1}{2}$ by 6 inches. 19. " Dressed " card of velvet, tinsel and scraps of the 70's. Size $1\frac{3}{4}$ by $3\frac{1}{2}$ inches. 20. S. Hildesheimer card of the 1880's. Size 3 by $4\frac{5}{8}$ inches. 21. Embossed scrap of 1870. 22. Santa Claus of the early 1870's. Nast's chromolithograph from one of six spreads (original size about 9 by 11 inches), published by McLoughlin Brothers, New York. *E. Willis Jones collection.* 23. Folder card of the 1890's. Size $3\frac{1}{4}$ by $4\frac{3}{4}$ inches. 24. Canton scrap of *c.* 1866-7. 25. Frosted Mansell scrap, slightly embossed, 1870. 26. Gold background chromo published by Joseph Mansell, 1870, 3 by $4\frac{1}{2}$ inches. 27. Embossed and scallop-edged chromo card published by Dean in the late 1860's. Size. *c.* $2\frac{1}{2}$ by $3\frac{3}{4}$ inches. 28. Goodall chromo of the 60's, probably by Bennett. Size $3\frac{3}{4}$ by $2\frac{5}{8}$ inches. 29. Jewelled, scallop-edged and embossed folder, a private card of the 1890's ($4\frac{1}{8}$ by $3\frac{1}{8}$ inches). 30. De La Rue card (1879, reprinted in 1881) of a set of three, No. 186. Size *c.* $3\frac{3}{4}$ inches square. 31. Chromo of 1870 or earlier ($3\frac{1}{2}$ by $2\frac{1}{2}$ inches). 32. Composite " made up " card of scraps, gilt lace-paper, oval of the 1870's. About $3\frac{3}{4}$ by $5\frac{1}{2}$ inches. 33. Scrap of the 1880's. 34. From a set of three designs (" Apparition of Father Christmas ", No. 216, De La Rue), probably by Kilburne (1879 or 80). Size 5 by 3½ inches. 35. Walter Crane's design, 1874-5, size 4⅛ by 2½ inches. 36. Scallop-edged, tint background card of the 60's (size 2⅝ by 3½ inches). 37. Saul Steinberg's pen and ink " Christmas Tree "—a folder card published by The Museum of Modern Art, New York, in 1949. Size 5 by 7 inches. 38. Chromo card of 1880. Size 3⅝ by 4⅝ inches. 39. Sulman card with added chromo partly stuck on. 1860's, 2¾ by 4 inches. 40. Marcus Ward card from a set of six, also published as a concertina-booklet entitled " Ye Newe Yeere Greetynge " in 1870 or 1. Embossed silver edges, gold background. Size *c.* 4 by 2¾ inches. 42. The second of the " Father Christmas and His Little Friends " set of cards, but with different margins. Size 3⅞ by 2¾ inches. 42. Scrap of 1878. 43. The third of the " Father Christmas and His Little Friends " set with yet another embossed border decoration. Size as No. 2. 44. Folder card of the late 1890's with cut-out or partly shaped top page. Size of the card 5 by 3⅜ inches.

I (a) Petter & Galpin colour lithograph of the 1850's (4¾ by 3⅛ inches).
(b) Colour lithograph of the 1850's (*c.* 4¾ by 3⅞ inches).
(c) Goodall card by Luke Limner of the 1860's (*c.* 4⅝ by 2¾ inches).
(d) One of a set of Baxter process cards (4½ by 2¾ inches).

II Chromolithograph of the early 1870's.

III (a) and (b) A pair of pin-pricked cards, one of them dated 1864. Size 2½ by 2½ inches.

IV (a) Scallop-edged, embossed card with stuck on chromo (about 1860) of 2⅝ by 3¾ inches.
(b) One of the first Bennett cards published by Goodall in the 1860's. Size 2⅝ by 3¾ inches.

V Chromo from a set of three, on Marcus Ward mount (1870). Size 3¼ by 4⅝ inches.

VI§ Luke Limner design with S. C. Hall sentiment, published by M. Ward (1860's). Size 2¾ by 4¼ inches. (Sometimes mounted on fine lace-paper).

VII§ Baxter process print of the 1860's (*c.* 3½ by 4¾ inches).

VIII Walter Crane's " Fortuna " of 1875 (*c.* 4¼ by 3⅛ inches).

IX Kate Greenaway's design published by M. Ward in 1876 or 7, one of a set of two. Also issued with different border design. Size 3½ by 5¼ inches.

X W. S. Coleman card (De La Rue, No. 415) from a set of three (1881). Size 3¼ by 7 inches.

XI (a) American card of the 1880's, *c.* 3¼ by 7¼ inches.
(b) Dora Wheeler's prizewinning card published by Prang (in 1881) with C. Thaxter sentiment on reverse. Size *c.* 7 by 8¾ inches.
(c) Red background card of 1878, published by L. Prang. Size 3½ by 8¼ inches.
(d) American card published by John A. Lowell (No. 16 A) in the 1880's. Size of engraving 6⅝ by 4½ inches, but printed on larger mounts.

XII§ Lithograph printed in six or seven colours, combining hatching, stippling as well as flat colours in the 1860's. Original size. *Marsden collection.* Its reverse is blank and the card was " folded in three " to fit the envelope fashionable at the time.

XIII (a) One of a set of two Eyre & Spottiswoode cards of the 80's. Size 4½ by 3⅛ inches.

HALF-TONE PLATES

ILLUSTRATIONS

ILLUSTRATIONS

ILLUSTRATIONS

ILLUSTRATIONS

ILLUSTRATIONS

ILLUSTRATIONS

ILLUSTRATIONS

176* Five in one tab card with Kate Greenaway's "winter" design from her Flowers and Fancies set of four cards of 1875. Size when fully extended 7¾ by 11¼ inches.

177* "Dissolving views" type of embossed, deckle edge trick card in original state. Size (not including small tab at bottom of the card) 4¼ by 5½ inches.

178* Transitional state of the same card, when the tab is half pulled out.

179* Complete change of the picture mounted on the card. *H.M. Queen Mary's collection.*

180* Two mechanical cards including metal tab constructions. *Victoria and Albert Museum.*

181* Scallop-edged tab card, with cut out oval centre, of the 1870's. Size of front (without 1½ inches long tab) 2¾ by 4 inches. Depth, when animated, 1¼ inches. *Leonard collection.*

182 Scallop-edged, richly gilded mechanical card of 1875-6, when animated. Original size 3 1/16 by 4½ inches, 3 1/16 by 6¾ by ⅞ inches when "animated."

183* Shaped and "porcelain enamelled" oval facsimile card of a dish (1880). *Victoria and Albert Museum.*

184 "Daring" mechanical card of the early 1890's, probably published by Faudel, Phillips & Sons. Size (without tab) 3½ by 4¾ inches.

185* Trick card folder of *c.* 2⅜ by 5⅛ inches, partly opened.

186* The same card fully opened.

187* Three dimensional jewelled and embossed animated card published by W. Hagelberg in the late 1880's and early 1890's. Size originally 5 1/16 by 4⅛ inches, with 1¼ inches depth when extended. *H.M. Queen Mary's collection.*

188* One of the first "private cards" by J. Goddard (1876). Size 5¾ by 6¾ inches. *Astley Clarke collection.*

189* Gold bevelled black card of the 1880's with reproduction (mounted gold panel). Size 2½ by 5 inches. *Fr. Daly Briscoe collection.*

190* One of three angel head designs of 1881-82 by James Sant (Tuck cards). Size 5⅜ inches square.

191* One of a set of three angel head designs of 1880-81 by Rebecca Coleman (Tuck cards) with Eden Hooper sentiment on back of cards. Size 4 9/16 by 5 1/16 inches. The set was issued also in editions of 3¾ by 4⅜ inches.

192 Gold background single page card published by Goodall in the early 1870's. Size 2 13/16 by 4 9/16 inches.

193* Madonna and Child by Alice Havers (Hildesheimer and Faulkner card of 1886). *Victoria and Albert Museum.*

194 Madonna and Child card, pen and ink design by Aubrey Beardsley. Published in *The Savoy*, January, 1896.

195 Madonna and Child card, wood-engraving (printed in red with black lettering) by Eric Gill. Published by Hague and Gill, High Wycombe, 1930's.

196* French wartime card of 1915, designed by Louis Vallet and published by "Le Rire Rouge". (Burning red heart used as a lighter.) *H.M. Queen Mary's collection.*

ILLUSTRATIONS

ILLUSTRATIONS

LINE BLOCK FIGURES

Photographs of the cards for plates and figures marked by an asterisk (*) were taken by Pamela Booth, F.R.P.S., those marked by § were taken by J. Allan Cash, F.I.B.P., F.R.P.S., and those marked by † by Keith Ewart.

The half-tone blocks for Plates 1, 8, VI, VII, XII and Plates II, V, VIII, XV, were very kindly lent by the Editor of *The Geographical Magazine, London*, and the Odhams Press Ltd., London, respectively.

"MY CHRISTMAS CARDS"

The following is a small sentiment, written by Miss Burnside, a prolific Victorian Christmas card poet, for a Christmas card printed in the early 1880's which was stuck—as a motto—on the first page of many old scrapbooks of the late Victorian period.

" My Christmas cards,
              Oh while I look
My store of pictured
                treasures through,
As in the pages of a book
I read kind greetings,
                sweet and true
And faces rise upon
                the waves
Of mem'ry, that o'er
                Time's dim sea
The treasures of its
                nooks and caves
Are softly bringing
                back to me—

And some are gay
                and some are sad—
Yet cannot bring me
                thoughts of pain.
'Tis only memories
                sweet and glad,
That Christmas cards
                bring back again.
For all are fraught with
                hope and love.
So may the card
                I send to thee
In some hereafter
                Christmas prove
A happy memory
                of me."

Introduction

"AMONGST the many odd things about the Christmas card is the fact that the phrase does not occur in the Index of the *Encyclopaedia Britannica*", stated a recent delightful fourth leader in *The Times*. Further on in the same article it is mentioned that " it would seem . . . that the moment has come for a centenary celebration ; and who would withhold tribute from an institution which has brought so much harmless pleasure—and no annoyance beyond the occasional humiliation of having been beaten at the post-box by one's friends and so put in the position of a mere returner of compliments ? "

This charming tribute to a popular institution with international implications of goodwill and friendship was well in line with the traditional attitude of the public towards Christmas cards. Another leading article published in the same columns in 1883, and written in the same spirit, if in the to us somewhat archaic language of those already far-away years, began as follows :

" The spirit of good fellowship which the Christmas festivities engender among every class may fairly be taken as one of the best results of this ever-popular and welcome season. It may, of course, be true to a certain extent that the universal practice of wishing one another the compliments of the season, is followed in many cases out of mere conventional necessity, but, on the other hand, there can be no doubt that this wholesome custom has been more frequently the happy means of ending strifes, cementing broken friendships and strengthening family and neighbourly ties in all conditions of life. In this respect the Christmas card undoubtedly fulfils the modern method of conveying Christmas wishes and the increasing popularity of the custom every year is for this reason, if for no other, a matter for congratulation."

But in spite of the pleasant notices which have appeared in the leading papers, a more comprehensive survey on the story of the Christmas card is yet to be attempted. It may be argued that since Christmas cards are ephemeral their curriculum and interest is necessarily a slight one. Nowadays the lifetime of the Christmas card is that short period of conspicuous display from its arrival just before Christmas to Twelfth Night, when, according to tradition, all Christmas cards and other festive decorations are cleared away. It is generally thought that the oblivion into which they then fall should be complete and undisturbed.

This attitude of the present generation does not, however, resemble the attitude of their parents, grandparents and great-grandparents towards Christmas cards of their day. The new cards in the shop windows were often reviewed in the Press of the last century, the Christmas cards arrayed on a family mantelpiece were not only examined, discussed, enjoyed or criticised by all the family and guests (an appreciation which was often more genuine and intimate than that accorded to the pictures hung on the walls !), but the treasured existence and appraised charm of the season's favourite cards continued to be cherished for years after the critical first Twelfth Night in their career. They were stuck with much loving care into precious albums and scrapbooks often given as Christmas presents for this purpose to Victorian children, who were taught to fill the pages year by year with their cards, scraps and mottoes, often noting under each the year and the name of the sender, Mamma, Papa, Auntie, and so on. Many of these albums still survive to bear witness to the tender care with which they were compiled, as well, as evidenced by the well-thumbed, dog-eared pages preserving the fingerprints of many generations, as proof that no doubt on special occasions or on very wet days they were brought out and enjoyed over and over again.[1] An aura surrounds these old albums, and one cannot but regret a little that some of the sentiments and the leisure required thus to express them are forever past history.

[1] In her " Letters from Broadlands " Blanche discloses a new and more mercenary reason for collecting cards in the early 1900's. " People are simply most immensely mean about Christmas cards," she wrote. " A year ago Aunt Goldie sent me the card I'd sent her the Christmas before. C'est bien elle ! I sent it to her again this Christmas."—More recently Harold Nicolson alluded to " the problem (which) arises when Twelfth Night has passed and all these bits of cardboard have to be taken down." (Spectator, December 31, 1948). He sends his to " an institution of inebriates " who " enjoy cutting out the pictures and pasting them on screens ", but describes the still more delightful method devised by " a versatile and inventive friend." " The moment he receives a Christmas card he puts it in an envelope and posts it on to someone else. If the card has been inscribed by some affectionate hand, " Love from Pamela " or " With the compliments of Messrs. Rickshawe, Court Hairdressers," he does not trouble to erase these inscriptions. He merely adds the words " and Richard." He contends that this method . . . gives added pleasure to his friends. Not only do they get their cards, but they are left wondering who Pamela may be."

INTRODUCTION

Most Christmas cards may be of little interest from one year to the next, but are certainly not without interest when inspected in a longer perspective. Victorian cards were an integral part of the Victorian Christmas ; they were in the focus of the most intimate annual holiday for all ; they were carefully chosen and individually considered by their senders and no less carefully studied in every detail when received. How could they fail to tell us many interesting things of their time and people—if only we try to understand their language ? Once we approach them with some understanding of their own conventions, these old witnesses of past decades will reflect forgotten aspects and intimate corners of life and mind. Those little items of fashion which held the day, those sentiments and attitudes, wit or pose which were almost second nature to those who lived generations before us, and which, because they were so very trivial and obvious in their time, were nevertheless part of the atmosphere of the period, though easily over-looked by chroniclers of the more prominent events.

Moreover, in the manufacture of Victorian Christmas cards we witness the emergence of a form of popular art, accommodated to the transitory conditions of society and its production methods. Popular art is often thought to be identical with, and exclusive to, the folk art of the not yet industrialised, peasant communities. It is thought to be dependent on the Nature-near and diffuse outlook of the peasant. But the same needs which inspire folk art in a peasant stage of society still exist in higher phases of its development. Forms of expression could be found, and these may take advantage of the possibilities of new media and production methods. Broadsides and chapbooks were, for instance, manifestations of genuine " popular art " surviving the Industrial Revolution. Printing did not extinguish popular art automatically, but in broadsheets, etc., became its medium. It is therefore not absolutely essential for popular art products to be hand-carved or hand-painted individually. They could, and in an industrial society would indeed, be also made by machinery. But it is essential that the products should be inspired by and fit into the way of thinking, the tradition system, and ordinary life of the common people. The latter should be able and willing to determine the character and trend of production by " imposing their own tastes on the products of the craftsman or the machine, in contrast to the more sophisticated art

3

made by specialists for wealthy patrons ", to use a recent definition of popular art. In this sense a good majority of the Victorian Christmas cards may be properly classified as popular art in a highly industrialised society.

This recognition should prevent us from attempting to apply to Christmas cards the same kind of criticism which would be applicable to canvasses in a fine art gallery or museum.

" It seems perfectly unnecessary to explain here the objects of a Christmas card ", wrote G. White in the special number of the *Studio* devoted to the subject in 1894. To-day it is equally, if not more, superfluous to define the Christmas card and its purpose, which is just as well, since a definition with any degree of scholarly accuracy would be no easy task.

Manufacturers of early Christmas cards could not dream of the revolution which was to take place in the means available for the transport of the descendants of their product. Nevertheless, just as a letter remains a letter however it is passed on, so the Christmas card also retains its essentials, whether transmitted by telecommunication, aeroplane, helicopter, ocean liners, steam or electric trains, road transport or by simple hand-to-hand delivery. Neither can Christmas cards be defined according to their substance or size. The majority are made of pasteboard or paper, but satin and silk and a great number of other materials were frequently used in their manufacture—even real dried codfish skin, produced for a Gloucester, Mass., firm of fishmongers. Thus no definition can exclude any on account of the material used in its manufacture. Neither can any definite size be taken as essential for a Christmas card. Victorian publishers produced sets of pretty Christmas cards not larger than an ordinary postage stamp. But the smallest Christmas card that I know of was a grain of rice, given to H.R.H. the Duke of Windsor (then Prince of Wales) in 1929,[2]

[2] It was stuck on a paste board of $3\frac{1}{4}$ by 2 inches and the text on the actual grain of rice, inscribed in Indian ink, read :
" To His Royal Highness
The Prince of Wales,
Sincere Christmas Greetings
From The
Joseph G. Gillott Pen Co.,
London, England
Season 1929."
(This unique " card " is preserved in Queen Mary's collection.)

and perhaps the largest was the card sent to President Coolidge in 1924, which was a folder of 21 by 33 inches, designed by Merton Wilmore of the Rust Craft Company, the well-known modern American Christmas card publishers. No production process, style of design, subject of text or decoration could be described as *the* characteristic of Christmas cards.

For the purposes of this book I take as a Christmas card any variety designed as such and which was at a given period and by a fair number of people considered as such. This draws attention to the necessary limitations of a book devoted to this subject. During the Victorian period alone (which is, of course, our main interest in this book) tens of thousands of different patterns of Christmas cards were published. " To identify and collect a specimen of each might exhaust a lifetime ; to classify and appraise them would be like compiling a dictionary ", wrote White. Jonathan King, the Nestor of all Christmas card collectors (who, in addition to trying to buy samples of every card published in his time, even managed to buy up some of the manufacturing firms in the latter half of the nineteenth century), aimed at possessing a copy of every single design, and gathered a collection of immense proportions, turning his houses in Islington into a " museum " of Christmas cards, but even he could not see his dreams realised. In the 1890's his collection, " weighing collectively between 6 and 7 tons ", included about 163,000 varieties of Christmas cards published between 1862 and 1895, but mainly after 1880.[3]

My aim as a collector or as the author of this book is not so ambitious. If knowing a little more about the things we love makes us appreciate them a little more, then I trust that my efforts to gather together some data and information will not have been wasted for those who are interested in a pleasant tradition, now growing old, and which is essentially a tradition of affection and goodwill towards all.

[3] In addition, King collected valentines and toy theatre sheets. The latter were presented by him to the London Museum in 1912, the year before his death. His Christmas card and valentine collections, on the other hand, were stored until, in 1918, the greater part of them was destroyed by fire. Some of his albums, etc., however, were purchased by Frampton and other London print-sellers and " . . . many fine specimens have been slowly seeping into this country ", states R. W. Lee, the American writer (1952).

" THE FIRST "
Christmas Card

L I T T L E more than half a century ago, Gleeson White, the prominent writer on art in the 90's and Editor of the then new art magazine, the *Studio*, gave 1846 as the date of the first Christmas card. " The origin of the Christmas card ", he said, " is fortunately for its future historians not lost in the mists of antiquity, that popular hiding-place of all sorts of origins." Unfortunately, another sixty years have been long enough to prove that this assumption was incorrect. The first Christmas card, as we now know it, was produced in 1843.

John Calcott Horsley (later made a Royal Academician) designed it on the initiative of Henry (later Sir Henry) Cole. It was printed in lithography by Jobbins of Warwick Court, Holborn, London, and hand-coloured by a professional " colourer " named Mason. The edition was " published at Felix Summerly's Home Treasury Office, 12 Old Bond Street, London ", by Cole's friend and associate, Joseph Cundall. According to Cundall, " many copies were sold, but possibly not more than 1,000 ". The price was 1s. per copy.

There is also some confusion in Sir Henry Cole's own memoirs as to the exact date of the first Christmas card. In the first volume[1] he alludes to the official G.P.O. figures, which showed an increase of more than 11½ million letters over and above the ordinary correspondence and 4 tons of extra registered letters in Christmas week, 1880, representing a total postage revenue of £58,000. With some pride, he adds : " The net revenue from Christmas cards has been largely increased by the card designed for Felix Summerly by John C. Horsley, R.A., in 1845." In the second volume of the memoirs there is a reproduction of it (between pp. 162-3) and in the caption 1846 is given as the date of the Cole-Horsley card.

Henry Cole was a very colourful character of the Victorian era: an energetic reformer, educationist and ardent improver of public

[1] *Fifty Years of Public Work of Sir Henry Cole, K.C.B.*, 2 vols., edited by his son and daughter (Alan S. and Henrietta), London, 1884.

taste. His name was closely associated with the Great Exhibition, the foundation of what is now the Victoria and Albert Museum, and many useful reforms, including the penny post, perforated postage stamps, postcards, etc. He had to fight for his ideas all his life, and was " one of the best-abused men of the century, so far as things artistic are concerned ". The tone of his memoirs, its extensive documentary material, suggests that it was written in answer to bitter contemporary critics, who, for example in the columns of the respectable *Art Journal*, would label him " a man of wild theories and vague speculations, which are Utopian in their character ", charging him with " unfitness " and " utter incapacity for the duties he undertakes " !

Cole's enterprise, the Summerly's Home Treasury, received similar attacks. It is true that in its " Announcement " Cole himself described " most of the Children's books published during the last quarter of a century " as " hurtful to children " and " Peter Parleyism ". " The many tales sung or said from time immemorial, which appealed to the other, and certainly not less important elements of a little child's mind, its fancy, imagination, sympathies, affections, are almost all gone out of memory and are scarcely to be obtained." Summerly's Home Treasury purposed to produce illustrated books, " but not after the usual fashion of children's books, in which it was assumed that the lowest kind of art was good enough to give first impressions to a child ". Amongst the books published there is an early volume of traditional nursery songs illustrated by Cope, Redgrave, J. C. Horsley, T. Webster and Linnell, and such books as *The Ballad of Sir Hornbook, Chevy Chase* with notes and music, *Little Red Riding Hood, Beauty and the Beast, Jack and the Bean Stalk, Cinderella, Jack the Giant Killer, Reynard the Fox*, and so on, illustrated, besides those already mentioned, by Corbould, Tayler, Townsend and Mulready. But Summerly did not confine his Treasury to books. Cole aimed at the imagination of the child. He put on the market perhaps the first " Colour Box for Little Painters " equipped with " the ten best colours ; Slab and Brushes ; Hints and Directions and Specimens of Mixed Tints ". Another important novelty originating from the Home Treasury was a box of terra-cotta playing-bricks, " geometrically made, one-eighth the size of real bricks ; With Plans and Elevations ", and a set of " Tesselated

Pastime ", " A Toy formed out of Minton's Mosaics with Book of Patterns ". All these, together with his numerous reproductions of the works of the Old Masters and contemporary foreign artists, speak for the character of the pioneer work done by Henry Cole in the field of child education and recreation. At this time of Summerly's endeavours to cultivate " the Affections, Fancy, Imagination and Taste of Children " the masses of the population were still more or less illiterate, and it was not until the 80's that people generally could read street-signs, shop-boards and notices. Some contemporaries, however, who could read and write used their accomplishments to attack him, for example, on his appointment as Superintendent of the School of Practical Art, as " Mr. Cole, of Felix Summerly notoriety ", " one whose taste, knowledge and experience are of a singularly low order ", blaming his " very crude theory relating to the Schools of Design, and his peculiar mode of trying to ' wed Art and Manufacture ' ".

It is not surprising that in such an atmosphere of bitter attack and counter-attack the to modern eyes certainly innocent, perhaps too innocent, subject of the Cole-Horsley Christmas card did not escape sharp adverse comment. This came on account of its supposedly dissipating influence[2] by " encouraging drunkenness ". White also alludes to this charge, but he doubted " if we investigated all the cases of drunkenness in all these years, could we find a single one remotely traceable to this design of Mr. Horsley's, or any of its fellows ".

In the 1880's, when Christmas cards were most fashionable topics and their manufacture big business, Horsley, by then an elderly man himself, wrote a letter to the Editor of *The Times* : " In your article of the 25th inst. upon Christmas cards, you refer to the fact that I designed and drew the first of these cards in 1846. I think it right to explain that I did this at the suggestion and request of my friend, the late Sir Henry Cole, who, at the period named, devoted much time and

[2] In fairness, it should be mentioned that when his turn came in the 1880's, it was Horsley, by then a celebrated Royal Academician, who led the equally ill-natured campaign against the nude model, or, more exactly, against the use by artists of models in the nude. He called this immoral, an undesirable infiltration of the mentality of Paris into the artistic world of England, and his agitation gained for him the nickname of " Clothes-Horsley " amongst artist friends. Whistler's " *Horsley soit qui mal y pense* " was a characteristic comment !

The first real Christmas card, designed by J. C. Horsley in 1843 at the suggestion and request of his friend, Henry Cole. The photograph shows a particularly interesting copy : it is the one sent to Henry Cole by the artist who signed the card by a small caricature of himself with palette and brushes. The date is clearly "Xmasse, 1843".

PLATE I

PLATE 2   The British Museum official photograph of another copy of the Cole-Horsley card, also sent by Horsley, signing himself by a palette and brushes, in 1843, to "his friends at . . . (undecipherable)."

PLATE 3
(left)

Two anonymous early designs probably from the early 1840's, carrying New Year's greetings.

PLATE 4
(right)

PLATE 5   A section photograph, much enlarged, of the signature and controversial date of the Egley card in the Victoria and Albert Museum.   The question is: Is it 1842, 1848 or 1849?

PLATE 6 One of the original pencil sketches for the Egley Christmas card design, now in the collection of the Victoria and Albert Museum.

PLATE 7 The much-debated Christmas card designed by W. M. Egley. For some time this design was thought to be older than the Cole-Horsley card and thus to be " the first " Christmas card.

PLATE 8

An ironical Italian New Year's greeting for 1703, engraved by M. Mitelli, of a Utopian paradise where rivers flow with milk and honey, trees produce clothes and finery, tables load themselves with delicacies, carriages move without horses, and so on. Only the man attempting to work is imprisoned (see: bottom left corner)!

PLATE 9
(left)

A baroque "emblematic New Year's card" for 1738, designed to hang on the wall. Its ambitious composition contains world-political aspirations in pictures and text.

PLATE 10
(right)

An early example of a print-merchant's *quodlibet*. Note the print with a figure in black whose posture conveys the greeting.

PLATE 11 The defence and security of Zurich is stressed on this card of the Constaffler Association of that town in 1703. Its object was to obtain support, probably both moral and material, for the association.

PLATE 12 An early nineteenth-century print illustrating the New Year's " visitors ", with cards and bills, at the house of a prosperous burgher.

PLATE 14 Christmas letter notepaper heading illustrating the seasonal pleasures of "Youth and Age", one of the immediate predecessors of the manufactured Christmas cards.

PLATE 13 (left)
A New Year greeting of "The Model", by Joseph Bergler. Note the unmistakable supplication in the attitude and inverted hat.

PLATE 15 The Japanese interpretation of a celebrated Japanese beauty. A *surimono* by Gakutei.

PLATE 16 A Victorian representation of Japanese beauty on a celebrated Christmas card by Rebecca Coleman, published in 1880.

PLATE 17

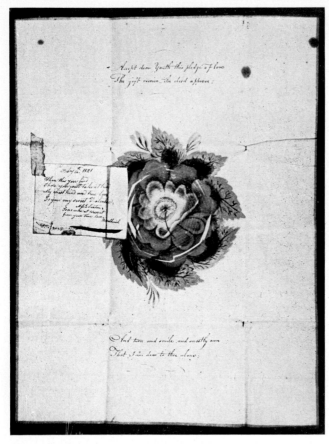

A charming example of "Grandfather's love-making" as described by its owner. It was sent by a tenant-farmer in the wilds of Devon for February 14th, 1821, and is about 7 by 9 inches in size. The deep red rose encircled by green leaves is partly painted, partly stuck on the sheet of pink-edged notepaper. The petals of the rose were cut into fine strips, so that when the attached silk string is pulled, the cut lines are elevated, and through them can be seen two co-joined hearts enclosed in a blue lover's knot, burning on their own fire. Above and below the design is written in fine small letters:

" Accept dear Youth this
    pledge of love
  The gift received, the
    deed approve ;

" And turn and smile, and
    sweetly own
  That I am dear to
    thee alone "

On a small scrap of paper in tiny letters is the note originally hidden behind the rose petals :

"When this you find   My most kind and true love
    I hope you will take it kind   To you my sweet Valentine,"

after which comes the name of the girl.

PLATE 18
Made up from various ready-made elements and scraps, this small (4½ by 3 inches) card well combines the hand-made valentine and the earliest Christmas card. Note the layers of real lace and sparkling silver, also the silk oval with the greeting text and holly wreath in red-and-green embroidery.

PLATE 19 A selection of tiny notepapers and envelopes decorated with brilliantly coloured and gilded Christmas designs in colour-lithography and diestamping. Most of the designs are by Luke Limner.

PLATES 20 and 21 Fashionable small visiting cards were decorated with an engraving of a vista in Rome or symbolic figures in the late eighteenth century. The handwritten "Captaine Shirley" occupies the space reserved for the visitor's name.

PLATE 22 "Mrs. Robin" sets forth to pay a visit. Humanised robins seen out visiting, going to church, giving red holly berries to "poor" robins and enjoying Christmas dinner, were popular on early cards.

PLATE 23 Dignity and Impudence are meeting in the farmyard on this small and old Goodall card. Probably designed by Crowquill.

PLATE 24 This small card appears in almost every scrapbook of the  early 70's. It was produced by Marcus Ward in soft, warm colours.

PLATE 25 "A bird in the hand is worth two in the bush !"

PLATE 26 Two charming postcard size surprise or "voiced" bird cards which look as though they were printed on somewhat thicker cardboard. Only when held in the hand and a little pressure is applied does the trick appear. This is a concealed whistle which chirps like the robin or quacks like the duck and so on, according to the bird pictured on them. These were given to Queen Mary by her mother, Princess Mary Adelaide, in 1878.

PLATE 28   The peacock, whose feathers were much coveted by the aesthetes, was destined to be a fashionable bird for a time on Christmas cards.

PLATE 27   Jacob, the goose, a mascot enlisted at Quebec in 1838 and died on detachment at Croydon, 1846, adorns this military Christmas card.

PLATE 30

PLATE 29   A card of three robins in the rain : two are sheltering under bracken, the third, a cock robin, is bravely facing the storm on a bramble. Note the pairs of butterflies in each corner of the border designed by Thomas Crane.

PLATE 30   It is difficult to understand the wide popularity in the 1880's of Christmas cards picturing small dead birds, often robins (on the right). The mottoes, " Sweet messenger of calm decay and Peace Divine", and " But peaceful was the night, wherein the Prince of Light, His reign of peace upon the earth began" hardly help to solve the puzzle.

PLATE 29

MAY LOVE AND FRIENDSHIP BRING THEE CHRISTMAS CHEER!

PLATE 32

A HAPPY CHRISTMAS

In Jesus there is
boundless store,
The Cross of Christ
is mercy's door.

PLATE 31   An early visiting-card robin design produced by R. Canton in the 1860's.

PLATE 32   A decorative small design of ferns and holly around a wooden cross from the early 70's. Many variations of this type followed in succeeding decades.

A MERRY CHRISTMAS AND A HAPPY NEW YEAR

PLATE 31

PLATE 35 One of a set of three attractive De La Rue Christmas cards by Robert Dudley. The pearl of the mistletoe is personified by a pretty girl with gossamer wings, against a pretty end of the century decorations.

PLATE 34

The inside page of a small and naïve Christmas card made up of various scraps and cut-outs stuck into a home-made folder, including the amusing dancing scene under a gigantic bunch of mistletoe. (1870).

PLATE 33 A typical Christmas card by Thomas Crane. The almost "documentary" spray of mistletoe is well brought out against the richly gilded and "architecturally" designed background.

PLATE 36   Queen Wilhelmina of Holland usually designed her own cards for Christmas, which were frequently reproductions of her own attractive landscapes.   The one reproduced was made for Christmas, 1943, a pleasant forest scene sketched in 1932.   Note "*Ipsa fecit*" in Queen Wilhelmina's handwriting.   Size, 6¼ by 5¼ inches.

PLATE 37   In the style of the "modern" *quodlibets* of the 80's, this Marcus Ward card combines in its design winter and summer motifs. Note Kate Greenaway girl in one of the panels.

PLATE 38.   A delightful Marcus Ward card of 1874 with very decorative flower design which is emphasised by the pale landscape in the background.

PLATE 39 Lilies of the valley painted in thick white paint so as to have the effect of reliefs, are the feature of this attractive, richly embossed and silk-frilled card. Its size is 4¾ by 4 inches, and when the folder is opened two hearts outlined by wreaths of similarly painted lilies of the valley, forget-me-nots and delicate green leaves are seen combined. Published by Marion, date, 1895.

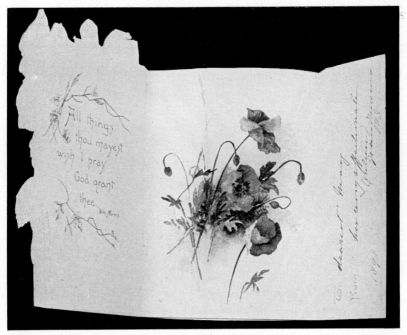

PLATE 40 A charming folding Christmas card featuring poppies, loosely "bunched" in the artistic manner of the 90's. The right-hand panel bears the handwritten dedication by Queen Victoria to Queen Mary, then Princess May. Note the motto by William Morris on the left-hand panel.

CHRISTMAS.

THE COLLECTOR.

In the morning, and the nice Roast Beef,
And then the Goose of noble style,
Who wish for us, with hearty good,
Come us, from the far country.

Old Christmas gives then, as they come in,
And gathers from our plate of quick
A tithe for all the poor.

The little Pigs grunt and the Geese all quack
Upon the Charity Bonzes they feast,
And will give to those who wish most.

THE PUDDING THAT CUT AWAY

Such a pudding how what do you say!
Runs, pudding that would run away,
But hastened on with his knife and fork.

It was a good pudding you may be sure,
Just wired himself up for the old good flavour,
And just from the dish if you wish for crumbs.
So from all good people the like of hish.

Remember that when egg pudding time comes,
You scrape the dish of the very last crumbs,
If it should so come who wish our part,
You must make a pudding to cut away.

PLATE 42 (*above*) A Goodall triptych card (1860's) designed by Crowquill, with Father Christmas as "the collector", and the personified Pudding "that cut away".

PLATE 41 (*on the left*) The two cards on the top are from a series called "Christmas Advances". The bottom picture is from a set of much-praised designs by H. Stacy Marks, R.A., made for Marcus Ward in 1873.

A Merry Christmas and a Happy New Year.

PLATE 43 Weeping piglets carry in the traditional boar's head on this tiny visiting card size Christmas card of the early 70's.

THE COMPLIMENTS OF THE SEASON, AND ALL GOOD THINGS IN REASON.

They're doomed for Christmas frowns and chine, for rigs must die that men may dine.

When the old lady who sits high and dry,
Picks the white feathers, Christmas is nigh.

PLATE 45 The anticipation of a plentiful Christmas dinner was a popular subject. This card from the 70's shows Father Christmas as the King of Misrule courtiered by a turkey, rabbit, goose, piglet and a couple of wine-bottles in full dress, knighting with his sword a huge "Sir Loin" of beef seen kneeling before the throne.

PLATE 46 (*right*) A delightfully coloured and printed decorative design for a "white Christmas" card.

A merry
Christmas
to her friend,
Mayst thou its
days right
gaily spend

PLATE 44 The punch-bowl was, of course, a frequent subject on Christmas cards, enjoyed not only by dwarfs, as in this card.

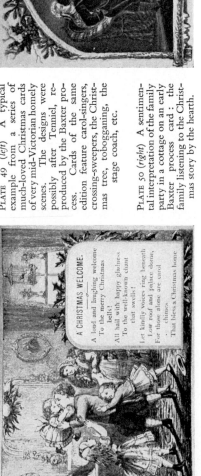

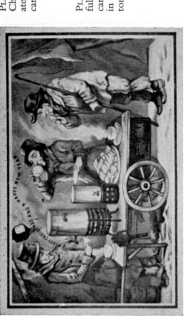

PLATE 47 (*left*) A Dickensian Christmas atmosphere emanates from this De La Rue card showing the humbler pleasures of the poor.

PLATE 48 (*right*) A delightfully produced De La Rue card, surprisingly well printed in the 70's in many pale and toneful colours. Size, about 6 by 3¾ inches.

PLATE 49 (*left*) A typical example from a series of much-loved Christmas cards of very mid-Victorian homely scenes. The designs were possibly after Tenniel, reproduced by the Baxter process. Cards of the same edition feature carol-singers, crossing-sweepers, the Christmas tree, tobogganing, the stage coach, etc.

PLATE 50 (*right*) A sentimental interpretation of the family party in a cottage on an early Baxter process card : the family listening to the Christmas story by the hearth.

PLATE 52

PLATE 55

The "innocent mirth" of two Victorian belles, in which Father Christmas plays a rather pathetic part.

A vigorous coach journey taken in his childhood by "Grandpapa", "going to *his* party", by G. Cruikshank, (Jun.), 1882.

PLATE 53 A white Christmas dominates the design on this visiting card size, lace-edged Christmas card from the late 60's.

Etched card by Tristram Ellis, "Father and Mother Xmas on the Ice !" of about 1880.

The Christmas coach laden with passengers and presents of game and other good things, a feature of the old-time country life, and thus of Victorian Christmas cards.

PLATE 51

PLATE 54

WISHING YOU A JOLLY CHRISTMAS.

PLATE 56 A newspaper boy in tattered trousers and bare feet riding a penny-farthing and cheerfully "Wishing you a Jolly Christmas" with the Latest News of the late 1870's.

PLATE 57 A little girl offering a nosegay to a little boy riding a tricycle. The lace framed oval picture can be lifted by means of a ribbon attached to its top and behind appears the sentiment, ending :
"Accept then in this bleak December,
A merry Christmas Dear, from me."

WITH GREETINGS FOR THE NEW YEAR.

PLATE 58 Another form of "transport" is demonstrated on this delightfully period Christmas card of 1880.

ingenuity in getting artistic treatment applied to ' unconsidered trifles' as well as to weightier matters.''[3] He confirmed this also in another letter addressed to Jonathan King. In this letter (published by James Laver in 1938) Horsley states that " Mr. Henry Cole . . . conceived the idea of an illustrated Birthday (not Xmas especially) card, which in 1845 or 1846 I designed and carried out for him ", and goes on to say : " There is no question that this was the first illustrated card issued. The idea was Cole's, the execution of the trifle mine." The dates in these letters, as well as Gleeson White's date, also 1846, are probably all based on Cole's references to the card in his memoirs.

More recently, however, three originals of the Cole-Horsley card have been discovered bearing the date 1843, written quite clearly by people who sent it to their friends for that Christmas. I know of four finished and three unfinished, proof copies of the Cole-Horsley card, all of which—except one—I was able to examine. Of these three (all finished versions), are dated by their sender, bearing the year 1843, three have no date on them and one, a proof copy, was given away in 1845.

The official photograph of one of the cards, then in the collection of the late Mrs. L. F. Strongitharm, was taken by the British Museum (Plate 2). I am also reproducing here the original of the card sent by Horsley to Cole. It, too, clearly shows the date, and includes a charming handwritten " sentiment " which runs with appropriate alterations after the nursery rhyme, " Old King Cole " :

" To His good friend Cole
Who's a merry *young* soul
And a merry *young* soul is he
—and may he be for years to come !
hoo-ray ! "

The same spirit is expressed by the artist in his special " signature " for this card, i.e. a self-caricature. It is followed by " Xmasse, 1843 ", also handwritten (Plate 1).

Sir Henry Cole's granddaughter, to whom I am indebted for the loan of this unique card, was also good enough to allow me to inspect another copy which she had found amongst her father's papers. It was

[3] Published on December 28th, 1883.

also sent to Sir Henry, but by another artist, T. Webster, R.A., whose illustrations were included in Summerly's list. Except for shade differences of the hand-colouring and, of course, the written inscription, this copy is a replica of the other two, and although it is undated, it comes from the same edition and was probably sent at the same time.

The two proof copies are of a larger and thinner paper. No " To " and " From ", dotted lines, or publisher's name, etc., are included on them and they are, of course, not coloured. One of them was given to Miss Henrietta L. Cole by her father in 1865. The other proof copy on its wider margin carries a posterior handwritten note : " Designed by J. C. Horsley, R.A., about 1845/The first Christmas Card " (" first " underlined).

The Cole-Horsley Christmas card was printed from a lithographic stone on a single stiff cardboard of $5\frac{1}{8}$ by $3\frac{1}{4}$ inches. The ink was probably dark sepia, now mellowed a little, so that the general impression is not unlike an etching. The rustic trellis frame, reminiscent of the " Gartenlaube " style, encloses the main centre scene and two narrower panels on each side of it. The main panel shows a homely family party in progress, including three generations, in true Victorian fashion. We can count eleven people, including four children. They are toasting the health of the absent friend, the addressee, with red wine, and only the three smallest children are not holding wine-glasses, but are busily engaged in tasting the plum pudding. The greeting text, " A Merry Christmas and a Happy New Year to You ", is placed on a pink curtain draped beneath the central panel in the foreground of the composition. The side panels represent the spirit of Christmas charity. On one the poor are obviously being fed and on the other given warm clothing. The design includes a dotted line above for the name of the addressee, and another, below in the right-hand bottom corner, for the sender's signature. The publisher's name and address are printed in the bottom left-hand corner. These do not appear on the proof copies. The reverse side of the card is left blank.

The conviviality of the party is also conveyed through the trellis-work, up which vines are growing. The whole makes a very charming picture of the period atmosphere without conscious emphasis on costume. The designer, J. C. Horsley, was a well-known artist, and a number of his larger compositions are in various public collections.[4]

The fact that 1843 has been established as the date of the Cole-Horsley card automatically excludes some others whose names have been brought forward to claim the distinction of having designed the first Christmas card.[5] For example, the often repeated suggestion that W. Dobson, later one of Queen Victoria's favourite painters, made the first Christmas card can no longer be entertained. All we know about this card is that, instead of his usual Christmas letter to a friend, Dobson drew and sent a sketch as a token of appreciation at Christmas, 1844 or 1845 (references vary). Also, for some time it was claimed that the card designed and sent out for Christmas, 1845, by Edward Bradley, or " Cuthbert Bede ", the author of that charming Oxford book, *Verdant Green*, and *The Curate of Cranston*, was the first Christmas card. His lithographer, Lambert of Newcastle, is said to have issued the drawing as a card for general sale in 1847. (Bradley was eighteen when he went up to Durham in 1845, and " Cuthbert Bede ", his pen-name, became known only in 1853, when the first part of *Verdant Green* appeared.)

A design is said to have been made by Thomas Sturrock (sometimes erroneously spelt Shorrock) and his friend, Charles Drummond, of Leith, Scotland, some time before 1846. The date, however, was not known to White, nor to Jonathan King, who told him about it and said that the card bore a laughing face and a Scottish New Year greeting, " A Guid New Year an' Mony o' Them " (Plate 3). Daniel Aikman, an apprentice in an engraver's workshop in the North, is also referred

---

[4] Horsley was a member of the Etching Club and contributed to the illustrations of Goldsmith's *Deserted Village* (1849) and Tupper's *Proverbial Philosophy*. He made a few pictures for the *Churchman's Family Magazine*, the *Poems and Pictures* (1846), Adam's *Sacred Allegories* (1856), and in 1857 six illustrations to the famous illustrated edition of Tennyson's *Poems*, published by Edward Moxon, which included Rossetti, Millais, Hunt and other celebrated artists of the period. In 1881 he was amongst the Royal Academicians who were invited by R. Tuck to design Christmas cards for their special series, and Horsley contributed some picturing children.

[5] It is indeed quite remarkable how great interest is shown by the general public far beyond the natural interest of collectors in this question of " the first " Christmas card. I have several hundred British newspaper " cuttings " and American " clippings ", a great number of them letters to editors, giving most varied and contradictory information about this subject.

to as the possible engraver of this or a similar card. Several such " laughing face " designs have survived, also with the text, " Wishing You a Merry Christmas and a Happy New Year " or " A Merry Christmas and a Happy New Year to You ". They are usually from the early 1840's ; some even earlier. (One tooth is seen to be prominently missing on most of them ; no doubt this was meant to increase the comic effect.) These designs were really notepaper headings, i.e. forerunners and not actually Christmas cards in our sense of the word.

On Plate 7 I reproduce a very charming card of about 3½ by 2½ inches in size. It is a handcoloured engraving of a girl not unlike Hayter's celebrated " females of Scott " holding in her hand a small card wishing " A Happy New Year and Many Returns of the Season ". Probably there were versions with valentine and Christmas texts also and although the exact date cannot be established, this pretty card must be considered amongst the earliest of its kind.

The date 1829 is clearly incorporated in the pattern of a very fine Anniversary card reproduced on Fig. 1. Its lettering, " To . . . on the ANNIVERSARIE of . . . day From . . . " leaves blank spaces for the insertion of the names of the addressee and the sender as well as for " Christmas–", " New Year–", " Birth–" or other words, suitable for the occasion. The twelve letters of ANNIVERSARIE are cleverly interlaced with tiny scenes and figures representing the twelve months of the year, including, between the final E and the sign of the Cross, scenes of the Nativity and the Adoration of the Magi. The card was designed by W. Harvey and engraved by John Thompson. In spite of its prior date it cannot really claim to be " the first " Christmas card as it was apparently designed to be used for other anniversaries as well ; it is, however, a very close forerunner for that coveted title.

A much more formidable competitor for the title of the first Christmas card appears to be the card designed by W. M. Egley. His much-discussed design was quite unknown to White in 1894, and it can be assumed that it was unknown also to his sources, including the then greatest collector, Jonathan King. A copy of Egley's card was presented to the British Museum in 1931 by Miss F. L. Cannan, together with some delightful skating prints and drawings (Plate 7). Another imprint, as well as two original pencil sketches for it, were presented to

Fig. 1. A very rare engraving made for 1829. The blank space enabled the sender to use it as Christmas and New Year card or for any other suitable anniversary.

the Victoria and Albert Museum by H. J. Deane, a relative of the artist. The design is very nearly the same size as the Cole-Horsley card, and its general treatment is also somewhat similar. Like Horsley, Egley uses a rustic trellis and vine leaves as a frame to divide his space into smaller and larger panels or sections. The greeting text is identical except that an " & " is substituted for " and " on Horsley's design, and, like Horsley's, it is shown on a hanging drapery covering the lower centre foreground of the card. The space left for the name of the addressee is again on the top centre of the card, while that for the sender's signature is directly beneath it, at the bottom. In the right bottom corner Egley's signature is etched, just before the four numerals representing the date of the design. The last figure is responsible for the extensive controversy as to the priority of this card. While the figures 184 are perfectly clear, the fourth figure falls on the edge of the plate in the angle formed by the side and bottom lines. It is obviously cramped a little and could easily be taken for a 2, an 8, or even a 9, each slightly distorted. Although there is no agreement in this respect between the experts of the most authoritative institutions, i.e. the print and drawing departments of the British Museum and the Victoria and Albert Museum, my own view, and some further evidence confirms, that Egley's design was etched in 1848.

Mr. H. J. Deane, who presented the scrapbook with the Egley card to the Victoria and Albert Museum, in his own words, " happened to be the possessor of a good deal of Mr. W. M. Egley's relics, such as his diaries, scrapbooks, sketches, etc." Amongst these were two prints of the Egley Christmas card, one of which is still in Mr. Deane's possession. This is in a frame, on the back of which is an inscription in Egley's own handwriting. It runs : " Christmas Card—the Second ever published. Designed and etched by W. Maw Egley, 1848, India Proof." The note also includes the reference number " 140 ". In the first volume of Egley's carefully recorded chronological catalogue of his works, against the number 140 is the following entry : " 140— Design for a Christmas Card.—The second ever published. Etching on copper.—India Proof below. Size $3\frac{1}{4} \times 4\frac{3}{4}$ in. Fin. 1848 : Dec. 4." To this is added : " The first Christmas Card was designed by Mr. J. C. Horseley [sic] and published by Mr. Henry Cole, under the name of ' Luke Limner ' ".[6]

These notes by the artist himself[7] are conclusive. 1848 is also confirmed by our photographic enlargement of the respective corner of Egley's etching (Plate 5).

[6] There is an irrelevant confusion between Cole's pen-name, Felix Summerly, and " Luke Limner ", the pen-name of John Leighton, another pioneer artist in the history of the Christmas card.

[7] A letter by Mr. Deane containing some of these details was published in the *Sunday Times*, London, on January 13th, 1935. Egley's " Catalogue of Pictures, Drawings, and Designs " is now in the Victoria and Albert Museum.

William Maw Egley was the son of W. Egley, the miniature painter. Hence "Junr." in his signature. A. M. Hind recalls that he became a regular exhibitor at the Royal Academy, and justly describes his work as having "something of the qualities of Dicky Doyle". His Christmas card is a fine etching, both in composition and execution.

The trellis-work is so arranged as to provide spaces for eight larger and smaller scenes depicting various traditional seasonal activities. The two main scenes occupy the upper and larger part, while the space below is occupied by five smaller scenes. Besides these, Harlequin and Columbine form the centre, and individual little figures of charm and humour fill every available corner. On the top left corner a young lady is writing her Christmas letter, which, in the opposite corner, her young man is reading. The two main scenes depict a large family dinner party in an elaborate dining-hall full of pictures, servants and butler (the size of the family has noticeably increased between the first sketch (Plate 6) and the finished etching!), and the Sir Roger de Coverley danced after dinner by a still larger number of guests. Beneath we see a Punch and Judy show, feeding the needy, skating adventures and waits. One of the two little cherubs smokes his pipe dangerously near the drapery on which the good wishes are conveyed! Egley also included mistletoe and holly, etc., amongst his decorations, motifs which later appeared in abundance on Christmas cards.

The Christmas cards designed by both Horsley and Egley represent a high standard of contemporary craftsmanship and convey the essence and atmosphere of the season as enjoyed in the period. [8]

[8] Original copies of these early cards are now extremely rare. The Cole-Horsley card was reissued in a facsimile edition in 1881 by De La Rue & Co., printed in chromo-lithography. This enabled it to be produced for 2d. and sold at 3d. per copy. More recently R. Tuck & Sons reproduced on a folder card a copy of the Cole-Horsley card. According to the handwritten inscription, its original was sent—just over a century previously—to a "James Peters, Wife and family" by "John Washbourn and his Wife" of "22 Theberton St., Islington" on "Dec. 23/'43". In an interesting article, Charles Carter, Director of the Plymouth Museum and Art Gallery, explained that while "machine-printed reprints" "are plentiful and of little value", a genuine specimen of the Cole-Horsley card realised £50. (*The Bazaar*, December 15th, 1936.)

THE FORERUNNERS
of the Christmas Card

WHETHER the present view that the Cole-Horsley card of 1843 was the first is correct, or whether other claims yet unknown will turn up to put the question once again in doubt, one cannot say. That it took a number of years after the first card before the Christmas card entered the market as a considerable commercial proposition is certainly a curious fact. Even when they did appear, it is remarkable how little some of them resembled the cards designed by either Horsley or Egley. The dissimilarity is the more conspicuous since Horsley's and Egley's designs were so very similar to each other, both in subject and composition. They were of the same size (" the usual size of a lady's card " in the 40's), and although the Cole-Horsley card is lithographed and hand-coloured, the design certainly has the character of an etching and might easily have been one originally, as Martin Hardie also thought likely. They both much more resembled the fashionable notepaper headings than the bulk of the Christmas cards of the 60's. These were considerably smaller in size and were in fact " gentlemen's visiting cards " embossed and decorated with the addition of a Christmas message, or direct descendants of the popular valentines of the period. The function, however, was the same : a convenient substitute for the older custom of the Christmas letter or personal visit to convey the compliments of the season. This has been the main purpose of the Christmas card ever since. The gentle family party toasting absent friends in Horsley's version differs very little in this respect from the recent airgraph Christmas greetings.

The urge to greet relatives and friends at Christmas, the homeliest holiday of the year, and to wish them happiness in the coming year is so general and deeply imbued that it is difficult for many to realise that our pleasant and convenient method of doing so was invented not much more than 100 years ago. The results of a small-scale mass observation test which I carried out showed that the majority thought that Christmas cards and the invention of book printing coincided. Many others believed that Christmas cards date back to the time of the introduction of engraving. Some 10 per cent. of those interviewed were of the opinion that Christmas cards had existed in Europe much earlier, but were first brought into Britain by the Prince Consort and became popular in the United States at the same time.

The study of the history of the forerunners of the modern Christmas card proves that the tradition of exchanging charms or small tokens of good luck at this time of the year goes back to very ancient times. In fact, we should have to go back to pre-Christian times, when the festival was not yet celebrated as the anniversary of the Birth of Christ, but as a feast for the winter solstice. People then celebrated the reawakening of Nature, anticipating the coming of spring and longer hours of daylight. They associated with it their various forms of beliefs in the victory of life over death, light over darkness and green verdure over snow and ice. The solstice season was the time of magic for men, and they could then, from the signs of their gods, read portents and foretell coming events during the New Year. The feasts and rites thus aimed to propitiate the friendly and disarm the unfriendly gods or spirits. Mummers and their plays, mistletoe and the kiss beneath it, the yule log and its kindling, the wassailing of fruit trees, a number of traditional dishes, such as the boar's head and mince-pie, all have their origin in these ancient rites. It is the nature of human customs and habits to survive long after their original meaning and significance have been forgotten.

Available archaeological material indicates that it was usual amongst the Egyptians to give small symbolic presents conveying wishes of good luck with allusions to the New Year. Small blue-glazed bottles were found in the tombs of the Pharaohs, probably scent-flasks, bearing inscriptions about flowers and the approaching New Year. Some scarabs with hieroglyphs, " *au ab nab* " (all good luck), were also probably New Year presents.

In Rome it was an ancient custom for all those who were connected with a household to visit it on the first day of January to exchange greetings and presents. Originally these were branches of laurel or olive, picked from the holy groves dedicated to the ancient Sabine goddess of health, Strenia. Her name probably represents the origin of the word *strenae*, as Roman New Year presents were called. Later the presents usually took a more practical form, such as dates, figs and other edibles, which were sometimes coated with gold leaf (mentioned by Martial) and were symbolic of good omen for the New Year. From Ovid's *Fasti* it is clear that, for example, honey as a present meant the wish that the coming year should be as sweet to the recipient as honey itself (*Fasti*, I, 185-8). A little further on, however, Janus suggests that a present of cash would be even sweeter than honey, pointing to the changing habits under the Caesars. The presents conveying the greetings were more and more frequently actual coins with a Janus head on them, or bowls, oil-lamps and other objects.

A characteristic type of these, a lamp decorated with the winged figure of Victoria, with a laurel wreath on her head and a branch in her left hand, carries the following inscription : " *Anno novo faustum felix tibi sit* " (May the New Year be happy and lucky for you)!. The goddess rests her hand on the medallion bearing the motto. Behind her is the traditional coin with the Janus head. The design includes a small pot, probably for honey, and above the medallion a pine-cone and a bundle of fruit. It is interesting to note how, at this stage, the various traditional *strenae* are employed as mere decorations (Fig. 2). Coins with New Year wishes often abbreviate the greeting and simply put " A.N.F.F. ", followed by " Hadriano ", or whatever the name of the respective emperor might be. The coin with the Janus head, known as *as*, which appears amongst the decorations of the New Year oil-lamp just described, was originally a valid currency and became perhaps the most popular token to express the compliments of the season. (It will be remembered that January was named after Janus.)

The advent and spread of Christianity and the continued adherence to pagan January celebrations concurred for some time within the realm of Rome, but as time passed the pagan saturnalia was replaced by Christmas, the celebration of the Birth of the Saviour. The Christian Christmas spirit introduced a slow but truly remarkable transformation, and seasonal elements which survived from previous times were enriched by new meaning and new content. This enabled them long to outlast the ancient gods, Osiris, Mithras, Strenia, Janus and Frey, in whose cults they originated.

Besides the performed and vocal customs, the giving and receiving of tokens of good wishes continued, and remain a feature of the winter solstice. Generally speaking, those countries whose language belongs to the Latin group, such as France, Italy and Spain, continue to observe January 1st rather than Christmas Day as the appropriate date for the exchange of *strenae*, and the French word *étrenne* preserves their continuity. In some European countries, apart from the annual distribution of tips to servants, etc., only New Year cards and

Fig. 2. A Roman oil-lamp bearing a Latin New Year greeting. The winged figure of Victory is surrounded by ancient seasonal symbols of good luck.

New Year visits sustained the Roman tradition. In these countries the New Year cards did not include references to Christmas and were sent out after the 25th, intended to arrive on New Year's Day.

The English seasonal greeting card was, on the other hand, different, since it conveniently combined Christmas and the New Year with the emphasis on Christmas, whatever its actual subject and design. These cards were meant to be delivered on or before Christmas Day and to convey greetings for the Christmas festivities and the following year, thus unwittingly and from the very beginning emphasising also the significance of the Christmas festivities as in some way the successors of the old winter solstice celebrations.[1]

The history of the printed cards of good wishes for the New Year takes us back to the early years of European engraving and printing. One of the first of these is a delightful line engraving by the famous fifteenth-century artist known as Master E.S., and is dated 1466. Master E.S. was a truly admirable engraver whose name, probably Ribeisen, was not discovered until quite recently, and he is usually referred to by his monogram. More than 300 of his engravings are known, including some which were formerly ascribed to the Master of the Sybil. One of these, the celebrated Madonna of Einsieldeln, has, in addition to the date, 1466, his family coat of arms. This and other proofs established that he came from Strasbourg.

Master E.S.'s New Year engraving (Fig. 3) shows Jesus as a little boy with a halo, wearing a loose mantle and stepping forward on the calix of a decorative flower. Behind Him is the wooden crucifix. "*Ein guot selig ior*", meaning a good and happy year, is engraved on a floating scroll. The language is from Lower Germany. The print must have had a great appeal when it appeared, for a number of copies and similar cards followed it, amongst them one by I. von Meckenem, the other great master of the century. It is significant that the wording on these early designs is confined to New Year wishes, while the chief subject of the design is usually the Infant Jesus, clearly alluding to Christmas. So these old prints are equally forerunners of the later divided Christmas and New Year cards.

The majority of fifteenth-century "cards" now known were printed from wood-blocks and were usually coloured by hand. They usually picture the Boy Jesus, a custom which was only interrupted by the Reformation. On some He is shown sitting on a decorated cushion playing with a bird, probably a cuckoo, one of the birds popularly

[1] In this connection it may be interesting to recollect that the Christian calendar was said to have been introduced to England by St. Augustine in the year 596, but was not generally adopted until 816, when it was enforced by the Council of Bishops at Chelsea. The new year was reckoned to begin on Christmas Day as late as the thirteenth century. Thus the connection between Christmas and New Year's Day was throughout the early centuries of Christianity so close that it meant practically the same thing.

Fig. 3.
The Christ Child on a flower with New Year greeting (for 1467) on a floating scroll. A copy of this extremely rare engraving by the famous and mysterious "Master E.S." is in the collection of the British Museum.

Fig. 4.
Anonymous fifteen century woodcut of a ship sailing from Alexandria with the Baby Christ and the figure of Charity on board.

credited with certain prophetic powers. So birds and flowers appear early on these printed forerunners of our modern Christmas cards.

Another interesting woodcut shows a ship sailing on the high seas from Alexandria. (Fig. 4). The Infant Christ is working the sails, and points to the scroll which bears the good wishes for the New Year. The ship carries also an apparently holy young woman, who, according to the catalogue of the Viennese Hofbibliothek, represents Charity. The design includes another figure and two winged angels, one fixing the pennant to the mast, the other blowing a beflagged horn. The port of embarkation and the Crusader-like flags and the allusion in the text to the wealthy cargo attach a particular interest to this fifteenth-century woodcut.

There appears to have been a marked decrease in the production of these cards in the sixteenth and seventeenth centuries. At least very few of them are known to-day. This may be partly due to the Reformation or to mere accident. (Most of the cards produced in the second half of the fifteenth century may have survived simply because they were treasured and stuck into Bibles as devotional pictures.) The prominent German collector, von Zur Westen, knew only one sixteenth-century print which he was able to classify as a New Year card. This is a finely executed oval woodcut and shows Jesus as a boy, with halo, wearing a long light robe and standing amidst flowers. He holds the cross in his right hand and the globe in his left. The numerous engravings picturing the goddess Fortuna standing on a globe were, according to some experts, New Year greetings, but this is as yet unsubstantiated.

There is, however, in the Forrer Collection an interesting woodcut, a legal calendar for 1600, which Westen reproduces. It is decorated with a number of national arms and allegorical figures. According to the inscription, the Gerichtsprokurator Bonaventure Schlech presented this print to his friends and clients with his best wishes for " a good and lucky New Year ".

The next phase in the history of New Year greeting " cards ", also rather little known to-day, was the introduction of large prints, actually calendars, which were meant to be hung on the walls, and smaller, less pompous engravings with a lighter approach to the subject of the coming year. I reproduce an example of each type showing two tastes and alternative ways of wishing good cheer for 1703 and 1738 respectively.

The first is an Italian copperplate engraving, made by G. M. Mitelli. The eighteenth-century *Biographical Dictionary* by Joseph Strutt gives the following account of this artist's work : " He etched in a very slight, feeble style, without effect. The naked parts of the human figure he did not sufficiently attend to ; neither did he mark the extremities correctly. Yet his works prove him to have been a man of genius . . . and worthy of the attention of the curious."

Mitelli's delightful plate (Plate 8) gives an imaginary picture of a Utopian world where, as he shows, rivers are flowing with milk and honey, dinner tables perpetually replenished with a variety of delicious dishes, trees producing, besides fresh fruit all the year round, coats, dresses, precious stones and jewellery, and so on—in fact, everything one could desire of a happy New Year. The only motif in the picture from a non-Utopian world is the forbidding round-tower prison, a slight memento of those *carceri* so familiar from the engravings of other Italian masters. But even the prison has, to Mitelli, an apparently Utopian use, for only one man, he who dared to work, is about to be imprisoned in it ! It is indeed delightful to follow in detail the little pictures and texts drawn, no doubt, with an ironical grin, but nevertheless unwittingly disclosing something of the man in the street in the early eighteenth century.

The second illustration from this period comes from Bavaria (Plate 9). It is characteristically baroque and of a very different type. Its title is " The Situation in Europe. Its Hopes and Longings. An Emblematical Wall Calendar for 1738 ". The drawing is by L. L. Hayd, and was engraved by J. A. Pfeffel, the one-time much-admired court engraver to the Emperor at Vienna. This large print is an equally imaginary representation of the state of affairs, of expected and hoped-for events in the New Year, 1738. Unlike Mitelli's, these are presented without the slightest sign of conscious irony—on the contrary. In the centre, between the title plaque and the explanatory verses, an historical tableau is recessed. On it we can see, on the left, a session of the memorable Conference of Nimirov still discussing the famous issue whether " Congressus or Congressio " is to seal the fate of the heathen Turkish rule over parts of south-eastern Europe, while on the right the Sultan's throne is seen already toppling over. The rest of the composition celebrates in an undisguisedly persuasive manner the anticipated success of the alliance between Russia and the Emperor of Austria. Anna Ivanovna, Empress of Russia, is on her throne, surrounded by figures symbolising Justice and Power[2] in the left upper part of the picture. At her feet a winged cherub is handing her the document of the alliance and the pen to sign it with. On the opposite side symbolic figures celebrate the chances of a peaceful solution and the god of the Danube watches over the safe passage of the allied fleet towards Constantinople. In the bottom left corner Themis holds out the handcuffs for the Turk, while in the right Neptune is passing the key of the liberated seas to the cherubic little figures representing the two great powers.

The prophecy, as is known, did not materialise, and the Austrian Army was seriously defeated in 1738, but the calendar remains an interesting relic, representing the phase when baroque enthusiasm and pathos, equally dominating text, design and political conception, turned even the previously more modest New Year greeting into big, poster-like designs to gain support for contemporary power politics.

At the beginning of the eighteenth century the *quodlibet* or *trompe-l'œil* joined the various forms of seasonal greeting cards. British art dealers were probably the first to circulate amongst their customers *quodlibets* picturing in a very realistic manner an array of their prints, drawings and similar wares, seemingly carelessly grouped, but in a cunningly contrived disorder, as if they would be lying on a desk or table. These were used for advertisement and were in fact a sort of illustrated catalogue. The engraving occasionally included a portrait of the dealer amongst the prints he offered for sale, posing as though he was receiving and greeting his customers. Sometimes the name and address of the merchant replaces his portrait, tucked away in a corner. Enterprising dealers who used the *quodlibet* were quick to take advantage of it as a greeting card and included text or motif conveying the compliments of the season.

The *quodlibet* here illustrated (Plate 10) is probably an early eighteenth-century example. One of the engravings "advertised" on it was published

[2] In actual fact, during her ten years of reign she was known as "Anna the Cruel", and thousands of Russian noblemen were sent to Siberia for alleged political crimes.

in 1703 or 1704. (It is the work of George Bickham, Sen., the engraver who died in 1769 and whose portrait of Sir Isaac Newton, decorated with emblematical ornaments, made in 1752, and some engravings after Rubens, are well known.) It also contains a portrait of the print merchant with his hat in his hand as though welcoming his clients. The idea of the *quodlibet*, though it had declined in Europe, continued to remain an attraction in America throughout the nineteenth century, and at least on Christmas cards has survived even to the present day.[3]

Switzerland contributes the interesting New Year greeting reproduced on Plate 11. It was designed in 1703 by J. Meyer, a Zurich printer and engraver, better known for his engravings of " The Fountains of Rome ". His card was made for the Constaffler Association in his home town, an organisation concerned with the defence of the place, and it is thought that the card was printed with a view of promoting its aims and of raising money. The two main figures are symbolic and represent respectively peace and plenty and the havoc of war. The latter shows a soldier with a spear in hand, leaning on a shield and trampling on a helpless baby. Behind him a house is in flames and the horrified face of a woman is just visible. The small pictures which frame the centre-piece show the gradual development of security in the home by a series of drawings beginning with a single stone house. The next little picture shows a single house surrounded by a high wall, and so on to the most up-to-date security measures in 1703—that is, the whole town enclosed within a system of fortifications giving collective security to all its citizens.

There is a certain similarity between this and the print-sellers' *quodlibet*. Both " advertise " their goods and ideas with the view of obtaining support or custom. Soon several other groups began to use the convenient form of a New Year greeting to promote their interests, chiefly financial.

Town-criers, bellmen, firemen, lamplighters, newsvendors and ballad-sellers, certain craftsmen and their apprentices, messengers, theatre attendants, etc., began to have neatly printed greetings, sometimes entitled " A Copy of Verses ", consisting of prick song prose or a poem,

---

[3] The work of the recently re-discovered W. M. Harnett (1848-1892) is being celebrated by some as a kind of forerunner of surrealist composition.

possibly a woodcut or two, each more or less appropriate for the occasion, which was a steadily increasing appeal for a tip. These greetings, usually in the form of broadsides, were offered personally, or left at the door at every house in the parish at Christmas. They were a kind of Boxing Day activity advanced to Christmas, in exchange for the surely expected annual tip on Boxing Day.

There is a charming broadsheet with twenty-three verses with which Bellman Thomas Law greeted all householders of " St. Giles, Cripplegate, within the Freedom " in 1666. Another, dated 1683-4, entitled " A Copy of Verses presented by Isaac Ragg, Bellman, to the Masters and Mistresses of Holbourn Division, in the Parish of St. Giles's-in-the-Fields ", is embellished by a woodcut picture of the bellman with his pointed pole, lanthorn and bell and, of course, a series of verses chiefly proclaiming his services, such as :

> " If any base lurker I do meet
> In private alley or in open street,
> You shall have warning by my timely call,
> And so God bless you and give rest to all ! "

Hone gives the text of " A Copy of Christmas Verses " " Presented to the Inhabitants of Bungay, By their Humble Servants, the late Watchmen, John Pye and John Tye " (1823), which ends as follows :

> " . . . Thus, whether Male or Female, Old or Young
> Or Wed, or Single, be this burden sung ;
> Long may you live to hear, and we to call,
> ' A Happy Christmas and New Year to all.' "

An early nineteenth-century Viennese print gives a rather pathetic vista of " The First Day of the Year " from a typical burgher's point of view (Plate 12). He is seen overwhelmed by well-wishers and congratulators, all offering him cards as well as bills on New Year's Day. His bewildered expression as he dips into his money-bag shows clearly enough the reluctance with which he dispenses seasonable obligations of such dimensions.

The cards distributed by the various professionals and public servants often emphasised the nature of their work in the pictures as well as in the verses. Tower watchmen would have a print of a church tower, the higher the better; the broadside-seller a kind of news-sheet. The latter followed a more or less set pattern. The main body of the sheet of paper was occupied by longish verses giving the latest news of peace and war, events at the courts, some weather forecasts and other useful information of disasters away and good tidings nearer at home. The text was headed or surrounded by, usually, woodcut illustrations. These were either small scenes of topical interest or Scriptural illustrations.

One such New Year greeting broadsheet, the *Sächsischen Boten*, produced for 1798, begins by calling upon the spirit of peace, shown as a small cupid with an olive branch, to shut the door of the temple of Janus, and imploring Mars to break his bloodstained sword, as Europe had had enough of wars. The rest describes, in picture and text, the blessings of peace. One picture indeed shows a cherub bringing a new-born baby from heaven, i.e. "an heir to the throne of brave Saxony". A woman is shown awaiting him with open arms. An early Victorian folio broadsheet which, in addition to the charming cut of the bellman and his dog on their rounds, was decorated with fifteen smaller cuts of mostly Biblical subjects, was entitled: "A Copy of Verses for 1839, Humbly Presented to all my Worthy Masters and Mistresses, of the Parish of Saint James, Westminster, By Richard Mugeridge, 20 Marshall Street, Golden Square." The verses alluded to the great events of the year (including some addressed "To the Queen", Victoria, for her Coronation)—for example, to the great achievement of the *Great Western*. It is worth quoting, as it is a characteristic example of these broadsheet-type seasonal greetings, combining reportage and popular comment, although the intentions are usually much better than the rhymes:

> "Well, despite of some thousand objections pedantic,
> The *Great Western* has cross'd and *re-cross'd* the Atlantic,
> Nor is *this* the first time—to the foe's consternation—
> That the deeds of our tars have defied calculation.
> Though few of our learned professors did dream
> That our seamen in steamers would reach the Gulf Stream
> Yet a fortnight's vibration, from Bristol to Cork,
> Will now set us down with our friends in New York;
> And a closer acquaintance bind firmer than ever,
> A friendship which nothing on earth ought to sever!"

Some large decorated sheets, called " Christmas broadsides " were in fact better described as " Christmas pieces ", which was their other name. During the first half of the nineteenth century these decorated sheets were filled in, in the centre, with handwritten greetings by school-children. They were presented for Christmas, and parents were appreciative of these proofs of their children's " proficiency in penman-ship ". But large purchasers of Christmas pieces were the " Charity boys", who used to exhibit them in the parish and collect small tips as a reward for their diligence (Fig. 5).

The anticipated reward is more directly suggested and with greater economy of the engraved word and line in an excellent engraving by Joseph Bergler (Plate 13). He spent his student years in Italy, and later was well known as the head of the Prague Academy of Arts. " Il Modelo " was made for New Year's Day, 1810. It shows a young professional model, seated, holding a large black hat in his hands in a manner quite unmistakable. Possibly the artist allowed his favourite model, whose features appear again and again in his drawings, also to use this picture as his own card, whether or not Bergler used it himself.

As the custom spread, European and especially Viennese card manu-facturers, visiting card and colour printers began to produce an increasing number of New Year greeting scraps for the general public. These were produced for the retail market, to be sold in more or less the same way as they are to-day in smaller places.

The cards themselves are quite small, often printed by the dozen in one sheet of about 7 inches square, each containing a little design and verse. The purchaser, by cutting along the dividing lines, obtained the twelve separate cards. These little cards, often hand-coloured, showed, for example, a smiling peasant girl wearing a big straw hat and holding in both hands a basket of flowers in the centre of which stands a small, naked baby holding a scarf with the inscription, " Luck ". Beneath the figure is usually the verse.

Other little cards were decorative woodcuts of love boughs, bouquets of flowers or engravings of one or two—seldom more—naïvely drawn figures, often coloured. A single- or four-line motto, usually of a rather sentimental or personal character, completes them. They were no doubt meant to be handed over personally to the recipient, or enclosed in a letter. There is hardly any space, except on the back, for the sender's name. Individuals for some time very likely received few, if indeed more than one, of these personal cards from their admirers. As in the case of valentines, the omission of any space for signature was probably deliberate, to permit the pleasurable speculation as to the identity of the sender.

Fig. 5.

" Charity boys " used to exhibit Christmas " pieces " or broadsides and collect small tips as a reward for penning a greeting or motto in the central space left blank on the printed sheet. (1840-50.)

These little cards, made for the retail market, had, amongst others, one interesting feature in common with the modern Christmas card. They bore no date. This was no doubt for the practical reason that those left over from one year could still be sold the next. A few English Christmas cards, also made for the retail market, sometimes had the year of publication printed on them. In the early 70's this was retained, but modified, by at least one firm in a rather clever manner. Instead of printing the date in full, only the first three figures were printed on the card itself. The fourth and actual year of dispatch could be added by means of a little cut-out scrap bearing the required number and designed to correspond with the shape and style of the preceding figures. This might be stuck on by the purchaser, and was supplied with the card at the time of purchase.

The invention of lithography in the last year of the eighteenth century and its rapid popular development greatly facilitated and increased the production of New Year cards in Europe. C. Haller von Hallerstein designed one of the earliest examples of a lithographed New Year card (Fig. 6.) as his own personal greeting for 1816. It harked back to the Roman mythology—a fitting move at that date—and featured a " modernised " two-faced Janus head with four women, probably representing the four seasons, dancing around it in a true Regency fashion.

In the 1830's Adolph Menzel, whilst still a young man, made a number of satirical designs for New Year cards, published in Berlin. These were lithographs, and both the drawings and the poems printed beneath them made fun of the professions, such as the Civil Service, law, medicine, art, trade and so on. Both poem and picture made the satire quite obvious, though perhaps not so vulgar as some of the so-called " comic " valentines later on. A similar though less offensive design by A. Schrodter shows the Old Year as a jovial little man with wings outspread as though ready to fly away. His departure, however, is delayed by the middle-aged women who take no notice of the New Year, represented by a spry young dandy in the background. All their efforts are directed towards the retention of the Old Year, thus deferring for a little their own advancing age !

I cannot hope to give here a complete survey of all the less direct forerunners of the modern Christmas card. There is, however, one non-European forerunner of it which must be mentioned. This is the Japanese colour print known as the *surimono*. Gleeson White mentions the " temptation to find precedents in the everlasting great Japan " even for the Christmas card, but withstands it, as " the dignity of our native products might suffer if set side by side with the exquisitely dainty prints familiar to collectors of Japanese art ". The " aesthetes ", it will be remembered, were rather biased in favour of everything Chinese or Japanese. The tremendous enthusiasms of the late Victorians for

Fig. 6.

An early lithograph featuring a two-faced Janus head and the dancing
figures representing the four seasons,—a private card for 1816.

collecting or possessing Japanese fans, blue-and-white china, porcelain
and other fragile treasures, and the vogue of the Japanese colour schemes,
the "greenery-yellery", had perhaps an even more general influence
than the popularised Rossetti and Burne-Jones manner which the aesthetes
inherited from the Pre-Raphaelites. Du Maurier, that most precocious
of British cartoonists, who was perhaps saved from becoming an "aesthete" himself merely by his French descent, and who, instead, carried
on a persecution campaign against the movement in *Punch*, found in
the aesthetic craze for Japanese preoccupations a sitting target for his
particular satire. One of his drawings shows an aesthetic wife, suitably
draped and with a transcendent expression on her face, intensely
holding an old china teapot, while her husband, equally aesthetic, stands
in front of her pleading, " I think you might *let me* nurse that teapot a
little *now*, Margery ! You've had it to yourself all the *morning*, you
know ! " Another cartoon, also in *Punch*, showed another of these women
deeply mourning over a piece of broken china. Her set of six small and
delightful children stand nearby, obviously puzzled and shocked. The
mother tells them that they cannot make up for her loss, as now her set
of china is incomplete.

Besides the general craze for imported Japanese products and their
home-made imitations, which, of course, soon followed, there are also

definite indications to prove that printers and publishers, as well as others concerned with art production, were familiar with Japanese prints and colour woodcuts, including the *surimono*. Walter Crane, one of the best representatives of "the modern idea" in the late Victorian period, writing about his first contacts with Edmund Evans, the important printer and publisher, "himself a clever artist", who aided his (Crane's) efforts "in the direction of more tasteful colouring", recalls that his first illustrations for children were designed with solid black or blue backgrounds. "Gradually more colours were used", he says, "as the designs became more elaborate under various influences, among which that of Japanese colour prints must be counted as an important factor."

In spite of the contention of some experts on Japanese prints that the art of the *surimono* was not sufficiently appreciated by Western collectors, a certain familiarity with the *surimono*, sufficient to exert an influence on Christmas cards, did exist in the latter part of the nineteenth century, at least amongst those responsible for the designing and marketing of Christmas cards. Walter Crane's references and the fact that he was with many of his friends, associated with Christmas card production (his brother Thomas made hundreds of decorative designs for the Marcus Ward firm), makes it clear enough that, beyond the general fashion for Japanese art, the inclusion of the *surimono* amongst the forerunners of our modern Christmas cards is not unjustified.

The delightful and exquisitely finished Japanese art of the *surimono* is the result of a slow development of printing during the long centuries which preceded it, and to the variety of external influences absorbed by the Japanese before the final degree of perfection was attained. Block-printing, the transitory phase between the handwritten copy and press-printing, like so many other inventions, originated in China. The Japanese learnt this first from the Chinese and used it, as examples from the eighth century prove, for printing in various colours bird and flower decorations on silk. The first printed texts, quotations from Buddhist scriptures, were printed in Japan in or before 770 to the order of the Empress Shiyau-toku in a "million" (which probably stood for "very many") copies, and used Chinese writing with Sanskrit language. With the steady increase in paper-making, book-production developed, yet it was not until centuries later that the admirable series of Japanese colour woodcuts began to appear in the early eighteenth century.

Shiba Gokan, who was probably born in 1737, was said to have been the first Japanese to make copperplate engravings. This art he learnt, together with the use of linear perspective, from a Dutchman. His master was Harunobu, whose son, Gakutei Harunobu, was already a well-known *surimono* designer. Gakutei's master, Shunsho, was himself a celebrated designer of these cards, and passed on his art to many of his pupils. One of these, Shunman, is famous for his very fine flower designs. Gakutei was said to have been well educated also as a man of letters, and inspired the great Hokusai, another pupil of Shunsho, and himself an excellent *surimono* designer, whose pupil he later became when he took up art as a profession. Besides his *surimono* designs, he was much interested in illustration, and his work in both spheres is most distinguished. One of his *surimono* cards (Plate 15) shows a Japanese woman seated against a decorative background, playing a guitar. The landscape artist Hiroshige also made popular *surimono* designs.

Although Japanese prints are usually signed, so far from simplifying, this appears to complicate their identification, since it was a custom to change names frequently, sometimes taking the name of the artist's master. The artist of one of the best-known *surimono* designs is a fair example. He was Toyokuni's son, Naogiro, who studied art under his father. At first he took the name of Toyoshige, later used his father's name, and, again, often signed himself as Gosotei Toyokuni, while many of his father's other pupils also took Kuni as their prefix.[4]

The seven gods of good luck and their ship were favourite subjects for the *surimono*. Other subjects considered to be most suitable were birds, plants and flowers of good omen, traditional scenes and episodes from folk-stories, musical instruments, domestic tools, household implements and women. The text of the *surimono* was usually specially designed to suit the print as a whole, and a little poem was frequently

---

[4] In an article, "Notes on My Own Books for Children", published in the *Imprint*, February, 1913, Walter Crane mentions that "the sight of some Japanese prints by Toyokuni gave me fresh suggestions for treatment, but it was not until about 1869 or 1870 that the results became very evident, and the bold outlines and flat colour with the occasional use of solid black which characterised the style of my children's picture-books became fully identified with them from that time onward".

included. At first their size was small, hardly ever more than 6 inches in length, and the brilliant colours and a lavish use of gold, silver and other metallic coating on embossed surfaces made these little prints very attractive. Their production and finish was perhaps more delicate and refined than other Japanese colour prints, possibly due to their size and purpose.

It was first thought in the West that the *surimono* was exclusively a New Year card. It was, however, realised later that the messages it conveyed were not confined to seasonal greetings, but were from time to time special announcements. They were a means of congratulation and celebration—for, in fact, any circumstance thought to be worthy of a special and distinctive form of communication. For example, a *surimono* by Giokuyan for an actor announced to his patrons that he had adopted a son, giving his name. Another, by Niho, announced the recovery of sight by the man who ordered it and who had been temporarily blind. The *surimono* was also used to report a change of name or use of pseudonym. In these respects, the Japanese *surimono* more closely resembles the function, though not the form, of the old European custom of the Christmas letter, and perhaps the great variety of modern American greeting card production.

Most, if not all, Christmas card publishers in the 1870's and 1880's produced at least one or two sets of cards with a Japanese setting or flavour amongst their novelties every year. Some were indeed charming in their interpretation of Japanese art and style—as they appeared to Western eyes, imbued with Victorian vision. In the 1870's the Marcus Ward firm produced a clever imitation of a Japanese lacquer cabinet with folding doors, designed by T. W. Wilson; also " natural flowers on cleverly treated diaper patterns in gold and silver " by P. Tarrant; and " a similar set in blue and white "; or designs, " though based on Japanese art, not transcriptions of genuine patterns, but ' exercises in the style of Japan ' ". The De La Rue firm in the 1880's published an attractive series of " Japanese Belles " by Rebecca Coleman, a popular designer of the time. I reproduce one of these, as it can pleasantly be compared with and contrasted to the original Japanese conception of the same subject. My illustration (Plate 16) is taken from a print on fine silk depicting a Japanese girl with features somewhat Europeanised to appeal to the Western idea of exotic beauty. The conventional kimono, sunshade and flowers complete the design of an attractive "Japanese Christmas card" made in England in 1882. Ernest Griset, a very clever and nowadays unjustly overlooked artist, designed another successful set of " Japanese drawings ", which were published by the same firm in 1876. Most other firms also produced " Japanese sets " regularly. Sometimes, when the face of the Christmas card was in no way associated with Japan, the reverse might still have a decoration " à la Japan ", either in black and white or, other editions of the same card, printed in gold and silver. With the advent of the black-background cards, comic Japanese and Chinese subjects appeared on some American cards of this type, an idea almost entirely overlooked by the European publishers who catered for the fashionable " Chinamaniacs ".

THE "FULLNESS
OF TIME"

I T is said that technical inventions and novel conceptions are not
sufficient in themselves, but are bound to be without consequence until
they coincide with that which is sometimes defined as " the fullness
of time ", the given moment, when advantage not only could, but would
be taken of their potentialities. The term is perhaps too grand for
such a small and factual phenomenon as the Christmas card. But if it
is merely meant that the introduction of new goods and ideas can only
be firmly rooted and established if and when the technical, social and
economical, including psychological, conditions of a given community
are such that the new goods or ideas fulfil and satisfy an existing, though
not yet expressed, need or demand, then it can be said that the first
decades of the second half of the nineteenth century provided the
" fullness of time " for the Christmas card.

I do not suggest that the early Christmas card manufacturers were
in any way aware of, or indeed anticipated, the tremendous volume of
trade which was to follow their first tentative efforts to put this new
feature on the market. On the contrary, it was on their part merely
a sideline or by-product of their established trade in playing cards,
notepaper and envelopes, needle-box and linen labels or valentines.
When, in 1894, G. White collected the material for his review in the
special number of the *Studio*, many of the leading personalities of the
earliest Christmas card firms were still alive, but he could obtain
surprisingly little exact information from them as to the first decades
of their manufacture. No records had been kept and no sample books
preserved. White, in his characteristic manner, remarks " they [i.e.
the early manufacturers] took no trouble to secure for themselves a complete set of their wares, duly annotated with information concerning
the artist and his design. Their appreciation for any old design you
will find is apt to be coloured by the amount of profit it earned. Hence
the few that come back to their memory as triumphs are apt to be quite
insignificant things ; so trivial that if the name of their designer

chances also to have escaped oblivion, it may be left to the limited immortality of the manufacturer's memory, or ", as White, I am afraid somewhat prophetically, continues, " to be hunted up in future by some overzealous collector who is omnivorous ! "

To the early manufacturers Christmas cards appeared to be a merely ephemeral business. As they experienced a positive reaction to and growing demand for them, they were quick to follow up their chances in the most expedient manner. These early manufacturers considered Christmas cards as only a temporary vogue which would pass as unostentatiously as it began, and so concentrated on a quick turn-over " while the craze lasted ".

The lapse of a century may enable us to inquire into the possible circumstances to explain why the Christmas card, which had so many early forerunners from the time of the Pharaohs and the Caesars, took so many centuries to appear in its apparently final form in the middle of the nineteenth century. To this seemingly irrelevant factors contributed.

One of these was the birth in 1804 of George Baxter, son of a printer and publisher in Lewes. The boy first illustrated his father's books, but in 1830 set up independently as a wood-engraver in London. He was an ambitious young man, determined to find a method of printing illustrations in colour as well as black and white to meet the growing demand of popular taste. There were, of course, others struggling for the same end when, after four or five years' work in London, he succeeded in inventing a process. He was quick to patent it, and guarded its secrets so jealously that his own apprentices were forbidden to use it. This is rather reminiscent of the great Gutenberg, who, almost exactly four centuries earlier, had forbidden his employees to give away the secret of his experiments in printing, and how desperately he had tried to hide the fact that his first Bible had not been hand-written. Gutenberg's secret, however, could not be kept after his bankruptcy and the quarrel with his creditors at court.[1] Neither could Baxter's process for colour printing remain a secret. Nor was it, either, an entirely new process in the strict meaning of the word. It was more an ingenious combination of an elaborate four-point register and of elements already

[1] The book to be printed in his press when his creditors took over was a *Psalterium* (1457), and by then it was openly stated—nay, claimed—that it was produced " without the use in any form of a writing pen ".

familiar in printing—that is, the joint use of the aquatinted metal key or foundation plate and oil colours printed from many (sometimes as many as twenty) separately engraved wood-blocks, copper, zinc plates, or litho stones. At first he printed mainly religious subjects for missionary societies, or book and magazine illustrations. Later he began to produce delightful small and comparatively cheap prints for every kind of industrial use, and also supplied large quantities of small prints for scrapbooks, needle-cases, box-covers and similar uses.

The more or less " colour-starved " early Victorian public reacted to these delightful, bright prints in a manner quite beyond expectation. They soon discovered a thousand and one uses for these gay or melancholy but always finely finished and brilliantly coloured trifles. Manufacturers and individual shoppers vied with each other for them. Naturally, other engravers and printers—some " Baxter licensees ", others using their own similar patents—soon joined in the production. Little is yet known about early English colour printing and about these firms, their chronology and interrelations in particular ; even less about the artists who designed their manifold products. Illustrations in black and white were in those days already recognised as a form of art, and most of the best artists had made and usually signed them. Some were well known, and indeed better, in this medium than in the oil paintings of their Academy pictures. The colour prints in the middle of the century were, on the other hand, usually unsigned, and only a few better-known artists could be identified by their style, sometimes familiar in other mediums, as having designed them. Courtney Lewis, Basil and Nicolette Gray and others who wrote on Victorian colour printing suggested that the majority of their designs may have been the work of non-professional artists. I believe also that sketches and " unconsidered trifles " by better-known artists were freely altered and redrawn for these purposes with, or more likely without, the consent of the original artist. Details, and certain motifs or figures from the works of popular artists of the day were borrowed, and with suitable, sometimes only slight, alterations were made into independent scraps or other small prints by their manufacturers. In those days, long before the photo-mechanical process, the craftsmanship of the engraver, blockmaker, and colour printer, as well as later the lithographer, resulted in a certain uniform appearance of most reproductions, sometimes with a closer similarity of manner to each other than to their originals. Borrowed elements, the style-creating effects of the print-maker's craftsmanship and the inventiveness of amateur designers intermingled happily in these popular colour prints. That they are a curiously genuine " popular art " is due to this composite origin, a combination of anonymous and collective taste, and the wide range of uses which made them readily conform to every kind of contemporary requirement and gave them their liveliness and so characteristically human touch.

Children and grown-ups who loved their toy theatres, their " penny plain and twopence coloured " from the very beginning of the century, and went on from the 1830's loving their tinsel pictures of actors or other figures, preferably on horseback and, if possible, in a melodramatic pose, and who throughout the century delighted in cutting out and pasting in bits of engravings, hand-coloured or pin-pricked papers and silhouettes, pieces of velvet, plush or silk, and who found sufficient time for and took real pleasure in doing it, proved to be a natural public for the new colour prints. These prints were simply destined to be cut out, and sooner or later found their way into scrap albums, where many of them may still be discovered to-day, whether they had originally decorated music-covers, needle-cases or cards. It was only one step further from these popular usages to apply these little colour scraps and cut-outs to visiting cards, either by the individual or by the manu-facturer. It did not take long before the same and similar pretty colour prints, either pasted on to or printed directly on visiting cards, began to appear with the added brief greeting text, " A Merry Christ-mas ", etc. Baxter licensees and others, such as William Dickes, J. M. Kronheim, Benjamin Fawcett, Leighton Brothers, Sulman, Le Blond, Stannard, Day & Son, Mansell, Tymms and Audsley and a number of others, began to produce little pictures of scenes and subjects considered seasonal and suitable for Christmas, printed in their respective processes from wood or metal blocks. These did not become a special line at that time, but occur frequently enough. Courtney Lewis reproduces, for example, a set of needle-box prints, probably made by Bradshaw and Blacklock. The last of these shows a young woman with a child in a wintry scene and a little bird, probably a robin, in the snow. Another small print, one of a set made also for a commercial use, shows a cook with a big Christmas pudding in his hands and four children rushing round him trying to press sprigs of holly into the round pudding. In size, technique and atmosphere, these little prints are similar to—in fact, identical with—many of the early Christmas cards which appeared on the market a decade or so later, in the 1850's or 1860's. In some cases actually the old blocks must have been used for printing.

A small print, about 2½ by 2¼ inches in size, marked only as " Baxter's Oil Colour Printing ", was on the title page of a *New Year Token and Gift of Friendship*, by Mrs. Sherwood and others, published by William Darton & Son, Holborn Hill, in 1836. It is a rare print and highly valued by Baxter collectors, but it is also interesting from our point of view, since, like others just mentioned, it is a perfect prototype of later Christmas cards. It shows a little boy with a bird's nest, while the parent birds anxiously watch the intentions of the angelic little brute.

The Le Blond ovals, especially some small versions of rural romance and country scenery, which became so famous more than a century ago, could also be taken—when the words " A Merry Christmas " were added—as typical Christmas cards in the 60's. Some of these were in fact made into Christmas cards by a little scrap label, bearing the greeting text, being attached to them ; others were stuck on Christmas cards as added decorations. The London firm, Le Blond, became a Baxter licensee in 1849. Up to that year this originally very small firm specialised in metal-plate engravings. Later, commencing with a delicately produced Pastoral Almanack for 1853, they made a great number of exquisite Christmas cards for the famous perfumer, Rimmel, including some of those which were accredited by fashionable people of the day to have been the " produce of France ".

Some of the popular " reward cards " distributed to children attending Sunday school offered themselves also as suitable prints for Christmas cards. In the 1840's and 1850's they were produced in many sizes, and perhaps the nicest were those printed by Dickes, Dean and Nelson. The last-named firm was reputed to have had a colour-printing process of their own, combining steel engraving and lithographic tinting, which enabled them to print great numbers at comparatively little cost. The Sunday school in those days included every imaginable kind of

PLATE 59 The corner of the cloak of the artist, J. A. Boerner, is caught in the closed door, which hinders him from proceeding. As he cannot thus call to pay the compliments of the season personally, the text explains, he is sending the print instead!
(1811-2.)

PLATE 60 New Year coming in (1870's) in true popular art style on this Christmas card
"With lots of good cheer
And plenty of toys,
For both girls and boys."

PLATE 61 Railway train photographs enter the field of Christmas card decorations about the turn of the century. This card was sent to Queen Mary by the Duchess of Connaught from Ottawa, Canada, for Christmas, 1912.

A " floating object " with the word MINE visible above the water causes some consternation on the *Tirpitz*. The clue emerges in the narrow strip picture below, when it appears that the mine is a case of mineral water.   Date, 1917.

PLATE 63

BORNE ON THE WINGS OF FRIENDSHIP TRUE
THE BARK OF GOOD FORTUNE IS WAFTED TO YOU.

The Best Wishes for a Merry Christmas and a Bright New Year

From Susan & Lou

PLATE 62

An attractive example of the expensive, richly " jewelled " ship Christmas cards which came in vogue in the late 1880's.   Note the pearls and tinselling shown remarkably well in the lettering.

PLATE 64 Two different types of ship cards. The upper is in the most fashionable style at the turn of the century, sent to Queen Mary by Edward VII in 1901. The card was published by Faulkner & Co., London. The lower is a postcard type card of a German battleship in Bergen Harbour, and was sent and dedicated by William II of Germany.

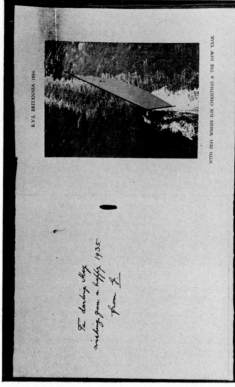

R.Y.S. BRITANNIA 1934

WITH BEST WISHES FOR CHRISTMAS & THE NEW YEAR

PLATE 65 A very attractive photograph of the Royal Yacht *Britannia* racing in a delightfully calm seascape decorated the Christmas card sent and dedicated to Queen Mary by King George V in 1934. The size of the folder card is 7 by 8½ inches.

1901

WITH BEST WISHES

Den tyske Eskadre i Bergen. — S.M.S. Kaiser Friedrich III.

PLATE 66 (*above on the left*) A card of the late 70's with a pronounced popular art flavour. It shows Father Christmas merrily distributing presents in the most progressive manner of the time : from an "airship".

PLATE 67 (*above on the right*) The private card of Mr. and Mrs. G. R. Sims for Christmas, 1901. The airship and the Edwardian figures make this little more than fifty-year-old design almost as "old-fashioned" as any of the Victorians. Note the Atlantic Ocean conveniently reduced to fit into the otherwise naturalistic composition.

PLATE 68 An airman dreams of Christmas stockings in this **airgraph** cartoon Christmas card from Egypt in 1941.

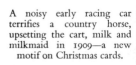

A noisy early racing car terrifies a country horse, upsetting the cart, milk and milkmaid in 1909—a new motif on Christmas cards.

PLATE 69

PLATE 70 Princess Elizabeth
—as Her Majesty then was—
and H.R.H. Princess Mar-
garet brought the microphone
into the picture of Christmas
card subjects. (The photograph shows the Queen making her unforgettable first
broadcast speech, with her
sister beside her, and it
formed the Princesses' Christmas card to Queen Mary in
1941.   Note the hand-
painted Christmas motifs on
the mount of the card.)

A charming photograph of
the Crown Prince Olav
of Norway on skis when a
little boy. This was his
own card, with a hand-
written personal dedica-
tion on the back to King
George V and Queen
Mary.

PLATE 71

PLATE 72 An early Joseph Mansell card printed by the Baxter process.

A Merry Christmas.

PLATE 73 (*left*) Two girls shelter from the icy wind under a big umbrella, but radiate the full warmth of Victorian sentimentality from their small persons !

(*On the right*) A small chromo card of the 60's. The good son of the well-to-do family feeds the shivering son of the poor.

PLATE 75 (*left*) "A Heavy Fall"— by the once well known artist, Onwhyn. Note in the background the "To be sold" board, referring to "Holly Lodge". Date, 1850's. Others in this set were barefooted Christmas carol-sellers contrasted to the butcher's shop full of huge joints, etc., entitled "A Christmas Carol," and similar cards.

(*On the right*) A good-humoured snowman is the ideal target for a snowballing match and the snowballs have cherubic little faces with wings.

A HAPPY NEW-YEAR.

PLATE 74

A HEAVY FALL.

A HAPPY NEW YEAR

PLATE 76

Wishing you a Bright and Happy Christmas.

PLATE 77 A precarious foothold on the ice and four fashionable young women holding hands as they slide down it. One of a popular Hildesheimer set of the adventures of four girls (1880).

PLATE 78   An informal family photograph made into a private Christmas card for 1911, of three generations of the British Royal Family, including Edward VII, George V and George VI.

PLATE 79   The Christmas card of an English family, which was embellished each year by a family photograph and a poem about the year, composed by themselves. This particular edition was made for 1916 and a drawing of stage and ships by the eldest boy, Albert, decorated the cover of the folder.

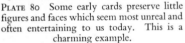

PLATE 80 Some early cards preserve little figures and faces which seem most unreal and often entertaining to us today. This is a charming example.

PLATE 81 Two of the "perfect" children so much loved by the Victorians decorate this old card, one of a set of four, published by Eyre & Spottiswoode. (Size 2½ by 3⅝ inches.)

PLATE 82 An early, possibly American, card with a little boy who, instead of toys, shows off an outsize "letter" carrying the seasonal greeting. A great number of similar little cards invaded the scrapbooks in the 70's. Some have black and others gold backgrounds.

PLATE 83 Children showing off their toys as though posing for a photograph were frequent on Victorian Christmas cards. This card was produced by Vallet, Minot & Co. of Paris and is now in the collection of the British Museum in London.

PLATE 84   Child sentimentalism of a slightly different kind emanates from this small, gold-edged card designed by a pleasant woman artist, Linnie Watt : a lonely little girl gazes out to sea. Two years later, in 1882, Miss Watt won First Prize with her Christmas cards of *two* children, a girl and a boy, building sand-castles, and day-dreaming in a forest.

PLATE 85   The portrait of a little madame probably by Rebecca Coleman, perfectly "chromo-lithographed on the finest white satin"—a delicious De La Rue Christmas card published for Christmas, 1880.

PLATE 86   The perfectly printed chromolithographs decorate the inside pages of a delightful, expensive card of children with toys of 1880. The cover of the 6½ by 5 inches folder is rich apricot silk plush, fringed with silk of the same colour.

PLATE 87   A one-time popular children's pastime, and an even more popular subject equally in Burlington House and on Christmas cards. The little girl and boy on this delightful early folder card of the 1850's are not a bit interested in anything except their bubbles.

PLATE 88   An example of the representation of children as miniature grown-ups on Victorian Christmas cards : a small chromolithograph with black background directly introducing mistletoe in the children's relationship. Note also the repeated occurrence of " awfully " in the wording.

PLATE 89   Children preparing a surprise for their parents are pictured on this postcard size De La Rue card (1880's).

PLATE 90   Jane M. Dealy designed a number of summery and rather feminine Christmas cards with dainty little girls playing or picking flowers or fruit and similar subjects from 1880 onwards.

PLATE 91 A perfectly self-explanatory Christmas card from the early 1880's.

PLATE 92 A glorious pillow-fight enjoyed by the
numerous children of Victorian families when
"home for the holidays". Note the change of
sentimentalism towards children (1881). The verse
on the back of the card, by A. J. F., begins : "What can you expect from six boys in a bedroom, And only one bed, where they scarcely find head room? "

The Marchioness
was celebrated by
Watts and Land-
seer as "the first
amateur in Eur-
ope."

PLATE 93 Children in a holly decorated balcony distribute oranges on this brightly coloured Tuck
"oilette" card of 6 by 5 inches (smaller versions were also produced) by Louisa, Marchioness of
Waterford.

PLATE 94
(*left*)
Designed by
E. Manby.

A charming little cricket enthusiast (about the
time when it became fashionable for women to
play the game), wearing a dark blue dress, bright
red sash and cap and long black stockings and a
sweet smile.

PLATE 95 One of Kate Greenaway's most
charming designs : a little page conveys the
Christmas greeting. Note how well the small
figure fills the space, providing not only a
captivating little person but a pleasing rhythm
of lines and colours.

One of W. S. Coleman's set of three designs which in the publisher's catalogue was listed as "*The Bathers*, after refined and original water-colour drawings in the classical style of

A tripping, fair, light-hearted girl,
Not yet the ripened woman quite,

bathing; ... printed in gold and colours, and inscribed with a suitable verse and Christmas Wishes." (1882.)

WITH THE COMPLIMENTS OF THE SEASON

PLATE 97

A charming though less typical Coleman Christmas card of a young girl picking apples.

PLATE 98

W. S. Coleman's carefully undressed little girls carried the same penetrating period flavour as Kate Greenaway's deliciously overdressed damosels and with their somewhat artificial innocence, both were immensely popular in the 1880's.

PLATE 96

PLATE 99 Two varieties of a well-known Kate Greenaway design, used by Marcus Ward both for valentine and Christmas card purposes. Between the two finished chromolithographs, the third, *i.e.* central version, is *the original* drawing made by Kate Greenaway in water-colours. It is interesting to compare the artist's drawing and the finished products. Note the change in the girl's expression, also the sizes of their feet, etc. (The original Kate Greenaway drawing is the joint property of two enthusiastic collectors, Miss Flanagan and Mr. G. Camm.   Each of them treasures it for six months every year.)

PLATE 100 Two cards from a pretty set of four of the 80's featuring a little girl receiving, reading and crying about a letter. The 6 by 4 inches cards are printed in fine pale colours, with pink, blue and gold border decorations in the fashionable style of their time.

PLATE 101

Three examples of booklet Christmas cards illustrating Shakespeare, Dickens, etc., characters.
Dolly Varden and Little Nell in words and pictures are seen here, representing Victorian
womanhood entering the Christmas cards in the early 70's. The folders are 3¼ by 5½ inches,
and contain ten pages each with four "Character Sketches".

PLATE 102   Couples illustrating the four seasons decorate a concertina Christmas card by Walter Crane,
published by M. Ward in 1878.   Crane, like others of the Art Workers' Guild, took a great interest in the
technique of reproduction of his designs.   His complaints about the results of some designs due to inter-
mediaries between the artist and the reproduction illustrate the problems confronting illustrators, especially
in those days.   About a set of his valentines he wrote :

"... They were copied on to the stone and much of the character lost in the process,
under which they had caught a certain lithographic-mealiness which is very objectionable ".

PLATE 103 The so-called Royal Academy cards were perhaps the first to feature grown-up women as the principal subject on Christmas cards. This is one of a famous set by W. F. Yeames, made in 1881 and published for Christmas, 1882.

PLATE 104 E. J. Poynter, R.A., seated his ladies in the centre of his Christmas card designs. Note the Chinese lanterns amongst the narrow columns, also the screen behind the figure. A snow-covered English hamlet is pictured on a narrow panel below the oriental carpet under the lady's feet. These big—7 by 4¾ inches—cards were printed in many rich colours and gold.

PLATE 105 Elihu Vedder's design, " Prang's American First Prize Christmas card ", with a portrait of the artist's wife. " Thy own wish wish I thee in every place " is part of a sixteen lines sentiment printed on the back of the card. The design includes scrolls left blank for the name of the sender and addressee.

PLATE 106 Women on the Christmas cards designed by Marcus Stone, R.A., were usually deeply melancholy, sitting by themselves on lonely benches or by their equally lonely fireside. This design was so popular that it was later reprinted as a picture postcard.

PLATE 107 The *Art Nouveau* treatment of female figures and Christmas cards. The former were often made to stand or sit beside an—at that time mostly fictional—swimming pool. The monochrome inset is surrounded by a heavily embossed, gilt frame and the floral decoration is also embossed in gold and colours.

PLATE 108 An example of A. Gray's pen-and-ink drawing Christmas cards caricaturing sophisticated young women of the aesthetic period. Note the china plate on the wall decorated by Crane's signature : a crane, caricatured.

PLATE 109 A characteristic end-of-the-century woman—and design—by Georges de Feure; a private card of Octave Uzanne, the well known fashion historian, for 1897.

PLATE 110 The old-fashioned round Christmas pudding and the up-to-date woman seated on it, offer a characteristic taste of the first years of the Edwardian "Merry Xmas" card.

THE VALENTINE
and its effect on Christmas Cards

M A N Y early Christmas cards which have survived from the 1850's and 1860's are almost identical with valentines of the same period, repeating their tricks and sentiments, with only the additional Christmas and New Year greeting to distinguish them.   One of these transitional valentines, with a small red " W " stamped on the back, shows that it was one of the early American cards, produced by G. C. Whitney, of Worcester, Mass., who at that time used to import lace and embossed paper "blanks", scraps and swags, etc., from Europe, chiefly from England.   They were composed (in America) into valentines, and a copy in my collection shows how a little Christmas scrap of a robin replaced proper valentine motifs on some of them.

Valentines were no longer novelties in the middle of the century. On the contrary, symptoms of decline in their career were beginning to appear.   For instance, at that time almost as many " comic " valentines were produced, sold and dispatched as those which remained faithful to the old tradition of St. Valentine's Day, and which were often the only means of affectionate communication between admirer and admired of opposite sexes.   The comic valentines took advantage of the old tradition to make fun, often with rough and rather cruel jokes, of the older opportunities offered on this day.

The customs connected with St. Valentine's Day are very old, and once again take us back to ancient practices which " lovers have observed and poets have honoured from time immemorial ".   The observance is much more than seventeen centuries old, when " the Christian Valentine was beaten by clubs and beheaded, at the time of the great heathen festival of love and purification ", as Dyer, in his *British Popular Customs*, states.   There is a legend which asserts that, while awaiting his execution, Valentine befriended the daughter of Asterius, his jailor, and on the eve of his execution sent her a farewell note signed " From your Valentine ".   But nothing more factual is known to explain any association between the third-century martyr and saint and the St. Valentine's Day customs. The ancient Roman ceremonies must have been observed also in Britain during the Middle Ages, and Alban Butler describes that " to abolish the heathens' lewd, superstitious custom of boys drawing the names of girls in honour of their goddess, Februata Juno, on the 15th of the month (the drawing being on the eve of the 14th), several zealous pastors substituted the names of saints on billets given on this day ". The *Paston Letters* illustrate that the custom was alive in English country houses in the fifteenth century. One of these written in 1477 by John Paston's future wife is addressed : " Unto my ryght welebelovyd Voluntyn John Paston Squyer ". In another, written to him by her mother, Dame Elizabeth Brews, we read : " . . . And, cosyn, uppon Fryday is Sent Volentynes Day, and every brydde chesyth hym a mate, and yf it lyke yowe to come on Thursday at nyght, and purvey yow y^t ye may abyde y till Monday. I truste to God y^t ye schall so speke to myn husband ; and I schall pray y^t we schall bryng the matter to a con-clusyon." Early in the seventeenth century, St. Francis of Sales is said to have severely forbidden the " custom of valentines, or giving boys in writing the names of girls to be admired or attended on by them ", and in 1645 Lord North describes as " costly and idle " the custom, " which by tacit generale consent wee lay down as obsolete ". Pepys, on the other hand, writes in his diary for February, 1661, that " My wife to Sir W. Batten's, and there sat a while ; he having yester-day sent my wife half a dozen pair of gloves, and a pair of silk stockings and garters, for her Valentines ". Other references also confirm that in those days it was quite customary to give and receive substantial gifts as valentines. Pepys mentions that Evelyn told him that Mrs. Stewart, who he believed " to be as virtuous as any women in the world", received from the Duke of York, when he was her valentine, a jewel worth £800, and Lord Mandeville, her valentine in 1667, gave her " a ring of about 300*l*."

In view of these rather extravagant valentines, one may appreciate Pepys's comment for the same year when he writes : " I find [that] Mrs. Pierce's little girl is my Valentine, she having drawn me ; which I was not sorry for, it easing me of something more that I must have given to others." At the same time Pepys refers to a custom, new to him, which presaged the later valentine *cards* : " But here I do first observe the fashion of drawing mottos as well as names ; so that Pierce, who drew wife, did draw also a motto, and this girl drew another for me. What mine was I have forgot, but my wife's was ' Most virtuous and most fair ', which as it may be used, or an anagram upon each name, might be very pretty." Pepys also mentions another type of hand-made valentine when he writes, " this morning come to my wife's bedside, I being up dressing myself, little Will Mercer to be her Valentine ; and brought her name writ upon blue paper in gold letters, done by himself, very pretty ; and we were both well pleased with it ". " But I am also this year my wife's Valentine, and it will cost me 5*l.* ; but that I must have laid out if we had not been Valentines ", he characteristically added. There are many other interesting aspects of the valentine customs in the seventeenth century, which are revealed by Pepys's diary. In 1665 he records that " this morning called up by Mr. Hill, who, my wife thought, had come to be her Valentine—she, it seems, having drawn him last night ; but it proved not. However, calling him up to our bedside, my wife challenged him."

Little Will Mercer's " very pretty " valentine of blue paper and gold letters and the mottoes drawn at Mrs. Pierce's party were considerably developed in the eighteenth century. In 1782 *The Diary of a Country Parson* records the note : " this being Valentine's Day gave 52 children of this Parish as usual 1 penny each—0.4.4. Gave Nancy this morning 1.1.0." At the same time sentimental valentines, engraved in ornamental lettering, entered the field.[1] Mrs. Willoughby Hodgson quotes one of these. It begins : " Dearest Fascinating Being, A willing captive I have been to your matchless charms and graces . . ." and ends : " Your devoted Love."

[1] There is an interesting handwritten valentine dating from the late seventeenth century in the Malcolm Stone collection (U.S.A.). It is possible that it was a sort of layout design or sketch for a copperplate engraving. The sheet, published recently by Ruth Webb Lee in *A History of Valentines*, New York, 1952, shows three attempts at a little verse, the third being dated and signed also, as follows :

" Good morrow vallentine,
God send you ever
To keep your promise and
bee constant ever   1684, October 25 "
The signature reads : " Edward Sangon, Tower Hill, London."

Later on valentines consisted of a picture and verses, combined with or hidden amongst a decorative composition of paper snippets and bits of silk and lace. With the advent of machine-made lace-paper embossed cards and printed scraps of posies, etc., the valentine became as complicated and as full of little surprises as possible. A favourite type of these, if such a word as " type " can be applied to such a rich variety, was the " cobweb ", a paper flower stuck on the sheet by its outside edges. In the centre of the flower there was a little tassel or a silk ribbon, which, when pulled, revealed that the paper flower was cut in the shape of a spiral, or a net, or indeed a cobweb, consisting of a great number of finely cut curves and circles (Plate 17). When fully expanded, the hidden motto, a more personal pictorial message, cupids or lovers kissing, etc., could be seen beneath it.

Printers did not for long leave the composition of valentine cards entirely to the public. Ready-made valentines soon began to be available on the market, complete with scraps of florist flowers, embossed hearts and true love knots, professionally cut-out and embossed, mounted or directly printed on frilled-edged sheets or blanks—all in the style and spirit of those made by individual artistry, only improved by the machine-made devices, especially in an age which was proud of its technical progress. For those who experienced difficulty in expressing their sentiments, valentine guide-books, *The Young Man's Valentine Writer* or *The Quiver of Love* or *Saint Valentine's Sentimental Writer*, etc., were published both in Britain and in America. The skill and care of the home-made valentines and the personal touch was reduced to the selection of the right card from a variety of exquisitely manufactured examples, which nevertheless conveyed the same sentiments. Thus the old custom of confessing love by giving a pair of gloves, which once favoured the glove-maker's trade, was now gradually expropriated by the fancy stationers.

According to the old tradition, the first young man encountered on St. Valentine's Day by a girl was expected to present her with a pair of gloves for the following Easter. An old Devonshire rhyme, many versions of which were known also in other parts, records the custom :

" Good morrow, Valentine, I go to-day
To wear for you what you must pay,
A pair of gloves next Easter Day."

Another old rhyme, published as early as 1598 by Hall, makes a joking reference to the same theme :

> " Love, to thee I send these gloves,
>   If you love me,
>   Leave out the G,
>   And make a pair of Loves."

An old rhyme collected in Oxfordshire in 1849 has the more flowery compliment to go with the old gloves :

> " The rose is red, the violet's blue,
>   The gillyflower's sweet, and so are you.
>   These are the words you bade me say,
>   For a pair of new gloves on Easter Day."

These rhymes would seem as though quoted, not from folklore or scholarly folklore publications, but from any of the early manufactured valentines, inscribed beneath pull-up or sliding-off scraps of flowers. No doubt they were. The real Easter gloves were sometimes replaced, or preceded, by a paper cut-out glove or a silhouette, lightly stuck on a sheet of paper, covering a written love message.

The machine-made valentines and the fact that they were offered in increasing numbers in the shops naturally induced more and more people to express their affections in this form. In the *Mother and Home*, Helen Macdonald recollects the story of " an old gent who waxed indignant at what he considered this waste of money " when he heard that in 1821 the Post Office delivered an average of 200,000 extra letters " at 2*d*. a time " in London alone on St. Valentine's Day. His daughter explained, " That's just the number of young folk there must be in love with one another in London ! That's the way to reckon."[2] The valentine circulation was even more extensive in the United States. Esther Howland's old firm alone sold $100,000 worth of valentines annually, and when later, in 1910, fire broke out on the premises of the other big American valentine manufacturers, the Whitney Company, nearly $200,000 worth of stock-in-trade was destroyed.

[2] An angry correspondent to the *Mirror* (March 20th, 1824) estimated £2,343 15*s*. as " the whole emolument flowing into the Treasury for one day's Folly *in London only* "... In the 1870's over a million and a half valentines went through the post on February 14th.

These figures give some indication of the increasing volume of the valentine makers' trade. But from the stationery manufacturers' point of view the valentine in itself represented a certain limitation to their sales. It confined their sales to shoppers within an age group, and even amongst these only to those individuals who happened to be in love in a particular year! Even then a loving couple would consume one or two valentines a year, and, as James Laver says, " an attractive girl, or as the phrase went, ' an elegant female ', might and did receive half a dozen valentines, but she had the right to expect that their senders had sent to no one but her ! " Thus when the Christmas card was also introduced by some of the valentine manufacturers, its less amorous but much wider appeal of friendship and impersonal compliment was bound to supersede the numerical demand for valentines. Its popularity with the publishers and shopkeepers was natural.

The comic valentine, to a certain extent, paved the way.[3] The " true ", expensive and elaborate love-bearing valentine would be sent only to the real queen of the sender's heart, but a punning joke, a toy-like trick valentine, or a design with comic figures in it would be suitable to many amongst everyone's friends and acquaintances. They would amuse young and old, and thus the comic valentine could be and was sent to a number of people simultaneously—to friends and to those of whom the sender wished to make fun.

When, for example, Dean's first brought out a large variety of comic valentines called " The Sixpenny Movables " in the early 50's, the sales were very much increased and, according to a contemporary report, day by day " quite a crowd assembled under the tree in Cheapside to look at a row of these valentines ", which " took their title from the moving eyes and mouth of the figures " on them. About the same time Goode Brothers were said to have been the first to bring out the " long-strip comic " valentines. They had a good demand for them and " printed 1,200 reams of double crown or double demy

[3] In the U.S.A., Robert Elton and Turner and Fisher began to produce comic (lithographed) valentines in the 1830's, to be followed from the 40's onwards by Thomas W. Strong and in 1850's by T. Frere with truly remarkable woodcut comics. In England bigger issues of comic valentines began to appear in the early 40's with lithographs and woodcuts, published by Park, Elliot, Harwood, Marks, Dobbs and Kidd, and others.

in a season ". The firm of Dobbs, Kidd & Co., of Fleet Street, produced over 1,000 varieties of comic valentines, printed on their fine-patterned lace-paper sheets. They were on sale at many West End shops in London and were exported in quantities to America.[4] The main joke lay in their contrast to the serious valentine and its essential senti-mentality. They were considered very witty if, for example, they resembled the sole of a boot made of brown paper and bearing the inscription, " You are a good old soul as ever trod ", or a couple of soles, one of a man and the other of a woman's shoe, side by side, and with the legend, " May you and I walk through life together. I am ready." Another popular comic was a cut-out watering-can with water seen splashing out of it. The motto reads : " My tears will ever flow like this, unless you stop them with a kiss ". A " clever " valentine gave the embossed picture of a pickle-jar with a slender rod in it and the legend, " I have a rod in pickle for you ! " or the top of a table with a bell and a wedding ring on it and the words : " May I ring the Belle ? " Another group of these popular but crude valentines used a flap to conceal the joke. When this was turned or lifted, it produced a transformation of the picture. For example, at first one sees a young, amorous couple on one of these valentines. When the flap is moved the same couple are seen aged, quarrelsome, toothless and bald. The unmistakable reproduction of unmentionable articles of clothing also played a prominent part on some of these valentines. (Actually, many of these were used also as Christmas cards of the same order.) For example, the cut-out, real lace and paper image of a pair of underpants with the wording, " My heart pants for thee ! " or a pair of miniature braces with a capital " M " superimposed, explaining that the sender is always ready for her love's em-braces ! These valen-tines were certainly in every respect very far-fetched from those earlier

[4] Under the title " English Valentines, Per *Hibernia* ", an American firm " advertised " in a Boston paper on February 9th, 1847, that they have " just received by the above steamer, the greatest assortment of Valentines to be found in Cupid's regions ", including the following varieties, " Comic, Sentimental, Lovesick, Acrostic, Funny, Burlesque, Curious, Characteristic, Humorous, Beautiful, Heart-struck, Witty, Arabesque, Courting, Serio-Comical, Bewitching, Poetical, Heart-rending, Love-encouraging, Trifling, Caricature, Heart-piercing, Serio-tragical, Laughable, Silly, Spiteful, Original, Enlivening, Heart-aching, Suicidal, and many other varieties " !

sentimental beauties, or indeed the later elaborate " mechanicals " and " special favourites ", which, for instance, had " in the centre of snowdrops, orange blossoms, grass, wild flowers, weeds and suchlike decorations, a small mirror, with these words printed on a scroll beneath, ' Take but a peep and you will see, one that the world holds dear to me ' ".

The practical jokes and ridicule not only signified the end of the sentiments from which sprang the valentine's previous popularity, but themselves contributed to their decline, until the custom was finally replaced by the sending of Christmas cards. Much of the sentiments as well as some of the cruder jocularities of Victorian valentines were inherited by Christmas cards.

CHRISTMAS LETTERS
and the Postcard

M A N Y of the early sentimental valentines were originally delivered by a trusted messenger or by the interested party himself, who handed it over early on St. Valentine's Day, as little Will Mercer did to Mrs. Pepys in the seventeenth century, or were discreetly slipped under the door at the house of the beloved,[1] or were left at an agreed hiding-place for the exchange of confidential love messages. Later, of course, the post was used. It still remained a superstitious custom for the sender himself to put it into the pillar-box for " greater safety ".

The precondition for the custom of sending out dozens or hundreds of Christmas cards was necessarily the greater reliability and quickness, as well as the cheapness, of the postal services. When postal charges were high and were paid by the addressee on delivery, letters of conventional compliments in quantities were not always welcome. Wordsworth was once charged £7 on receiving what is now called " fan mail ". Postal duties in those days varied according to distance, and additional charges were made according to the number of enclosures or sheets. The introduction in 1840 of the penny post throughout the United Kingdom resulted in a tremendous increase in correspondence by letter. Between 1840 and 1845 their numbers increased from 170 to 300 millions, and for some time, at the Christmas season, little Christmas greeting cards were enclosed with many Christmas letters.[2]

Soon after the extension of the penny post, printers began to produce notepapers with an engraved and printed heading. These were not address headings, familiar to-day, but illustrations of fashionable watering-places, seaside resorts or other attractive landscapes. At first

---

[1] Letter-boxes and slits in the hall door were not a familiar feature before 1840. They were then introduced at the suggestion of the Post Office to save the letter-carrier's time. The Marquis of Londonderry, annoyed by the idea, wrote an angry letter to the P.M.G. asking if he was expected " to cut a slit in his mahogany door " !

[2] In the U.S.A. reduced postal rates were introduced in 1845, but uniform rates only in 1862. The equivalent of the " penny post ", 2 cents, did not come into force until 1883.

these were probably intended to be sent by people living or spending a holiday at the places illustrated, as souvenirs, similar to those little prints sold in the streets on public occasions, royal weddings, thanksgivings, which were so much treasured by the Victorians. Later the pictures on these notepapers had no particular connection with any one place, but became simply decorations. Cartoons and engravings of humorous incidents, some after Leech and other well-known artists, became popular. The headings often incorporated in the design a date, or the name of the month, a development of the custom of giving the date of publication of the engravings. Some sets, containing twelve or more sheets with various designs for each month or so, soon included at least one design suitable for use at Christmas. The upper half of the first page, sometimes even two-thirds of it, was taken up by the engraving. One of these, from a series of seaside incidents, shows a naked child standing in a few inches of water and obviously reluctant to go further in, and howling with either fright or rage. Mamma or Nannie, armed with a child's spade, is admonishing him to " Go in do, you naughty boy ". The sheet, dated " Dec 23rd 1853 ", had already been used more as a card than a Christmas letter. The personal text on it, written in a somewhat shaky old handwriting, only conveys "Grand-Mothers Love to all the little Children that are good ".[3]

The popularity of bathing scenes may seem somewhat misplaced on Christmas letters, but this shows once again that the season never altogether lost its association with the winter solstice and the reminder of the spring and summer to look forward to. But I reproduce a notepaper heading made definitely to illustrate Christmas activities (Plate 14). The treatment of the subject, " Youth & Age Keeping Ye Merry Xmas ", is similar to Horsley's and Egley's cards, although here the rounded panels are encircled by holly branches. The picture in the

[3] One of the many seaside patterns, with the motto " Mamma is not the least timid of the sea ", shows a rocky seashore, and in the foreground a stout Victorian mamma, fully dressed in crinoline, jacket, scarf and a large picture hat, holding up her skirts, showing her bare feet, paddling somewhat timorously in the shallow water. Two little children are seen paddling with her, but obviously enjoying it much more than she is. Another notepaper heading, inscribed " Return from Bathing ", pictures the back view of three girls covering almost the whole space with their crinolines and with their hair flowing over their shoulders, followed by a little dog barking at them, whilst in the background three young men are watching them with far from unfriendly curiosity.

left-hand circle illustrates a game of blind man's buff being played by a group of small children, charmingly Victorian, while on the right-hand side an old couple are playing cards and other elders are telling stories. In the centre, above the two circles, a young man wearing the fashionable whiskers of the 40's is with his sweetheart under the mistletoe.

The introduction of die-sinking for printing notepaper and envelopes with decorative embossed designs provided a further step towards the real Christmas card. A group of these little Christmas notepapers was published by Charles Goodall & Sons in 1862 (Plate 19). Some of the designs were by John Leighton and included embossed, die-stamped decorations and flat-surface printing combined. The colours are usually delightful, and resemble the rich and bright colouring of medieval manuscript illuminations as well as the colour scheme of traditional, popular art. The sizes were usually small, the whole note-paper being 7 by 4 inches—or even smaller, about 4 by 3 inches. On one there is a wintry composition of bare branches and carol-singers and the text: "Now with Carol and with Lay—Let us welcome Christmas Day". Another shows a little robin and a spray of ivy with a parish church in the background. Its text, printed in bright red, is :

" Listen ! for my song shall be
May Christmas Blessings bring to thee."

A small notepaper represents a stage still nearer to the Christmas card proper. Its decoration occupies the centre of the front page of the tiny folder with a delightfully bright flower and scroll design and the text :

" May Blessings Flow
From God Above
To You And All
Who Christmas Love,"

leaving only space enough for the signature of the sender on the margin of the small page. Personal messages could be written only on the inside page of this tiny folder. It was not intended for even a short " letter ", but just as a conveyance of good wishes, i.e. as a Christmas card.

Notepaper and envelopes often bore the same little emblems. This increased the charm and interest of the envelopes, but somehow reduced the interest of the card inside and was not really justified. As the ornaments on the notepapers and cards grew larger and larger, the early custom to repeat them on the backs of the envelopes had to be abandoned. But the envelope itself is an important inheritance of the modern Christmas card, and it is inherited from the Christmas letter.[4]

In this connection, perhaps it should be mentioned that the first envelope-making machine was patented by W. De La Rue, inventor son of the founder of the firm of the same name, and Edwin Hill, brother of Sir Rowland. Later on the De La Rue firm played a prominent part in the development of the Christmas card in England. The size of the first editions of cards was no doubt determined also by the charming small envelopes this old machine was designed to produce.[5] Almost all the decorations I saw for ornamental Christmas notepapers and envelopes were also used either simultaneously or later on visiting-card-size little Christmas cards. The small Christmas letter, however, went out of fashion soon enough. It was at this stage no longer a letter, and for the conveyance of a greeting without correspondence the single Christmas card was obviously more suitable.

The next important development in the history of the Christmas card came with the introduction of the common postcard in 1870. It represented a further 50 per cent. reduction in the postal charges, and although Christmas cards continued to be dispatched in envelopes, if these were unsealed the facilities applied to them. The disadvantage was, and is, that it can be read by all and sundry. A contemporary writer in the 70's maliciously suggested that this handicap could easily be overcome if Greek letters were used on postcards, his contention being that this would be equal to a cipher in his day of a declining

---

[4] The general introduction of the envelope more or less coincided with the penny post. Previously envelopes would have been considered as enclosures or second sheets, and thus double the postal charges. It will be remembered that the first Post Office envelopes were ornamented with the designs by W. Mulready, R.A., a friend and collaborator of Henry Cole. Cole himself was in all these innovations closely associated with Rowland Hill, later Secretary to the Postmaster-General.

[5] The first machine was recently exhibited in London. It was in perfect working order, and envelopes produced on it were presented as souvenirs to visitors to the exhibition.

classical education. It is interesting how concerned people were about this point. A handbook on *The Art of Secret Writing* was promptly published, and its publisher placed a full-page advertisement of it in the December (1870) number of *The English Society*. " Every reader ", it claimed, " is shown various simple Modes by which open Correspondence can be carried on without being intelligible to any person not in the secret . . . a great service under the New Postal Law " !

But by the 70's the more personal messages had already been discarded in favour of a printed text on the Christmas card. Actually the words " Christmas card " for some time still did not necessarily mean Christmas card in our meaning, but, inheriting the functions of the Christmas letter, was used to describe mainly ordinary postcards received at Christmas-time. Mr. Punch indicated that ungenerous financial considerations prompted the growing frequency with which Christmas letters were replaced by mere cards. There is a sarcastic list of " Christmas cards " which a writer was supposed to have received in 1874 : " . . . an invitation to dinner (which the experience of many winters tells you will be formal, heavy, and tedious, mild in its *menu*, and mysterious in its wines) " ; another invitation " to an ' At Home ' (where you will meet with no one you know, and from which you will make your escape with relief) " ; one from the " only genuine and authentic Waits of the parish of St. Maxim's, soliciting you for some small pecuniary compliment in return for their musical services during the past month " ; a postcard from a cousin in Norfolk " announcing that in consequence of a mysterious disease which has made great ravages amongst his Turkeys, he will not be able to send you one this Christmas " ; " from Aunt Uggathorne to say that she intends to spend the day and stay all night on Thursday (when you expected the Granby Palmers and ten other people to dinner) " ; and, finally, one from the incumbent of the Parish of Grabthorpe, in Northumberland, asking your kind assistance " towards the restoration of an ancient Campanile, the only known example of the Arabesque period in Architecture " ! I have summarised this account as it is curious that a whole selection could have been made of " Christmas cards " at Christmas, 1873, without reference to a single true Christmas card as we now understand the term. In a few years' time, in 1879, *Punch's* book review gives some considerable space to notices on Christmas cards, and in the following years several articles deal with them. One of these begins like this : " More Christmas Picture Cards ! What games of cards everywhere ! It must be overdone *at last*, and then discarded for ever—till the fashion returns." In January, 1880, under the title " More Cards Already ", Mr. Punch complains :

> " The mighty MARCUS, scarcely breathed
> From sleet of Christmas card,
> In card-house of St. Valentine
> Holds us again at WARD ! "

In long verses he complains that " the sleet of Christmas cards " was hardly over when publishers began to put on the market " three weeks in advance ! " their novel valentines, " With Hearts and Darts and Loves and Doves, and Floating Fays and Flowers ".

> " With too much of them thrust on us,
> E'en soft sweet things seem hard.
> Must Punch, must England, old and young,
> Henceforth ' live by the card ' ? "

Instead of the prophesied decline in the popularity of Christmas cards, however, *Punch* itself began to present its political cartoons in the form of full-page " GRINaway Christmas Cards " in 1881, recognisibly caricaturing some of the almost naked girls of the then fashionable Coleman, Dudley, etc., cards shivering in the wintry Christmas weather.

The comparatively rapid change in *Punch's* attitude was, as usual, very characteristic. Nothing more clearly shows how quickly Christmas cards became the subjects of general interest and public comment in Britain in a single decade. In addition, the cards crossed the Atlantic— by this time, both ways. The previous export to the New World was from the mid-1870's reciprocated by an ever-increasing volume of Christmas cards exported from America to " the old " continent and elsewhere, and in 1875 the " Father of the American Christmas card " began to produce American cards also for the American home market. This proved to be of a decisive influence on the development of the Christmas card—everywhere.

OLD CHRISTMAS
Card Makers and Creators

T H E London *Times* in its Christmas Number in 1883 published a long article on Christmas cards. Parts of this notable article are quoted elsewhere in this book, but I am summarising its concluding passages here as these represent a reasoned account of the whole trade as seen seventy years ago :

" Although the popular use of Christmas cards is no doubt condemned by stern philosophers of the unemotional school as so much worthless sentiment, it is not only . . . productive of considerable moral benefit, but it also works in operation a substantial good by the development of a new department of art. It has created quite a new trade, and has opened up a new field of labour for artists, lithographers, engravers, printers, ink and pasteboard makers, and several other trade classes."

The article goes on to explain that—

" The work, too, is perennial. . . . All the year round brains are at work devising new designs and inventing novelties. . . . The very cheap Christmas cards come, it is true, from Germany, where they can be produced at a much cheaper rate, but all the more artistic and more highly finished cards are the result of English workmanship. Science and mechanics, too, play an important part in this work. . . . Nor must we forget the host of trained and skilled work-people required for successfully carrying out the necessary operations. . . . And last, but by no means least, let us remember the poet, who, as can be imagined, has his inventive faculties well tested in providing Christmas sentiment for the million and more individuals, each with a taste of his own."

Then the writer turns, as Sir Henry Cole did in his memoirs, to the increase in postal revenue :

" It is a not unpleasant result of the extensive use of Christmas cards that the revenue of the country is considerably benefited by the custom, thus indirectly reducing taxation.

" Perhaps the chief cause of this wonderous popularity is [according to the writer] that Christmas cards are sold at a range of prices calculated to meet any pocket. The poor may indulge in art to the extent of one half-penny—nay, even less, we believe—the rich, if so minded, may expend five guineas on a single card. . . . It is, of course, a necessary condition of the custom . . . that popular requirements should be studied in every respect, but we are inclined to think that at the present time the more artistic and highly-finished cards, and consequently more expensive, find even a readier sale than those of a cheaper description.

" It is open to question . . . whether the ultimate value or benefit of such expensive gew-gaws is proportionate to their cost ; but, on the other hand, we must remember that the extensive use of artistic cards has stimulated this class of trade and manufacture and has, indeed, created a new and rapidly expanding field of enterprise, for which these days of overstocked markets, there is really much cause to be thankful,"

concludes the writer of this comprehensive article at a time when the European and, indeed, world problem was to find a way to sell.

Who were the men and makers who established this new and rapidly expanding field of enterprise and how did it develop into a trade the scope of which could not be anticipated ? Not much is known about them. Sometimes even the names of artists, poets and manufacturers who made the cards are difficult to discover or identify. The Christmas card was an essentially anonymous trade—as anonymous as the folksong of the olden days or the ornaments of a merry-go-round, or a barge on the Grand Union Canal.

In the absence of reliable and more definite contemporary evidence we are once again in difficulty if we want to give the title " the first " unequivocally to any publishing firm. The possible claimants are numerous amongst the early publishers. Relying on John Leighton's information in a letter to the Editor of *The Times* in 1883 (in reply to the article quoted above), also on Gleeson White's assertion, and finally on a review, " Minor Topics of the Month ", in the *Art Journal* of December, 1862, one can say that probably the first more ambitious, and in volume considerable, edition of a variety of Christmas cards for the ordinary market was published by Messrs. Goodall, the playing-card manufacturers of Camden Town, London, and that the year was 1862. If, however, Leighton's suggestion that the first Goodall editions were decorated only with text, with no robins and holly branches, embossed figures, etc., which, according to his recollection, " came later ", is correct, these must have been previous to 1862. The critic of the *Art Journal* praises the " great variety "—" all being in keeping with the season". He even goes into some detail by relating that by this he means "holly and ivy . . . predominating". The selection was obviously in front of the reviewer as he wrote for the magazine, " an extensive series of cards, notepaper and envelopes, of an exceedingly pure and beautiful character". The alternative dates given by G. White were 1862 *or* 1864 : as he said, his " authorities vary ". It should be mentioned that the production technique used on most of these small 1862 cards for stamping reliefs in two and more clean colours and gold was invented just four years before, in 1858.

Our contention as to the priority of the Goodall cards and the date does not in any way mean to exclude the probability that before Goodall's fairly extensive edition of Christmas cards was put on the market editions by other publishers were already doing business on a smaller scale. Amongst these could be numbered several Baxter licensees, well known at the time also as chromolithographers, such as Kronheim, Dickes or Mansell, whose work on cards and other smaller surfaces compared favourably with their larger and sometimes less-refined prints. Christmas letter headings as well as small, visiting-card-size comic Christmas cards, sometimes signed with " D & S " or not at all, and produced by Dean & Sons, were certainly on the market at the beginning of the 1850's. Most hand-coloured lithographed and wood-cut cards date from the 50's. So were the Petter and Galpin cards, as we have seen. The early colour printers, Bradshaw and Blacklock, whose large-size *Pictorial Casket of Coloured Gems*[1] was perhaps even more treasured in many Victorian homes than its famous predecessor, Chapman and Hall's Baxter-printed *Pictorial Album* of 1837 and R. Canton of London, a firm well known from the 1840's onwards for valentines and other small prints, added Christmas greetings and seasonable rhymes to their colour prints, embossed lace-paper valentines and the " Poetical Cards " which he claimed to have first introduced to the public. (Canton's intricate " laced borders " were actually manufactured by George Meek.) About the same time, Schipper of London and Elliott of Bucklesbury began to use small chromolithographic pictures for their so-called " made-up " cards, which, in addition to valentines, reward and birthday cards, included some with wishes for, or symbols of, Christmas. Some of the scraps used by these firms were imported from Germany and France. Some of the motifs—piglets for luck, four-leaved clover for good fortune—were better known there.

One of the first firms to produce stationery decorated with embossed and die-stamped relief ornaments and lithographic colour prints was Sulman. Their lovely visiting-card-size, embossed, often fancy-edged cards are similar to, and can easily be mistaken for, the Goodall cards. Joseph Mansell of Red Lion Square, London, was another Baxter licensee (after 1849) who combined early colour printing with embossing and produced a considerable number of small-size Christmas cards, some of which were contemporaries to, others a little earlier even than, the 1862 Goodall edition. There was also the well-known firm of Leighton Brothers, which flourished between 1850 and 1885, and which was controlled by G. C. Leighton, who learnt his craft from Baxter. He exerted a great influence on the *Illustrated London News*, and in this respect he and his firm were the real successors of Ingram and the great Victorian printer Vizetelly. Leighton Brothers printed some of the best mid-Victorian magazine covers and colour illustrations,

[1] This was first issued in monthly parts and reproduced in one volume in 1853 or 1854. It advertised that a " magnificent coloured portrait of H.M the Queen would be presented gratis to every subscriber ", but on the back of the same wrapper charmingly offers an alternative, i.e. " The subscriber, if preferred, may have the option of choosing an equally beautiful coloured engraving of H.R.H. Prince Albert ".

as well as commercial designs. They employed first-class artists and their colouring was "richer than that of any other printer". Their contribution to Christmas cards was in the form of colour prints which were superimposed on cards of several early publishers. Thus, as far as I can trace, their name is not printed under them, as is the case with their larger plates. But collectors are often lucky enough to come across with very pretty, usually embossed and die-stamped cards of about 3½ by 2½ inches, not unlike the Goodall production, produced by the old firm, C. and E. Layton.

I should mention Vizetelly himself amongst the men whose work was important in the development of the Christmas card, although he made none as far as I can discover. His *Christmas with the Poets*, "embellished with 53 tinted Illustrations by Birket Foster", had, I believe, a considerable influence on the whole Christmas card manufacture and on their designers. The book was very popular, new editions of it were widely reviewed, and it must have contributed considerably to the popular revival of the " old Christmas " atmosphere, customs and traditions which were in any case so apt to the spirit of the mid-Victorians that, if they could not have been unearthed, would have been indeed invented. Contemporary critics agreed that this was "*par excellence* THE book for Christmas", adding, however, characteristically, " albeit we live in more sober times than those to which it specifically refers " and that " there are two or three songs and poems it would have been judicious to omit, at least for general reading. . . ." The book was compiled mainly from old poems and carols, and the pictures showed ancient Anglo-Norman carol-singers, while in the background other figures bring in the loads of food and drink ; the entry of the boar's head into the old hall ; a scene of " Old English hospitality to the Poor " ; the wassail bowl ; the yule log ; tenants bringing presents to the landlord ; the shepherds of Bethlehem ; wassailing of fruit trees ; " Christmas Sports " ; " A Merry Christmas to you all ", etc.—an obvious treasury of sources for subjects and motifs for the Christmas card designers. Both directly and indirectly, Christmas card producers made use of the ideas contained in this book, while its popularity paved the way for the appreciation of Christmas cards recalling traditional scenes when this type of card began to appear on the market. Similar mutual benefit was gained when in the 70's Washington Irving's book, *The Old English Christmas*, was re-published by Macmillan's with Caldecott's illustrations. In this the American author describes his recollections of a Christmas spent in England with an affection and humour which made his chapters within a few decades nostalgic to read. Dickens, whose contribution to the mid-Victorian Christmas through his own *Pickwick Papers* (1836) and *A Christmas Carol* (1842), etc., is too well known to be specially emphasised here, is said to have declared : " I don't go upstairs two nights out of seven without taking Washington Irving under my arm."

Publicity in those days was not so extensive as it is to-day, but " interested parties ", artists, writers and publishers, were usually friends or acquaintances more frequently than is the case to-day. For example, Birket Foster built his half-timbered " Elizabethan " house, in the middle of a garden, so close to that of Edmund Evans that " one could walk from the grounds of one house to the other ". It was in Evans's villa at Witley, in Surrey, " pleasantly situated on the brow of a hill commanding a view of Blackdown and the sunny Weald ", where Walter Crane and Birket Foster met, and " it was there that the general idea and the size and bulk " of various early Crane and Kate Greenaway picture-books were discussed and " settled upon ", as Crane recalls in his memoirs. All such coincidences and, of course, the public reaction to the various small—one might say, experimental—Christmas card publications are significant and had a certain bearing on the development of the early Christmas card production.

In 1865 and 1866 Josiah Goodall ordered four new designs each year from the Marcus Ward firm to be printed in colour lithography.[2] These were designed by C. H. Bennett, who " by the testimony of all his contemporaries was unequalled in his peculiar walk as a draughtsman "—to use the words of the notice on his *Wit and Humour, Done in Permanent Lines for Posterity*, a volume of more than 100 engravings

[1] Some last-century references suggested that the first Goodall cards and notepapers were produced in France. Actually, many of them bore the trade mark of the Marcus Ward Ulster Works. The widespread belief that they were imported from France or Germany possibly increased their sales in those days, but cannot be substantiated.

published soon after his premature death.[3] Bennett's Christmas card designs represent a further stage, if not in technical perfection, at least in general appearance. The cards were still small and oblong in shape, but the lithographed designs were on all eight varieties upright and practically filled the whole face of the pasteboard. Additional personal messages and even the signature of the sender could only be written on the reverse. The cards are now extremely rare, and as far as it is known no collector possesses the whole set.

The first of the first four designs pictures a merry group of bellringers and big bells of a somewhat Heath-Robinson-like mechanism; the second a jovial elderly man bowed down by the weight of a huge Christmas pudding which he is carrying on his back, on which the Christmas message is written; the third portrays a characteristic mid-Victorian " Grandpapa " with mutton-chop whiskers, high colour and a broad smile; while the fourth shows two little boys carrying between them a large flower-pot in which a heavily laden Christmas tree is planted. The brief, conventional Christmas greeting is written on the front of the pot. The 1866 set is technically somewhat better. The first of these shows a rather fat, winged boy with spade standing deeply entrenched in a great round plum pudding, shovelling pieces of it into a wheelbarrow, while another lad, also with wings, is waiting for the barrow to be filled. The second is a joke on women's fashions of the day. On the top of the card four bells are suspended from a holly and mistletoe decoration, on which the conventional greeting is written. Beneath them the back views of three female " belles " accentuate the bell shapes. The motto " Christmas Bells " completes the design (Colour Plate IVb). The third card illustrates a group of waits packed into a crescent moon, and the greeting seems to be formed of the notes coming out of the various musical instruments. The last is another Christmas pudding, complete with a head emerging from a holly collar, wine-bottle legs, mince-pie hands with a huge knife and fork. The greeting is included on the front of the pudding. . . . The size of the Bennett cards is $2\frac{5}{8}$ by $3\frac{3}{4}$ inches. The

[3] His work includes a small book of lithographs entitled *Christmas Shadows*, published by D. Bogue; *Proverbs with Pictures*, Chapman and Hall, 1858; " The Excursion Train—a Series of Studies of Character ", *Cornhill Magazine*, 1861. He was a regular contributor to the pages of *Punch*, etc.

colours are very pleasant, but the printing suggests the 1850's rather than the 60's. The dates 1865 and 1866 are based on White's survey, and while it is a most helpful and indeed fundamental source for the whole subject of old Christmas cards, dates and names given by him are not infrequently erroneous.

The very next year, in 1867, Marcus Ward & Co. opened a London house and began to publish their own Christmas cards. Their sample books had " survived only in portions " at the time of White's survey, but no Christmas card collection which has survived will fail to contain a fair number of Marcus Ward cards. Once most fashionable in the eyes of the general public, these cards are now treasured by all collectors.

In the hands of this firm, Christmas card production ceased to be a side-line, but became instead a great and expanding industry, intelligently exploring possibilities of both production and market. Though they never ventured into the field of the more complicated mechanical and animated trick cards, their Christmas cards nevertheless embody in their actual design and general make-up a definite period flavour as well as a quality of design which are sought after to-day. While naturally supplying the market with popular patterns, Marcus Ward combined this with a surprising insistence on a certain standard of taste and art well above the average, and—succeeded in selling it. White writes with much appreciation about William H. Ward, one of the partners, known personally to him, and to whom he attributes the full exploitation of technical facilities, a permanent decorative interest, and the discovery and employment of first-class artists as designers as his deliberate policy. The latter included Thomas Crane, the brother of Walter, who became the director of the firm's department of design. He was an excellent designer, and was responsible for hundreds of attractive ornamental designs and flower decorations of a good standard, including a number of those which distinguished the borders and back pages of the Marcus Ward output. Some of the other artists who regularly designed Christmas cards for Marcus Ward were H. Arnold, Miss Georgina Bowers, the popular cartoonist of horsy and hunting scenes, Walter Crane, S. T. Dadd (humorous animal sketches), Robert Dudley, E. Duncan, Edwin J. Ellis, who also wrote some of the sentiments, Thomas Goodman, Kate Greenaway, A. M. Lockyer,

H. Stacy Marks, R.A., Fred Miller, W. Tasker Nugent, Henry Ryland, Moyr Smith, Charlotte Spiers, Percy Tarrant, Patty Townshend and T. Walter Wilson, who designed the once-famous " Christmas Cabinets ", folding triptychs in a series called "Christmas in the Olden Times ", and several others. No wonder, therefore, that *Punch* commented (in 1882) that " Marcus Ward is to the front with his show, and *all* his Christmas *cards* are—trumps ! " In 1884 a series of original drawings, used for Christmas cards and a few valentines, when auctioned at Foster's, fetched £1,798. Included amongst these were two sets of drawings by Kate Greenaway which then sold for 10 guineas each. In 1897 the Gold Medal of the Victorian Era Exhibition, Earl's Court, was awarded to Messrs. Marcus Ward & Co. for their exhibit of lithography and stationery, " embracing samples of their world-famed Christmas cards from 1867 to the present time ".

Like the Goodall firm, which abandoned the production of Christmas cards after some years of pioneer work, so did Marcus Ward, though after a longer time of extensive business. These precedents were followed by a third, important pioneer of large-scale Christmas card production—namely, the De La Rue firm. They commenced this line of their business under their own name in 1875 and ceased publication as such ten years later, in 1885. These figures are based, once again, on White's information.

De La Rue's had a very distinguished career, not only in the Christmas card trade, but in many other fields. The founder, Thomas De La Rue, came from Guernsey, where he obtained his training as a printer, and in 1815, when only twenty-two, joined Champion's, his brother-in-law's firm. A year or so later he came to London and began by making straw hats and bonnets of embossed paper. Later he returned to fine art printing and was helped by a loan from his old friend, Robert Westall, R.A., whose work he used to engrave in Guernsey. This enabled De La Rue to explore many new fields. He was full of inventiveness, and he is reputed to have discovered how to make very white and shiny surfaced cards of fine quality, the type used most by publishers for the small, visiting-card-type Christmas cards later on, and a new process for printing cards, including playing cards, etc., besides various novel printing inks, embossing methods for bookbinding, etc. The envelope as it is known to-day was manufactured exclusively by De La Rue for a number of years. Although Thomas De La Rue died years before his firm began to publish Christmas cards, his enterprising character and the technical achievements were retained when the firm began to manufacture them. Like Goodall and Ward, De La Rue remained loyal to the principle that the Christmas card should be a *card* and its appeal should be in its picture, its harmony with the text and frame ornamentation rather than in animation or tricks. Gleeson White, who had the opportunity of studying all their sample books (most of which were destroyed during the Second World War), praised De La Rue for being, together with M. Ward, aware of the difference between the schools of " decorative art " and " natural art ", their designs being " ruled by architecture, rather than painting ". They brought out a greater number of women or " female " artists, as their society was then called, than either Marcus Ward or Goodall, and achieved a great popular success with sequences of charming Christmas cards picturing little girls in their early adolescence who, as a contrast to the equally fashionable Kate Greenaway school of much-overdressed and befrilled children, were partly or altogether naked, but curiously wrapped in the same rather sentimental Victorian atmosphere of innocence.

Amongst the regular contributors to the De La Rue cards the following artists should be mentioned : Aubert, who was responsible for the general make-up of many of the cards (he had been a pupil of Owen Jones, the famous early Victorian designer), Gordon Browne, W. S. Coleman (who specialised in the dainty little nude damosels just mentioned), Rebecca Coleman, J. M. Dealy (the artist of many very pretty children subjects drawn with a charming feminine touch), Robert Dudley, E. H. Fahey, Ernest Griset, Alfred Hunt, G. J. Kilburne, J. Lawson, Major Seccombe (one-time popular sentimental cards of military life and " soldiers' dreams "), and F. S. Walker, a member of the (Royal) Society of Painter Etchers.

The De La Rue cards were almost exclusively confined to figure compositions, but no such limitation marks the designs of the Christmas cards produced by Raphael Tuck & Son, the still flourishing pioneer publishing house. This firm began to publish Christmas cards on a considerable scale in the early 1870's, probably in 1871, and aimed at providing a card for every shade of taste and choice with suitable designs and at a variety of prices to suit every pocket. It is a pity from the point of view of the student of popular art that, according to Gleeson White, Tuck " has not kept for reference even a series of its catalogues, much less a complete set of its thousands of publications ", as he thought that " even Mr. King's collection does not include all the various items published by this house ". This and the " enormous quantity " of the firm's publications caused White in 1894 to attempt only a slight review of the Tuck cards. To-day only those examples can be studied which were preserved in individual collections, since all the remaining sample books and records of the firm were lost during the Battle of Britain.

Raphael Tuck brought new features into the Christmas card trade. While establishing their large-scale production, ingenious direct and indirect methods were also introduced to gain and increase public interest in Christmas cards. As early as 1880, the firm carried out a big competition to encourage new designs, and various prizes were offered. Well-known Royal Academicians of the day, Sir Coutts Lindsay, H. Stacy Marks (who was himself one of the early designers of cards published by Marcus Ward) and G. H. Boughton, sat on the jury. Nine hundred and twenty-five designs were submitted. They were exhibited at the fashionable Dudley Gallery, which was second only to the much-debated Grosvenor of the aesthetes in the eyes of the artists of the contemporary idiom at the time. £500 were distributed as prizes, and in addition Tuck purchased a selection of designs for £2,500. The significance of this enterprise and the considerable impetus it must have given to designers directly, and to the general public indirectly, will be appreciated if one compares the sum paid out to these competing artists with the fees earned by designers a few years before. The publisher of Kate Greenaway's first valentine set " sold upwards of 25,000 copies of it in a few weeks ". According to Spielmann, her biographer, " her share of the profits was probably no more than £3 ", and " she painted many more on the same terms that year and the next ". (An article in the *Windsor Magazine* discloses that in 1897 the fee for an average Christmas card design was three guineas.

" If it is particularly good or original, the price goes up from four to six guineas, and a clever designer, whose work is known in the trade, can make a steady income of from £500 to £900 per annum.")

In 1881 Tuck's Christmas card production consisted of 180 sets, representing, according to White, 700 designs for that year alone, while in 1882 *Punch* reported in its " Booking Office and Christmas Card Basket " that " Raphael Tuck & Sons have gone in for Royal Academy Christmas cards, the best being those by Mr. Marcus Stone. This comes of having been Christened RAPHAEL, which must be at once suggestive of the highest Art." This, of course, alludes to the famous Christmas card designs which a number of popular R.As. were commissioned to do for this firm. Although their sales figures may not have been as high as some expected them to be, the venture was much discussed and advertised, and thus raised the popular reputation of Christmas card art as such. Gleeson White came to the conclusion that " it would seem as if, two designs of equal merit being offered, the public preferred the work of the outsider to that of the honoured member of the Royal Academy ".

Queen Victoria granted Raphael Tuck & Sons a Royal Warrant in 1893, and for some years they regularly produced Christmas cards for her and for other members of the Royal Family. " It is very interesting to learn the manner in which the Christmas card is regarded by the Queen ", says an article in *Home Chat* in 1895, based on information from Tuck.

" Not only does she procure at great expense cards for all her royal relatives—and we know how numerous they are ", reports *Home Chat* charmingly, " but she buys not less than thousands to send to her neighbours at Windsor and Osborne." In 1895 Queen Victoria chose a typical animated design of period children dancing, but of an even more elaborate card " Her Majesty has ordered nearly a hundred for her relatives in all parts of Europe. . . . This card may be said to have reached the culminating point in Christmas cards. Standing up properly, it occupies a space of 12 inches high by 10 inches wide and 8 deep. . . . It represents the offering by the Wise Men of the East of gifts to the infant Saviour. . . . The whole is got up in a most lavish manner and leaves the beholder in wonder as to how the Christmas card of the present day can be improved upon ", declares the writer. The same article gives an account of " a large number of Christmas cards " ordered by Mrs. Cleveland, the wife of the United States President. " The designs are peculiarly interesting, inasmuch as they are all of more or less Puritan nature or time, and are unequalled for chaste simplicity and good taste. Thousands of Americans will be the proud recipients of these cards this Christmas time from their President and his wife ", concludes *Home Chat*.

Raphael Tuck & Sons, in contrast to most other early Christmas card publishers, continued Christmas card making without interruption from the time of their commencement to the present day. Thus the changing fashions and design types are well reflected in their output, and if the complete series of their cards could ever be collected and shown in chronological order, it would give a very descriptive panorama to illustrate the development of popular taste during the last seven decades. Some of the designers of the Tuck cards, including the " Royal Academy Series ", were : R. J. Abraham, T. H. Allchin, E. A. Bailey, H. M. Bennet, G. H. Boughton, A.R.A., E. Barnard, Sir G. Clausen, R.A., R. Coleman, W. S. Coleman, M. Croft, W. C. T. Dobson, R.A., J. C. Herbert, R.A., G. D. Leslie, R.A., H. S. Marks, R.A., H. J. Miles, J. M. Morse, C. Noakes, V. Norman, E. J. Poynter, R.A., W. Pilsbury, Sir H. Rowlandson, S. Rankin, K. Sadler, H. Sandier, J. Sant, R.A,. A. Squire, M. Stone, R. A., K. Terrell, P. Townshend, W. J. Wainwright, Louisa, Marchioness of Waterford and W. F. Yeames, R.A.

Most old Christmas card albums contain numbers of cards bearing the name of Hildesheimer, their publisher. There were several firms of this name, and it is not quite clear what their relation to each other was.

One of them, S. Hildesheimer & Co., is stated to have begun publishing Christmas cards in 1876. Albert Hildesheimer published also about the same time, while Hildesheimer and Faulkner, which later became C. W. Faulkner & Co., probably published Christmas cards even earlier, though the bulk of their enormous output came in 1880 and the following years.

S. Hildesheimer & Co. were at first thought to have produced only two Christmas cards of their own. The rest of their trade in this field consisted of cheaper imported Christmas cards, which at that time began to appear on the market in great numbers. In a couple of years, however, this firm also began to produce large numbers of their own designs, and in 1879 created a precedent by introducing in large quantities a set called " The Penny Basket ". It was at this time that the distribution of Christmas cards went through a decisive change. Previously they, together with other kinds of stationery, were mainly on sale in booksellers and stationery shops. Towards the end of the 70's and in the early 80's, however, tobacconists and toy-shops began to take up big selections of Christmas cards for sale, and soon they began to appear also in other shop windows, together with the multitude of fashionable gold-painted alloy bric-à-brac which used to be spread in various baskets on the pavements in front of larger and smaller drapery shops. Contemporaries, including Gleeson White, attached a great, though not favourable, importance to the interest drapers began to take in the Christmas card trade and sale. In spite of the tremendous impulse given to the production and distribution of Christmas cards by the placing of single orders of £10,000 worth of cards, for instance, by Bollen and Tidswell, the first drapery firm to enter into the competition, some came to the conclusion that the subsequent price cuts as well as " the less enlightened " standard of the new middleman, " who disposes purely material products " as compared to those who sell books, would eventually lower the artistic qualities of the Christmas card. The fact remains that it was this tremendous extension of the market which resulted in the real mass production of Christmas cards. The effects were both good and bad.

Besides introducing the new " Penny Basket ", S. Hildesheimer & Co. scored a great success, and in the opposite direction, with an ambitious new type of Christmas card, reproducing etchings and water-colours by Wilfrid Ball, a member of the (Royal) Society of Painter Etchers. These cards were just about the size of a postcard, but on single paste-boards, and half surrounded, in the then fashionable way, by floral decorations. The set was in the form of a miniature sketch-book, in imitation leather binding and containing eight pages, all of which could be turned as a real sketch-book. The pages contained little landscapes and notes, seemingly handwritten. Six patterns of these cards were published in 1884 with sketch-books each illustrating a different beauty spot, such as Burnham Beeches, Epping Forest, Hampton Wick, Putney, Richmond and Windsor. The one about Putney, for example, contains tiny water-colour sketches of the Toll House, Putney Church, Boat-houses and Fairfax House and Windsor Street; pages 4 and 5 are covered by facsimile handwritten notes beginning: " Mr. Whistler, the finest living etcher, was the first to show us the picturesque quaintness of old Putney Bridge, now so soon to be demolished. . . ." Gleeson White, commenting on the success of these novel sketchbook cards, states that " the indirect reward for these dainty little things came in the form of almost instant fame. When a signature is attached to tens of thousands of copies of prints carefully preserved and prized, a draughtsman whose appreciation has hitherto been limited to artistic circles becomes a ' man of the town ' at once, with all the profits and penalties of the distinction." He " greatly applauded " Wilfrid Ball on his pleasant little essay and his " sane " and " somewhat daring " reference to Whistler, and " for his courageous attempt to gild a pill that the British public had not then learned to swallow as if they liked it ".

Hildesheimer and Faulkner published a great number of cards of " popular academic " rather than " aesthetic " taste, to use the terminology of contemporary criticism. They, too, arranged a prize competition and exhibition of Christmas card designs in 1882. Their exhibition was held in the Suffolk Street Gallery, now the Royal Society of British Artists' Gallery, and they paid out £5,000 in prizes. The first prize of £250 was awarded to Miss Alice Havers for a card entitled " A Dream of Patience ". She thus became one of the most celebrated Christmas card artists, a position she maintained well up to the 1890's in addition to regular work as an illustrator of books and magazines and a frequent exhibitor at the R.A. and elsewhere. One of her early designs is prominently preserved in one of Queen Mary's albums of earlier cards.

Hildesheimer and Faulkner employed a great number of well-known artists, amongst them many of the most popular Christmas card designers of the day, such as J. E. Barclay, H. W. Batley, Miss Bennett, Alfred Bower, the political cartoonist Bryan, A. W. Cooper, H. H. Couldery (whose " sympathy with kitten nature down to the most appalling depths thereof " and " tact and sensitiveness to the finest gradations of kittenly meditations and motion ", wrote Ruskin in 1875, were " unsurpassable "!), C. Davison, Jane M. Dealy, Mme. Dubourg, Mrs. Duffield, S. T. Dadd, J. Nelson Drummond, Mrs. Fellowes, Miss E. Folkhard, Frank Feller, G. C. Fraser, Ernest Griset, M. L. Gow, G. C. Haite, Alice Havers (Mrs. Fred Morgan), W. J. Hodgson, F. Hines, Reginald Jones, E. K. Johnson, G. C. Kilburne, E. Blair-Leighton, A. Ludovici, Jr. (designer of amusing cards of " intense aesthetes "), Lizzie Lawson, E. Manly, Margery May, W. J. Muckley, Fred Morgan, F. C. Price, T. Pyne, Octavius Rickatson, Henriette Ronner, J. McL. Ralston, Percy Robertson, R.E., Martin Skipworth, R.E., G. Sadler, H. Sandier, Mrs. Staples (" M.E.E."), Henry Reynolds Steer, H. J. Stock, St. Clair Simmons, B. D. Sigmund, Percy Tarrant, Alfred Ward, Miss Linnie Watt, A. W. Weedon, Ernest Wilson and others.

When the so-called " classics " of the British Christmas card industry developed the Christmas card into a commodity of truly general interest and at the same time a typical product of the 70's and 80's of the last century, Louis Prang, " the father of the American Christmas card ", originated the production of Christmas cards in the United States. It can now safely be said that this became an important, indeed decisive, turning-point in the history of the Christmas card. The Christmas card ceased to be a mere European or English peculiarity, with the limitations this necessarily involves. Prang's plant in Roxbury, a suburb of Boston, and his production of cards designed and printed in America, not only established a line of trade which grew into the tremendous American greeting card industry of to-day, but led to the creation of a market and an extension of the custom on such a world-wide scale that it now can almost be described as universal.

Before Prang, Christmas cards used to be exported from Britain and other European countries, just as valentines had been previously, to America and the British dominions overseas. But just as even the more ancient custom of the valentine could not really become rooted and general in the New World until local producers, naturally more familiar with the tastes and requirements of their compatriots, joined in the publication of these " lovers' missives ", so the Christmas card could not become really established until it was " home produced ".

The Esther Howland and the George C. Whitney, as well as the T. W. Strong and Turner and Fisher, of the development of the American valentine card was, in a single person, an energetic and versatile, intelligent and undefeatable German immigrant, Louis Prang, for the history of the American Christmas card. He arrived in New York in April, 1850, after the failure of the 1848-9 revolutions in Europe, with the optimism and determination and an idealistic faith in the New World so typical of the exiles at that time. Unlike many who shared his fate and hopes, but lost their way later, Prang was able to use his knowledge and experience combined with the reformer's idealism in building up an industry, which not only became highly prosperous in his own lifetime, but helped to improve the standard and appreciation of art and to contribute to the general and particularly the art education in his new country. Besides being an ingenious publisher and first-class lithographer, his name is also remembered in America as the promoter of the so-called " Prang method of education ", which was a system to awake and develop the creative impulse in the young and on which he spent considerable time and large sums of money.

After a number of short-lived ventures in publishing and other trades, including work as a wood-engraver under Frank Leslie at Gleason's Pictorial, he set up as a lithographer under the name Prang and Mayer, Boston, in 1856, but four years later, in 1860, his partnership with Julius Mayer was dissolved and the now better-known " L. Prang & Co." was established. During ten years of hard work and much experimentation both in the fields of production techniques and of marketing, he succeeded in perfecting a process of lithographic colour printing, usually from eight, but sometimes from as many as twenty plates,[4] which gained for him the admiration of experts on both sides of the Atlantic.

True to his principles, shared by many enthusiastic reformers of the period, that the facilities to mass-produce colour prints should not

---

[4] " I have used zinc plates for nearly all my colour plates since 1873, and am positive that I have saved thereby fifty thousand dollars", stated Prang in the Chicago *Lithographer and Printer* in 1884. " I should have had to erect another building long ago if I had not used zinc plates", he added. Zinc as a substitute for lithographic stones was a much-discussed " new improvement " in the 80's, and the Editor of the periodical found it timely to comment that " Prang's work is known, and therefore nobody can say good work cannot be printed from zinc plates".

debase art, but, on the contrary, that cheaper production should bring art and good taste into the lives of the masses and the everyday life, he made every effort to make the best contemporary artists interested in designing for his purposes. He originated the first open competitions for Christmas card designs in 1880 and successive years. The considerable prizes he offered to winning designers (the first prize $1,000, second $500, and a number of smaller prizes of $300 to $200 !), and the great publicity enjoyed by the exhibition of the entries at the American Art Galleries, New York, the appointment of people like Samuel Colman, Richard M. Hunt, E. C. Moore, John La Farge and Louis C. Tiffany as judges and, in 1881, the introduction of additional equally big prizes to be awarded by the public itself by popular vote—all these had the desired great impression on designers and distributors as well as the general public everywhere. Prang's enterprise, his anticipation of a publicity campaign and modern projecting and merchandising methods, as it would be termed to-day, were certainly remarkable in the 1880's, and had an immediate effect also on his chief competitors, the leading publishers in Britain. Some of these took up the challenge : Tuck, Hildesheimer and Faulkner and S. Hildesheimer & Co. themselves inaugurated prize competitions and exhibitions of designs and introduced novel attractions designed to have a wide, popular appeal amongst those who began to talk about the superiority of imported designs, for example, the costly introduction of the so-called " Royal Academy Series " and various other selling devices ; while others, unfortunately including such pioneer producers as Marcus Ward or De La Rue, who could not or did not want to join competition on this new and extensive scale, soon abandoned the production of Christmas cards altogether.

At the beginning, from 1875 to 1879, the Prang cards were usually small, single cards (3½ by 2 or 4 by 2½ inches were the most frequent), printed on one side of the card only. Flowers, flowers and birds, decoratively grouped, but seldom stylised in the manner which was the fashion at the house of Marcus Ward and others in London ; the greeting text, couplets or prose, usually fairly brief, but varied to suit every possible requirement, the letters, usually rather elongated to give " elegance ", but, considering the period, not too fancified, and always worked in as part of the whole design, and, finally, the usually faultless register and perfect finish lend a definite character and attraction to these cards.

One of the novelties in design which swept into great vogue, lasting for several years on both sides of the Atlantic, was the black background Christmas card. Prang began to produce these in huge numbers in 1875, but probably brought out some in the previous year, when, publishing only for export to Britain, the year of copyright was not yet dutifully printed on all his cards as in later years. The contrast made the bright colours and contours of the emblems, scrolls, flower or bird designs stand out brilliantly from the solid black background of these cards.[5]

Similar to the black background cards, Prang produced some small and large oblong cards with a brilliant plain red background. These, somehow resembling the general effect of the old Roman wall decorations, provided the same contrast with the actual pattern as the black background cards, but the red lent a festive gaiety to the cards, perhaps more seasonable than their black counterparts.

By the end of the 70's, the typical Prang card became more and more elongated, $5\frac{1}{2}$ by $2\frac{3}{4}$ and $6\frac{3}{4}$ by $2\frac{1}{4}$ inches being characteristic measurements, usually considered particularly artistic at the time, while, especially from 1880 onwards, when designs submitted to the prize competitions were included in his annual output, cards rather large in both dimensions (6 by 8, 7 by 10 inches, etc.), became the features of the Louis Prang production. At the same time, rather fine, usually monochrome decorations began to appear on the reverse side of the cards, occasionally incorporating longer sentiments or verses, the name of the designer of the card and details of the competitions. Though

[5] It is interesting to note how old and successful patterns seem to recur again after many years. The black background Christmas cards, which used to be extremely popular from 1875 well up to the late 80's, but were afterwards completely forgotten for nearly thirty years or so, were reintroduced again, though without the previous lasting success, in 1923. " The black background card will be one of the most popular this season ", said the London paper, the *Daily Mail* (October 17th, 1923), in an interesting survey of new designs, adding : " the rich lacquered effect being a most effective backing for any subject, from a glass bowl of flowers to a group of kittens and puppies or a beautifully painted robin perched on a twig of holly. The choice of ribbons on these cards helps to complete a most artistic effect. . . . The terra-cotta ribbon on a black card with a bowl of wall-flowers on it . . . a particularly happy example. . . ."

always representative of the artistic conventions of their period, these reverse patterns are often even more attractive, at least to our mid-1960 taste, than the ambitious and colourful pictures on the obverse, their real attractions sixty-odd years ago.

Perhaps it should be added that Prang, like Marcus Ward and De La Rue and a few other manufacturers in Britain, would not venture into the field of trick or mechanical cards, and his artistic *credo* forbade him to produce cards composed of layers of lace-paper and different materials, which he no doubt considered vulgar and of bad taste, and even his comics were of the rather arty, caricature type as opposed to the cruder jocularity of both American and British valentine and Christmas card production of this type. To him the Christmas card was and remained a *card*, embellished by its pictorial design and the lettering of the greeting text or sentiment, and his way of increasing its beauty was to select a design and sentiment which, according to his best knowledge and that of his advisers, was more beautiful than the previous one, rather than deliberately accumulating styles and materials in order to achieve greater attraction. Nevertheless, as if to prove that there is no escape from the spirit of an age, all the larger and more ambitious Prang designs were produced and available with or without the wide silk fringe, the distinguishing mark of the elegant and expensive greeting card of the 1880's.

Amongst the American Christmas card designers whose work was published by Louis Prang, the following artists should be mentioned : O. E. Whitney (who did the first, mainly flower cards for him), Rosina Emmett (winner of the First Prize at the 1880 and the Fourth Prize at the 1881 contests), Alexander Sandier, Alfred Fredericks (an artist noted for his woodcuts for school text-books, etc.), A. G. Morse, Elihu Vedder (the winner of the First Prize at the 1881 competition, and about whom Walter Crane wrote in 1872, when he visited Italy, as " chief among the circle of American artists " and " whose work was already known in England " ; Vedder's design, as one of his lunettes, may be seen at the head of the stairway in the Congressional Library, Washington, D.C.),[6] Dora Wheeler (winner of $2,000 in 1881), Charles C.

---

[6] " (They) took their place as part of the architecture of the building more perfectly than any others ". *The History of American Painting* by S. Isham, New York, 1944, p. 554.

Coleman, L. B. Humphrey (one of the first group of women book-illustrators in the U.S.A.), Walter Satterlee, Fred Dielman (later a well-known illustrator), F. Taber, J. C. Beckwith, E. H. Blashfield (the painter), R. F. Bloodgood, I. H. Caliga, T. W. Dewing, F. W. Freer, I. M. Gaugengigl, W. St. John Harper (illustrator of Keats's *Endymion*), Will H. Low (the celebrated illustrator of Keats's *Lamia* (1885) and *Odes* (1887), who was also responsible for some valentine designs published by Prang), Leon and Percy Moran, Thomas Moran (the popular landscape painter), H. W. Pierce, A. M. Turner, D. Volk, J. Alden Weir (the distinguished etcher who was also one of the first " painter lithographers " in the U.S.A.), the cartoonist C. D. Weldon (who won the First Prize at the Prang Christmas card design competition in 1884, when the prizes were awarded by the ballot of dealers, in place of juries composed of artists and art critics and the popular vote of the general public of the previous years), E. K. Johnson, F. S. Mather, Newton Macintosh, G. Schackinger, R. M. Sprague, Fidelia Bridges and Henry Sandham (the painter).

These and several others contributed to designs for the Prang cards, and thus to the first, momentous epoch in American Christmas card production. Naturally, the standard of Prang's cards varies according to the quality of the artist, the nature of the design and its price, as is the case of most publishers. Their technical excellence, however, and their perfect finish as chromolithographs hardly ever falters, and this makes them particularly sought-after items for the intelligent collector, even if he or she may never venture to compete with the seventy odd volumes of Prang cards in the American Antiquarian Society's collection at Worcester, Massachusetts. But every collector will find it worth while to include in his collection a selection of Prang cards, not only as they represent the first era of the history of the American Christmas card, but on account of their interest and quality in themselves. The distinguished critic and first Editor of the *Studio* of London, Gleeson White, writing of Prang cards, says, amongst other things, that " both for their intrinsic merits and the influence they had upon English taste, it is not easy even now [he wrote in 1894] that their novelty has faded to speak of them except in superlatives. . . . Indeed, it would be a somewhat difficult task to find a dozen examples published in England that could be set forward as worthy rivals to the best dozen of the Boston cards. . . . The prices obtained for copies were also very much higher, so that it is hardly fair to set the results in direct competition with those produced for half or quarter the cost on this side. But considering them apart from any comparison, how good they are ! Not merely in design, but in colour, they have, for the most part, a singular charm. Their designs are delicately finished without niggling detail. The charm of the colouring is not to be attributed entirely to a larger number of colour printings, or superior chromolithography ; both these factors no doubt helped to give the peculiarly harmonious result ; but one can feel beyond this, that the artists employed recognised from the first the limitation of all mechanical reproduction, however perfectly manipulated, and designed accordingly."

Frank Weitenkampf, in his authoritative work on *American Graphic Art* (Macmillan, New York), refers to New York Press comments as to the " very real influence in the education of taste " exerted by " these bits of pasteboard " and " the spirit of the projector who laid so many well-known or promising artists under contribution ". This foremost American expert sums up the significance of the Prang Christmas card production as follows : " Here was one example of the application of art to things near at hand, the entrance of art into daily life. The problem of such service on the part of art without a loss of its ideals, a service just to both parties, is always with us."

Actually a recently discovered design, " the first *American* Christmas card ", is an interesting early example of the idea of combining practical use, in this case business advertisement, with " A Merry Christmas And A Happy New Year ". It is a lithograph produced probably in the early 1850's by R. H. Pease, of Albany, New York, and the design includes a picture and prominent display-lettering advertising " Pease's Great Varety [*sic*] Store in the Temple of Fancy " as well as spaces provided for the name of the addressee and the sender. (For description see Appendix, List of Christmas card publishers.)

Apart from the production of Louis Prang of Boston, most of the rest of the American market was supplied by imported Christmas cards during the nineteenth century, and no American publisher is recorded by Chase or other American writers between Prang, who gave up publication of Christmas cards during the 1890's, and the second era of the American Christmas card, which began in the early 1900's with the attractive " Cornhill Dodgers ", which, in the changing manner of the times, continued the deliberately artistic approach in their general appearance (Fig. 7), and with the establishment of the still-flourishing firm, Albert M. Davis & Co., in Boston, whose extensive output exercises a decisive influence on the most popular Christmas card types both in the U.S.A. and elsewhere.   But I think that there is every justification to include amongst the early Christmas card manufacturers the Boston firm of James A. Lowell & Co., who produced extremely finely executed and printed steel-engraved Christmas cards in and about 1880, and Messrs. Farmer, Livermore & Co., Providence, R.I., of about the same period.   These designs were usually printed in black or dark grey on tinted paper, though occasionally one also comes across coloured examples.   They anticipate in their general style the layout designs consisting of smaller and larger panelled pictures grouped in and amongst rather loose sprays of flowers or branches or decorative grasses, a convention which became so universal in magazine illustration and every sort of "artistic" design in the 1890's, including, of course, the designs of thousands of the " more refined " type of Christmas cards.

In Britain another firm, worthy of our special attention, began to produce Christmas cards on a large scale in 1878.   This firm, now better known as general book publishers, is Messrs. Eyre and Spottiswoode Ltd., London.   In 1882 *Punch's* reviewer, in " Our Christmas Card Basket ", includes their publications amongst the most prominent of the year, and after describing some of the other cards turns to verse :

> " There are none much sublimer
> Than those of Hildesheimer.
> Likewise very good
> Are those of Spottiswood(e)."

The identification of the Eyre and Spottiswoode cards is easy : the publisher's name usually appears clearly printed on the margins. Most of their artists, amongst them Harry Arnold, I. Brindley, Frank Feller, Elizabeth Folkhard, C. M. Jessop, T. R. Kennedy, B. Maguire, H. Stacy Marks, R.A., J. Proctor, Percy Tarrant, Linnie Watt and A. Whymper, were also known for their designs made for other Christmas card publishers.

An apparently smaller but rather original selection of Christmas cards was published in the late 1870's and during the 1880's by Alfred Gray, most of them actually designed by himself and the cartoonist W. G. Baxter. He specialised in hand-coloured, smallish cards, printed on parchment. Many other cards by him were from pen-and-ink drawings, about postcard size, seldom printed in more than two colours, gold or silver and black being the most frequent.

Fig. 7. Alfred Bartlett, Boston, began to publish his attractive " Cornhill Dodgers " in 1900. For some time sales were much handicapped on account of their fine deckle edges. " The public merely glanced at these edges and refused to buy. They looked upon them as marred, frayed, or mutilated." (The second colour is omitted from this reproduction.)

Some of these caricatured the fashionable Walter Crane and Kate Greenaway drawings, the " new furniture " and other topical subjects of the " yellery-greenery " days.

At about the same time, Angus Thomas of London began to produce his innumerable comic and usually humorous trick cards. They were to appeal to a considerably less highbrow but much wider public, and were not produced very finely in either design or execution, but their wording made full use of all possible, and often impossible, puns and spelling tricks afforded by the language. Wishes for " Good (four) tunes " were conveyed by four tiny manuscripts of popular songs attached to one of the cards, " *warmest* Christmas greetings " expressed by a miniature thermometer attached to the card, with the additional quiz as PS. : " What is the Highest Known Temperature ? "—the answer : " 2 (Two) in the Shade " hidden under the thermometer, and so on. In the 1890's, at the time of the big publicity campaign of the London *Daily Mail*, Angus Thomas was quick to provide " an UP TO DATE " and " MOST SUCCESSFUL " Christmas greeting, including a miniature replica of the *Daily Mail* itself, and with the wish : " May BEST OF NEWS for you be found,/Telling a GLADSOME TALE,/Not only when CHRISTMAS TIME comes round,/ But, by ev'ry DAILY MAIL." Similarly, when the violent argument for and against cleaning pictures in public galleries was raging, Angus Thomas produced a replica of a bogus Old Master painting of a young woman smiling out of the richly gilded frame, half of the canvas " cleaned ", i.e. printed in lively, bright colours, while the other half is pictured as shadowed by the darkened varnish, the sentiment being : " May Christmas Joys RESTORE all bygone pleasures and Paint Your Future in Sunny Tints ! "

Space does not allow me to give a detailed account of the many other publishers who manufactured or commenced to produce Christmas cards during the nineteenth century, and I must confine myself only to mention some of those whose work I have come across, and refer the reader to the List of Christmas Card Publishers, p. 262. A. Ackermann of London was associated with L. Prang of Boston, and cards actually produced and printed in America sometimes appeared in London under the name of this firm ; Adam & Co., Newcastle ; J. Beagles & Co., London ; Birn Brothers, London ; J. Bognard, U.S.A. ; Book Society, London (chiefly religious cards with Biblical quotations, mostly printed in Austria) ; Brooks, London ; Bufford's Sons, Boston ; Burke, London ; Byrne & Co., Richmond ; Campbell and Tudhope of Glasgow (with chiefly religious subjects and verses) ; Castell Bros., London (usually actually printed in Bavaria) ; C. Caswell, Birmingham (early publisher of mainly religious cards with flower decorations) ; Cayer & Co., Paris ; Charles, Reynolds & Co. ; S.P.C.K., London (publishers of suitable religious cards of flower decorations and lettering); F. Guy Corke ; Davidson Brothers, " whose books are in excellent taste and full of dainty inventions ", according to Gleeson White ; J. B. Day, London ; G. Delgado, London (still flourishing) ; Dietrich, London ; T. Dupuy, London and Paris (cards probably produced in France) ; F. Edwards & Co., London ; Faudel Phillips & Sons ; C. W. Faulkner & Co., London (the successors of Hildesheimer and Faulkner from the 1890's onwards, and still flourishing) ; Griffith, Farran & Co., London (associated, I believe, with Ernest Nister) ; W. Hagelsberg, Berlin (who produced a great number of cards with English texts, often religious subjects of the guardian angels watching over children or flying about wintry towns type, but also novelty cards to commemorate the Colonial Exhibition at South Kensington in 1886, or picturing Punch and Judy shows which appear on a blank white panel when the card is held up against an electric light, itself still a novelty) ;[7] Hamilton, Co., London (publishers of " For the Empire " Series, etc., in the 1890's) ; Hawkins, London ; Horrock and Hetherington, London (who published Tristram Ellis's etched cards) ; International Art Publishing Co., New York and Berlin (Christmas postcards) ; Harding, London (who, according to *Punch*, " hit on a very original notion in his Hunting Christmas cards, which are full of life and spirit, and, like the horses depicted, ought to go well ", 1880) ; Jarrold & Sons, London ; Leadenhall Press, London ; R. J. Mackay (U.S.A.) ; W. Mack, London ; W. McKenzie & Co., London ; Albert Marks, London ; Meissner and Buch, Leipzig ; Misch and Stock ; Mowbray & Co., London and Oxford (who started their still-flourishing production, " Christmas Cards of a character definitely associated with the central fact of the festival—the

[7] It is interesting to recollect the announcement of S. Hildesheimer that " Foreseeing that designs selected solely by Artists, who, however eminent in their profession, had no technical knowledge of the Art of Chromo-Lithography or practical experience of the wants of the Public, would fail to satisfy the demands of the Trade —who require Christmas Cards to be not only artistic in design but *perfectly printed* and suited to the popular taste—we determined that one of the three Judges to whom we entrusted the award of the principal prizes in our Exhibition, should be a practical authority in all matters appertaining to the reproduction of Works of Art by Chromo-Lithography. We were fortunately enabled to obtain the valuable services of W. Hagelberg, Esq., of Berlin, a gentleman of great experience, and occupying a foremost position amongst Fine Art Printers, to assist the eminent Royal Academicians, G. D. Leslie, Esq., and Briton Riviere, Esq., in the selection of the designs ; thereby securing not only the highest artistic but the best practical judgment for this important trust " (1881).

Holy Incarnation ", with the publication in about 2,000 copies of the Nativity of Our Lord, by W. H. Hughes, in 1880) ; M. H. Nathan & Co., London ; Newman & Co., London ; Ernest Nister, London and Nuremberg ; Ollendorff, Germany ; Ough, London ; Parkins and Gotto, London (one of the early " private card " specialists) ; Pearson, Bath ; Philipp Bros., London ; Religious Tract Society, London (who issued a good number of Christmas cards in addition to their other familiar cards and booklets, with an emphasis on the religious significance of the anniversary in the text of the cards) ; Rolph, Smith & Co., Toronto (one of the first Canadian Christmas card publishers, whose cards were " Entered according to Act of Parliament of Canada in the year 1881 . . . in the Office of the Minister of *Agriculture* " !) ; H. Rothe, London (with cards printed mostly in Germany, I believe) ; Saunders, McBeath & Co., Dunedin, N.Z. (who commenced producing Christmas cards in 1882, including a card illustrating the comet of 1882 as seen in New Zealand ; also verses describing that December is a summer month there, etc.) ; Schipper & Co., London ; Gibb, Shallard & Co., Australia ; Smith, London (imitation cheques, etc., drawn on the " Bank of Providence, Branches all Over the World ", " Three-hundred-Sixty-six Days of Health and Prosperity " and similar cards) ; Sockl and Nathan, London (" The Originators of the famous ' Colonial and Indian Exhibition Cards ', ' Colinderies ' for Xmas, New Year and Birthday ", also " The Edinburgh Exhibition Cards for the Scotch Buyer " in 1886) ; Stannard & Son, London ; Thomas Stevens, Coventry ; Terry, Stoneman & Co., London (for whom Dickes frequently made the colour prints) ; R. Thomson & Co., London ; True & Co., Augusta, Maine ; John Walker & Co., London ; W. Wheeler, Jr., Cork ; Wheeler Brothers, London ; Geo. C. Whitney, Worcester, Mass. (the famous valentine producers, who, from about 1880, added Christmas cards, calendars and various illustrated booklets to their list, some of which were published in co-operation with the London firm, Hildesheimer and Faulkner) ; Wirths Bros. and Owen, New York ; Yates, Nottingham.

The scope of the present work does not permit the inclusion in any proportionate detail of the various Christmas and New Year card publishing houses on the Continent, apart from those already mentioned and a few of those whose cards, often printed also with greeting text in English, found their way on to the British and American markets from 1870 and 1880 onwards.

Some of these cards were the products of publishing houses with business establishments in Britain, later on also in America and on the Continent, such as Marion & Co. or Th. Dupuy, both of Paris and London, or Cartler, and others. Some firms, such as Aubry, the Paris publishers of the 1870's, had some arrangement with Messrs. Marion and Co., and at one time with Raphael Tuck, for instance, and many of these cards—but by no means all—bear the trade-mark of both firms, one on the left, the other on the right bottom corner of the same card. There were many others, amongst them Blot, Duprey, Vallet, Mirrol & Co., Bonasse-Lebel & Fils and Massin, all of Paris, whose Christmas cards were apparently imported and entered at the Stationers' Hall in London. In a similar way, Christmas cards were imported from Germany and some from Austria-Hungary. To mention only one and one of the most successful German firms, Meggendorfer of Munich, for instance, sent over during the 70's, 80's and 90's perfectly finished and very expensive trick cards which sold at high prices in London and in America.

Although a few of the publishing houses mentioned in this chapter are still in production to-day, the great majority of them were in the Christmas card business only for longer or shorter periods during the nineteenth century. The tremendous increase in the number of Christmas card publishers which followed the turn of the century and the fact that these are almost contemporaries means, I am afraid, that they must be omitted from individual mention here, but allusions to the publications of some of them are made in connection with particular cards reproduced or referred to as examples interesting as, or illustrative of, special trends or ideas in design and fashion.

A MICROCOSM
of the Age

WHEN one turns the pages of an album of old Christmas cards, one experiences sensations not unlike those experienced by the alert observer on an eventful journey. The mental journey provided by thousands of such cards takes us, however, not merely to places near and far, to the unexpected discovery of hidden beauties, charming people, strange customs and unfamiliar ways of life. The route opened up for us offers a little of all these experiences to the sympathetic traveller, with the addition of the subtle pleasure induced by the entry into another dimension at the same time—namely, that of *time*. Old Christmas card collections may relate little of importance to the material of ordinary history books, but certainly reveal and preserve almost every other aspect of life and atmosphere, fashion and the changing panorama as seen through the eyes of their contemporaries, and thus provide a realistic background to the appreciation of the more momentous events of the period. Besides an objective documentation of habits, customs and costume pictured on them, popular Christmas cards also disclose many unconscious attitudes and predilections without wishing to do so, and thus perhaps with less distortion. The picture presented by the mosaic of old Victorian cards is composed of a multitude of minute but nevertheless real elements. However casual and unsystematic each may appear if considered separately, considered together they form an integral whole, with sufficient incongruities to be as convincing as life itself. They not only present, but represent the taste, style and perception of their age.

Christmas cards represent in a condensed, microscopic panorama the macrocosm of the endless variations, contrasts and divergencies so characteristic of the latter half of the " glorious century ". From a distance it seems that this unconscious period touch, a peculiar and recognisable flavour with which these cards depict their world, is the only common denominator of the Victorian Christmas card. In other ways, the designs may differ in everything, including the fact that since the 1880's Christmas cards are very often folders of four, eight or more pages, not strictly cards. Neither were they necessarily all made of cardboard or paper. A considerable number of patterns were painted or printed on silk or satin. Others, again, were composite products of real lace as well as lace-paper, seaweed, shells, dried grasses and flowers, velvet or chenille, metal plates, tinsel or celluloid, crewelled work and many other materials applied on a paper or silk base, but in such a way that the latter played a negligible part, if in fact it was used at all. Nor were old Christmas cards limited in any way as to subject or style of their pictures or decorations. In this respect they differed still more widely than in the material substances used in their make-up. The very indiscriminate choice of subject (habitually criticised by contemporaries generation after generation), which ranged from appropriate Christmas topics, Nativity scenes, holly, ivy and mistletoe, Father Christmas and the Christmas tree, wintry scenes, robins and family parties, etc., through flowers, plants and bouquets, animals, birds and insects of all kinds to comic or serious illustrations of contemporary public figures, popular characters, novelties (such as electricity, the bicycle and the telephone, the airship, or that " new monstrosity from France ", the " autocar " or " automobile "), customs or habits, makes a collection of old Christmas cards a treasury of illustrations for any social historian. There are few subjects, if any, which concern themselves with the outlook or conditions of the last 100 years which could not be very well illustrated almost exclusively by contemporary Christmas cards. If a novel type or subject was the popular favourite one year, it would almost certainly be followed by another novelty the next, both on the Christmas market and on the succeeding pages of old Christmas card albums everywhere. An interesting fact in this connection is that although novelties appeared in fairly rapid succession and achieved greater or less popularity, the old ideas, both in subject and design, were usually produced for years, if not decades, after they were said to have been " out of date ". Many new features—as, for example, " frosting ", which appeared in 1867, and was perhaps most frequently used in the 90's,—reappeared again and again on Christmas cards. The same happened to many other novelties, including the various trick ideas, spelling jokes, acrostics, etc., which, though they were never really discontinued, periodically regained a burst of popularity.

The first Christmas cards in the 1840's, it will be remembered, were single rectangular pasteboards with lithographed or etched drawings, including the text, as well as the space for the names of the addressee and sender, printed on one side of the card only. The typical cards of the 50's and 60's, on the other hand, were either die-stamped designs again combining ornament and lettering in one harmonious unit, in which the Victorians were admittedly great masters, even though our taste in lettering and typography is very different from theirs, or small chromolithographs often superimposed on embossed valentine sheets and lace-paper, with short greeting texts in simple capital letters, frequently printed in black. These two main types were most usually of the small visiting card size, with embossed, perforated or fringed edges, except, of course, in those cases when these designs were used, not for cards, but for the miniature notepapers from which these Christmas cards descended. The third "typical" group, if the term can be used at all in respect of Christmas cards, at that time is represented by the first comic Goodall cards designed by Bennett and printed by Marcus Ward. These were rectangular paste-boards, again printed on one side only. The design attempted to be more pictorial and less ornamental and covered the whole page, incorporating into its design a short greeting text or other suitable legend. The Christmas card of the 60's seldom provided a dotted line for the addressee's or sender's name; they were larger editions made for a wider public which at that time had not yet generally mastered writing with ease, while the first Cole-Horsley, Egley, etc., cards were for a much smaller circulation confined to literate middle class or, rather, educated people.

In the 70's, although the smaller still remained popular, the trend was for a larger card of the then introduced postcard size or bigger, especially amongst those who were keen on the most up-to-date. The small folded cards, which began to appear in greater numbers about this time, consisted of two, four or even more pages, frequently printed on one strip of paper and folded like a concertina. They were sold complete with suitable, usually fully decorated, envelopes. The same sets could also be obtained as two, four, or eight separate cards—that is, each page separately. One of the first of these was the set called "Little Red Riding Hood" (Marcus Ward), which was very popular. Also a set of "Christmas Dreams", a humorous set in six parts, "Christmas with Punch and Judy", a set of five units, "Robin Hood and the Black Bird", and others. Most of these were published by Marcus Ward, and some were designed by Kate Greenaway at the beginning of her career. Examples of them have survived in almost every larger collection, but complete sets are seldom to be found in any one album. They tell a simple, witty or "dainty" tale in pictures, somewhat on the lines of modern strip cartoons. Other folded cards, sometimes opening out from the centre so that they appear as triptychs when opened, and many trick cards differing from each other not only in the trick, size and motif, but in style and finish also, originated in the 70's.

The padded cushion or sachet Christmas card became the vogue, I believe, in the late 60's and early 70's. Amongst Christmas cards they perhaps most closely resembled the sentimental valentine. Usually 3 by 4¼ or 4 by 5½ inches in size, these little envelope-like sachets were richly decorated with gold, silver and blue or other colour ornaments, and printed on embossed or lace-fringed paper. In many cases the flaps of the envelopes were not stuck down, so that the recipient could unfold them. Then he, or, more usually, she, would find another picture and a motto. Beneath this, or simply enclosed in the envelope, was a little pad of cotton-wool or soft tissue paper scented with a drop of perfume, tonquin beans, orris root or lavender powder, which has by now, of course, long since evaporated. It would seem that the famous perfumer of the period, Rimmel, was in no small way responsible for these as well as for many other ingenious perennial novelties.

We have to combine the incongruous adjectives "perennial" and "novel" in describing Christmas cards in the later Victorian era. A new trick or a novel idea which achieved success with those who received it would certainly be tried out on others, if not, as records prove, sent again and again to the same people in successive years! The great and genuine delight the Victorians took in conjuring tricks and the very latest novelties determined the popularity of these cards.

To begin with, Christmas cards were novelties in themselves. If, as a shrewd critic of the Victorian era said, " a novelty was a device for effecting some very simple purpose, like that of striking a match or sharpening a pencil, in a highly elaborate and ornamental way ", and if those novelties " looked as if they had cost more than they had cost ", then a great number of ingenious Christmas cards fitted in perfectly. Their coloured pictures and text at the time when bright colours, after the earlier Victorian greys and browns, constituted almost a revolution in mode, and when literacy in general was just beginning to be flaunted as a new ability, must have seemed the very thing ! If, further, it was " essential to a novelty that it should masquerade as something different from what it really was " (for example, " if you wanted to strike a match, you had a large pig framed in relief, and under him the legend, ' Please scratch my back ' ", and if " you then started rubbing your vestas against the pig, and with good luck you might get the fourth or fifth to ignite "),[1] then the earlier as well as the later Victorian trick cards were undoubtedly the most appropriate tokens to send with your compliments of the season to loving friends and relations at Christmas ! If the choice was made with some care and suitable circumspection, with due regard to the peculiar sensibilities of devoted aunts and the formidable prejudices of beloved uncles, then you could be sure that your Christmas card will go down well in family history.

Christmas cards were as diverse in their artistic designs as in size and medium, materials and manufacturing processes. They were, in fact, as varied as the ingenuity and taste of their designers, publishers and manufacturers *could* make them, and just sufficiently so to be welcome to both the middle-man and the buying public. The tendency of all concerned was to go one better than anyone else and to surpass their own latest efforts ; to provide every year " the latest " in taste, style and technical perfection—a dangerous trend in a period of general

---

[1] Some who are inclined to believe that such descriptions are the result of *satirical* licence on the part of a type of writer about the Victorian period will be interested to know that Geyer's *Stationer*, an advanced trade journal published in New York, " among the novelties in pocket match-safes ", described " one cutely representing a pig dormant ", and the London counterpart of the periodical was eager to reprint the notice, for the benefit of European readers, " among the most novel " and " exquisitely modelled " attractions of the month (*Stationer, etc., Register*, May 12th, 1890).

and almost continuous mechanical discoveries. But those who lived in the second half of the nineteenth century truly felt that all the achievements and craftsmanship of past ages were at their service, easily available in museums and books. As it was pointed out, never before had a people known so much about the past. The astonishing thing was that they felt sure that they could still improve on what they admired.

The same confidence which prompted the Pre-Raphaelites to improve the development of art was present in the hearts of the manufacturers, who were not slow to exploit the possibilities inherent in the advance of machine production. The small band of Christmas card manufacturers was typical of this type. It is rather pathetic sometimes to read their advertisements or the description of their goods. If the words " Christmas card " were replaced by the name of some more decisive human achievement, these essays would still sound rather pompous to-day ! They quoted Ruskin and spoke of Art with a capital A. No decorative style, past or present, which came to their notice remained untried in the mass production of Christmas cards. No possible, and impossible, material or process was omitted without first being tried out. When some of the best men, like Crane, finally withheld their support, the Christmas card manufacturer had to rely on the lesser leaders of contemporary arts and crafts. These might have been secondary to the great names, but, as the public reaction to their works clearly proved, were very near in heart, if not identical with, the period taste and the actual popular attitude towards " the beautiful ". The famous Victorian, especially late Victorian, idea of beauty, the almost arithmetical multiplication of in themselves pretty elements, regardless as to whether they harmonised with each other or not, enabled Christmas card designers and manufacturers to explore any and every combination of pretty things. The ingenious could, of course, " accumulate " a great deal of beauty on a building or monument, but what limitless possibilities there are, and how easily obtained for the use of the maker of Christmas cards and similar minor *objets d'art* ! Thus the production of Christmas cards became one of the characteristic projects of their time. Why ? Here was a *charming* custom to greet friends with a *pretty* card, embellished with *brilliantly* coloured *beautiful* pictures of *dainty* subjects. An *enchanting* or *edifying* sentiment would convey the tender thought, and there were further limitless possibilities for adding qualifying *prettinesses* in the form of attractive natural or manufactured flowers, grasses, materials, and thus achieving an ever-increasing *perfection of beauty*. If a card printed in two bright colours was attractive, a few additional inks should make it even more so. The principle seemed sound enough, and it was convenient to work on. It was, of course, not confined to colours. It applied equally to all other factors, including style : a combination of " Egyptian ", " Gothic ", " Rococo " and a touch of " Japanese " in one single card, if it was to be particularly beautiful. The result could not help to be more attractive than a design in any single style could attempt to be !

Gleeson White, writing in 1894, maintained a firm and very high standard of aesthetic criticism. He firmly divided the thousands of Christmas cards which he examined into two groups : cards of artistic merit, and cards without it. The latter were not only completely rejected by him, but, apart from a few general comments, not even discussed in his paper. This is all the more to be regretted, since this group contained not only by far the greater majority of the old Victorian Christmas card patterns, but the most popular and thus most typical cards of the last century. No one can, of course, blame Gleeson White's principles. He was a really distinguished leading art editor of his day, a fighter, and perhaps too much involved in the " contemporary " movement in the arts and crafts of the 90's to visualise that only a few decades later their evaluation might change, if not be reversed. From this distance many of those cards which to the critic in the 90's were most or exclusively artistic may seem only equally often much less characteristic period pieces than those which he simply declined to notice. Moreover, if we look at Christmas cards as representing a stage of popular taste, then the cards designed and appreciated only by a small circle of rather sophisticated individuals of a rather mannered period must be considered less interesting than those which were owned and beloved by the many. Nevertheless, it would seem worth while to recall the most attractive points. Gleeson White contrasted the later and more embellished Christmas cards with the early Marcus Ward type, which he described as " architectural ". By this he meant that " its treatment should be more nearly allied to the surface decoration of buildings than to transcriptions of nature, which are in theory, attempts to imitate the outlook from a window of the building. This latter, usually held to be the aim of the pictorial artist, cannot be employed without degradation upon mechanically produced reproductions in colour ; but the artificial convention—the idea of decorative as distinguished from pictorial art—wherever you find it for stained glass, mosaic, enamel, inlay or colour printing, has another purpose to fulfil, which is more admirably achieved when the limitations of the material are duly observed." This was indeed an admirable principle still worthy of the consideration of decorative designers, even though most Victorian " transcriptions of nature " seem to us to-day markedly dated and in a way hardly less " stylised " than their purposely decorative art. The difficulty about its practical implication was, however, that at the time when White wrote architecture was itself perhaps the least " architectural " of the whole century.

It is indeed interesting and instructive to observe from the 1860's right up to the early twentieth century the same selecting, or rather " mixing ", methods which are apparent both in external and internal architecture and in the make-up and design of Christmas cards. Besides other manifestations of contemporary taste, it would be tempting to make comparison between the various old cards, Victorian buildings and pieces of furniture. This is, however, beyond the scope of the present book. On the other hand, it should be pointed out that while, owing, perhaps, to the more permanent character of architecture, Victorian buildings often distress our modern eyes, in the Christmas cards of the same era the same elements, which clearly manifest unity of a not very style-like style, are generally less offensive. If not pleasing, they entertain rather than offend the modern spectator. The ambition to provide " the maximum of veneer for the minimum of cash " and the indiscriminate over-ornamentation which still seems so unforgivable in architecture arouses a certain sympathy, not untinged with admiration, when seen in such ephemeral phenomena as Christmas cards. Perhaps to a certain extent this is also due to the Surrealist experiment in recent years. Our eyes are once again trained not to abhor the third dimension when we see it added to the flat surface of a canvas or a page.

Nor are we entirely unprepared to appreciate free and surprise associations of heterogeneous symbols : the Surrealists taught us to enjoy once again the " collection of concepts co-existing in the mind of the artist ".

A certain parallel and decorative unity existed in all manifestations of the quickly changing period taste throughout the Victorian era. Thus, especially from the 70's onwards, an undated Christmas card collection could be placed in more or less accurate chronological order from the " dated dress " of the various cards. By the " dress " of the Christmas card I am not alluding here to the dress of the people illustrated on the cards, but to the whole " outfit ", the appearance of the cards themselves, such dated properties as glass- or aluminium " frosted " surfaces, fancy edges, superimposed layers of lace-paper, sparkling ornaments and other fripperies.

From the early 1880's a number of these elaborations were transmitted to folded cards. From that time top covers or, in the case of the triptych, flaps were not only extravagantly embossed, " jewelled " with sparkling surfaces, and cut into every imaginable shape, often with scalloped edges and fringes, but the career of the silk-fringed Christmas cards also began. These were either single cards or folders framed with bright, dark or even multicoloured silk fringes. The folded ones were usually equipped with silk cords and tassels, ostensibly to facilitate opening the folder or to tie it up, but in fact still more to adorn them. As far as I can discover, silk-fringed cards were introduced almost simultaneously by Marcus Ward, Stevens, Raphael Tuck and Hildesheimer in England and Prang in America.

Later in the '80's and throughout the 90's the cord and tassel were replaced by a wider silk ribbon band and bow on the increasingly popular folder type of Christmas cards. As the number of pages were by then usually eight or more in one folder, the cord or ribbon was not only decorative but served to hold the pages together, just as it does in certain Christmas cards of this type still popular to-day. The decorative element was sometimes enhanced in true period fashion by the use of two or more ribbons of different colours on one single card. For no apparent reason, a change in the method of fixing the ribbon took place just before the turn of the century. Instead of its being passed, as hitherto, around the whole fold of the card, it was made to pass through circular holes in the cover and then tied in a bow or slip-knot. Sometimes only half or a third of the ribbon previously required was used in this way ; even less when the ribbon went through two holes about one inch apart. The economy in the silk ribbon was slight compared with the additional labour required to attach it, so I fear that this novelty, which rapidly achieved success, could not be explained by economy or functionalism ! This was the time of the Victorian renaissance of the " rococo ", when erratic curves and dancing bands dominated fashion, houses, furniture and Christmas cards. The shimmering and flamboyant extravagances of this taste could not tolerate a straight line, even of silk and ribbon—not even around one side of a small Christmas card !

It should be made clear, however, that while the new " rococo " flourished there was still a steady and probably increasing public for almost all the earlier types and fashions of Christmas cards. Ever since 1843 there have been a number of people who would prefer to convey their Christmas greetings with the old type of a rectangular, single card, the changing taste being apparent in the design on the card and not in its basic shape. There were also many who would continue to choose a small ornamental card, similar to the old " gentleman's visiting card ", or a simple white folder, decorated in the centre by a small, die-stamped design, such as a coat of arms or professional guild or service emblem, out of the greatest selection of modern patterns. These cards, which are still very popular, represent an unbroken line of succession from those earliest little die-stamped designs of the late 50's and early 60's. Die-stamping (combined with hand-colouring) was still perhaps the most usual process in the production of the huge American Christmas card business in the 1930's.

Similarly, frosting, jewelling and many other once-popular novelties have survived in many present-day cards, although in succeeding years their production was much simplified.

In more recent years there has been a new and increasing demand, especially in Britain, for good colour reproductions of the paintings of Old and New Masters. This fashion was probably started in 1884 by Raphael Tuck, when the firm first began to use for Christmas cards fine reproductions of Raphael's pictures. Marcus Ward produced a Fra Angelico and a few others, while a number of publishers, such as Mowbray, the Medici Society and others, specialised in producing this type of Christmas card. In Britain the recent enterprise of the Trustees of the British Museum and other public galleries, and in the U.S.A. the Museum of Modern Art, who bring out masterly reproductions of art treasures in their collections as Christmas cards, has achieved a well-deserved popular success, while *The Times* and several other publishing companies also produce yearly delightful photographs of English landscapes, usually in the form of calendars which have a wide public support.

Another type of the modern Christmas card, which a leading article in *The Times* rightly says is " the fashion of the day ", is the woodcut or wood-engraving, especially in higher-brow circles and those of modern taste. This fashion was the result of the modern revival of the ancient art of the woodcut. It came to its own again when towards the end of the nineteenth century mechanical block-making obviated the use of the wood-block for reproductive purposes, and made this medium once again exclusively available for creative artists.[2] Cheaper ones, imitating the effect of original wood-engravings, are in fact reproductions from scraper-board drawings. Some artists turned again to chromolithography, and produce Christmas cards (as well as other prints) in the contemporary idiom which this little more than a century old process carries as well as it did the old Victorian patterns. The important qualities people usually look out for to-day are attractive designs and text as brief as possible. It is frequently said that there are only a few to whom the subject of the picture really matters, or who would select their cards on account of the " sentiment ", that is the greeting text, on them. But publishers who specialise in Christmas cards have a different story to tell. One of them who produced reproductions of modern painters tells me, for example, that in his experience pictures by the most modern French masters go down well with the general public as Christmas cards if they are, however vaguely, associated

[2] Sets of modern wood-engraving Christmas cards were published, amongst others, by the Redfern Gallery, the Greggnog Press, the Golden Cockerel Press, the Hague and Gill Press, High Wycombe, the Ward Gallery, and Gordon Fraser, Cambridge.

with fishing or sailing boats or flower studies. Some of those who are quite ready to buy these subjects on Christmas cards would never dream of buying or appreciating, either as Christmas cards or as pictures for their walls, reproductions or originals of other subjects by the same masters ! In other words, many people even to-day will easily tolerate a style and interpretation on account of the subject interest or sentiment, whereas without it they are hostile or at least unappreciative.

This attitude is very well in line with a characteristically Victorian heritage, although even before that the story told in a painting or sculpture, to say nothing of drawings—especially illustrations—was always disproportionately a greater incentive to popular imagination than any other virtues in them. The British tradition in this respect is, perhaps, older and more positive than that of other countries, both for artists and public. Within this tradition, the Victorians were certainly the most conspicuous, and definitely expected the products of visual arts to provide a story or an anecdote, to have a literary conception or a moral content. The Christmas card picture was no exception. On the contrary, the subject or story of the picture and sometimes the text on the Christmas card was, perhaps, the main and decisive factor in the choice of cards. Contemporary references, memory and correspondence pay far more attention to the subject and sentiment of the Christmas card than to its other peculiarities. If the more specifically technical and artistic nature of the card is mentioned at all, it is done in a generalised manner of secondary importance. The greatest collector of Christmas cards and similar objects, Jonathan King, the thoroughly Victorian citizen of Islington, grouped his huge collection in albums according to " subjects ". One of his contemporaries describes an occasion when he was shown " ten volumes of robin Christmas cards ", " a volume of snowmen ", another " of insects ", another of " donkeys, velvet birds, birds made of real feathers, political cards ", and so on, in an endless array of subjects with only slight attention to other features, such as animation, the materials used, etc. Very few, if any, were grouped according to their designers, artists or even manufacturers. This treatment is, of course, in line with the view that Christmas cards are a form of impersonal popular art, and were treated as such by the public.

Even Gleeson White, who was, perhaps more than anyone of his time, concerned with the " how " in addition to the " what " of the artist's work, often contented himself with descriptions, such as " Children kneeling ", or " Guardian Angels ", or " Little Maids from School ", or " Fairies in Mid-air ", " Children decorating the Home with Holly ", etc., and here and there an additional " dainty " or " charming " or " admirable " is not infrequently the *only* comment on the craftsmanship.

The tendency to select or reject designs on account of their subject unavoidably leads to otherwise unjustifiable selections. Gleeson White, for example, who was interested in either floral decoration or suitable figure compositions and landscapes, did not include a single Christmas card featuring the robin redbreast or other bird. It shows, no doubt, admirable restraint in view of the immense popularity of these little birds on Christmas cards from the 50's onwards. " Why these simple studies of single birds against a gold background should have been so extremely popular is not easy to see " is his characteristic comment.

I am quoting this here not merely to justify the next chapter of this book, which deals mainly with the robin Christmas cards, but also to illustrate how our whole approach has changed, and to show the risk I am taking in adopting the traditional Victorian principle of grouping material according to the main subjects of the Christmas cards. However, this seems to be the appropriate way for this review, and I believe it would please both their makers and the Victorian public which loved them so dearly.

ROBIN REDBREAST
and other Feathered Favourites

THE REV. CANON GILBERT ELLIOTT writes from Sussex in a recent letter : " I recall my mother saying that she remembered my father coming in to her and saying : ' The Jacksons have sent me a card with the picture of a little bird on it. Do you think they imagine I am getting silly ? ' This must have been his first experience of a Christmas card." The charming episode took place in the very early 1860's, and from this we may assume that " the Jacksons " were amongst the first to choose a Christmas card with a robin design.

Most authorities agree that the firm of Messrs. Goodall & Son was the first, apart from Summerly's Treasury Office and a few scattered, small enterprises in the 50's, to publish Christmas cards for the market as a commercial proposition. Gleeson White gives the alternative dates 1862 or 1864 as the commencement of this enterprise, but I think now it can be taken that 1862 was the year. Two independent references confirm this date. The first is the already mentioned " Minor Topics of the Months " in the *London Art Journal* of December 1st, 1862. It refers to " An extensive series of cards, notepaper, and envelopes of an exceedingly pure and beautiful character ", which were produced by " Messrs. Goodall & Son, card manufacturers of Camden Town, for Christmas and the New Year ". The Editor goes on to say that " They are in great variety—all being in ' keeping ' with the season ; holly, ivy, of course, predominating in designs charmingly executed, and brilliantly coloured ; and generally by excellent artists ".

The second reference is in a letter by " Luke Limner of Regent's Park ", published in *The Times*. It is written in reply to the article on " Christmas cards " printed on Christmas Day, 1883, on which Luke Limner comments as follows : " The writer of your article upon the origin of these missives is hardly explicit enough. Occasional cards of a purely private character have been done years ago, but the Christmas card, pure and simple, is the growth of our town and our time. It

ROBIN REDBREAST

began in the year 1862, the first attempts being the size of the ordinary gentleman's address card, on which was simply put ' A Merry Christmas ' and ' A Happy New Year ' ; after that there came to be added robins and holly branches, embossed figures, and landscapes. Having made the original designs for these, I have the originals before me now ; they were produced by Goodall & Son." From these authentic sources it may be accepted that it was in 1862 that robin redbreast appeared— that is, immediately the Christmas card manufacturers began to elaborate the formal greeting text.

This little feathered favourite has maintained its popularity, though sometimes sharing it with the wren, right up to the present day, in spite of the thousands of new and most varied subjects which were and are used by designers searching for novelty. It is remarkable what a hold the robin has on the sentiments of the general public, particularly in its association with Christmas, including the rather dignified leader-writer of *The Times* of the 80's. In describing the Christmas cards of his day, he wrote, after recalling the influence of Father Christmas : " Nor indeed, we are happy to note, is the feathered favourite the cock-robin altogether absent from the designs of the present day, and so far as can be judged, he does not seem likely awhile to lose his favoured hold upon the popular mind and sentiment." Further evidence, if needed, is supplied by the correspondent of an altogether different paper, the *Daily Gazette* of Islington. He visited Jonathan King, the local resident who filled his two Essex Street houses with his collection of Christmas cards and valentines. " We turn over ten volumes of robins, revealing robins red in all imaginable styles ", he reports, " comic robins, perky robins, robins in the snow." He saw also sheets of robin stamps for sealing envelopes bearing various seasonable greetings. One of these reads as follows :

> " Dear Sister, my love I send to you,
>   And kisses, one, two, three ;
> And in return, I hope a few,
>   You will send back to me."

Another one-time visitor to the same collection tells us of another use of the Christmas robin. These were made and printed as sheets of scraps, which were sold together with batches of small printed cards. The scraps were then simply stuck on the cards by an edge, usually the bottom, but according to taste, hiding a chosen greeting text or sentiment. The following is a rather interesting example :

" My wishes come by Robin's rhymes,
Since he has pleased so many times ;
For London poor are still in need,
Whom Robin's crumbs may help to feed.

" Or if the missions we would aid,
By Christmas cards and sheets now made,
The Robin gladly will take flight,
With wings of love he'll bear your mite.

" Each Christmas offering to our King,
Each feeble prayer may blessings bring ;
May blessings rest on you, my friend,
True Christmas joys that never end."

The thousands of various robin designs on Christmas cards and their prominent place in the old albums and scrapbooks which I have seen make me feel that it is justifiable to deal with them at some length ; not so much on account of their purely artistic merit, but for reasons underlying my whole approach to the subject of Christmas cards, considering them to be one surviving form of popular art in our highly industrialised society. In popular art new motifs and new subjects seldom appear by accident. When innovations are accepted, it is very likely because they fit into a recognised, or perhaps subconscious, chain of traditions, survivals and superstitions, which somehow became associated with them. The quick and lasting grip of the robin motif on the Christmas card public and manufacturers cannot be entirely due to the fact that " Luke Limner " happened to use one as a model for some of his early Christmas cards.

Folklore and popular tradition can, indeed, vouch for many associations between the robin and the Christmas season, for this little bird is revered amongst the most distinguished in the feathered world. While animals in general were thought by the ancients to possess various magic powers denied to human beings, as many still not extinct superstitions bear out, the birds, which could fly, always had a particular appeal to the imagination of pedestrian men. The robin, the wren and the swallow were the favourites amongst them. British folk-lore contains much data to show that they were considered sacred birds until quite recent times.

> " The robin and the wren,
>   Are God Almighty's cock and hen.
>   The martin and the swallow,
>   Are God Almighty's bow and arrow "

is the ancient rhyme from Warwickshire. The Shropshire version of the same ends with the following couplet :

> " The martin and the swallow,
>   God Almighty's scholars."

From Essex comes another delightful old folk-rhyme of the same kind :

> " Robins and wrens are God Almighty's shirt and collar,
>   Martins and swallows are the two next birds that follow."

Even young boys were taught to respect the superstition which protected these birds and their nests from their explorations. An old Essex rhyme records it :

> " The robin aye the redbreast,
>   The robin and the wren,
>   If ye take out the nest,
>   Ye'll never thrive again.
>   The robin and the redbreast,
>   The martin and the swallow,
>   If you touch one of their eggs,
>   Bad luck will sure to follow."

Similar rhymes expressing similar beliefs were collected from all over the British Isles. In the northern counties they say :

> " The robin and the wren,
>   Him that harries their nest,
>   Never shall his soul have rest."

In Cornwall :

> " He who hurts the robin or the wren,
> Will never prosper sea or land,
> On sea or land will ne'er do well again."

The superstitious protection, however, is not effective on one day of the year, and curiously enough on that day it was a popular rite to hunt and kill a wren or sometimes—as a result of more recent confusion—a robin. It was a ceremony shared by all the young and old men of the village, who carried the dead bird in procession on a pole, decorated with evergreens and red braid, or in a glass case on an improvised small hearse. Villagers who obtained a feather, a protective charm, were supposed to have good luck throughout the coming year. This custom is a late survival of the ancient sacrifice of the king of the tribe to avert disaster, originally a human sacrifice, which was modified later by mock substitutes, while the red cloth and wheels are fire symbols. The songs sung by the hunters during the procession also commemorate the original sacrifice for the common good. One version is :

> " We hunted the Wren for Robin the Bobbin,
> We hunted the Wren for Jack of the Can.
> We hunted the Wren for Robin the Bobbin,
> We hunted the Wren for everyman."

Originally the custom was observed on December 24th, but during more recent centuries it usually took place on the 26th, St. Stephen's Day.

A charming old legend tells how the robin's breast became red. The little bird, in trying to ease Christ's suffering on His way to the Crucifixion, pulled out a thorn from His crown of thorns, and in so doing a drop of His blood fell on his chest and has remained there ever since. Another and even more ancient tale explains the robin's red breast in a different but equally emotional way. According to this, it was the wren who flew to Hell to obtain fire for men. When he returned he was himself in flames and the little robin rushed to his rescue, and in beating out the flames scorched his breast, and that is why it remained red.

COLOUR PLATE I Christmas cards from the early 1850's and 1860's.

a. One of the now very rare Petter and Galpin cards, direct descendants of the Cole-Horsley design.
b. One of a set of charming early cards (publisher unknown).
c. A delightful Goodall card by Luke Limner.
d. One of two charming early cards illustrating Christmas-tide "at home and abroad".

COLOUR PLATE II Dating from the early 1870's, this Christmas card derives its bright colours and naïve decorative patterns from the popular art of the period.

a

COLOUR PLATE III *a* and *b*

Pin-prick decoration, which became a popular home-craft in the 1830's, was occasionally used for ornamenting Christmas cards.   These are two charmingly naïve examples, tinted with water-colour.   One is dated 1864.

A unique little card which, in spite of its rather naïve craftsmanship, well conveys the excitement and pleasure of the children in choosing their own Christmas cards.

a

b

One of the first early Goodall cards designed by C. H Bennett.   It contrasts the shapes o Victorian bells and belles (a very rare card to-day).

COLOUR PLATE IV

COLOUR PLATE VII A delightfully dated moral-
izing Christmas card. Each Commandment was
thus translated into "modern" terms of the 1860's.
Probably Kronheim print.

THIRD COMMANDMENT
Thou shalt not take the name of the
Lord thy God in vain:
for the Lord will not hold him guiltless that taketh his name in vain.

COLOUR PLATE VI
A characteristic John Leighton–Luke Limner card of the
early 1860's.

A Merry Christmas
God bless our friends, wherever they be,
on land or sea;
Angels tell them, where they roam,
think and speak of them at home To-day!

COLOUR PLATE V One of a set of charming early
religious cards meant for children. These little chromolithographs were sometimes superimposed on to scent
sachets or envelopes containing other cards belonging to
the same set.

LISTEN WHILE TO YOU IS TOLD
A TALE STILL NEW ALTHOUGH SO OLD.

COLOUR PLATE VIII   A decorative card of a Victorian " Fortuna " designed by Walter Crane in 1875.   She is no longer a mere symbol : the face is almost a portrait of a young woman of the period.

COLOUR PLATE IX   " My lips may give a message better Of Christmas love, than e'en my letter " is the coy legend on this delightful Kate Greenaway card of the late 1870's.

COLOUR PLATE X   One of the attractive W. S. Coleman Christmas cards—though few would consider it very seasonable to-day.

COLOUR PLATE XI A Selection of American Cards.

a (*top left*) An elegant and elongated "boy meets girl" card of the 1880's.

b (*top right*) This card, designed by Dora Wheeler in 1881, won two First Prizes, *i.e.*, $2,000 at Prang's Competition. Described in the chapter, "Women on Christmas Cards", p. 150.

c (*bottom left*) An attractive red background card produced by Prang in 1878 (see pp. 77 and 114-5).

d "This *bears* witness to my love for thee" is one of the charming and brilliantly engraved Christmas cards produced by John A. Lowell & Co. of Boston (about 1885).

The boys and a
snowman enjoying
themselves. Girls
were conspicuously
absent from cards
of similar subjects
in the 1860's.
Note the charac-
teristic Victorian
lettering.

a

Here's happiness to all,
Abroad and at home;
Here's happiness to all,
For Christmas is come.

Compliments of the season.

b

c

To wish you
the old, old wish
A
Merry Christmas
and a
Happy New Year

From

Merrily
speed
the
Hours

d

COLOUR PLATE XIII

a and *b* (*on the top*) Later Victorian fashionable Christmas parties and cards. Note the absence of children from both parties and cards (1880's and 1890's respectively).
c When the lady-cyclist invaded the road in fabulous bloomers they were made targets of both adoration and fun also on Christmas cards.
d Speed and motoring on a Christmas card of the early 1900's.

A Victorian family outing in the early 1880's. According to the sentiment on the back of the card such an event was a definite joy and fun to old and young!

A MERRY CHRISTMAS TO YOU ALL.

COLOUR PLATE XIV

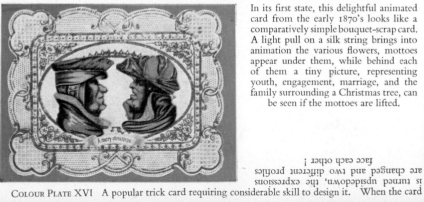

In its first state, this delightful animated card from the early 1870's looks like a comparatively simple bouquet-scrap card. A light pull on a silk string brings into animation the various flowers, mottoes appear under them, while behind each of them a tiny picture, representing youth, engagement, marriage, and the family surrounding a Christmas tree, can be seen if the mottoes are lifted.

COLOUR PLATE XVI A popular trick card requiring considerable skill to design it. When the card is turned upside-down, the expressions are changed and two different profiles face each other!

These few examples will indicate the long-standing connection between the robin and his fellow, the wren (both connected with fire in popular tradition), and celebrations at Christmas, which is perhaps responsible for the robin's continued and exceptionally privileged position on Christmas cards. Nor is it quite unlikely that " Luke Limner " was himself familiar with these traditions. Basil Gray, in *The British Print*, says that " He represents the great undercurrent of popular art . . . grown articulate." We know also from contemporary sources that he was, both as an artist and as a man, of a considerable intellectual standard, had a keen interest in antiquities and heraldry, lectured on " Libraries and Books ", and, besides his work on *The Unification of London, with Maps and Plans*, wrote a book on various styles and suggestions for decoration in 1853. He was a life member of the Society of Antiquaries and the London Archaeological Society, and many " kindred associations ". So it is probable that he was familiar with the folklore publications which not long before his time began to record regularly the type of folk-rhymes I have quoted. He also travelled extensively, and studied Byzantine art in Russia, Caucasia and Georgia, where his already aroused interest in folk art must have been further stimulated by the peasant arts and crafts still flourishing there.

I am including amongst the illustrations cards almost certainly by " Luke Limner ", which show a robin in the design, and combine a characteristic balance of decorative skill, realistic detail and brilliant colours (Colour Plates Ic, VI, and Plate 19). Some of the early robin cards clearly show the transition of the " made-up " Christmas card from the valentine (Plate 18), with perforated paper combined with hand-made real lace, silk and superimposed robin scrap. Some robin cards show the first adaptation on small cards of the designs originally used as headings on Christmas notepaper and on the backs of envelopes. These were printed obviously from the same dies in brilliant, clean colours. The little rhymes, called " sentiments ", appeared soon afterwards. It is interesting to note that on the early cards the sentiment usually referred to the robin whose little picture decorated the card, whereas later the design and the sentiment were very often quite independent. Their appearance on the same card became accidental.

THE HISTORY OF THE CHRISTMAS CARD

In the early 70's the comic robin began to share the realm of the sentimental. It was at that time that he first appeared harnessed to a little cart filled with holly, a chromolithographed card I found in almost every old album I went through (Plate 24). Previous to this we also find robins pulling the old round plum pudding or a Christmas cracker, reminiscent of the mice in *Cinderella*. There were a great number of dressed-up robins (Plate 22), usually couples, wearing bonnets and top-hats, sometimes completely clothed and struggling against wind and snow, but still paying their Christmas visits, and doing almost everything human beings do at Christmas. Some extremely well-drawn cards of this type were designed by R. Dudley, a prominent artist of many subjects. Mr. Punch had a witty comment to make about these humanised robins when he gave some seasonable suggestions for Christmas *cookery*. " Cards ", he states, " form a welcome and dainty addition to the Christmas morning breakfast. To prepare take two plump robins (*boned, so as to stand in impossible attitudes*), a church tower with bells, and holly to taste. Season the whole with a couple of cheap rhymes and sprinkle thickly with frost. Serve in half a sheet of note-paper, ' With Best Wishes from All at Homeleigh ', enclose in an envelope and garnish with pink stamp." " A more economical version of the above ", advises Mr. Punch, " omits the Best Wishes and garnishes with a green stamp " (an allusion to the letter and card postage). The frosting which Mr. Punch alludes to was first employed on robin cards in 1867, and soon caught the public fancy, invaded all sorts of cards, and was indeed often overdone.

In the late 1870's manufacturers striving to outdo each other in inventiveness managed to introduce the sound of their birds in addition to their appearance on Christmas cards. I am reproducing the two most successful of these from H.M. Queen Mary's personal collection. They were sent to her by her mother, Princess Mary Adelaide, for Christmas, 1878, when they first appeared on the market (Plate 26). They are slightly smaller than an ordinary postcard of to-day. Between the boards was hidden an at that time ingenious flat suction whistle, which chirped when the boards were lightly pressed together and released. The little bird is pictured standing on a writing desk covered with folios, an ink-stand, quill pens and half-written letters, but his attention is concentrated on a little picture in an open book. It shows the portrait of another little robin in the bush, with a short poem printed under it, while the left-hand page is used for the text conveying the sender's good wishes for a happy New Year. The same card was also published bearing Christmas wishes. The card demonstrating its use in the same illustration shows the corner of a farmyard, with geese and a magpie, and the sound it makes is more like a squawk. On the robin card a tiny black bead is inserted for his eye, and, together with its novel sound effect, this card must have delighted children of all ages. The *Bazaar* of December 11th, 1878, reviewing these "voiced" Christmas cards published by Goodall & Son, mentions that they vary from the robin to a double-faced baby, the squeak in this case coinciding with the appearance of the less agreeable of the two faces.

Fowls and robins both appear on one of the early cards of the De La Rue Company, one on the dish and the other in the bush. This bird doesn't squeak, but speaks for an altogether changed attitude. It is made so that one might almost smell the goodness of a roast turkey, a dominant feature of the chromolithograph, which the chef is seen just carrying in to dinner (Plate 25). The robins are here relegated to the background. We can just see them outside the kitchen window. But the motto explains everything : " A bird in the hand is worth two in the bush ". From the mouth of the chef comes the scroll wishing " A Merry Christmas ". This was one of the early De La Rue cards. A whole set was devoted to proverbs interpreted in a similar, topical manner.

Christmas cards with turkeys and geese, particularly in roasted form, and comic allusions to their contribution to the happiness of Christmas are also very numerous. The Joseph Mansell firm, which, in addition to their famous valentines, was one of the earliest Christmas card publishers, also published a number of cards of turkeys and geese, mostly humorous and sometimes including foxes dressed in uniform. A card entitled " Dignity and Impudence " shows the two popular fowls of the Christmas dinner in some disagreement with each other (Plate 23).

No fear of becoming a Christmas dish, however, threatened the mascot " Jacob the Goose ", a rather exceptional fowl, whose picture from an old contemporary drawing adorned regimental Christmas cards in the 1930's (Plate 27). His distinguished, though brief, *curriculum vitae* is printed opposite the portrait. It runs : " Enlisted at Quebec, 1838. Came to England with the 2nd Battalion, 1842. Had one Good Conduct Ring. Died on Detachment at Croydon, 1846."

As time went on and Christmas card production became a huge industry, gradually almost all subjects, and amongst them almost all imaginable birds, became at some time or other subjects of the little pictures which Christmas cards now are. One by one swallows, owls, love-birds and parrots, then hens, cocks, ducks and wild ducks, and so on and on, all joined the original robins and wrens, and later geese and turkeys, on Christmas cards as winged messengers of the Christmas cheer.

The peacock, whose feathers were the much-coveted properties of the wardrobes in every fashionable house in the 1880's, was destined to be at least for some time also a feature of Christmas cards. It was the heyday of the aesthetes, and the peacock feather, together with the sunflower motif, became the symbol of those who belonged to " the advanced ", those who were " intense " for intensity's sake. Thus the peacock feather was a kind of materialised pass-word by which people " of the same feather ", so to say, recognised each other. Under this sign, conversation could be freely " utterly utter ". Men could speak with assurance about the sins they so diligently read and wrote about, but seldom really committed. Women could pose and behave as though perpetually in a trance—in fact, trying to resemble as closely as possible the women in Rossetti's and Burne-Jones's pictures. Many Christmas card designers belonged to the first, second and third ranks of the aesthetic movement. So the peacock soon appeared on their cards, and on these actually outlived the craze by many years (Plate 28). Mr. Punch and Messrs. Gilbert and Sullivan no doubt helped to speed the passing of the utterly utter by ridicule, but at the same time focused attention on them by witty words and catchy tunes. The Christmas card of P. J. Billinghurst, the artist, was made in the last year of the century, and depicts the peacock as Vanity and the owl as Wisdom. The pen-and-ink design is also filled with a number of other symbols and as a whole well illustrates that which was considered " highly artistic " in those days.

No survey on the "feathered favourites" Christmas cards, however brief, could leave out all those dead birds with which we are so familiar on Christmas cards.

From the early days there were, of course, Christmas cards picturing roast turkeys and geese, served on dishes or hanging in rows at the poulterer's, as on one of Stacy Marks' best archaic Christmas cards. These, and also the joints of raw meat, often with comic arms and legs attached, were prospective Christmas dinners, and as such were meant to convey good cheer, just as the popular hunting and shooting cards, or simply the bag of wild duck or pheasants, carried " good luck " in these sports.

The cards which are difficult to understand to-day, in spite of my allusion to the curious St. Stephen's Day custom of bird-killing, are those which show a single dead bird as the only feature of the card, lying on its back, alone, as on a bier (Plate 31). The texts, too, often sound rather morbid. Yet, in spite—or could it be because?—of the thoroughly sentimental sentiment of the Victorians, these cards, judging by their repeated publications, seemed to have enjoyed a considerable vogue.

THE INCIDENCE
of Holly, Ivy, Mistletoe and Floral Subjects

I T is not difficult to explain the popularity in Christmas card designs of those evergreens which are still generally used for seasonal decorations in the home at Christmas. Their close and direct association with the Christmas festivities and that of the old winter solstice, though as old, if not older, than that of the robin, is still a very much alive and flourishing tradition to-day.

The holly, with its gay red berries (as an old ballad now in the British Museum says, " Holy hath Berys as red as any Nose ") and its dark green stalk and strong, prickly leaves, is certainly a most cheerful decoration in the gloom of winter. Evelyn refers to holly as " that incomparable tree ", and as the British variety is no doubt incomparably richer in colour and lasts longer than its Continental cousins, it is easy to understand how holly became the favourite Christmas decoration of the British home. For centuries the sharp-thorned holly leaves and its blood-red berries were associated in the minds of the devout with the suffering and blood of Christ, giving to holly a certain religious significance, and thus making it still more suitable at Christmas.

Ivy, another popular Christmas evergreen, is found everywhere, and is for ever connected with holly in the delightful old carol, " The Holly and the Ivy ". As a symbol of constancy, it occurs frequently in the classics, although during its growth it passes through the most varied phases of all plants. Once it is established, however, it clings indeed constantly to tree-trunk, wall or hedge and shows great determination to survive. Long before the Christian Christmas was celebrated, both holly and ivy were favourite household decorations during the winter festivals. Holly was considered particularly lucky and propitious to human beings, since its prickles frightened away witches and other malevolent spirits.

Mistletoe also from the earliest times has had a mysterious hold on the imagination of mankind. Its parasitic growth used to be found most frequently on both wild and cultivated apple trees and, though more rarely, amongst the branches of that " most highly favoured tree ", the oak, with which so many very ancient heathen rites and traditions are associated. The rite of cutting mistletoe was attended by great and solemn ceremonies in ancient times, in which the Druids, who in their visions were said to have been able to locate mistletoe, proceeded from tree to tree. If in the process a bunch fell to the ground, or if none was either seen or envisaged for a long time, it was believed to be a bad omen for the whole community. Mistletoe was an important plant in Norse mythology and was also revered on account of the healing properties attributed to it. Former enemies sealed their peace beneath it with a kiss, which in primitive civilisations was a form of total exchange of souls and personalities. A late survival of this ancient heathen custom is the still-practised kiss under the mistletoe, a favourite privilege at Christmas-time. Thanks to this custom, shy young men and blushing Victorian damsels more than once found each other as a prelude to a romance or a happy lifetime together. It is therefore not surprising that the mistletoe, and the kiss beneath it, became such a popular subject on Christmas cards in the nineteenth century. In addition to its peace- and love-making implications, according to popular tradition, mistletoe hung on oak beams was thought to prevent the building being struck by lightning. The Swedish word *donnerbesen*, meaning " thunder besom ", shows that this belief was fairly universal in northern Europe.

Both mistletoe and holly first appeared on Christmas cards as early as the 1840's, when Egley produced his charmingly etched Christmas card. A bunch of mistletoe hangs from the rustic branches of the panel which frames the Sir Roger de Coverley dancers and a branch of it fills the space on the bottom right corner of the card, just above the signature and the much-discussed date, 1848 (Plate 7). In the opposite bottom corner a branch of holly can be seen. A more dominant part is played by both holly and mistletoe in some of the designs of those Christmas letter headings which, as we have seen, were the immediate forerunners of the Christmas card industry. One of my illustrations of these shows a design with three round panels separated from each other, not as in the Cole-Horsley and Egley designs by a rustic framework, but by clearly identifiable, in the case of the two lower pictures, holly wreaths, whilst the upper is covered with an extensive, though rather loosely drawn, spray of mistletoe (Plate 14).

Holly, ivy and mistletoe motifs occurred frequently on the early " Luke Limner " cards produced by Goodall, and later on those by Marcus Ward and most other early publishers. So there is little justification for those recent disparaging remarks, based, no doubt, on Gleeson White's report, that " Father Christmas, holly berries, and snow appear to have come in, unfortunately, only with the decadence and vulgarisation of the institution of which they seem so clearly an integral part, and with the import of cheap cards from Germany ". As it happens, apart from the Cole-Horsley card, wintry evergreens occur frequently on very many early cards. Some of the more characteristic designs incorporating them occur on many cards as motifs, though not necessarily the main features. If space permitted, hundreds of designs could be included to show the really prolific use of holly, ivy and mistletoe on the early Christmas cards. Their decline only began somewhere in the '90's, partly on account of imported foreign cards, partly due to the indifference and superiority of the " sophisticated ", who despised the use of such simple natural features in an age boasting of its mechanisation.

There are some interesting holly-decorated cards, bordered by very fine embossed and perforated and partly gilded white lace-like paper frames, with an old gold oval, on which are attractive bright green holly leaves with the greeting " A Merry Christmas to You " composed entirely of red holly berries. These designs date back to about 1870 or 1871, which was the year when the use of the holly berry for constructing the letters of text had just been introduced. The holly Christmas card reproduced on Plate 32 is of the same date. Its background is blue of two shades, the darker merging rather abruptly into the lighter owing to the primitive manual " dot-reduction " technique of the " chromos " of the time. The fronds of bracken are silvery white, and in the centre, just below the greeting and motto texts printed in black, is a dark brown wooden cross wreathed in bright green holly leaves and red berries. Variations of the same subject were frequently met with in the early 70's, emphasising the familiar association between holly and the Saviour's crown of thorns and blood. In the early 80's larger and more ambitious cards of the same motif had on them silver birch crosses standing upright, surrounded and entwined by bright spring and summer flowers instead of holly. The centre of these cards is usually an oval or circular panel of a miniature landscape, while later in the 80's, the wooden cross is usually replaced by one of gold or silver, and the brilliantly coloured flowers by white or pastel shades. Both these latter types clearly tried to " improve " on the original motif, but while doing so lost the original significance of the Christmas holly and cross combined as symbolic mementoes.

A very attractive card using the mistletoe motif is at the same time a good example of the so-called " architecturally " designed Christmas cards (Plate 33). The background consists of a finely designed pattern of ornaments and lettering printed in gold, silver and various pale colours. The sprig of mistletoe which is the central attraction at first sight is so realistically drawn and coloured across the card that, with its shadow, it looks like a real sprig of mistletoe laid on, in the third dimension, an ornamented card and photographed by a modern techni-colour cameraman. The card is one of the celebrated patterns " designed so excellently well " by Thomas Crane for the Marcus Ward firm in the 1870's, to quote White, who deservedly praised this type of card by saying : " For legitimate use of the mere materials, cardboard and printer's ink, for the easy method of securing true decoration by the most direct means, it would be hard to find in European colour printing anything that fulfilled its purpose more completely. Here, and here only, one feels, has the limit been recognised, the question of economic production faced and conquered and a simple bit of lithography made admirable art, not because of its superb drawing or refined colour, but because of its simplicity, dignity and absence of imitation." Its text reads as follows :

> " Fair Mistletoe !
> Love's opportunity !
> What trees that grow
> Give such sweet
> Impunity ? "

and a brief " With Christmas Greeting " incorporated in the design of the lower part of the card's ornamentation. A similar card with ivy leaves instead of the sprig of mistletoe was also designed by Thomas Crane.

Robert Dudley, an artist of considerable reputation at the end of the last century and also designer of many favourite Christmas cards in those years, including some " human robin " cards, as already mentioned, made for the De La Rue firm a delightful set of oblong cards on which the various evergreens were personified by charmingly drawn young figures. One of these is " A Pearl of Mistletoe " (Plate 35). Its size is 4 by 6 inches, printed on a white pasteboard with a pale grey background. The lettering and the characteristic line decoration are a darker shade of the same colour. The feature of the card is, of course, the design within a very pale gold oval. The figure of a young girl, lightly draped in a gossamer robe, with transparent wings, is fluttering in the air, holding in her left hand a spray of mistletoe, apparently just picked from a growing bunch of it, which forms the decorative background to the figure. Pearls of mistletoe are braiding her tresses. Another design of the same set called " A Sprite of the Ivy " is similar, but shows another charming little girl, also wearing the briefest light drapery, sitting in a swing of ivy tendrils surrounded by ivy leaves and holding a bunch of ivy berries in her left hand. The motto printed in a single line across the bottom of the card is : " In smooth bright current may thy days glide on." These little cards are gems of artistic chromolithography, and no wonder they were much treasured in their time.[1]

An early Louis Prang American Christmas card with holly and mistletoe decorations was copyrighted in 1878. It was a long card about $3\frac{1}{2}$ by $8\frac{1}{4}$ inches in size, with a rich red background. The design consists of a sepia monochrome drawing of six children of various ages, with two white doves each with a blue streamer waving from its neck with the inscriptions " Joy ! " and " Mirth ! " on them. The whole is enclosed in a frame of holly leaves and berries and one or two sprigs of mistletoe. The greeting which appears on a white panel beneath the picture consists of six lines, characteristic of the American style,

---

[1] Their success prompted Hildesheimer & Faulkner to publish—probably in 1884—a set of nude children on holly and flowering branches, playing with large insects and birds. These were designed by Alice Havers and the four cards were entitled " Choice Studies " (Series No. 491).

which from the beginning very much emphasised the sentiment on the cards. It says :

> " Ho ! for the merry, merry, Christmas-time,
> With its feast, and fun, and its pantomime,
> When good humour reigns, and a gay content
> Is boon companion in all merriment.
> Such a CHRISTMAS bright, with its frolic joys,
> Belongs to all good little girls and boys."

The vibrant plain red background lends a festive gaiety to this early American design (Colour Plate XIc).

By the end of the last century evergreen motifs were augmented by the addition of sprays of the fir[2] on Christmas cards, and early in the twentieth century the poinsettia made its appearance on Christmas cards produced in America. Since then the popularity of this decorative plant has steadily increased, and to-day it may be said that it rivals holly as a Christmas card ornament in the U.S.A. Just as legends motivate the more conventional evergreens associated with Christmas (holly, ivy, mistletoe), so a charming legend is attached to the poinsettia. This legend, incorporated in Joseph Henry Jackson's attractive story, *The Christmas Flower* (Harcourt, Brace & Co., New York), is about a poor Mexican boy, Pablo, who had nothing to take to the shrine of the Nativity. He picked a branch of these " leaves of the forest weed " as his offering to the Christ Child. The topmost cluster of the branch turned into brilliant scarlet after it was placed under the altar, turning, like a miracle, the poor boy's humble present into a most beautiful, star-like flower.

But the plant world was not confined to evergreens on Christmas cards—far from it. Possibly no single subject recurs more frequently on old Victorian Christmas cards than flowers and plants, shrubs and trees of every kind, grouped without much regard to coincidence of growth or season, and not infrequently arranged in such strained and unnatural positions that one cannot place all the blame on their designers.

Although flowers were very much subjects of affectionate admiration throughout the nineteenth century, not only in poetry and art, but in the gentle and refined conversation of the gentle and refined in general,

---

[2] Various representations of the Christmas tree are provided on the array of Father Christmas cards (Dust Jacket).

their abundant use for the pictorial embellishment of Christmas cards was continuously the cause of unfavourable comment on the grounds of their apparently slight association with Christmas sleet and snow, even amongst those who were quite willing to applaud flower imitations in iron or stone in contemporary architecture.

How can we then reconcile bright spring and summer flowers, grasses and autumn leaves conveying the " Compliments of the Season " with the demands of " Ye Olde Christmasse " of bleak ice and snowed-up roads outside and the cheery warmth of huge fires and extensive family jollity within.

One explanation, of course, readily comes to the minds of all students of old rites and customs—namely, the coincidence of our Christmas season with the ancient winter solstice traditions. Spring and summer subjects on Christmas cards fit well into this theory, envisaging amidst wintry cold and sleet the promises and pleasures of the coming year.

I reproduce, for example, a charming Marcus Ward card dating from and typical of the late 80's which combines winter, spring and summer motifs, curiously recalling the general effect of old *quodlibets* (Plate 37). The sentiment on it suits this argument well :

> " Coldly the north wind is blowing,
>   Fast beats the snow on the pane,
>   Darkly the river is flowing,
>   Yet Summer will come again.

> " The west wind's breath will awaken
>   The blossom on meadow and plain,
>   Long is the sleep they have taken,
>   Yet Summer will come again."

Similarly, the sentiment by A. Smith on a much earlier little Dickes card with rather naïve mistletoe, etc., decoration in the British Museum begins :

> " Christmas is come, and in every home
>   To summer our hearts can turn it."

Another very attractive Goodall card contains within a frame of lilies of the valley as its sentiment the following lines by Coleridge :

> " . . . Kind hearts can make
>   December blithe as May . . ."

Another reason, and probably more directly in keeping with the Victorian mentality and with the many social repressions of the period,

OCTOBRE.

Beauspine f.   **Réséda.**   *Victor sc t*
Vos qualités surpassent vos charmes.
Héliotrope.   **Œillet Rouge.**
Je vous aime.   Amour vif et pur.
Vos qualités surpassent vos charmes :
je vous aime d'un amour vif et pur.

Fig. 8. Engraving from a tiny Language of Flowers book edited by Charlotte de Latour and published by Audot, in Paris.

may be found in that delightful but not now much required " language of flowers ", which was and had been for many generations not only the gallant and attractive way of expressing affection for members of the opposite sex, admiration and other sentiments, but very often the only way practicable. " Yes, flowers have their language ", the Editor of *Forget-me-not* assures us in his introduction to one of the dainty old books on the subject, dedicated to the Duchess of Kent, which ran into fifteen editions in quick succession just over 100 years ago. " Theirs is an oratory that speaks in perfumed silence, and there is tenderness, and passion, and even lightheartedness of mirth, in the variegated beauty of their vocabulary." He goes on to explain that " no spoken word can approach to the delicacy of sentiment to be inferred from a flower " and that " the softest impressions may be thus conveyed without offence " and " at a moment when the most tuneful voice would grate harshly on the ear. . . . " I have studied more than sixty different editions of these delicate handbooks, all published between the 1820's and 1890's. Many of them seem to have been reprinted year after year, which indicates continuous public demand for, and the popularity of, these grammars and vocabularies of the floral language of international vogue (Fig. 8).

It may be taken for granted, therefore, that amongst the people who exchanged greeting cards at Christmas the emblematic significance of plants and flowers was a known and understood convention, just as the rules of etiquette and contemporary "observances of the best society " were known.

Victorian writers on the language of flowers were eager to point out the ancient origins of the practice, tracing it back to the classical Greek and Roman times and the dream-book of Artemidorus, and the even older use of flowers to convey love and other messages is said to have been practised by Eastern peoples of long ago. They recalled how the laurel wreath which used to crown the victor came to be identified with honour and glory itself. They record that it was the very interesting correspondence of Lady Mary Wortley Montague (1689-1762), which " first told our country-women how the fair maidens of the East had lent a mute speech to flowers, and could send a letter by a bouquet ".[2]

[2] " There is no colour, no flower, no weed, no fruit, herb, pebble, or feather, that has not a verse belonging to it ; and you may quarrel, reproach, or send letters of passion, friendship, or civility, or even of news without ever inking your fingers ! " she wrote in her letter from Pera, Constantinople, to a friend in England on March 16th, 1718. " I have got for you, as you desire, a Turkish love-letter, which I have put in a little box, and ordered the captain of the *Smyrniote* to deliver it to you with this letter ", and from the list and rhymes and their literal translation which follows we learn that it included a little pearl, a clove, a jonquil, a bit of paper, a pear, a soap, a bit of coal, a rose, a straw, a bit of cloth, cinnamon, a match, a gold thread and a hair, a grape and a gold wire, " and, by way of postscript : ' Pepper ' = ' Send me an answer.' "

THE INCIDENCE OF HOLLY, IVY, ETC.

In a time-worn old copy (an old Christmas present) of *The Hand-Book of the Language and Sentiment of Flowers*, by Robert Tyas, F.R.B.S., printed in 1850, I found the following charming floral dedication, hand-inscribed in 1856 by an Edward to an Emma :

"Dear Red Rose bud, you are to me the sweet moss rose, bless me with your Red double Pink and with us may the Honeysuckle and the Linden never die."[3]

Another way in which the language of flowers used to be employed to convey similar communications at times when Mamma or Papa would exercise strict censorship on any written correspondence, and the meeting of loving couples usually took place in the presence and under the supervision of an elderly chaperone, often, if not always, rather disagreeably inclined towards the niceties of affection and love-making, was to draw and paint the flowers which represent the sentiment the sender wanted to convey, or to stick suitable flower scraps or, best of all, pressed and dried flowers and grasses in the desired order.

With the help of the numerous tiny "dictionaries", a flowery Christmas card could be read as a letter and the hidden message was often the reason why some otherwise rather absurd greeting cards were placed in a prominent place in many albums.

Thus, holly, ivy and mistletoe have innumerable rivals to share their popularity, all of which, although in different ways, were equally appropriate to the Christmas card. It would be impossible to attempt to enumerate the endless variety of Christmas card designs picturing individual flowers or bouquets, lifelike naturalistic reproductions or flowers used as decorative elements, or represented in various individual styles and periods, or the actual applications of dried flowers, leaves and grasses, to say nothing of those attractive landscapes where wild flowers as well as cultivated flower gardens show an abundance of colour and vegetation. All these in a cold and dark late December are harbingers of spring, and gaily arriving on Christmas cards announce the coming end of snow and sleet, and winter winds, and the awakening of that most ancient and most-loved Sleeping Beauty of mankind, Nature.

[3] According to the vocabulary *Red Rose Bud* stands for "Pure and Lovely", *Red Double Pink* = "Woman's Love", *Honeysuckle* = "Bonds of Love", and *Linden* = "Conjugal Love".

THE CHRISTMAS CARDS
of "Ye Merrie Olde Christmasse" at Home and Abroad

NATURALLY, a great number of old Christmas cards had as their subjects scenes from the celebrations customary at Christmas. Both Horsley and Egley in their respective cards concentrated on these homely scenes, and both gave prominence to the Christmas dinner being enjoyed by a big family party. Later cards often give us an insight into the other traditional activities, games, dances and other customs associated with the season.

In respect of the Christmas dinner itself, the principle of the *pars pro toto* is fully worked out ! A chef holding a steaming dish with a roast turkey or a huge sirloin of beef or the ever-popular Christmas pudding, which appear on Christmas cards in a thousand and one forms, all tended to convey the same idea of a happy Christmas through a plentiful dinner. On the same principle, many designs anticipated the sumptuousness of the Christmas dinner by illustrating rows of killed birds, turkeys and geese, or the butcher surrounded by his choicest joints of raw meat. These in themselves not very " dainty " subjects for the drawing-room chimneypiece were nevertheless very popular owing to their implications. These neutralised the natural revulsion from the appearance of carcasses. A number of these cards were really meant to be humorous, and some were. H. Stacy Marks made a famous set of four very decorative " old costume " cards, of which two concentrate on prospective Christmas dishes. One of these shows a poulterer welcoming a couple to his shop, in which are displayed a fine selection of turkeys, geese and pheasants. The other shows a swineherd and a buyer looking at a fat pig and fatter piglets (Plate 41c). The caption reads, " The Compliments of the Season and All Good Things in Reason ", while below the following philosophy is proclaimed : " They're doomed for Christmas brawn and chine, for pigs must die that men may dine ! " Joints of meat, in company with bottles of wine equipped with feet and arms, made to look rather like disproportionately fat and jovial old men, were also frequent motifs

on Christmas cards. The round Christmas pudding also lent itself
well to such humorous designs which personify the characters of Roast
Beef, Plum Pudding, etc., and probably derive from the old masked
pageants in which people dressed themselves up to represent these
Christmas ingredients in the procession of the traditional Lord of
Misrule, a side-line ancestor of Father Christmas[1] (Plate 45).

A set entitled " Christmas Advances ; A series of 4 Subjects illustrative of Beauty and Good Cheer ", by W. T. Nugent (Plate 41a, b),
shows pretty young women being courted, or tempted, by tiny
creatures of this type, representing Roast Beef, Old Port, Plum Pudding
and Mince Pie respectively. The verses give an idea of the type of
humour that went down well in those days :

> " Let not Roast Beef be
>   Carelessly passed by.
>   At Christmas hold him in
>   Esteem most high."

> " Fair Girl be warned
>   When Christmas comes
>   Reject that pudding
>   Stuffed with Plums."

> " Old Port implores thee
>   To his suit give ear,
>   And sip a bumper
>   With thy Christmas cheer."

> " Resist ye blandishments of
>   Hot Mince Pie,
>   Or surely you'll repent it,
>   By and by."

In the late 60's a very popular type of card first appeared. Their
designs alluded to the ancient Christmas dish, the boar's head, which

---

[1] A Goodall triptych card (Plate 42) designed by Crowquill in the 1860's
picturing Father Christmas as " The Collector" of the Christmas fare and the
pudding " that cut away ", in one of the accompanying verses assures us that the
would-be dishes are rather pleased to be of service in a good cause :

> " The little pigs grunt and the Ducks all quack,
>   And the Beef runs on to the roast,
>   Knowing that Charity blesses the feast,
>   And will give to those who want most."

was always attended by great ceremonies, carried in procession to the banqueting hall, heralded by trumpeters and dancers. Many early cards, but later ones, too, pictured this ceremony in the " archaic " manner of historical nostalgia (Crane, M. Smith, etc.), but the set I am now referring to takes a comic line. One of these cards (Plate 43) shows the boar's head, decorated with rosemary and holding a lemon in his mouth, being carried on a dish supported on the shoulders of four piglets as though it were a bier. The little pigs walk as solemnly as they can and dry their tears on large white handkerchiefs.

A delightful card of the 70's interprets the " white Christmas ". It shows, finely drawn, the " old lady who sits high and dry " on a cloud amongst golden stars, and as she " picks the white feathers [of a goose] Christmas is nigh " (Plate 46). Snapdragon and punch were also popular subjects on many small cards, and are usually shown with sprites, dwarfs or gnomes carousing around them (Plate 44).

Spirits in a different meaning and more obvious form dominate a delightful early English card which bears a German translation of the greeting text (Fig. 9). It was designed by Kenny Meadows and signed by his initials, and engraved on wood by W. J. Linton, with whom Walter Crane and many others spent their years of apprenticeship. Meadows was a well-known illustrator for the Vizetelly Brothers' three-volume *Shakespeare* (1843), etc., and used to design valentines, which are now rather rare and valued, at about the same time or before. It is possible that this card is directly connected with the early " laughing face " notepaper designs, and it is quite likely that copies of it were issued with English, Scottish, etc., texts.

The Falstaffian joviality of the Kenny Meadows design has little resemblance to the fairly early (Series No. 193) De La Rue chromo-lithograph reproduced on Plate 47. This card shows the merry Christmas as enjoyed by the men of the street. They are standing round a hand-barrow on which are two large urns being kept hot by braziers, and a huge dish of sandwiches. The three men, two in top-coats and top-hats, though obviously not very well-to-do, and the third in a wagoners' smock with his whip in his hand, are all drinking or about to drink steaming cups of coffee. It is one of a set of three cards entitled " Wayside Caterers ", all showing the humbler enjoyments of the poor. One of the others shows a number of poorly dressed, shivering men enjoying the warmth of potatoes baked in their jackets and eating them with evident relish. The third, also in a wintry setting, shows some working lads buying chestnuts from a jolly old woman sitting by her brazier. This type of card was as representative of the social sentimentalism of the century as the cards picturing large and happy family gatherings. They were meant to be attractive for the well-to-do, who were to be frequently reassured that the "decent poor" none the less enjoyed themselves in their own way, at least at Christmas.

But the real Victorian Christmas atmosphere was the privilege of those who were lucky enough to share amiable company, good food and drink, dancing, games and other jollifications of the season in their

Fig. 9. A large Christmas card designed by Kenny Meadows and engraved on wood by W. J. Linton. Late 1840's or early 50's.

own homes, whether they were large and comfortable or small and overcrowded. In the former, splendour and gaiety, fashion and plenty, in the latter, warmth of intimacy and the quiet enjoyment of the Christmas story, etc., provided the essentials to the same holiday consciousness. The " holiday at home " and the " longing for home " aspects became permanent features of the Christmas card, Victorian or modern (Plates 48, 49, 50 and Colour Plate XIIIa).

Many typical World War I cards show groups of soldiers round a brazier in a dug-out, toasting absent friends—recalling the toast on the Cole-Horsley card of 1843 in very different circumstances. Some of these cards were completed by small pen-and-ink drawings in the margins, showing some of the absent friends, including a small dog sitting by his master's hat and gloves at home.[2]

The Victorian Christmas party, and consequently the cards depicting it, was not only remarkable for the toys and candles, holly, ivy, mistletoe decorations and the lit-up Christmas tree, the Christmas dinner and other activities. It was not confined to the type of well-ordered family party where, as, for example, an early Baxter process card shows, an elder brother dutifully kisses his little sisters, one by one, under the mistletoe and under the solemn and dignified supervision of their parents, the whiskered Papa seated by a table as an authentic daguerreotype while, at a sufficient distance from him, Mamma is engaged in doing her habitual needlework (Plate 49). The Christmas tide was also the time of seasonal visitors as well as the season for visiting.

Perhaps it is no exaggeration to say that especially to the young in every houshold the most welcome of all seasonal visitors from the time of his first appearance was an old man, both fact and fiction, Father Christmas. He turns up with his jolly, laughing face beneath a fur cap or hood; his bushy white eyebrows, moustache, beard and clumsy movements, due to age as well as to the thick, fur-trimmed robe, appeared early enough on Victorian Christmas cards. But his magic

---

[2] A popular American invention carried the Christmas kiss of the sender to the fronts over the seas. These First World War cards were decorated with the Stars and Stripes and there was a space on them, prepared with gum coating, for the " kiss ". The mark of the lips, as when giving a kiss, could be impressed on this surface. The verse underneath told the happy recipient :

> " For Uncle Sam you're fighting
> And it makes me love you so
> That I send a kiss in the space above
> To take wherever you go ! "

Another small card pictured a soldier. His feet in France, he is seen reaching across the Atlantic and embracing a girl in America.

> " What's a little Ocean between friends
> When it's Christmas—OVER HERE ?"

explained the motto.

personality, even his costume and general appearance, commonly thought to be one and unchangeable, has slowly but definitely changed, as witnessed in the long sequence of Christmas cards featuring him as the century grew older.

Father Christmas is only one of his names; some call him Good King Wenceslaus, other St. Nicholas, or Santa Claus, the latter being the American version derived from the early Dutch settlers' Sante Klaas. Wenceslaus was originally a King of Bohemia in the tenth century. St. Nicholas, on the other hand, was Bishop of Myra, in Asia Minor, *circa* 350, and became the patron saint of Russia as well as the city of New York and other places. He is also the patron saint of children, particularly of schoolchildren, and his day was celebrated throughout Europe. According to a legend, it was St. Nicholas who miraculously saved three poor girls by giving them each a gold bar when they were about to sell themselves. Thus they were saved from shame and servitude, and this is said to be the beginning of the tradition of the gifts which Father Christmas–Santa Claus places in Christmas stockings every year.

Even more striking than his complex " family tree " is his habit quickly to conform to the speediest and most up-to-date travelling conveyance of the age of progress in his eagerness to deliver his presents through the chimney ! According to old Christmas card pictures, while the traditional Nordic deer-carriage is still frequently used by our Santa Claus, beflagged railway engines, motor-cars, balloons and aeroplanes were soon used by him not long after their very invention. The machines themselves, if the contemporary Christmas card illustrations can be relied on, look very much like a cross between the actual early model of the vehicle with a touch of Heath Robinson and village fair mechanism added to it—altogether most entertaining to modern eyes. (A fair selection of old and new representations of Father Christmas on Christmas cards is reproduced on the dust jacket of this book.)

In the late 60's Marcus Ward published a charming series of cards entitled " Father Christmas and His Little Friends ". They were small cards, about 2½ by 4 inches in size, and their gold background and embossed narrow borders helped to bring out the flatly coloured pen-and-ink drawings. On one of the little cards Father Christmas is seen impartially distributing gifts to children drawn with charm and naïvety when " he unpacks and spreads around the newest things in toys ". Another card in the same set (which was also available as a folded concertina) pictured him as a benefactor to the parents, too, as " An hour before dinner Old Xmas employs Snowballing and romping outside with the boys ". Santa would not be the man he is if he could not appreciate a joke or two—even horse-play—directed against him. Thus we see on a popular little card, framed with holly and ribbon, a youngster holding the visiting card of " The New Year " and jauntily raising his hat in greeting to a tired and heavily bent Father Christmas, who, like a snowman, is melting away at the approach of the New Year. Another card, the third of a set of three called " Christmas Reprisals ", which have been preserved in a number of collections from the late 1870's, shows Father Christmas in an even more pathetic position. He has been rolled into a huge snowball by two demure young ladies of the period, who are playing this rather rough game with curiously sedate expressions, while the old man shows signs of alarm at their joke. The motto, " 'Tis innocent mirth that gives Christmas its worth ", probably added to the poignancy of the card (Plate 51). At the time of its publication, the set was described by its publisher as " representing the discomfiture of Father Christmas " and sold to retailers at 6s. per dozen. Nearly forty years later a design in some respect similar is a rather naïvely drawn card sent out by the South Wales Borderers for Christmas, 1917. It too shows a huge snowball in the centre, but it is being rolled by a British Tommy towards a fat German officer—representing the German Army in the form of a snowman, already disintegrating ! (Fig. 10.)

But, of course, Santa of the Christmas cards also shares in all the fun that human friends enjoy, and on one card, an etching by Tristram Ellis, we see him in the 1880's even happily married and skating gaily with " Mrs. Xmas ", to the delight of ordinary skaters in the background (Plate 54). Although attempts were made by some English publishers to popularise Old Mother Hubbard of nursery rhyme fame on somewhat the same lines as Father Christmas, this never really caught on on Christmas cards.

In the 1880's it was considered an objectionable " modern " habit for families to spend Christmas Day away from home. Father Christmas, in one of Sambourne's cartoons, is seen on the steps of a wealthy " Modern English Home ". He is loaded with cards and parcels, The butler with dignity informs him that " Her Ladyship is at Monty Carlo ; the young gentlemen are in the Halps ; and Sir John has taken the other members of the family to the Restorong "—a new fashion, clearly disapproved of by Father Christmas. But to visit relatives and

FROM·THE·52ND·GRAD·BATTN· *SOUTH·WALES·BORDERERS·*

Fig. 10. A more recent counterpart of the Victorian card on Plate 51. Is it possible that the amateur artist of this typical military card of 1917 recollected the former card in his grandmother's old scrapbook ?

friends and to stay with them was, no doubt, an even older custom than the sending of Christmas cards. Some of the early nineteenth-century European cards clearly illustrate, for example, the transition between the personal visit to convey the compliments of the season and the sent card. One of these shows in a pleasant line engraving the figure of the young Johann Andreas Boerner entering his friend's and patron's house with his hat under his arm, as he had gone personally to wish him good luck for 1807. In 1812 Boerner produced another card, another self-portrait, but this time we see him hatted and cloaked at the gates of a mansion, probably his own home. The corner of his cloak is clearly caught in the closed doors behind him, which prevents him from calling in person to pay the compliments of the season : he sent the etching instead (Plate 59).

Seasonal visitors, such as the waits and carol-singers, formed the subjects of Christmas cards from an early date, and have remained colourful motifs up to the present day. These motifs used to have a sentimental claim both to the designer and his public. They were reminders that Christmas is the time to remember the poor, who were originally fed and clothed, and later tipped, as the prevailing form of charity. The services of postmen and delivery boys frequently form the feature on Christmas cards in the Victorian times, but much less later. These subjects were probably inherited from the greeting bills submitted by public servants—such as watchmen and others (Plate 56).

There has always been something very attractive about candle-light, and to-day Christmas is readily associated with it. But lighted candles were used on Christmas card designs long before the Christmas tree, which was said to have been introduced into England at Windsor Castle in 1841,[3] became really popular. Shopkeepers long before this used to send presents at Christmas to their regular customers, and it was usual for these to consist of or include some candles, possibly as a contribution to the once-traditional Christ Child candles, which used to be put in the windows and lighted at sunset on Christmas Eve to show the Child the way ; or to the traditional kissing bough decoration, which included beeswax candles as well as apples and mistletoe.

The old horse-driven stage-coach is almost as much a property of the Christmas card store of subjects as travelling is to-day associated with the Christmas holiday. It was not, of course, the considerable discomfort of the coach journey which seventeenth-century writers so bitterly complained about, but the romantic and old-time associations which made their pictures on the cards so popular—in a century in which the use of the horse was slowly being replaced by the steam engine, and which ended up with the motor car (Plate 55). In 1629 John Taylor, the water-poet and publican, gravely wrote, " It is doubtful whether the devil brought tobacco into England in a coach, for both appeared at the same time . . ." and " The Lover of His Country " asked, " Is it for a man's health to travel with tired jades, to be laid fast in the foul ways, and forced to wade up to the knees in mire ; afterwards sit in the cold till teams of horses can be sent to pull the coach out ? Is it for their health to travel in rotten coaches ? . . ." This was certainly not the late nineteenth-century or the modern Christmas card conception of " coaching in the olden days ". Their picture is based

[3] Previously the Christmas tree was only very occasionally seen in Britain, mainly thanks to visitors from Germany. The custom did not become general before the 60's and 70's.

instead on the warm sentimentalism of which Washington Irving's
" Old Stage Coach " was typical :

"In the course of a December tour in Yorkshire, I rode a long
distance in one of the public coaches, on the day preceding Christmas,
[he wrote] ; the coach was crowded, both inside and out, with passengers, who, by their talk, seemed principally bound to the mansions
of relations or friends, to eat the Christmas dinner. It was loaded
also with hampers of game, and baskets and boxes of delicacies ;
and hares hung dangling their long ears about the coachman's box,
presents from distant friends for the impending feast."

Detailed descriptions followed of the coach, coachman, fellow travellers
and horses. Irving's delightful book was read in new illustrated
editions just about the time when old Christmas subjects were enjoying
so much success also on Christmas cards. Naturally, the same affectionate picture was the one which embellished Victorian cards in lines
and colours. In 1882 some pretty cards of coaching subjects by George
Cruikshank appeared. These are full of the same sentimental attach-
ment to coach and horses, but contrast the elegance and comfort of
modern, i.e. 1882, travelling to the romantic but trying adventures of
1828. The cards were printed on silk and were produced in pairs.
The first, called " Old Times ", shows a coach deeply mired in a snow-
drift, with additional horses harnessed to pull it out. The exposed
parts of the wheels and the top of the coach are heavily coated with snow
and ice, and the whole picture illustrates the struggle for survival on the
roads of those days. " Our Times ", the proud modern counterpart,
exhibits a similar coach rolling along at high speed on a made road,
showing all the travellers comfortably seated, instead of pushing and
pulling as in the former. Somehow the drawing conveys a tremendous
advance in progress. Another pair illustrated a family journey, showing
a numerous family, including the future Grandpapa, being driven by
a postilion in a carriage over a rough track. The card, " Grandpapa
going to His Party " (Plate 52), is coupled with a similar design entitled
" Going to Grandpapa's Party ", a scene which apparently takes place
some sixty years later. This pictures a similar carriage, but on its arrival
at a stately mansion, and the whole family party, including a number
of grandchildren, bringing toys and masses of presents, being welcomed
on the doorstep by a now white-haired, late Victorian Grandpapa.

I feel I should mention amongst these charming old coaching cards a unique card of this type in Queen Mary's collection. It was sent to her in 1934 by H.M. the Queen when she was eight years old. It is dedicated " To Granny from Lilibet ", and the design on the folder shows an old-time coachman holding the reins and a beribboned whip in his hands and with his scarf blowing out behind, suggesting speed, whilst beside him sits a charming young girl in bonnet and cape, holding a band-box in her hands. The design was hand-coloured (with crayons) by the little Princess herself. The driver was given a black top-hat and a deep lilac-blue coat ; the girl is dressed in a yellow coat with a bright orange bonnet. The inset panel for the greeting text is coloured pink, and the whole work has been done with great and apparent love and care to please Grandmother. A most charming little card.

Whereas in recent years the coach and its accessories are only picturesque reminders, in the 80's of the last century coaching was still an important means of travel. The pride evident in some of the coupled or contrasted cards was typical of the period. This was the time when electricity and the telephone, with their practical uses, began to be subjects of conversation and, correspondingly, targets for the usual practical jokes. The 1881 cartoon by Tenniel on the coming omnipotence of electricity was, of course, ironical, but typical of the thought of the day. He visualises some " fantastic " future uses for electricity, such as hatching Christmas turkeys by electric heat. Bicycles driven by electric power enable the riders on them to read the *Electric Times* instead of concentrating on the pedalling. The resuscitation of frozen beef from Australia becomes possible by means of it. A huge fish-shaped balloon is sketched complete with wings and a suspended basket to accommodate the passengers, all brightly lit up by electric bulbs, and, of course, propelled by electric power. Such a journey must have been thought of as a huge joke, for beneath it appeared, " London to Paris in two hours ! " " No sea sickness ! " and so on.

But while all these electrical gadgets must have seemed in 1881 fantastic, tricycles and bicycles, somewhat laborious, propelled by manpower, were already familiar features everywhere on the roads, and of course they had their share of publicity on contemporary

Christmas cards as well. Cards demonstrate them with neat little girls or boys riding on them with an expression of naïve bliss and concentration on their faces (Plates 57 and 58). The draughtsmen took great care to depict in detail the mechanism of these vehicles, no doubt in response to the public interest focused on them. Later a surprisingly great number of Christmas cards with pictures of bicycle adventures, sentimental and comic, were published, and a special impetus was given to designers when the lady cyclist invaded the road. They are featured in skirts or the fabulous bloomers, adorable or ridiculous, but usually with great gusto (Colour Plate XIIIc).

The railway was by then, during the second half of the century, no longer a novelty. Once again Christmas cards were eager to make use of the steam engine to convey Christmas greetings. For example, a charmingly naïve card shows a boy, representing the New Year, riding on a steam engine with a fully decorated Christmas tree behind him. (Earlier, in the 1830's, Cupids used to be seated on engines, in the same manner, on embossed Kershaw valentines!) In the foreground are hampers and toys and even bottles of champagne—the locomotive is obviously bringing in a happy New Year! (Plate 60).

The deep-rooted British love of the sea and ships, so clearly demonstrated also by the great popularity of Christmas cards with these subjects, somehow never seems to have been much extended on Christmas card pictures towards the big and beautiful ocean liners which were beginning to assume a great importance in the life of the 80's. Popular taste remained faithful to the old-fashioned sailing ships and rowing boats even in the last, progress-conscious decades of the century, at least in arts and cards.

Sailing boats appear amongst the early Goodall card decorations in the 1860's. A much later example of a ship card (Plate 62) is not only interesting as a characteristic illustration of the general preference for the old ships, with their picturesque rigging and billowing sails, on Christmas cards, but also, as the photograph brings out, the " jewelling " of the capital letters, etc., a much-admired feature of expensive Victorian cards, and the gleaming pearls which further adorn the jewelled surfaces. My next illustrations, on Plate 64, are more interesting from a general historical point of view. Both these ship cards were sent to Queen Mary in 1901. The upper is a Faulkner card and characteristic of the finely printed and fashionable style at the turn of the century. It is about 3½ by 5 inches in size and consists of a folder of four pages as the cover, with another four pages inside, held together by a silk ribbon. The design by G. S. Walters on the cover is a pleasant scene of the Thames Estuary, with a homely sailing barge in a misty seascape with a steamship in the distant background, and in the foreground a rowing boat with two silhouettes in it. The text on the inside folder includes the " sentiment " :

" Christmas fill your heart with gladness
Bring you joy and banish sadness.
New Year find you blithe and gay
" 'Til next you welcome New Year's Day."

The handwritten dedication is " To dearest May ", and the signature was added to the printed greeting, " Kind thoughts ", by King Edward VII. The card below this elegant card was sent by William II of Germany, and is dedicated : " Warmest wishes for 1902. Willy ". It represents a German battleship in a Baltic port, after a drawing by Paul E. Ritter. A similar picture postcard type card with " With every good wish for 1900 from Willy " pencilled on it, was sent by him in 1899. It was a reproduction of a water-colour drawing of a German cruiser steaming into the Bay of Naples. [4]

But this taste in naval Christmas cards was rather unique in Victorian times and more recent decades as well. Even such an expert and interested institution as the British Admiralty continued to reproduce on their regular Christmas cards old galleons, sailing barges, and if a naval engagement was the chosen subject, a reproduction of an old print of previous centuries seems to have been preferred. During the two great wars, however, naval pictures and photographs of various men-of-war appear on Christmas cards, and there were also a number of cartoons illustrating witty aspects of life at sea. One of these (Plate 63), an eight-page folder, sent out by the Dover Patrol in 1917, shows the powerful battle-cruiser, the *Tirpitz*, approaching a floating object. On this the letters MINE are clearly visible just above the water. The

[4] The German Emperor seems to have had a particular liking for this type of card for Christmas. Up to 1912, which is the year of his last preserved card and shows himself conferring with his officers on deck, he managed to find a different naval vessel annually as the main attraction for his compliments of the season.

cartoon shows signs of panic on the deck. In the narrow strip drawing below we see the next move—the *Tirpitz* in full flight. The " floating object " has by this time righted itself in the water and is seen to be a large wooden box with " Mineral Water " written in large letters on one side. The lid of the box has by now been raised, and a British A.B. is seen eating a Bath bun and drinking lemonade, and hooting at the departing ship.

In the middle of the 1890's a new conveyance joined the ranks of regular transport and a new motif emerged for Christmas card decorations. This was the " new monstrosity from France ", the " autocar ", " automobile ", or, as it was finally called, the motor car, furnished with chain-driven rear-axle, gear-box, countershaft and an alarm bell— as well as a maximum speed of twelve miles an hour. Like most newcomers, the motor car had at first to overcome general distrust and malice, though in the late years of the *fin de siècle* this was much easier in the case of a mechanical contraption than in any other ever since. The versatile pen of Sir Frank Lockwood was quick to sketch a car as his personal Christmas card in 1897, the first year when the red flag was no longer compulsory on the Queen's highways (Fig. 11). When the twelve-mile speed limit was replaced by twenty miles an hour, Professor Herkomer, the celebrated painter, made an " ultramodern " design as his personal Christmas card in 1903, showing a motor car travelling at full speed. James Laver aptly pointed out recently that the drawing " shows a remarkable modernity of handling, which has outlasted the one-time modernity of the subject ".

Another characteristic early motoring card shows a pleasant seaside resort. The scene depicts the arrival of a rather fantastic, up-to-date racing car of its time (1909), controlled by two padded and helmeted drivers (Plate 69). As a contrast to this modern sport, horses and riders, and beyond them sailing boats, can be seen in the background. In the foreground a terrified horse has just upset his milkmaid driver and the milk churns, and the cart is just about to turn over, a scene only too common on the roads in those days when the countryside was first being invaded by motorists. In 1912, C. W. Faulkner & Co. issued some humorous cards in colour by Dudley Buxton. One shows motorists held up by road repairs, whilst youngsters take advantage to beg for " cigarette pictures " and another for " a little drop of oil ". By this time, however, the motor car was no longer a subject for amazement, but an accepted fact. As it became more and more familiar on the roads, the novelty value, which for a time made the car a topic for the traditionalist but at the same time always novelty-seeking Christmas card designer, gradually fell out of special favour. No longer Tenniel's mythical, electrically driven balloon, half-fish, half-bird, but the real " airship " and aeroplane began to make their appearance as serious means of travel, and again the Christmas card was quick to use these

Fig. 11. Father Time " travels quickly " on this personal card by Sir Frank Lockwood (1896). Note the somewhat worried expression on the face of the passenger in contrast to the determination of the youthful driver.

as motifs. Their interpretation is naturally rather naïve, and this was probably a faithful reflection of the reaction of the ordinary people in those days.

The earliest cards which represent the first aerial adventures on Christmas cards usually approach their subject with the same wonder and fair-ground fantasy. An early card with two " dainty ", as they were called, children sitting in a brightly coloured fun-fair flying boat conveys the greeting on a scroll held by the little girl. A card from the 70's transports Father Christmas high above the clouds in the basket of a bright pink-and-yellow striped balloon (Plate 66). He is seen delivering his presents in this novel manner, but the card bears the strongest resemblance to the traditional fair-ground *décor*. The card designed by E. Walker in 1901 as the private card of Mr. and Mrs. Geo. R. Sims, the author and playwright, and produced in monochrome by F. C. Southwood, shows marked progress (Plate 67). It is certainly much more ambitious than its Victorian counterparts, if not almost pompous, and is in many ways characteristic of the manner of the fashionable Edwardian magazine illustrations. It is only the rapid march of fashion which makes it seem as naïve as its predecessors—indeed, rather pathetic—to us. London is landmarked on the picture by the cupola and towers of St. Paul's, just visible behind the mistletoe which, with holly in the opposite corner, decorate the frame. Behind the contours of St. Paul's, however, the Atlantic Ocean is visible, just sufficiently reduced to enable us to identify the Statue of Liberty on the other shore. But no flight across the ocean is indicated. These symbols of space and distance are only put in to emphasise the main feature of the card. It is the airship, a cross-breed between Giffard's " Steam Dirigible " of 1852 and Spencer's airship of 1903. A very Edwardian couple, evidently Mr. and Mrs. Sims, is seen each standing in a wicker basket. Mr. Sims is at the controls, while Mrs. Sims, with an engaging smile, is releasing Christmas cards from a postbag. A paper scroll not only conveniently fills in space in the design, but bears the greeting, " With Best Wishes for Christmas and the New Year ", which is, of course, the reason why Mr. and Mrs. Sims undertook this hazardous and no doubt much-admired venture in the air in A.D. 1901. In 1912 elegant folders appeared and were sold as ordinary " counter cards " (i.e. to be sold over the counter ; not private or personal cards, by this time in great vogue both in England and in the U.S.A.[5]), with the motto : " Bearing Greetings as of Old ". The cover was shared by a pretty monochrome picture of a stage-coach advancing in a wintry landscape, and above it the gold-embossed image of a biplane, loaded with holly.

The more recent variations of aeroplanes, both in fact and on Christmas cards, are too well known to us all to need recollection here, although

[5] Personal cards are cards which include the printed name and possibly address of the sender, while a private card, like Mr. Sims's, is made to order and often includes the ideas of the sender.

we are beginning to scent the period flavour in the surviving originals or pictures of the biplanes which were still the pride of the 1920's. Thus I conclude this group of Christmas cards by the reproduction of a good-humoured sketch drawn on an airgraph card sent out by a unit of the Royal Air Force serving in Egypt in 1941 (Plate 68).

All these motifs, which appeared from time to time on the Christmas cards of the day, reflect the interest taken in the means of transport, perhaps subconsciously, as the means also by which loved ones and friends may be reunited (Colour Plate Id).

Old Christmas cards bear witness that there were in the past, just as there are now, many ways in which Christmas may be spent " out " (Colour Plates XII, XIII and XIV, and Plates 71-77). The choice of these outings and the distance ventured would vary according to age, rank, respectability or other conditions in an ever-changing world. If it should prove to be a white Christmas, snow and ice for the young at any rate will provide in the neighbourhood of their homes all the incentive required for a glorious Christmas outing. The snowman and the snowball, as many Christmas cards both past and present testify, have a magnetic power of attraction for the bursting energies and exuberant spirits unable to find an outlet indoors. A seasonal target for these energies is the snowman, a creature who seems more than pleased, as one Goodall card witnesses (Plate 76), when snowballs fly about him from every direction. The mature wisdom and good humour of snowmen as represented on Victorian cards, whether frozen hard or beginning to melt, are comparable only to that of Father Christmas.

A great chance and attraction is provided by the universal slipperiness of ice and snow, with all the indignities and surprises which were apparently enjoyed by both the young and their elders. Skating, tobogganing and sliding down the hills were all much appreciated motifs on Christmas cards, including the tumbles. Cards usually depict boys and girls thus disporting themselves amidst scenery of snow-covered trees and cottages, village churches and belfries, chosen to bring out the daintiness and sentimentality of innocent merriment. To make them more delicate and the cards more compositely pretty, the artists often put sprigs of holly or mistletoe into the children's hands, just as these were put into the mouths of dogs and horses, besides the other Christmas touches, such as a border or mount and frosting.

Winter sports, both in life and on Christmas cards, were not confined, however, to the young. Randolph Caldecott, for example, made as a private card a water-colour showing a delightful old fellow of the Rip van Winkle variety gracefully bowing on the ice and wishing the compliments of the season. An apparently very popular set of chromolithographs designed by William Duffield and published in 1880 by Hildesheimer and Faulkner pictures four pretty young women, fashionably dressed in pale colours, making a chain of apparent insecurity on very icy ground (Plate 77).

Very characteristically, children of the poor were very frequently the subjects of Christmas cards. Their living conditions and miserable childhood was beginning to be felt by many to be a disgrace to society in the second half of the Victorian Era. Correspondingly, a sentimental aura is drawn around these poor, hard-working and much-exploited children, to whom ice and snow were no mere fun, but the cause of harder living and additional work (Plate 74). The artists usually · painted them on Christmas cards with the sympathy due to little ragged crossing-sweepers, tattered torchbearers or newspaper boys, though seldom with the force of social criticism. This attitude seemed natural enough in view of their public, and if they were the incentive to a larger tip or a hot meal so much the better. They were not aiming to reform the social evils of the day ; they were to supersede them for the duration of Christmas. It was, nevertheless, a genuine attitude, the relics of which are still pleasant to look at on Christmas cards, although no one to-day would consider it an appropriate answer to social questions or a serious contribution to a merry Christmas. In the words of an American expert, " cards are rarely published to-day [1926] that indicate or even intimate the idea that unhappiness exists. They would fall quickly by the wayside, for everyone is intent on scattering sunshine and joy."

CHRISTMAS CARDS
of Children

O N E of the characteristics of the Christmas card not specifically Victorian in origin, though it very easily could have been, is its recurring interest in children as prominent motifs in its design. The large Victorian families and the tradition which brings together several generations for the Christmas celebrations naturally laid an emphasis on the children at this season.

" It is a beautiful arrangement, derived from days of yore, that this festival, which commemorates the announcement of the religion of peace and love, has been made the season for gathering together of family connections, and drawing closer again those bands of kindred hearts, which the cares and pleasures and sorrows of the world are continually operating to cast loose : of calling back the children of a family, who have launched forth in life, and wandered widely asunder, once more to assemble about the paternal hearth, that rallying-place of the affections, there to grow young and loving again, among the endearing mementoes of childhood,"
wrote Washington Irving.

Nowadays it is only too often pointed out that family reunions on this scale were only possible for a comparatively small section of society in the past. Still, Irving's long sentence gives once again a good word-picture of the feeling which is characteristic of a great number of Christmas card pictures. In these great family parties, children, according to the rules of Nature, would secure at least a numerical dominance, strengthened by their superior shouts and laughter, easily satisfied pleasures and indefatigable energies. This in itself would explain why their charm, daintiness and, even when mischievous, lovable qualities, as they appear to their elders, were so often featured on Christmas cards.

But in this the Victorians were continuing and further developing the older tradition which associated Christmas and the Christmas card with the Child. It will be remembered that the old woodcuts and engravings, the forerunners of the Christmas card as we now know it, regularly concentrated on the figure of the Infant Christ, whose blessing

Fig. 12. A "calligraphic greeting" card of 7 by 5½ inches, printed in brick red. The design includes the seven members of its artist's family in 1946.

was evoked to make the New Year peaceful, happy and prosperous. These old presentations of the naked or lightly draped baby and child figures, although they were the representations of a definite Child, Jesus, and were, in accordance with the outlook of their age, definitely religious in significance and devotional in appearance, may also be taken as the forerunners of the child motif on Christmas cards. Even when the religious associations of Christmas are not frequently expressed on Victorian Christmas cards of children, the fact that they try to emphasise the purity and innocence of children in a way at least indirectly points to their descent from, and indicates the chief significance of the Christian Christmas, the Incarnation nearly 2,000 years ago.

The Cole-Horsley and Egley cards, it will be remembered, pictured whole family parties—not children alone. Actually, they carefully observed the disparity in age, and thus dignity, of the various generations of the family, placing each figure in its right place and relationship between the foreground and background in the composition. The Horsley and Egley procedure has been followed ever since on many Christmas cards. Drawings and photographs of family groups, composed with painful care to include all available members of the family, are still familiar to many of us. They have been used on Christmas cards almost without a break, especially within the greater family circle, and within this are to-day as frequent as ever, though the stiff and formal grouping, thanks to modern trends in photography, has been to some extent relaxed.

My illustrations show this type of card in various strata of society. They include a card, dated 1911, of King Edward VII and his family (Plate 78), including the late King George VI as a boy ; the card of the Green family of Herne Hill, who printed a versified record each year beside the annual photograph of the happily growing family group (Plate 79) ; and a modern version of the family-group Christmas card designed by J. R. Biggs, typographer and designer, as his private card for 1946 (Fig. 12). The last is composed almost entirely of clever spirals and loops by a playful pen, showing the artist, his wife and five children under similarly formed Christmas bells.

The portrait of the Victorian child as it appears in the illustrations on Christmas cards is very versatile, vivid and manifold. Christmas cards give us prototypes of the ideal, the good, the neat and tidy, rather meek child, as well as the mischievous and the mixed species. They disclose the attitude of the grown-up towards the child in succeeding decades, from the stiffly moralising and forbidding mid-Victorian times to the later, less-censorious period, when a certain naughtiness was considered charming and chic, a privilege of childhood and a sign of robust health. Later still some perky sophistication was particularly well received by their elders.

The earliest cards of children preserve little figures, faces and attitudes, some of which now one may find rather unreal and most entertaining. But some of them could have been the source of little amusement to their " models "—that is, the children themselves—who were to be impressed by the moral and the moderating influences in them. " The highly salutary precepts enjoined in books such as Mrs. Turner's *Cautionary*

Stories were in great favour—with parents ", remarks Lady Dorothy Nevill in her delightful memoirs. A few lines from this book (first published in 1807) illustrate the relationship between the Victorian tenets for children and the Christmas card pictures of them :

> " Mamma, why mayn't I, when I dine,
> Eat ham and goose, and drink port wine ?
> Eat pudding, soup, and mutton, too . . . ? "

To which the dignified reply is :

> " Because, my dear, it is not right
> To spoil the youthful appetite."

The little girl who could happily accept this answer could easily have looked like either of those little girls depicted on one old Christmas card with a " too good to be true " expression on her face (Plate 80), or the one seen on another old card, coming home under an umbrella held by her slightly elder brother. She would probably also have resembled the girl seen on another card (Plate 81) with her brother and the guardian angel beside her, both pointing to a picture of the Three Wise Men, to which she is obviously paying rapt attention. The masculine counterpart, the " good boy ", is well represented by the well-dressed schoolboy holding on to the hand of his elegant, top-hatted father or uncle (Colour Plate VII). They are witnessing a fight between two boys, one a poorly dressed peasant lad, the other a schoolboy. The latter is apparently responsible for the fact that the other boy's cap is on the ground. Whoever started the fight, the offence obviously provoked a swear-word which gave the old gentleman his chance to quote the Third Commandment, " . . . for the Lord will not hold him guiltless that taketh His name in vain ", accompanied by an appropriate gesture with his free hand. All the other Commandments were illustrated on similar, delightfully dated cards.

Compared to these edifying and perforce moralistic cards, the invariably well-behaved though pleasantly smiling (not laughing, of course !) little girls and boys posing for Christmas card pictures were signs of advance in taste in the ideal child. Their neat charm and prettiness, their childishness and their (though often somewhat faint and precious) affection for flowers, their dolls, bricks, rattles and other toys, expressing itself in the way they hold them, demonstrates that a sentimental representation of infancy was replacing the mere illustrated moral tenets of the earlier cards (Plates 82, 83, 86, 87).

In the next stage, though all these types appear to be intermingled with their predecessors and successors, children are presented on Christmas cards more pronouncedly as the " sedulous apes " of their elders, even as men of the world, but yet undeveloped grown-ups. Boys and girls are less often shown as little brothers and sisters, but as " couples ", young lasses and lads of the future, courting and paying compliments. Tiny boys, for instance, make love and give " a tiss " to tiny maidens under the mistletoe " tos it's Tismass ", as the text reads, or dance or skate together and do the things grown-ups do. Once again this sort of picture is far more entertaining for the elders than to children themselves, as experience shows, not only in practice, but as Christmas card *décor* also (Plate 100). This phase of the Victorian children-subject card automatically introduces the teen-agers and adolescents, their charm in the shyness and clumsiness of awakening sex transformed into popular Christmas card pictures. Designs dating from the 1880's onwards for some twenty years specialised in cards of this description. During this time both the extravagantly overdressed and startlingly undressed " youthful beauty " reached its zenith on fashionable Christmas cards. The latter under the title " classical ", the other under the name of " old-time " conquered Victorian hearts. On the one hand, Kate Greenaway's costume boys and girls and those of her numerous disciples populated one-half of the tremendously increased Christmas card output of children cards. On the other hand, slightly clad infants and little beauties, often draped only in their somewhat affected innocence and conveniently arranged postures, as created by W. S. Coleman and his followers, occupied most of the other half of popular successes. Whilst these types are a very long way from the earlier pictures of Victorian children, both the overdressed and befrilled and the " classical nudity " have, curiously enough, something of the same Victorian period flavour in their treatment.

Kate Greenaway's popularity and the influence of the costumes of her graceful child figures began in the 1870's, and culminated at the turn of the century. Her name was given to the fashion of children's style at least in two continents, and remains a household word up to the

Fig. 13. Du Maurier's cartoon of "extraordinary-looking" children in Greenaway dresses. It was implied that such garb encouraged arrogance.

present. But while our grandparents were mostly attracted by the picturesque reversion to the children's fashions of their grandparents' day, we must be grateful to her chiefly for the insight she gives us into the world of children in her own times.

Kate Greenaway's father, a well-known wood-engraver, very soon discovered her artistic talent, and even while at her first school in Clerkenwell she began to make designs for Christmas cards and valentines for publishers, such as Kronheim & Co. and others. None of these was signed by her later, well-known initials, K.G., and indeed show little formal affinity with her later, more characteristic style. Gradually both Kate Greenaway and her advisers discovered her genius for the innocent little faces and grace of childhood, so she began to concentrate on these subjects with the ambition and determination which was so characteristic of this energetic girl. The Rev. W. J. Loftie, one of her first patrons, after their first meeting, described her as " very small, very dark, and seemed clever and sensible, with a certain impressive expression in her dark eyes that struck every one ".

" No doubt it was in her first remunerative but anonymous work of designing valentines and Christmas cards that the possibilities which lay in childhood archaically, or at least quaintly, attired first presented themselves to her, but the goal was not to be reached without unstinted labour and active forethought ", wrote Spielmann, one of her biographers. " Her success rested upon the thoroughness with which she laid her foundations." If she was to specialise in children, she decided to do it properly. She was a good needle-woman and made the dresses herself, and by making her little models and lay figures wear them was able to study their movements, behaviour and habits in them. Whilst she surrounded herself with these living dolls, whose appearances were already creatures of her own imagination, she poured into her drawings all the understanding, love and affection she, a lonely woman, felt for these little friends. This is perhaps one of the clues to her outstanding success in making her tiny characters so human and convincing. Their success was certainly extraordinary. The " Day after Xmas, 1880 ", the great Ruskin wrote to her in response to her Christmas card, " Luck go with you, pretty lass " : " To my mind it is a greater thing than Raphael's St. Cecilia." The Victorian public was not in the position to read Professor Wilenski's explanations, one might say *apologia*,[1] that " this was not an art judgment, but the equivalent of saying, ' This little girl reminds me of Rosie—the child I fell in love with—a much sweeter Rosie than the pietistic Rose with eyes turned up to Heaven (like Raphael's *St. Cecilia*) who made me miserable in her later years.' " Neither could they differentiate between the authority of the famous Oxford Lecture, *Fairy Land*, delivered in May, 1883, and largely devoted to the art of Kate Greenaway, and Ruskin's other pronouncements on art. Finding their preferences confirmed by the greatest living expert, the public was eager to buy her work in tens of thousands.

Kate Greenaway's art was later chiefly associated with book-production. From 1878, when, after some quarrel with Marcus Ward & Co., her main publishers up to that time, her successful partnership with Edmund Evans, the famous printer, began, in the space of ten years her printed books reached the " grand total of 417,000 ". But it was before that, at a time when her work consisted almost exclusively of Christmas cards and valentines, that her artistic idiom took shape. It is a pity that she did not sign her designs or even keep a complete

[1] *John Ruskin*, by R. H. Wilenski, Faber and Faber, London, 1933, p. 174.

set of them. Neither did her various publishers. " After the success of her first popular series, it is easy enough to discard the too-faithful disciples who never once caught her peculiar charm", wrote Gleeson White. " But in the earlier of hers, when her manner was less pronounced, even the publishers are not always absolutely certain regarding the authorship of several designs." Neither White nor her biographers attempted to unearth and catalogue her Christmas card designs, and this is still a matter for the future.[2]

Amongst all Christmas card designers, Kate Greenaway was perhaps the most popular single artist whose name was known to her public and identified with her work for a long time. Every form of her art was sought after and anxiously collected by an ever-increasing number of fanciers from 1868, when she first exhibited in a public gallery in London. This took place at an exhibition of drawings in the famous Dudley Gallery, where W. Crane, Muckley, Stacy Marks and other artists known also as Christmas card designers used to exhibit. It was a reputedly " progressive " gallery and the *Art Journal* in its criticism of this exhibition only records, listed amongst others, the title, " The Fairies of the Caldon Low by Kate Greenaway ", since " restricted space" compelled the critic " to pass hastily on with mere recommendation ".[3]

Besides Kate Greenaway's designs it is interesting to see Du Maurier's cartoon, published in *Punch*, entitled " The Height of Aesthetic Exclusiveness ". It shows a procession of the young Cimabue Browns, walking disdainfully, proudly holding the emblematic peacock feathers and sunflowers of their aesthetic parents before them, and wearing " Kate Greenaway costumes " (Fig. 13). The text—without which Du Maurier's drawings could often be quite misunderstood—reads :

" EFFIE : ' The Cimabue Browns, Mamma. They're *Aesthetic*, you know ? '

" MAMMA : ' So I should imagine. Do you know them to speak to ? '

[2] Recently Carroll Alton Means, in a series of six articles published in *Hobbies*, an American magazine for collectors, identified a fair number of previously unrecognised Kate Greenaway valentines. His argument in most cases seems convincing (1953).

[3] Crane's exhibit is reviewed in the same article : " . . . a poetic though peculiar composition by Walter Crane, as a favourable, because not too ultra, example of the abnormal styles which find local habitation in the Dudley. . . ."

" EFFIE : ' Oh dear no, Mamma—they're most *exclusive*. Why, they put out their tongues at us if we only *look* at them ! ' "

No difficult long skirts, dust-collecting cloaks, coal-scuttle bonnets or other properties of " greenawisme " (a word coined in those days in the French language !) can be traced in the attire of the other group of young maidens, mostly in their teens, who appear on the popular cards designed by W. S. Coleman and his faithful disciples. Little is generally known about Coleman, though he was quite a celebrated artist in his time. He was first known as a naturalist, illustrating botanical works and studies on natural history. He was on the Committee of the Dudley Gallery, and is reverently referred to in several contemporary memoirs. His main theme in Christmas card design was also, like Kate Greenaway's, the quaint grace and charm of childhood, but unlike her, in that they were revealed by a budding adolescence and the transition from immaturity to girlhood. The titles of his attractive card sets also sound different from those of Kate Greenaway, and they seldom carry more than a line or so of text. Whereas her cards were identified as " Page in Red Costume ", " Damsels with Muffs " and " Lads in Ulsters ", etc., in the absence of more detailed titles, Coleman's were known as " Girlish Delights ", " Jocund Youth ", " Sylvan Sports ", " Youthful Graces ", " Eastern Damsels ", " Dancing Girls ", " The Age of Innocence ", and so on. A set consisted of three varieties of cards, and they were almost always of girls. If boys occur, they are very little. His figures always have a rosy or sunburnt skin in pleasant contrast to the bright blue sky or water and bright flowers around them. The latter are almost always identifiable— thanks to Coleman's learned interest in botany.

Coleman's Christmas cards certainly bring spring, youth and freshness into the winter season, and although they are not without the artificial innocence so characteristic of their time, they were certainly a great contrast to the early and mid-Victorian treatment of children in life and, as we have seen, on Christmas cards—a contrast which was the result of the gradual change which had taken place, not only in the habits and social status of little girls, but women in general. Esmé Wingfield-Stratford, the brilliant analist of Victorian trends, described this development after the end, in the 70's, of the phase of fashionable demureness : " The attractive girl was no longer round-faced and innocent-eyed, but pert and frivolous. To judge from the drawings of the time, quite an abnormal number of noses seem to have acquired an upward tilt, and their owners a corresponding boldness of self-assertion." This perfect observation, as most of the writer's other comments, can be well substantiated also by the evidence of Christmas cards of the time. On cards the " modern girl " made her appearance considerably earlier than, for example, she did in the columns of *Punch*. There, as C. L. Graves pointed out, " Leech's precocious children were almost without exception boys." The pretty little maids with the dreamy eyes, but no longer unself-conscious, which appear on the Christmas cards of the 1880's and 1890's are, however, undoubtedly in every respect " first cousins " of if not identical with the " young generation " and their "charming naughtinesses". as mirrored in *Punch* at the beginning of the present century. The child of this time, as it has been well remarked, " found out all about Santa Claus and is now going to look into this Robinson Crusoe business ".[4]

The changed manners of young girls were, of course, the reaction to their strictly prescribed place and the manners expected of them by the rigid etiquette of the earlier Victorian decades, just as their slovenly postures are in direct contrast to the straight-laced uprightness of carriage demanded of the girls in their grandmammas' time, as borne out by the illustrations at the beginning of this chapter. Later on, when education and sports abridged the gap between them and boys, much of the discrimination between children of the two sexes disappeared. But somehow the interest is seen to have diminished at the same time. Modern children when they appear on Christmas card pictures add comparatively little to the image of the child of our day. With the exception of photographic cards, they are either stylised without recognition or done in the manner and fashion of " olden days " or—plain caricatures.

[4] Little Molly, a child of this type, leisurely reclining in the armchair of Wallis Mills's cartoon, when asked by the Rector whether she would rather be beautiful or good, promptly answered, " I'd rather be beautiful and repent." Madge, another little beauty seen beside the lake in Kensington Gardens, answers the same question in much the same way. While pulling up the garter on her knee, she says, " I would rather be pretty, Miss Smith ; I can easily be good whenever I like to try." The " distinctive note of scepticism and revolt " by children can be detected in a cartoon by F. H. Townsend, also in *Punch*. His little girl has just shocked her Uncle George by saying that she hated all her lessons. Uncle tries to soften this. " Come now. You don't mean to say you hate history ?" " Yes, I do," replies the little niece. " To tell the truth, Uncle, I don't care a bit what anybody ever did . . . ."

WOMEN
on Christmas Cards

A N interesting sequence of the popular success of adolescents on Christmas cards was the entry in about 1880 of adult young women as their central theme. Previously, if featured alone, women were either immature girls or aged grannies. Otherwise they were usually included in a composition as part of family life, sharing the home with their children, dogs, cats and furniture. Christmas cards showed them as mothers or guardians of the little ones, or as affianced partners of men, under the mistletoe, or in the ballroom. On the comparatively rare occasions when they were featured as "female beauties" on Christmas cards, an aspect more frequent on old valentines, they were made to stand for allegorical ideas or sentiments and were dressed in classic or historic settings. The popularity of the Greenaway-Coleman types of Christmas cards and, of course, the freer part played by women in actual life paved the way for the appearance of pretty women in their prime as central subjects on many Victorian cards by the end of the century, just as up to that time the other beauties of Nature, such as children, birds and flowers, had dominated the card designs.

Early tentative attempts in this direction had been made as illustrated in a series of "Dickens' Characters" made up as Christmas cards, which included women figures, such as Little Nell, Dolly Varden and others (Plate 101). These were finely printed and neatly produced little booklets, with coloured drawings and word-pictures of each character.

In 1881, W. F. Yeames, the R.A., made a set for Raphael Tuck of still rather demure contemporary women, dressed as such, but with Cupids, rather like love-birds, in cages (Plate 103). On one of these cards the bars of the cage were transformed into boughs of mistletoe as a Cupid escaped into her arms. The set was much appreciated in its day. (It will be remembered that melancholy young ladies used to cut the wings of Cupids on some Victorian valentine

Fig. 14. A Christmas card designed by Walter Crane for Elemér Czakó, head of the Arts and Crafts Museum, Budapest, when Crane visited Hungary at the turn of the century. The flower motifs were the Hungarian equivalents of the peacock feather and sunflower of the *aesthetes*. Note Crane's dedication and crane-sign at the bottom. (The card was sent to the author in 1938.)

pictures). Another celebrated Royal Academician, E. J. Poynter, seated his women, in somewhat provocative manner, in evening dress in the centre of fantastic and fully ornamented golden alcoves, with columns, screens and recesses in abundance. His cards were called " Winter Cherries ", " Christmas Roses " (Plate 104), etc., and snow was added to their " classical " properties. Marcus Stone made a number of fully dressed pretty women of the time sitting by themselves on lonely benches in wintry gardens (Plate 106), or on lichen-covered rocks, or, with equal melancholy and loneliness, reading by the fireside. These cards were so popular that they were made into picture postcards also. G. D. Leslie's women were annually much praised and admired at Burlington House. It has been said that he " paints his heroines as if he were in love with them ". Leslie's Christmas card designs, charming direct portraits, bear the motto :

> " Thy joys be flowers that blooms tho' winds be bleak
> Like Christmas Roses on a maiden's cheek ",

or

> " Sweet in winter to remember
> What the summer smile can bring,
> May it brighten mid December
> Every feeling, every thing ",

which is the only clue to Christmas on the card. Elihu Vedder, the well-known American artist, made his favourite model, his wife, the centrepiece of his Christmas card drawings, which brought for him the $1,000 First Prize at L. Prang's famous Christmas card design competition (Plate 105), and Walter Crane contributed, somewhat earlier, his familiar, fashionably attractive tall, slim women to the galaxy of feminine beauty which towards the end of the century enjoyed such new favouritism on Christmas cards (Plate 102, Colour Plate VIII).

The fashionable beauty who is at the same time an adored mother was the contribution of American designers to the portraiture of pretty women on Christmas cards. Rosina Emmett won $200 in 1881 with her attractive design of this category.

> " Climb though and cling to reach Life's highest good ;
> Higher than mother's kiss thou canst not climb ! "

are the opening lines of the sentiment by C. Thaxter, printed on the back of the card. Both artists' and popular First Prizes, $2,000, were won in 1881 at Prang's competition by D. Wheeler with a design of a young mother with two children clinging to her in a wintry storm (Colour Plate XIb). They represent human poverty ; their bare feet and shadow rest on the globe. But they are looking up, and in the clouds with which some pretty winged cherub heads intermingle, the vision of the Holy Child, held by His veiled Mother, appears, under the legend, " Good tidings of great Joy ".

Naturally, the so-called " aesthetic craze " also left its mark. Both sides were reflected on Christmas cards. A. Ludovici designed some successful cards of this type. He concentrated not only on the feminine supporters of this fashion, but also on the " effeminate male " aesthete. The latter is seen on one of these cards in a pose of affected ecstasy,

Fig. 15. Mum and Dad acting for Santa Claus—a highly artistic black and white Christmas card of 1895.

adoring a sunflower. There is another card with an intense, long-haired aesthete holding a big white lily in his hand. Another typical set of cards by A. Gray are pen-and-ink drawings, printed in black and gold. On one of these a young painter is seen in a tight-fitting dress embroidered with sun and sunflower motifs, holding the palette and the brushes. It represents " Painting ", but both eyes are shut. The text reads : " A most intensely utter Christmas & Ecstatic New Year ".

> " A blue-and white damozel,
> A Japanese damozel,
> A China adoring, bric-a-brac storing,
> Dresden-and-Sèvres damozel "

by the same artist, is seen kneeling in front of a sunflower frieze, holding a peacock feather and emotionally admiring a blue-and-white dish on the wall. The design of the dish is a crane, caricaturing the signature made famous by Walter Crane (Plate 108).

Naturally, the " new woman " and the sportswoman, who were targets of both adoration and fun, the women of the naughty 90's, made their debut on the late Victorian and Edwardian Christmas cards. These subjects were also illustrative of the changing appearances and fashion, as well as the technique of reproduction on Christmas cards (Plates 107, 109, 110 and Fig. 15). This has continued right up to the present day, when modern photography contributes a new way of documentation, offering fresh aspects and emphasis, which seem entirely of our own age. An example of the latter is the Christmas card reproduced from Queen Mary's collection, with a photograph of the British Red Cross Society's march past in 1939 (Plate 112). A comparison between the first and last illustrations to this group of cards will indicate some of the changes in and towards women which had taken place in the space of a few decades.

CHRISTMAS CARDS
for Children

A S we have already seen, children on old Christmas cards reflected the changing and developing image of childhood. Some of these little pictures were, of course, genuinely appreciated by the children themselves, but in most cases they were of far greater entertainment to their elders. A separate group may, however, be selected of those cards which first of all succeeded in amusing the child of their time and were only secondarily concerned with grown-ups. Amongst these may be included many of the serious and most of the humorous animal cards, such as those of cats dressed up sometimes like dolls, sometimes only with ribbons, feasting and dancing or otherwise enjoying the Christmas party in the Louis Wain manner (Plate 113); or foxhunting scenes in which tiny monkeys, in full hunting dress, are mounted on the foxhounds (Plate 119), with all the hazards of the hunting field. Some of the humorous riding, hunting and horse-racing scenes, especially when the riders are children and the adventures are of a rather burlesque character, were cards for children, though sporting subjects of every description were also much loved by their elders. A series of old-fashioned bulldogs standing on their hind legs in the ring in full boxing kit, including gloves and shorts, were no doubt equally amusing to children and grown-ups (Plate 115). Similarly popular with all age-groups were S. T. Dadd's animal sketches, usually combinations of pets, such as monkeys and parrots, etc., in lively encounter (Plate 116). Dogs of every breed, like horses, frequently figured on Christmas cards. They were usually, just as in life, part of the human milieu, sitting by the fireside or sharing the games with the children or hunting.

Grotesque parallels and an emphasis on the similarity between animals and certain human characters and features were natural subjects to delight almost everyone (Plate 114). A witty one of this kind illustrates its motto : " A little more than kin and a little less than kind " (Plate 118). The idea of C. H. Bennett's once-popular " Christmas Shadows " and " Shadow and Substance " drawings (sets of human portraits and their shadows, the latter giving away the real character of the human model—for example, the shadow of a physicist, the silhouette of a duck (quack !), an old gallant (a goat), etc.), appears on some Victorian Christmas cards. But in these the shadow of a dog looks like the silhouette of a one-time policeman, in a cat's shadow the contours of a disagreeable old woman are visible, and so on (Plate 120).

The representation of animals, quite apart from their humorous potentialities for the amusement of children and kindred spirits, are, of course, perfectly entitled to a place on Christmas cards owing to their traditional association with the scene of the Nativity and its many legends. Even such seemingly irrelevant creatures as bees, generally credited with many great irrational qualities in the folklore of all nations, come within the circle of ancient Nativity legends. " In the North bees were thought to worship on Christmas Eve by humming the 100th Psalm in their hives, at the same time as the cattle fell on their knees in the byre, to adore the Child Jesus. Country people up to a few years ago firmly believed that both these events took place at midnight on Christmas Eve ", records C. Hole in her *English Folklore*.

Even more strange and unexpected than bees and other insects (Plate 122), which were at one time quite fashionable subjects on elegant, long Christmas cards, is the surprising number of rats and mice which decorate Victorian cards. Considering their universal unpopularity as pests and the specific war waged by women against them, their appearance on these cards is curious, even when it is only in the form of corpses, victoriously carried by those renowned hunters, the cat and the owl, as seen on a Christmas card from the 1870's (Plate 123).

Animals are frequently featured also in modern Christmas cards designed by distinguished contemporary artists, and these have a wide popularity even amongst those who otherwise do not particularly support contemporary art.

But, to return to the Victorian Christmas cards with a special appeal for children, we should mention some of the children's stories, told in pictures and verse, which, besides the trick cards, were much loved by all youngsters. One of the first of these was a small set called " The Story of Little Red Ridinghood's Christmas or How to keep the wolf from the door ", one of Kate Greenaway's early works, first published in 1868 (Plate 124). The set contained six brightly coloured little cards, each 2½ by 4 inches, framed in an embossed gold lattice, decorated with embossed holly and ivy motifs. The cards were sold in a nicely

Fig. 16. Less conventional animals appeared on this personal Christmas card for 1936 drawn in pen and ink by B.P., as Lord Baden-Powell used to be known affectionately to boy scouts all over the world. (9 by 6¼ inches.)

ornamented envelope to match ; they could be had either separately, or made up with pink ribbons into a booklet. The first picture shows Red Ridinghood's arrival at Grannie's cottage :

" Little Red Ridinghood comes to spend
The Christmas days with her ancient friend.
For well she knows her presence will tend
To gladden her Granny's Christmas."

In the second picture, Granny, in a chimney-pot hat and long blue cloak, leaves her to " try her maiden hand at a pudding or pie "while she goes " to buy some little odd things for Christmas ". Then we see Little Red Ridinghood carrying her three-legged pot to the old-fashioned open fire, and when she sits down and " blows the fire as though her small arms could never tire ", Father Christmas arrives.

When Granny comes back she finds, on the next card, Ridinghood and Father Christmas both seated near the fire listening to and telling " yarns and jokes of old Christmas " respectively. For the last picture, dinner is ready and—

> " There's plenty to eat and plenty to spare,
> And O such a merry time is there,
> With Red Ridinghood, Granny, and Christmas."

In 1871 Goodall brought out a couplet card on which the designs might have been taken from a pantomime scene. The first, bearing the title " Time's Footsteps for 1872 ", shows an aged Time with his scythe and hour-glass, doddering, whilst, leaping over his back, the New Year, in the form of a lively boy, " steps in " (Plate 125). The other card shows the Old Year " stepping out " head first through a trap-door, whilst Sexton Owl and Robin Redbreast look on. Behind, the curtains have just been opened by " New Year ". An example of a less "philosophical " but most delightful children's card type was sent to Queen Mary when she was a little girl in the 1870's. It is in the form of an illustrated imitation letter from Santa Claus in facsimile handwriting and chromolithographic sketches made in delightful clean colours and with surprisingly modern effect. The pictures fill in the left-out words in the text, a popular acrostic trick at that time. The four-page letter (Plates 128 and 129) reads :

" My dear *May* [May was added by the senders],—

" Wake up lazy bones and see who is sitting on the end of your bed [showing the picture of a little girl yawning and rubbing the sleep out of her eyes, and a sophisticated doll sits watching her at the end of her bed]. She has brought her [picture : trunk] with her, and inside you will find her best [picture : hat] and [gloves] and [cloak] and [shoes] and [sunshade]. Now jump out of bed and give her a [picture shows bathtub, can of hot water, soap, sponge, towel-horse and bath towel, indicating hot bath] and then let her take a nap in her [cot], for I see she is very [picture of the doll : tired] after her long journey. I hope you will love her very much and send heaps of thanks to your loving old friend,

" SANTA CLAUS."

The last sketch shows the little girl hugging a very clean and tidy doll in both arms. The card, one of a number of similar designs, was produced by Castell Brothers, London, but was actually printed in Bavaria. (" Alice " and " Charlie " are added signatures of the senders of the little card.)

" Christmas Dreams of Childhood " is a Marcus Ward card from another serial of four, showing the four main stages of life, with " appropriate " dreams expressed by little figures in the design around the central, sleeping character and with the help of the verses on the back of each card (Plate 126). The designs are in contours, filled in with bright colours. Holly, ivy and mistletoe alternate with the symbolic little figures. The first sentiment says :

> " In his Grandsire's easy chair
> A Boy sits sleeping there,
> And smiling through his sleep,
> What visionary joys
> Of festival and toys,
> The chief desire of boys,
> Upon his fancy creep ?

> " Oh, you may guess he sees
> Forests of Christmas trees,
> And Christmas cheer, good store !
> Dear Child, may earthly pleasure,
> Be sent thee without measure,
> And richer, better treasure,
> Within the golden door ! "

On the other cards of the set, " Youth " dreams of love and a convenient bunch of mistletoe, " Manhood " of unpaid bills of the Christmas feast presented by tradesmen (more like a nightmare !), while " Old Age " rests happily dreaming of his grandchildren.

Children must have loved the series of six small chromolithographs, " Christmas with Punch and Judy ". The successive drawings caricature Mr. Punch providing the goose for a " Jolly Christmas " and " committing it to Judy's tender care " :

" Behold, cried P., the fruits of my industry I bring of them to thee, my J.
> Dost thou not thank thy stars for such provider ? "

In the following pictures the goose appears burnt to a cinder, and Punch is seen mighty angry and hungry at the sight of " cremation applied to geese ", but finally all is well and they drown their sorrows in a huge bowl of punch " and drink goodwill to all mankind ".

A set of four larger oblong cards by Kate Greenaway, but not signed, were published by Marcus Ward in the 80's. They were made to illustrate " Robin Hood and the Blackbird—the Tale of a Christmas Dinner ". On the back of each card a rhyming commentary, in the style of an old ballad, recounts the ludicrous hunt for a Christmas dinner for Robin Hood and his Merry Men. The story begins on the first card :

> " A rhyme, a rhyme, a Christmas rhyme,
> Of what befell at Christmas time,
> To that bold hunter Robin Hood,
> Maid Marian, and the archers good.
> One year, whose date I don't remember,
> It froze and snowed all through December ;
> Birds small and great died off in pairs,
> The famished foxes ate the hares ;
> Deer were devoured by wolves and bears.
> Said Robin to his merry men,
> ' No game is left' ; said Marian then,
> ' For Christmas feast, some there must be,
> Remember you've invited me ! '
> So Robin donned his green and feather
> And a merry troop set forth together ;
> But nothing found all day, till, lo !
> A poor starved blackbird crossed the snow.
> Bold Robin stopped and bent his bow ;
> Then Marian cried, ' Forbear this time ! '
> But Robin shot—so runs the rhyme."

The second card shows the triumphal return of the hunters, led by Robin Hood with his bow and peacock feather (Plate 130), who has just said, according to the rhyme on the back of the card :

> " . . . I did my best ;
> To thee, Friend Friar, I leave the rest."

" Then follow me, and you shall see,
Said Tuck, how soon a feast shall be
Prepared for this gay company,"

sounds the answer, and

" So after Tuck, in merry time,
They piped and marched—so runs the rhyme."

The rest of the charming tale describes the dinner party and how, when the miserable blackbird proves too small and uneatable, Friar Tuck —" that nimble cook "—miraculously produces from a " secret nook " fat pasties, so they had a good Christmas dinner after all !

The illustration on Plate 127 belongs to another Kate Greenaway series of four oblong cards entitled " A Christmas Procession of Mirth & Good Cheer ", also published by Marcus Ward. The reverse of each card contains the actual Christmas greeting, while above the little figures, incorporated in the border decoration, there is a rhyme, printed in a single line, as follows :

" When high on the walls you have twined the green holly, let music resound and let all be most jolly."

" 'Tis time for good fellowship, mirth and good cheer, for Christmas comes only but once in a year."

" Brave butcher and baker, good health be to you, and to the candlestick maker, too."

" A welcome at Christmas as to every guest, but the warmest to those who bring frolic and jest ! "

These few cards have been written up in some detail, since each of them is representative of a popular type, which later, according to the vagaries of fashion, have unfortunately completely disappeared, though before the market for them had been exhausted. The new fashion was taking shape by the end of the 8o's and children's stories were directed into books and magazines for children.

SOME
CHRISTMAS CARDS
by Children

AFTER the review of Christmas cards specially designed for the amusement of children, it may be fitting to add a brief account of a few delightful Christmas cards made by children for their elders. At one time or another all of us experienced in our nursery days the creative impulse, especially about Christmas-time, which could not be satisfied until with much love and care it had found expression in some token of our own manufacture. Parents the world over love beyond all else these little masterpieces by the untrained hands but devoted hearts of their children, and enter into the conspiracy of secrecy even to the moment when the masterpiece is produced on Christmas morning and received with such apparent pleasure and surprise. These childish efforts are, of course, confined to a limited family circle, and are precious as little documents of the feeling which created them. They are put away safely, even by non-collectors, and treasured with the same devotion and warmth of heart which prompted the little artists to make them. Many years later they turn up in old family albums or amongst forgotten bundles of old letters, and bring back happy recollections, and perhaps a melancholy smile, of those far-off days.

It will, I am sure, give pleasure and encouragement to many small artists all over the world to know that princes and princesses, later to be kings and queens, share this ambition with them, and, with the same labour and affection, prepare for their parents and grandparents special hand-made " private " Christmas cards as a surprise for the great day. By the gracious kindness of H.M the late Queen Mary, I am delighted to be able to reproduce here some of the Christmas cards made by Her Majesty Queen Elizabeth II when she was Princess Elizabeth, made for and dedicated to her grandmother, Queen Mary, and also Christmas cards made by His Majesty the late King George VI and his brothers when they were children.

While these cards well represent the special characteristics of all children's cards, they are of great interest to all who make or are interested in Christmas cards, as they show once again that universality of the Christmas spirit and sentiment which has been a sub-theme throughout this book, as experienced in Christmas cards, and which unites all from castle to cottage in the goodwill of the season. In this spirit the following illustrations have to us all a special interest and significance.

The Round Tower of Windsor Castle is familiar to many, but the flag flying on top of it in King George VI's private Christmas card, jokingly made when he was young Prince Albert, is a delightfully original form of conveying his signature, sent to his father, King George V. The card has been hand-coloured ; the walls with grey, the grass and trees bright green and the road yellow water-colours, whilst the flag is outlined with a bright purple border and the name " Bertie " written across it in blue. The dedication " For Papa. 1904 " was also written with the paint brush (Plate 131).

In 1906 Prince George, the late Duke of Kent, made a most realistic brown bear as a surprise for his parents, making clever use of needle-work and water-colours combined. The outline of the 6 by 8 inches card is in back-stitch, as is also the outline of the bear, including his ears, mouth and neck. The other card on the same page in the album is a charming floral design of snowdrops and green leaves in water-. colours made by him in the following year (Plate 132). Prince Henry, now H.R.H. the Duke of Gloucester, painted a snow-covered red-brick cottage in pastel colours on dark brown wrapping paper in 1906, and a tempting dish of fruit outlined in back-stitch and coloured in crayons in 1907 (Plate 133). This card is neatly dedicated, " For dear Mama from Harry ". Little Prince John, when only five years of age, made some of the most charming little children's cards in needlework on cardboard. One of them is a formal evergreen growing in a flower-pot, and the other is a milkman rolling a milk churn. It is dedicated by the late Prince, who died in 1919, " For Mama from Johnny ".

I conclude this group of Christmas cards by children with two made by the then Princess Elizabeth for her grandparents.

The first, made for Christmas, 1933, is about 5 by 4 inches in size, and is an entirely self-made folder card. On the cover is a charming little design of joy bells and Christmas evergreens worked into a balanced composition. The bells and the two horseshoes in the corners are painted in gold, which is also used for the lettering. The sprays are in pale green and the berries bright red (Plate 134). The motto on the card reads :

> " CHRISTMAS JOY-BELLS
> ARE RINGING FOR YOU."

The inscription inside the small folder is in pencil :

> " To Grannie from Lilibet."

The date, 1933, was added by Queen Mary (Plate 135).

In 1934 the Princess prepared another charming card, size 5 by 4 inches, this time with floral decorations and two love-birds as the central feature. The colouring is crayon : the flowers bright yellow and the birds blue, as are the words " A Merry Xmas ". This card was dedicated " To Grandpapa, from Lilibet " in pencil.

The last illustration in this section is a card in a different medium. It is a lino-cut landscape with a figure and trees silhouetted against an orange and yellow sunset. The lino-cut is hand-printed in deep black and the spaces are hand-painted in water-colours in varying shades of red and orange, which on the cream mount of the card (5 by 7½ inches in size) make a very pleasing colour scheme (Plate 136). Inside the folder is the dedication written in ink : " With love to Granny from Lilibet." The sentiment on this card is, as my photograph shows, a poem by Robert Louis Stevenson, printed inside (Plate 137). The lino-cut was made to illustrate it, and the colours and composition of the little lino-cut are indeed in striking sympathy with the words of the poem :

> " In the other gardens
>   And all up the vale,
> From the autumn bonfires
>   See the smoke trail !
>
> " Pleasant summer over,
>   And all the summer flowers,
> The red fire blazes,
>   The grey smoke towers."

COMIC, ANIMATED
and Mechanical Trick Cards

UNDER this heading I am grouping some specimens of a very characteristic and extremely popular type of Victorian Christmas cards. It is difficult to define the limits of this group with any exactitude, and the cards which are included in this group have at least one feature in common—namely, the surprise element. They are usually made to appear very simple, yet by the pulling of a string or moving a lever, the turning of a page or other manipulations reveal the trick and at the same time disclose the sometimes unexpected complexity of their construction. Others at first sight appear to be authentic legal documents, cheques or banknotes, and only an examination of the text makes one realise that seasonal good wishes were being conveyed in these clever " forgeries " ! Other cards contain a hidden whistle and squeak or chirp when handled ; others, again, if held to the light, show an otherwise unsuspected picture, and so on.

The Victorians had a delightful childlike taste in what they considered artistic pleasures and enjoyments beneath the discipline in their daily lives. The animated Christmas cards were the direct descendants of similar valentines, which, long before the " movables ", had held the field since the eighteenth century. With the valentines, of course, the " trick " and messages hidden in bouquets of flowers, under silk and lace, or cobwebs, were essential. In these days " dear Papa " gave his eligible daughters very little freedom of movement. Letters addressed to them were rigorously censored by him, and letters from them were sent out by stealth. It was not customary to sign valentines, and the address was also often written in a disguised hand. Some early Christmas cards were almost indistinguishable from valentines, except for their Christmas message. Later, the animated and mechanical Christmas cards were no longer used as clandestine communications between lovers or sweethearts, and gradually became something like paper toys, aiming at the delight and applause which would surely follow their performance. They were certainly most popular and welcome in every strata of society and to all age-groups. Their ingenuity and inventiveness, to say nothing of the skilful craftsmanship and amount of work, often sweated female and child labour, invested in them make these cards at least as representative and documentary of the age as the more ambitiously " artistic " efforts. Unfortunately, my distinguished predecessor, Gleeson White, in his essay, which is our chief reference on old Christmas cards to-day, writes very scathingly about the whole of this group of cards. He declared that—

" we need not be concerned . . . with the large number of makers who delight in producing imitations of unlovely objects, luggage labels, cork soles, slices of blankets or of bacon, burnt ends of cigars, extracted teeth, and other horrors reproduced in realistic imitation to accompany a message of goodwill to their friends. Nor with those again [he continues] who issue cards with facsimiles of coins, or corkscrews, razors or hairpins, in low coloured relief, for the sake of a punning legend underneath. These things, concrete practical jokes of the feeblest order, have their scheme in the economy of life perhaps, so doubtless have black-beetles, earthquakes, fogs, and the omnipresent bacillus, but it is easy to forget them when they do not actively obtrude their unwelcome presence."

Some of these cards are indeed " unlovely objects ", but a large number of them are charming in design and express in every detail such a delightful period flavour that it is only to be regretted that so comparatively few of them have survived to the present day (some of the " movable " ones were moved into pieces by successive generations, who loved to play with them), and that contemporary critics, like Gleeson White, in contrast to the public who loved these kinds, considered them beneath their notice. The greatest collection of Christmas cards including a vast number of these animated and mechanical cards is no longer available to the student. I am, of course, referring to Jonathan King's famous " museum " in Islington. He used to show to his visitors an elaborate card which he considered to have been the first of its kind. It was outwardly quite a plain card, but when opened out flat, a full-rigged ship emerged sailing the high seas complete in every detail, with masts, rigging and sails. It was said that the inventor of this card made a fortune out of its sale, and eventually built a real ship from the proceeds in which he sailed to America, where he finally settled.

One of the earliest of these trick cards, based on similar valentines, was printed on quite common notepaper, folded in two, so as to look like a little letter. The first page is in fact a pseudo-love-letter in imitated handwriting to a " Dearest Love ". The last few lines on the page anxiously press for an early answer on a " most important question " so placed that the page must be turned at this point. When it is turned over, one finds no more of the sentimental love-letter. Instead, an unexpected caricature, a hand-coloured lithograph of an elderly spinster seated at a table in her nightdress, with both feet in a tub of hot water, appears on the next page. The caption beneath is, " And how are your poor feet ? ", a perhaps practical, but rather shocking joke after the solicitous sentimentalism of the beginning of the letter. The surprise picture on another card of the same kind (Plate 143) shows a rather corpulent, fierce-looking gentleman with bushy eyebrows and a very long red nose, seated in top-hat, top-coat, a pink muffler and top-boots, with his hands in his pockets : on the whole, neither friendly nor warm, but above it is the caption : " A merry Christmas to you and don't forget the Mistletoe."

Another very popular and extensively used idea for Christmas cards was the realistic imitation of banknotes, cheques, wills, railway tickets, I.O.Us., packages, postcards and envelopes, etc. Cards of this type were already on the market and popular in 1870, and have been and still are to be found amongst new publications even to-day. The actual words and often the decorations on these cards were always seasonal and joking, but the general impression was of such a close resemblance as to be almost deceptive at first glance. The card of the £5 " Bank of Love " note was so similar to its Bank of England counterpart that it provoked an action by the authorities, who feared that it might facilitate forgeries. These cards are now very rare, as they were both banned and withdrawn not long after their first appearance. The same fate followed the publication of American editions of dollar imitation Christmas cards and valentines. I am reproducing here a card of the same idea produced nearly fifty years later, caricaturing the French 5-franc note, " redrawn " by Frank D. Hawkes for the B.E.F. in France. The British Tommy and the American G.I., instead of the symbolic figures of the genuine note, are the main features of the jovial card which was sent for Christmas, 1918 (Plate 138). The cheque on the " Bank of Blessings, Unlimited " for " Ten Thousand Joys " was published by Angus Thomas in the early 1900's. The embossed " stamp " shows two clasped hands and " best wishes " (Plate 139). Thomas has specialised in similar trick cards, and enjoyed making jokes in spelling. The silver teapot realistically " tinselled " on the card has a lid which actually can be lifted up (Plate 140). A cheque for " Five Thousand a Year ", dated December 25th, 1895, is attached to it. (This closely resembles the idea of the celebrated " Tukkin " cards, published annually by the Rust Craft Company in Boston, which " never seem to lose their popularity ". To-day these cards consist of " four or five extra ones, tucked in as part of the message and design ".) The wording on the card is a play on drawing tea and cheques and other words reminiscent of teatime. A similar play of words is made use of on the card showing miniature facsimiles of *four* seasonal *tunes*, actually stuck on the card in such a way that the pages could be turned and the music played, wishing good *fortunes* (Plate 141).

There was a handy visiting card available to send as an answer if the addressee was not amused. Instead of the name, " U. R. Requested " is engraved, while the " address " read : " 2 Mind your own Business."

A less elaborate though charmingly naïve card shows the booking office of a railway station. A number of tickets are freely distributed. Two larger are " facsimiles " of real railway tickets except for their wording, which has " Prosperity " as the destination " From All Difficulties " on the " Christmas and New Year Line, Dec. 24. 1889-90 ". The tickets were " Available at all times " and " Transferable only to old friends ".

The conventional Christmas greeting replaced the name of the locality of the post office stamp, dated Christmas Day, 1883, on some cards, realistically embossed to look exactly like an envelope (Plate 144). A rosebud is attached to the package by a ribbon, also convincingly embossed. Cards somewhat similar to this Hildesheimer card of the

80's were published again in the 1940's, deliberately recapturing the Victorian atmosphere. The " postmark " on the modern version omits the year, a reasonable economy on the part of the publishers. In the old Victorian editions at first the date 1883 was clearly marked, but when further quantities were put on the market in the following years, the final figure was deliberately blurred so that the cards could be topical during the rest of the decade.

The trick of another early type of cards is almost obvious—once discovered. They consisted of one or two heads, usually embossed on small, lace-edged visiting cards. They were usually in profile, and their expressions were either excessively jovial or thoroughly disagreeable. The surprise consisted in the cleverness of the designs, which showed a profile whether held the right way up or upside down, with a friendly or forbidding expression, respectively. A popular design of this kind, if held the right way up, showed the head of a judge, fully bewigged, and when reversed the face of the culprit. The effect is accentuated if two profiles face each other, as seen on Colour Plate XVI.

A seventeenth-century engraver is said to have designed " landscapes " which, if looked in a different angle, appeared to be human profiles. There are Victorian cards employing the same idea. A card of the 70's at first sight is only a picture of a wintry landscape, but the design includes a striking face of Father Christmas which is immediately revealed when looked at sideways (Plate 147).

So far I have been describing mostly flat cards without real mechanical tricks. There are slightly more complicated types, although at the first glance they too would be taken for simple, flat cards. It is indeed a pity that I cannot always reproduce them both in their simple, flat form, as they were received, as well as extended or opened out, the very process of which discloses several additional surprises. One of the simplest and oldest methods of " animation " was to affix a cut-out picture of a child, or other suitable subject, in such a way that if it was held in the hand it could be raised from the card itself without becoming detached from it. Small strips of paper stuck both to the card and the cut-out, and not visible unless the card was held sideways, formed the trick. Whereas the simplest used only one cut-out or scrap in this way, the most complicated contained literally dozens of them, in layers built up to form a perfect picture in perspective when extended, and usually composed of paper, lace, silk and transparent materials alternately. The frosting and jewelling which completed these elaborate Christmas cards must have made them look like scenes from Wonderland in an age of flickering light and shadow even more than they would to-day in the cold, bright light of electricity.

A delightful card, published by S. Hildesheimer in 1880, illustrates a very simple idea. The perfectly flat card, when taken out of the envelope, on its face shows an old manor house, snow-covered, and in the forecourt guests arriving (Plate 145). The picture then is opened out from the middle, and inside we see the interior of the house and three exquisitely Victorian versions of " ye olde Christmasse " (Plate 146). The centre shows the guests dancing under a bunch of mistletoe to the music of a harp and violin, while the panels illustrate a young couple at a spinet on one side, and on the other a game of blind man's buff. (A similar card had " Bringing in the Yule log " on the top and " Grandpapa's story " in the central panel, " inside " the card—and the house.)

It is not difficult to imagine the thrill with which these simple cards were unfolded! The same thrill accompanied the opening of those also very extensively popular Christmas cards which were themselves the shape and size of a small envelope, usually about 3 by 4 inches. The four flaps were not stuck down, but just folded into each other and sealed with an easily removed scrap of a robin, sprig of holly or bunch of flowers of significance in the language of flowers. The other side of the envelope, on which the address would normally be written, was also very finely decorated with embossed ornaments in silver or gold, enclosing an oval which framed a poem or Christmas message, often printed on laid-in silk or satin. When the flaps were unfolded, the chief attraction of the card appeared. It was usually a colour-print stuck in fully or only on one side. If the latter, it could be lifted to show a further little poem, text or a chromolithograph beneath it. Occasionally the little picture itself invited additional discoveries : for example, when showing a house with shuttered windows in a moonlit garden, the shutters could be opened with a fingernail to reveal the loving couple, as on a valentine, within. Here again the workmanship was minute, and the ornamen-

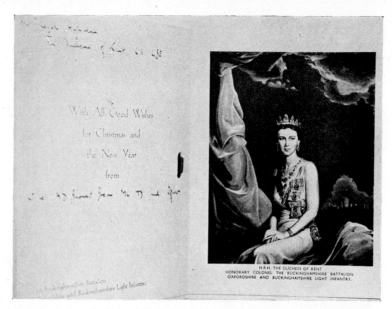

PLATE 111   A half-tone reproduction of a portrait of their Honorary Colonel, H.R.H. the Duchess of Kent, decorated the folder card of the 1st Battalion The Oxfordshire and Buckinghamshire Light Infantry for Christmas, 1939.

March past at National Red Cross Training Camp, 1939.

PLATE 112   The British Red Cross Christmas card for 1939 contained this photograph of the march past at a training camp in the same year.

PLATE 113 Performing animal cards had, and still have, a great popularity. These two are from a set of Christmas party cards. The same set include a dinner party in the barn : cats seated around a table and waited on by serving cats; they are eating roast mice on skewers. " After the Opera " shows a number of cats on the rooftops and an irate housewife complete with night cap preparing to douche them with a jug of water.

PLATE 114 A popular American card of a pug dog with a rather human expression, wearing a lace collar and the motto " Trusty and true, Is the friend for you ! " (Published by L. Prang for 1878.)

PLATE 115 Boxing bulldogs hold the stage on a curious set of animal cards.

PLATE 116 (right) Monkeys, whether two-legged or four, always get up to mischief. On Christmas cards S. T. Dadd specialised in them in the 1880's.

A MERRY CHRISTMAS.

Christmas bring you store of blisses,
Lucky hits, and pretty misses

PLATE 117 A curious Marcus Ward card with a cat and her trophy of a pigeon, while other cats are greedily watching. Another card of this set shows a cat anxiously watching a hen sitting on her eggs. The text on the latter runs :

"With interest all your plans are watched,
By friends who wish them safely hatched ! "

THE BEST WISHES OF THE SEASON TO YOU

PLATE 118 This card of a piggy pig and a humanised "pig" wearing a peacock feather in his hat quotes Hamlet : "A little more than kin and less than kind " !

PLATE 119 The hazards of a curious chase. Monkeys in full hunting kit and mounted on foxhounds are featured on this comic card. One mount has just unseated his rider into the ditch.

Be Christmas joys of substance made,
And troubles merely empty shade.

PLATE 120 "Shadow-cards" drew parallels between animal and human characters.

One of a set of four designs, published by S. Hildesheimer for 1881.

PLATE 121   Shepherd and shepherdess children and a favourite lamb decorate this charming American card of the black background type.

PLATE 122   In the 1880's some elegant floral designs included various insects in their decoration.

PLATE 123   Considering the perpetual war waged against mice, especially by women, it is curious to find so many Victorian cards featuring them either alive or dead. This card shows the triumphant return of two scavengers, the cat and the owl, with their bag.

PLATE 124
(*above*)
The "Little
Red Riding-
hood" set of
1868.

PLATE 125
(*left*)

PLATE 126
(*right*)

PLATE 127
(*below*)

*For
description
see text
pp.* 154-9.

PLATES 128 and 129
A delightful little girl's card in the form of a four-page letter from Santa Claus written in the manner of old Victorian love-letters (acrostics). *Described on pp. 156-7.*

PLATE 130
The amusing ballad of Robin Hood's Christmas hunt was illustrated by four scenes by Kate Greenaway. This shows the result: one poor blackbird. *(See below.)*

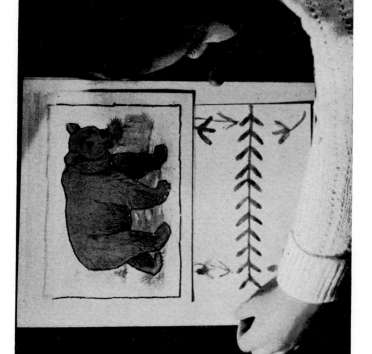

The picture postcard of the Round Tower of Windsor Castle made into a unique individual Christmas card by hand-colouring it and adding a painted flag. It was made and given to his father by H.M. King George VI in 1904, when he was the young Prince Albert.

PLATE 131

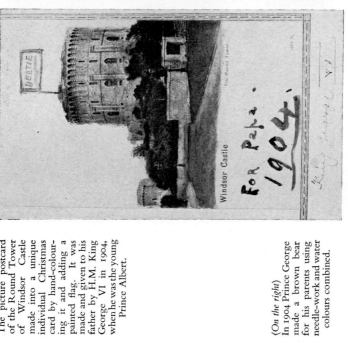

(*On the right*)
In 1904 Prince George made a brown bear for his parents using needle-work and water colours combined.

PLATE 132

CHRISTMAS·JOY-BELLS
ARE·RINGING·FOR·YOU

PLATE 134 H.M. Queen Elizabeth II, when a young Princess, designed and made this charming little Christmas card for her grandmother, H.M. Queen Mary, in 1933. (*Described on pp. 161-2*).

To Grannie

From Lilibet

1933

PLATE 135 (*on the right*)
The dedication written by the then Princess Elizabeth inside the (above) folder card. (1933 was added by H.M. Queen Mary.)

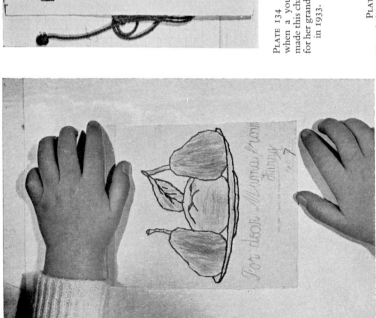

For dear Mama From Harry "7"

PLATE 133 A tempting dish of fruit outlined in back-stitch needlework and coloured by crayons was Prince Henry's Christmas card to H.M. Queen Mary in 1906-7.

GREETINGS.

PLATE 136

A colourful lino-cut landscape hand-coloured and illustrative of the R. L. Stevenson poem,
the sentiment inside the folder, was H.R.H. Princess Elizabeth's own hand-made card for
1936.

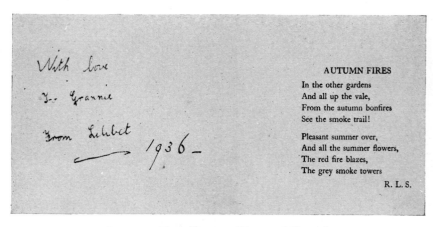

AUTUMN FIRES

In the other gardens
And all up the vale,
From the autumn bonfires
See the smoke trail!

Pleasant summer over,
And all the summer flowers,
The red fire blazes,
The grey smoke towers

R. L. S.

PLATE 137   The inside pages of the same folder card.

PLATE 138
(*above on the left*)
A jovial card imitative of the old 5-franc note.

PLATE 139
(*above on the right*)
An Angus Thomas "cheque" card drawn on "The Bank of Blessings, Unlimited . . ."

PLATE 140
(*left*)
Angus Thomas's tinsel teapot and Good Fortune Christmas cards.

PLATE 141
(*right*)

Descriptions on

PLATE 142 An innocent trick card sent to Queen Mary in 1907 from Marienbad. Outwardly it is in the shape of a pewter mug, decorated with silhouette figures drinking the waters. The card opens, and inside is seen the silhouette of the sender.

PLATE 143 The pseudo-love-letter trick card reveals its surprise element when the first, usually deeply sentimental page is turned and the joke appears instead of the expected continuation of the letter. This card (*on the right, above*) is typical of the latter.

PLATE 144 A Hildesheimer Christmas card for 1883 so realistically like a little package that one is tempted to undo it.

PLATE 145 An attractive triptych card published in 1880 by S. Hildesheimer.

The cover of the card shows the guests arriving for a Christmas party.

PLATE 146 The same card when it is opened out like the doors of a cupboard. The party is now in full swing *inside*!

PLATE 147 At first sight only a wintry landscape, but the design of the above card includes a striking face of a smiling Father Christmas which is revealed

when looked at sideways !

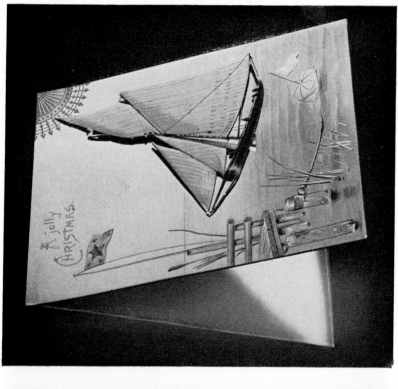

PLATE 149 A sailing boat trick card. The boat is a separate cut-out cardboard, and will rise and fall on the "water" if the pendulum "keel" is moved.

A jolly CHRISTMAS.

PLATE 148 A typical scented enveloped or sachet card. The embossed flaps can each be turned back, as seen in the illustration. The windows of the chromolithograph "house" can also be opened or closed with a fingernail.

If you hold up this picture
A light at the back
You will see the sweet cherub
That watches o'er Jack.
May God keep our sailors
So brave and so true!
May they spend jolly Christmas,
And I'm sure so may you!

Christmas 1886

PLATE 152 (*right*)

The reverse side of the same card, which explains the apparition, and includes Queen Victoria's handwritten dedications for this as well as another card fixed on the same page in Queen Mary's collection.

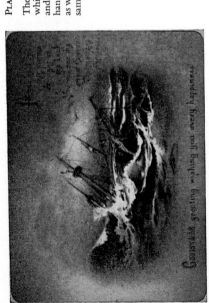

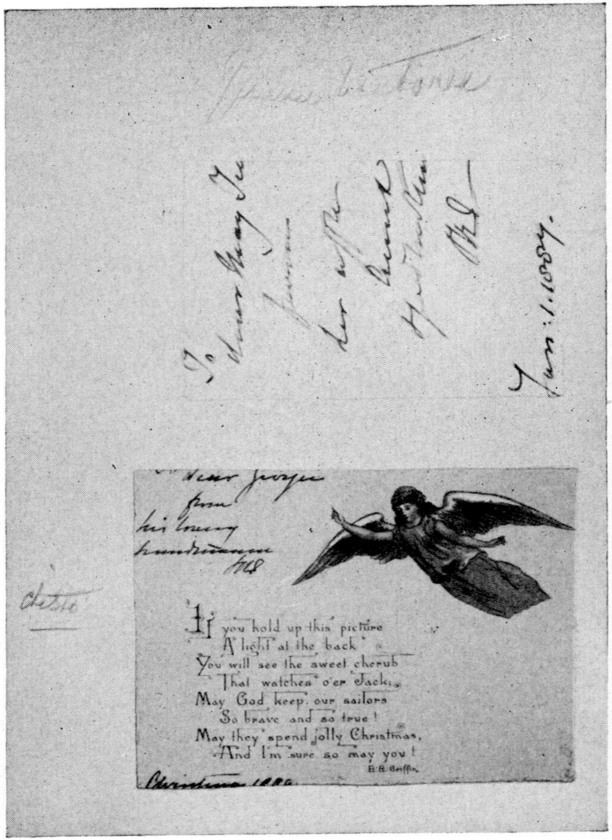

Christmas greeting wishing you every happiness

PLATE 150 (*above*)

A dangerous moment at sea is the apparent subject of this Christmas card sent to King George V in 1886 by Queen Victoria.

PLATE 151 (*on the right*)

When this card is held up to the light, a guardian angel in pale colours can be seen over the sinking ship.

Christmas greeting wishing you every happiness

PLATE 153 A little gem of advertising. The complicated mechanism of the eau-de-Cologne bottle is described on p. 169.

PLATE 154 An effective cut out or "shaped" Christmas card sent to Queen Mary by Queen Victoria in 1894. The two photographs of the same card make its "mechanism" clear. Note the rich jewelling and frosting, particularly the sparkling letters in "Christmas". The second photograph (below) shows the reverse of the card, including Queen Victoria's dedication and well-known signature.

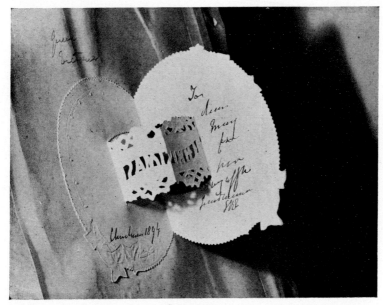

PLATE 155

PLATE 156 A delightful little concertina calendar sent to Queen Mary by Queen Victoria for Christmas, 1895. The delicate finish of the card is apparent from the photograph, which shows the card extended. The width of each panel is about 1½ and 5 inches in height.

PLATE 158
(below)

PLATE 157
(above)

The outside of a partly home-made "boxed" Christmas card. When the lid is opened, the characteristic complexity of lovingly accumulated Victorian symbols—moss, dried grasses, feathers—and numerous scraps appear, to say nothing of the layers of lace-paper and frosting (Plate 158). But one needs the soft light of a candle of 1871, the date of the "card", to see them at their best !

tation of the cards was itself often a work of art. It is no wonder that in the *Art Journal* of 1869 they were referred to as " pure and practical Art-teachers ", especially for the student of design. In addition to their decorative qualities, these little enveloped or sachet cards were often padded with an absorbent tissue impregnated with perfume or lavender water. This gave them an attractive, cushioned touch, and the treasured ones were used as handkerchief sachets. This combination of purposes was introduced by the Rimmel firm, the well-known London perfumers in the 60's (Plate 148).

A little gem of advertising under the cover of an enchanting Christmas card should perhaps be mentioned here. It belongs to the most complicated of animated cards. The card itself is in the shape of, and designed to resemble, a bottle of eau-de-Cologne, complete with seal and label (Plate 153). The neck of the bottle can be raised to expose the tucked-in greeting card which is the same width and depth as the " bottle ". As it is slowly pulled out, a bright red rose and blue forget-me-nots appear against a floral background. When fully extended, the cut-out rose bends forward, and as it does so it brings into view and animation a complicated series of colourful cut-outs, attached to each other invisibly, so that they all stand out in relief. A little angel holding a tiny cross made of flowers sits in the middle in a small carriage drawn by white doves, one of which is holding a sealed letter in its beak. The greeting text on the background can only be seen when the card is fully extended. The actual size of the " bottle ", or, rather, card, is 5 by $2\frac{1}{4}$ inches, and when pulled out, $7\frac{1}{4}$ by $2\frac{1}{4}$ inches. The illustration, with the help of a mirror, shows the card fully opened.

Two delightful ship cards in Queen Mary's collection were sent by Queen Victoria in the 80's. One of these, now rather rare designs (Plate 150) is to all appearances a simple card, about 6 by 4 inches, bearing a rather sombre chromolithograph of a sailing ship in very rough seas which looks as though it will be swamped at any minute. But the top right corner bears the text :

" If you hold up this picture,
A light at the back,
You will see the sweet Cherub
That watches o'er Jack."

The cherub does indeed appear, wearing a pale pink robe and with wings and arms outspread, in the sky just above the ship when the card is held up to the light (Plate 151). The construction of this card is simple (Plate 152), yet the effect was no doubt delightful and a surprise novelty at the time of its publication. The same idea—in fact, the same cherub pattern—appeared on another card published at the same time. On this we see the shepherds and when the card is held against a light the angel appears to be pointing to the Star of Bethlehem. (The patent was also employed in profane, sporting cards, too—without the cherub.)

The other card is folded in two so that it could stand like an inverted V. The design shows a calm sea with part of a jetty, a buoy and some rich " jewelling ". In the centre a yacht in full sail can be seen. It is printed on a separate piece of board, and only attached to the folder itself by its keel, which, instead of being in the water, passes through a slit in the card. This tongue of cardboard, not visible on the face of the card, moves like a pendulum with a little weight attached to it, and as it is moved so the ship rocks " on the waves " (Plate 149).

A very pretty card made for Christmas, 1895, shows a little boy in eighteenth-century costume, offering a partly cut-out bouquet. It looks like a long, narrow card, little more than 5 by 1 inches in size. One is tempted to take hold of the bouquet, and as one does so the card lifts and unfolds, rather like a miniature folding screen (Plate 156). The panels show in four sets the calendar for 1896, each one preceded by a young gallant with a bouquet, bigger and bigger, offered to a young belle. Little angels with golden-thread bell-ropes ring in Christmas on another animated, three-dimensional card (Plate 159). The window of the tower is of purple celluloid and transparent. Through it, when the card is made to stand, a ray of light shines on the sparkling angels. Their little figures are cut out, together with the ground and fence, from another piece of cardboard and hinged to the tower card, so that it can both stand by itself or be folded up and put back into an envelope.

Just as valentines were sometimes " home-made " even when elaborate ones were already to be bought on the market, so were Christmas cards. These were individual compositions of scraps drawings and paintings, and allowed for little personal touches which only the sender and the recipient would understand—for example, feathers or flowers and grasses, perhaps picked together, or other little mementoes of intimacy. One of such so-called " boxed " Christmas " card " before me as I write is built into a shallow cardboard box, about $3\frac{1}{2}$ by $5\frac{1}{4}$ inches and $\frac{3}{4}$ inch in depth, covered with old gold paper (Plate 157). The outside of the lid of the box shows a cut-out engraving of a knight of the time of the Commonwealth ; his dress is nicely hand-coloured. He is holding in his left hand a tiny square card with " A Merry Xmas to you " printed on it, but cut out separately and stuck on the surface as though the knight is holding it. Inside the box, under several layers of tissue paper and within a frame of white lace-paper, stuck on gold paper and fixed to small bits of cork, are arranged a number of scraps, including one of a cheerful Father Christmas and another of a robin. Moss and natural, as well as silvered, dry grasses are characteristically arranged, and behind Father Christmas is a scrap with the date, 1871, made up from red holly berries (Plate 158). A similar boxed card in my collection is combined with a small drawer. As the latter is drawn, the lid is automatically raised and a golden-framed mirror emerges from the box. The box also contains an affectionate sentiment addressed to the recipient and printed on a separate card. When this is lifted, a panorama of lace-paper and dried flowers becomes visible, like the one just described. A further Christmas wish is inscribed on a ruined-column scrap. This " Invisible Fairy Mirror " " card " was first published by Alexander Laidlaw for Christmas, 1865. Although it was a celebrated novelty, it sold at 2s. 6d. per copy.

Little decorative imitations of pocket purses were elaborately produced as more expensive Christmas cards. Some of these were carefully finished with every detail, including the lucky gold coin, which was made of paper, with a joking explanatory text (Plate 160). A design which appeared for Christmas, 1888, was of a little leather wallet. When it was opened with the help of cleverly arranged strings in the background, a number of cheques drawn for the following year and imitation coins, complete with the profile of the Queen, peeped out. Besides the Christmas greeting, the text on this card runs :

> " Who steals my purse steals trash,
>   Things are not always what they seem,
> Yet I'm as rich as misers are,
>   Whose wealth is but—an empty dream."

The open wallet is surprisingly decorative in a documentary manner, without any ornamentation, and resembles the effect of the old *quodlibets*. A fair number and variety of similar purse cards were published by several publishers (Plate 161). Their popularity prompted the enterprising Pears' Soap manufacturers to use this type of card in their famous advertising campaigns by inserting amongst the coins and cheques a small card " To introduce Pears' soap " printed on it in imitation hand-writing.

In the 70's, a much less expensive and also less elaborate card was the so-called " Black Christmas purse-card ", which, however, was not made to resemble a purse, but was a paper coin in relief fixed in the centre of a black visiting card. These were meant to be enclosed with a real purse, the latter being the Christmas present.

The first page of the first album of Queen Mary's great collection of Christmas cards preserves some of the earliest cards received by Her Majesty when she was a child. The page is charmingly arranged, and two of the four cards stuck on to it belong to the finest examples of animated cards (Plate 162). One of these, placed in the centre of the page, looks like a reproduction of an oval bouquet tied with light and dark blue ribbons. The greeting is in the centre of the symmetrical composition, framed in a wreath of flower scraps. The length of the card in this state is a little more than 5 by $1\frac{1}{2}$ inches at its widest point. That which at first glance looks like a number of buds on the point of opening at the top of the bouquet is actually the tail and wing feathers of a little blue bird which can be withdrawn from the little sheath-like case hidden behind the bunch of light blue ribbons of the card. When the little bird is fully withdrawn, his wings and tail spread out, and one sees that he is carrying in his beak holly leaves and berries, also tied with a ribbon. It is a charming card, and one of the earliest of this type. Her Majesty preserved it in perfect working order since Christmas, 1875, when she was eight years old.

Variations of this type of pull-out flower cards were amongst the most treasured Christmas cards. One from 1870 shows a bouquet of red, white and yellow roses held together in a gilded case, which carries the greeting. This case is made to resemble the handle of a fan, which indeed it proves to be when one of the silken threads hanging from it is pulled. The bouquet then opens out to more than twice its original size, and five rose petals, larger than the rest, form the shape of an open fan. On each of these flowers is printed a quotation from Wordsworth, Keats, Thompson and Scott. Each of the little verses is framed in lilies of the valley, as my illustration (Plate 164), showing the card fully opened, indicates. The other flower and fan card which I have chosen to illustrate the type pictures a bunch of violets placed in the centre of an embossed, lace-edged white paper card. In this case the handle pulls out, as the illustration shows, and can then be opened into a real miniature fan, also with mottoes and flower decorations on each leaf (Plate 165).

My next illustration is a card which in shape and appearance in its first state is similar to the bouquets already described. The handle contains an oval plaque with the conventional " A Merry Christmas to you ". When the card is handled, one soon discovers that the handle is made of two similarly cut cardboards, which are not stuck together. When one uses both hands, it will soon be apparent that the card can literally be turned inside out by bringing the two edges together again by a circular movement with each. The illustration (Plate 166) shows clearly enough the complete transformation which takes place when this has been done, including the shiny lantern-like paper, and the young beauty with a rose in her hand and gilded grass around her head emerging from the centre. Now also the hidden message can be read. It was written on the reverse of the more obvious greeting and says :

> " Christmas Holly and Mistletoe
> Whisper to thee
> My deepest affection
> Where ever thou be."

The only original I know of this card is in the collection of the Victoria and Albert Museum. I found the explanation of my next illustration also in the same collection. I do not include it in this chapter, for it is a simple, flat card, little larger than the ordinary postcard of to-day. It was one of a set of four designed by W. Tasker Nugent for the Marcus Ward firm of London and Belfast. The set was entitled " Greetings in Costume ", a frequent subject in those as in later days, and the one I am referring to shows a little boy dressed in pink, gold and white lace-frilled cloak and trousers, wearing a feathered hat. He is holding up a circular disk resembling a bouquet of tiny flowers. For some time I was inclined to suspect that its size and shape was really meant to save the artist from the vicissitudes of drawing another hand, since the hands on his designs, which he did not manage to cover up, indicate that the drawing of these was not one of his strongest points. But I recollected that I had seen similar bouquet features brought as Christmas presents on other old cards, but, as they were much smaller and less clear, I passed them over with little compunction as bouquets of real flowers not very happily drawn. A Christmas card in Queen Mary's collection, however, provided the solution. The little messenger in Nugent's design was carrying one of these animated bouquets cards in his hand, not as a camouflage, but as an especially valuable gift.

This, for me at any rate, unique card from Queen Mary's collection is illustrated here in two positions. The first (Plate 167), except for the invisible wedge which is used to bring out the filigree lace edging in the shadow, shows it in its inanimate form. It is made quite flat so as to fit into an envelope. In the second photograph it has been animated, and both in the card itself and in its shadow can be seen the intricate mechanism of its construction. Almost every flower is a separate minute scrap embossed and printed in many delightful colours. The butterfly in the centre of the manifold garland of flowers is so placed that she is at right angles to the two levers, the cords of which are clearly seen on the first photograph and which, when brought together beneath the surface of the card, bring into movement each separate garland and make even the butterfly appear to hover above, instead of settling on, the rose in the centre. Of course, this and many other cards illustrated in this book would have been seen to much better advantage if it had been possible to reproduce them all in colours, but I hope the photographs will give some idea of its delicate beauty and charm, even though the delightful colouring has to be left to the imagination (Plate 168).

A very elaborate type of the animated card has survived in considerable numbers, although their paper mechanism was also rather complicated and liable to break under the strain of repeated manipulation. The possible reason for their survival would seem to be that their means of animation did not prevent them from being pasted into books and albums.

The mechanical cards which I am describing here could perhaps be grouped as tableaux cards, for their composition and arrangement of figures and background closely resemble a miniature stage or the finale of a toy theatre. It is this theatrical effect which makes them appear much more complex than they actually are. Almost anyone with some imagination, enough scraps, neat fingers and time to spare, all of which the Victorians had in abundance, could produce their own. When the pages of a scrapbook are turned casually, these cards may easily be overlooked, since, apart from the fact that they are slightly thicker than the ordinary single-sheet card, there is nothing to distinguish them. Their surface design was often also published independently as a single-page card. Thus it takes a little more careful observation to see that these are not single, but double cards attached only at the lower edge, and that the first or upper card can be lifted until it forms a right angle with the second or base. This simple action reveals the tableau, which begins to take shape as soon as the cover is lifted, on account of the hidden strings or strips of paper which attach the individual scraps to both cards. The tableaux are often religious in theme, most frequently scenes of the Nativity. Occasionally there are quite secular subjects too, such as animated landscapes with houses, trees and streets, including men and animals. The examples which I am illustrating differ considerably, although two are scenes of the Nativity. In the centre of the cover card in this case a tassel is attached to facilitate the opening or dropping of the curtain (Plate 169). Another Nativity scene is the subject of the second tableau card, which has the same measurements (3 by 4½ inches) as the preceding one, but which stands vertically. A feature of this card is the two-storied effect, showing the stable with scrap figures inside and outside, and above two angels against a background of the comet and stars (Plate 170). The cover of this card was also very popular as a single-page card in the 1870's, if its frequent occurrence in many collections is any guide. It shows a night scene with a camel and the Three Wise Men following the Star of Bethlehem.

My third illustration of these shows a charmingly descriptive landscape of a medieval town built on the banks of a river on which sailing ships can be seen, and a four-horse coach in the foreground seems to have just crossed the hump-backed bridge. This card, sent to Queen Mary for Christmas in 1875, is in her collection, and is photographed with the other cards on this the first page of the first album of it (Plate 162).

A spray of lilac with no text, realistically cut out, decorates and at the same time forms the camouflage of a rather original mechanical Christmas card. To open, once again both hands have to be used. As the top and back are divided from the leafy end of the spray, a complete transformation takes place on the reverse of it. Instead of the lilac blossom, two chubby little hands, realistically embossed, appear, each holding one end of what seems to be a cracker in the shape of roses—the stalks representing the ends that are held and the flowers the body of the cracker. The rose petals are made of red silk and actually stand up when the card is in motion. Hidden amongst them, where one would expect to find the motto in a cracker, is a tiny, silver-edged envelope sealed with an even tinier red heart scrap. The blue ribbons round the wrists of the little paws complete the bright colour scheme of this dainty and clever card, which is illustrated here as representing one of many built up on similar lines (Plate 163).

It is difficult to visualise the clever working mechanism of the next group of animated cards, even with the help of the two photographs of the same card. It again presents a rather stage- or tableau-like arrangement of figures, trees and houses—in fact, a gay children's garden party (Plate 171). The cover, when closed and flat, consists of two decorative panels with bunches of flowers in ovals. This card opens from the middle outwards by holding the shells, clearly seen on the first photograph on either side of the flower panels, in each hand. As the panels slide away from each other, the three-tiered scenery unfolds. Like the top card, each tier is composed of two separate halves packed one behind the other in the original state and still slightly overlapping when the card is fully opened. The next photograph (Plate 172), taken from above, shows how the separate leaves fit into each other as well as the framework of the card.

A further variation of these cards with even more theatrical or peep-show effects used a concertina-like structure. The top and bottom cards were connected by transparent coloured paper pleated like the bellows of the concertina, and when fully expanded, and when the little door-like flap on the top card was opened, the animated scraps inside were seen in the light, coloured according to the colour of the transparent paper bellows.

The theatre is quite clearly suggested on some other somewhat smaller and older cards of much simpler construction, though opened up in the same way as the two-panelled card divided in the middle. These were printed on a single thin cardboard and the folding produces the double-card effect. When closed, only a draped stage curtain can be seen in an oval form. The card illustrated shows very clearly the long paper handles by which the curtains are " pulled back " and the single picture printed in the centre of the card behind them, which then becomes visible. These scenes were usually landscapes in the " Italian style " and were often rather fine colour prints (Plate 173).

A direct descendant of the animated valentine is again a simple, flat-looking card, with many flowers set in an oval, but without text on its surface. A silk ribbon attached to the bottom of the oval is in this case the handle which opens the card when lightly pulled. A delicately embossed oval golden frame comes forward as the cover is lifted, and behind it appears a picture of three little angels in a flower garland. At the same time, several of the flower scraps are lifted, revealing hidden mottoes of Truth, Constancy, Faith and Joy. The Christmas greeting text is on the reverse of the lace-edged oval top, and appears only when the card is open. The effect of this card is enhanced if seen, as it originally was, by candle- or gas-light, with their familiar shadows. A surprisingly great variety of these delicate cards existed and were treasured for decades, and it is a pity that I can reproduce very few examples of them in this book (Colour Plate XV).

The popularity of a novel type of Christmas card often resulted, not only in many imitations, but gave the leg-puller also an inspiration to make fun of it, very much in the same way as the original sentimental valentines were followed by rather broad, jocular valentine cards which competed with and later surpassed the popularity of the ones they intended to caricature. The Christmas card type just described was also soon followed by humorous varieties, which did not emulate the delicacy or finish of the production, but used the same mechanism for making fun. One of these caricature cards of the same overall size uses a woman's frilled nightcap decorated with bows of pink ribbons on top and bottom instead of the oval frame of its model. The text around it runs : " To wish you a CAP-ital Christmas and many a jovial NIGHT ". The nightcap can be lifted in much the same way as the flowery oval on the other cards, but here, instead of love messages and angels, there is only a glass with steaming grog bearing the caption, " A night-cap ". The text on the back explains in verse that—

> " Old-fashioned they may be,
>   But after all's said,
> On a cold winter's night
>   They're a comfort in bed ;
> So I'm sending a COUPLE
>   of NIGHT CAPS to you.
> I think you will find
>   You can do with the TWO."

A charming mechanical card from Queen Mary's collection, which has few rivals, employs a very good idea of construction. In its flat state it is an oblong card of about 3½ by 4 inches in size, with the decorative inscription " Joy and gladness attend your Christmas hours " on it, while above, as though resting on and looking over a wall, a couple of little winged angel heads, cut out of paper and delicately coloured, can be seen. When the oblong cover is brought down, a small tongue of stiff paper attached to it inside is automatically pulled slightly forward, and this, by means of an ingenious mechanism connected with it, raises a set of cut-out little angels not seen when the card is shut (Plate 174). They are fixed to a connected cardboard construction, and when the card is animated they look as though they are flying in the sky on little cushions of clouds. The sky blue inside of the card offers a very charming contrast to the little figures and their white cloud patches. The reverse of the cover carries the little sentiment :

" Naught, naught thy soul can harm.
    The Prince of Peace is nigh !
He shields thee with His arm,
    He shall thy needs supply.
Thine onward path with His care
Shall blossom like a garden fair."

Another animated card also with a Christmas subject comes from Queen Mary's collection, and was given to her when she was a little girl. It is made of a thickish cardboard imitating very realistically an oblong almond slice decorated with almonds and strips of angelica. To one of these is attached a silken tape which, when pulled, lifts up one side of the card, and on the reverse a jovial Father Christmas appears in his familiar red robes, with a large sack of presents on his back. When the tape is pulled still further, the upper part of the Father Christmas card comes forward, as though he was bending down to empty his sack, and on his back, which thus becomes a little flat platform, a series of small scraps, representing a Christmas tree, complete with angels and toys, a little Christ, a rocking horse, etc., stand up automatically. A little string in the back manipulates all these figures, just as another string helped Father Christmas to bend down. This card is photographed with the help of a mirror to show the picture of Father Christmas as well as the final scene on the top of the card (Plate 175).

A very large group of expanding cards of many forms and subjects, but having alike one feature in common—the tab which actually animates them—are known as " tab cards ". The simplest of these consisted of two thin boards attached round the edges with a round or oval opening cut out in the centre of the top sheet. The card around the opening was usually elaborately ornamented and surrounded in a gold- or lace-edged border. The tab in these cards was a cut-out or attached tongue of a third bit of cardboard between the other two. It was made to move up and down behind the opening in the centre of the top of the card. Thus when the tab was pulled a different scene or text appeared within the frame. For instance, if before pulling the tab a bunch of flowers could be seen behind the framed opening, this would be replaced by a greeting text printed under it or vice versa when the tab was pulled which, as it were, opened the shutter. On this simple little trick many more complicated structures were built.

A more complicated group of tab cards are those which, when the tab is pulled, no longer remain flat, but extend also in the third dimension, and a scene in perspective with some depth appears behind the opening cut in the top card. I reproduce one of these (Plate 181), and the original is indeed one of the loveliest little toys of its kind. The top card is of a delicate pale blue background with a garland of pink and gold roses and cherubs surrounding the oval opening, the whole framed with a gold-and-white embossed lace edge. When the tab is pulled downwards, it is as though one is looking into a vista, including the scrap figure of a boy bringing a bunch of flowers, in a cut-out garland of roses and forget-me-nots. In what seems the far distance behind him, we see a fountain against a background of trellis on which a quince in bloom is climbing. Three photographs are required to indicate the effect of moving the tab in a lovely children's card in Queen Mary's collection. The size of this pretty card is $4\frac{1}{4}$ by $5\frac{1}{2}$ inches, and the extension of the tongue, in this case of only 1 inch, produces a completely different picture on the card. Plate 177 shows the card in its unanimated form and the greeting, " A Sunny Happy New Year to you, dear ", and the motto, " May your Christmas be without a blot, And of what's behind may you have a lot ". The illustration on the card shows a little girl playing with her doll and other toys. When the tab is being pulled, it becomes apparent that the little picture is composed of four strips, each 1 inch in width (Plate 178). The movement of the tab produces a change of picture by drawing four other previously invisible strips over the original four sections. Thus the picture of the little girl " dissolves " into a group of children and a large dog skating on a frozen pond (Plate 179).

Once the trick in these cards is understood, they may appear much simpler than the effectiveness of their performance would suggest.

Their manufacture certainly required much labour, precision and care. In the 1850's the London firm, Dean, produced children's books of "Dissolving Views" on similar lines. By pulling a tab, a frightening view of a volcano was "dissolved" into a picture of a waterfall, complete with a peaceful angler. The idea of alternating scenes lent itself very well to comic subjects. A tremendous pillow-fight in a children's dormitory was the subject of one of these tab cards, with the sequence of all of them fast asleep in bed procured by the mere pulling of the tab. This was a very popular card, and although allegedly invented to amuse children, was most probably more appreciated by their parents.

Another frequently occurring and no doubt popular tab or pull-out card shows four tabs, one on every side of the rectangular original card. On these the tabs are quite short—just sufficient for a finger-hold. When pulled out, another complete little card appears from behind the central card on each side, thus making the one card into five (Plate 176). They all contain texts or designs, and on the same principle they could be, and indeed have been, extended almost indefinitely, since each card pulled out could have others tucked away beneath them.

The substitution of thin metal for the paper tongue of the tab opened the door for further developments in the design of these cards. I am illustrating two of these by one photograph, but here again a number of photographs taken from various angles would be necessary to give an adequate idea of the complexity of the ingenious and attractive little devices. The strength and firmness of the metal tab enabled the designer to build up on a small card a "mighty structure"—in some cases higher than the length of the card. The bottom card on Plate 180 shows a little girl sitting, surrounded by garlands of flowers. A slight pull on the tab releases a canopy of tightly packed scrap flowers which, when fully released, cover her like a many-coloured dome. The other card, when closed and flat, shows a carriage drawn by swans. A lady in classical dress sits in the carriage playing the harp. This picture lies very lightly on the face of the card and is attached to it only at its lower edge. A light touch will turn it over, whereupon, with the help of a tab behind the card, a wonderful edifice of a flowery bower rises up into the third dimension ! In front of it a lover and his lass can be seen. The little poem on the reverse of the cover offers :

" A toast to the mistletoe bough
That may ever at Christmas be seen
A love charm to sweet maiden fair
As it hangs amidst ivy so green."

There were many similar cards. One, when opened in the same way, raised a fully detailed chapel, complete with long, transparent " stained-glass " windows, altar, pews and angels. Others produced sedan chairs equipped with beautiful passengers ; others, again, ships and endless variations of flowery bowers of every possible description, including impossible ones—these being no more out of place than the others, since the aim of these cards was to surprise by the unexpected and to appear as miraculous as the transformation scene in a pantomime. The realistic touches were only put in to increase the unrealistic effect of the ultimate " animation ".

A few examples of a large group of " cards " which were not really mechanical should be included in this chapter. The trick as far as these were concerned is that they were realistic imitations of real things. Facsimile ashtrays, half-burnt cigars, shoe-laces, china dishes and plates, and an incredible number of other objects, sometimes naïvely, sometimes surprisingly well manufactured, with the conventional or, more often, witty greeting texts, have been popular features. They could not be treasured in albums and scrapbooks, as they were not sufficiently flat, but took their places on mantelpieces and other customary places for the display of titbits, such as china pots and plush cases, fans and feathers, daguerrotypes and calendars, etc. Many of these facsimile novelties were first displayed as such, but, as they were seldom thrown away, became affectionately treated mementoes of the " olden days ". A slightly torn card of this type which finally found its way to the Victoria and Albert Museum is a facsimile of a dish, made of finely glazed paper. Between a butterfly and some yellow rose and evergreen decorations is a printed greeting text, but on the reverse is preserved a personal but unsigned dedication, " With best love, 1880 ", in an old-fashioned handwriting (Plate 183). Some facsimile cards naturally lent themselves very easily to jokes. A favourite involved the Post Office, for it was the exact replica of a label with a severed string. On it was written all the details of the present : in one case a large Christmas turkey, with weight and value stated. In a corner of the label-card official " regret " is expressed that unfortunately the string broke on the journey and the precious bird flew away ! A clever but simple trick, permeated with the perfume of the period, distinguishes a small card which must have been considered rather frivolously piquant and risky when it appeared. It is, as received, a narrow little folded card, 2½ by 5 inches in size. The modest decoration of embossed wild roses in gold, with a cream border, surround the gilt lettering on the cover : " May all Christmas pleasures be *fetching* and above board ! " When the folder is opened a little, the picture inside shows a young gallant in a somewhat formal attitude helping a young woman in a noncommittal way over a stile. She is dressed in a red frock with the leg-of-mutton sleeves and the tight waist of the period, and wears a jaunty little hat of the late 80's. The left foot and part of the red skirt are printed on a cut-out flap, which is stuck to the folders in such a way that it lifts automatically when the folder is being opened. At an angle of about 75 degrees, the girl is seen with one foot already over the stile, but as the card is opened further one begins to see the reverse of the uplifted scrap and on it her leg lifting higher and higher, until, when the card is opened flat, she reaches the " high kick ", and one sees all her frills and furbelows, like a chrysanthemum in full bloom (Plates 185 and 186). The part of the skirt and right foot printed on one side of the scrap and the frills and the leg, in a black stocking, on the other are so well pasted on the pasteboard that while the top matches the rest of the dress perfectly, the other side of the scrap matches equally well the frilled underclothes. It is only the folding and unfolding of this little scrap of paper which " animates " the otherwise unaltered picture and is responsible for the—to us—rather comic attraction. Beneath the stile is printed the rhyme :

> " The friend of Fortune may you be,
> May nothing bar her smile,
> But hand in hand with you may she
> Show up in tip-top style ! "

The poet, well known on Victorian cards, signs himself as " S. K. Cowan, M.A." A somewhat similar end of the century card is manipulated by a tab (Plate 184). By pulling this in and out, the pasteboard legs of the young lady on the card perform a frantic dance. The contrast of the static upper and fast-moving (cut-out) lower parts of the figure look very comic, though few would consider the design " daring " to-day. In its time in 1892 this was known as " the Dancing Girl " card, and sold extremely well, but to-day it is very rare.

It is difficult to resist the temptation to go on describing the numerous other types of mechanical and trick cards, but as a line has to be drawn, I will draw it here, and merely allude to " cards " made of tin, brass, aluminium, cork and veneer, plush, leather and opals, velvet birds and silk and satin cuttings, aerophanes, or those with a mirror or a picture stuck on real glass. There were also many composite cards made up from a great number of individual Christmas cards into one complicated system of folding and unfolding.[1]

A visitor to Jonathan King's collection at Islington in the early 1900's records that he had seen one composite card in this " museum " of cards which consisted—for he counted them—of " as many as 750 pieces " of paper, cardboard, scraps, etc., all stuck on separately " to form the dainty, charming and finished article " ; to say nothing of the fancy wreaths and flowers made of coloured feathers and the many other fantastic ideas and materials which Victorian manufacturers and their public explored in their search for the " novel and beautiful ".

But perhaps the least cardlike Christmas cards were those " talking-machine records " which were published in America just before the First World War. According to Chase, they were prompted by the success of greeting texts set to music in previous years. They were sent

[1] An interesting though more modern version of this tendency of combining cards was the invention of the American " six letters " cards early this century.

> " There's six Christmas letters awaiting you here
> To bring you my wishes for glad Christmas cheer ;
> And if the directions you duly obey,
> I'll greet you by proxy six times through the Day "

read the sentiment on the covering, decorated sachet. It contained individual letters sealed in smaller envelopes, to be opened " in the morning, during the forenoon, at noon, in the afternoon, at six o'clock and at bedtime ", each containing further verses (written by H. W. Pingree) to greet the happy recipient.

in decorated boxes, and the sentiment explained :

> " This is no usual Record
>> But one that was made just for you ;
> And the message it brings
> Is the song my heart sings
>> To-day and all the year through."

The six-inch record itself, when played on the machine, greeted the
recipient in a rich baritone ; " it almost seemed as if Santa Claus
himself were singing the beautiful message ". The production was
discontinued in America the next year on account of wartime economy,
but in Austria and Germany the idea was revived and cardboard
gramophone records with the tune of " Heilige Nacht " were produced
as Christmas postcards during the 1920's.

But all the infinite varieties of sentimental or comic animated and
mechanical cards cannot be enumerated here. I shall therefore conclude
this chapter with the photograph of a delightful three-dimensional card
sent to Queen Mary at the beginning of the 1890's—a card which I only
know from her collection (Plate 187). When folded flat, the card will
just fit into an ordinary envelope of about 5 by 4 inches. It opens up, as
the illustration well shows, into a three-dimensioned little card structure
of a child's cot, with a winged angel, the guardian angel, standing
beside it. She is wearing a long pale mauve robe, slightly embossed
and embellished with the jewelling which had, by the 90's, become
very popular on more elaborate and expensive cards. The little girl
can just be seen lying in the cot, her picture being printed on and cut
out from a separate cardboard, which is attached to the head and foot
" rails " of the cot by a clever contraption, thus also reinforcing the
three-dimensional effect. The bedspread is draped over the foot of the
bed and on it in gold lettering is the greeting : " Christmas blessings
be thine ", while on the back of the card is a little rhyme, signed by
the initials E.E.G., which reads :

> " May Joy be Yours this Christmas-tide,
>> True Joy that never knows an end ;
> May Guardian Angels, at your side,
>> Your path direct, your steps attend."

RELIGIOUS
Christmas Cards

IT may be argued that, since Christmas is essentially a religious festival, all cards sent out for the occasion promote the festive spirit and contribute to the celebration, and thus become automatically of some significance which could be classed as religious. Nowadays, on the other hand, almost annually the Press contains letters from the public commenting on the comparative rarity of Christmas cards with

Fig. 17. Christmas card of the 1890's. Pen and ink drawing by Georgie C. Gaskin, printed in black and red. (5¾ by 4½ inches.)

a definite religious character. Cards which contain no definite allusion to the central subject of Christmas, the anniversary of the Birth of Christ, or do not represent motifs usually associated in the Christian tradition with Jesus and the Nativity, are sometimes called " pagan cards ", and their greater number is taken by many as indicative of a modern deterioration in the observance of Christmas. But it is doubtful whether it is indeed a fact that there are fewer religious Christmas cards now than formerly, and whether the number of religious cards is really significant of the attitude of the public towards the Christian emphasis on Christmas.

From time to time, publishers like C. Caswell, Campbell and Tudhope, Mildmay, Mowbray & Co., T. Nelson & Co., the Society for the Promotion of Christian Knowledge, the Religious Tract Society, Burns, Oates, the Catholic Truth Society, and more recently the Church Artists' Agency, etc., set out to produce decidedly religious Christmas cards. These, although they were always in the minority even in the most religion-conscious years of the Victorian era, have a distinct attraction which had a sure influence on the " general publishers ", who were prompted to bring out some, usually more elaborate " Scriptural " cards themselves. The motifs—whether the style is the old Bible illustrations or a modern interpretation—are concentrated on the scene of the Nativity, the Mother and Child, the angels, the Wise Men, the shepherds with their flocks, the manger in the stable or in a chapel, and similar subjects. Amongst them there are many reproductions from Old Masters (people are generally less shy about religious subjects by Old Masters than by contemporaries), but there are also quite a number of modern ones, consciously aiming at expressing and interpreting the message of the gospel in the up-to-date language of contemporary art. But however well these cards are often made up, the majority of the public, including those who are practising churchgoers, somehow do not choose them in the quantities one might expect. A study of a great number of Victorian scrapbooks and albums failed to disclose a much higher percentage of religious cards received by the average person in the last century, when the practice of Christianity was a so much more accepted—in fact, dominant—part of the daily life in all social grades.

It is in fact one of the most interesting puzzles in the history of the Christmas card that this token of goodwill in picture and text should not have been used more frequently to emphasise the spiritual significance of Christmas, the scene of the Nativity and all the beautiful episodes which throughout the centuries have inspired pictorial art of every shade, kind and quality. The explanation may be that the Christmas card from its beginning was more closely associated in the minds of the senders with the social aspect—the festivities connected with Christmas than with the religious functions of the season. Going to church was not confined to holy days, as it is often to-day, but was a regular observance widely practised. Reward cards, Sunday school mottoes, magazines and text-books, which all had religious contents, were not confined to any particular season, but were given and received throughout the year. It is therefore understandable that the Christmas card itself developed on somewhat different lines—without in any way expressing a lack of religious feeling in a devout age. It is indeed interesting to note that the comments which draw attention to the proportionately few religious cards only began to be made in the 1890's, and more especially in the present century,[1] when the life of the ordinary family began to drift away from daily family prayers and weekly church attendance : in other words, when religious observances became more and more concentrated on, or, generally speaking, confined to Holy Week and Advent.

In this connection, the " Statistics of an ordinary country Rector's Christmas cards " (in 1946) which I received from Sussex in the course of my researches is such a delightful account that I am giving it verbatim :

" *Religious* cards (all good and beautiful)

1 from a German, 1 from a Jew, 1 from an actress .	3

Ordinary, I : coloured pictures :

of homes, cottages, etc.	26
of dogs	18
of horses, coaching, etc.	14
of birds	7
of scenery and ships	9

---

[1] At about the same time criticisms against the use of " Xmas " instead of " Christmas " on Christmas cards and elsewhere began to appear in the Press. Correspondents considered " Xmas " an irreverent modern abbreviation, typical of the age, which, of course, may be the case of many. It will be remembered, however, that the early Victorian Christmas cards often used the abbreviation, which was then considered a reverent though perhaps somewhat mannered archaism. The early Fathers of the Church used X for Christ, but, of course, as it was recently pointed out by J. Ward (*Daily Telegraph*, March 29th, 1939), the letter did not represent the English X, but the Greek χ.

Ordinary, II : not coloured :

miscellaneous	19
Facetiously jovial (2 in very moderate taste) . . .	5
6 *Personal photographs* and 1 illustrated poem . .	7
5 *Original drawings and paintings* (all excellent) . .	5
Unclassified (from U.S.A.)	1
	114

Printed greetings without illustrations, parcels, calendars
and veiled advertisements . . . . . 23 "

Another representative analysis was sent to me by a Catholic priest from Surrey, and I am glad to quote its conclusions for comparison :

" Many of the cards had nothing whatever to do with either the Person of Christ or the Season of His Birth in the Incarnation, nor even of the Feast of the Epiphany ; they were not meant to be ' irreligious ', but conveyed no message of the peace to men of good-will. They could have been sent at any odd time of the year, and were sent because it was the fashion to ' send a card ' at this season of the year, and most of the offenders in this matter were women."

The actual classification of the Christmas cards received by the Rev. Father for Christmas (1946) was the following :

" Mostly of garden scenes with a wealth of flowers, and usually a gateway ; vases of flowers ; country scenes, a roadway with trees and a horse, with printed wording, ' Homeward Bound ' ; cards with a monogram, two or more letters intertwined so as to form a device or cipher, or a crest or coat of arms ; shepherdesses ; snow scenes, sometimes with a church apparently lighted for Vespers or Evensong. *About* 20 *distinctly religious* in character. An increasing number of letters." (About 120 cards.)

If the totals of these and other similar analyses I received are added together, a curious fact emerges when the average is taken : the average proportion of the definitely religious Christmas cards received in the 1870's and 1880's is approximately the same as in the 1910's and to-day, and if anything there is a slight increase in the percentage during and after the Second World War.[2] It is hoped that this trend will be maintained and indeed further increased in the future. We must recognise, however, that the bulk of the Christmas card production today is governed by the ordinary rules of demand and supply. It is therefore essential that all those who feel that the religious significance of Christmas should be more emphasized in present day Christmas cards, should not be shy about it, but make their preference clear by choosing their own cards accordingly. This would assist the development also of religious graphic art of the contemporary idiom, which is doubly handicapped today.

Examples of old Christmas cards which express the religious significance of Christmas are also grouped in various other chapters of this book. Naturally, religious subjects appeared in every style and type and throughout the whole history of the Christmas card, and it would be artificial to confine these cards in one chapter.

[2] " One of the most successful and perplexing art contests ever held in France " was arranged by the Hallmark Greeting Card Company of Kansas City, Mo., U.S.A., in 1949. The *New York Herald Tribune* reported (June 16th) that more than 5,000 artists sent in 5,121 entries. The company announced that ten paintings would be selected and reproduced as Christmas cards and that the winning artists would receive 10 per cent. royalties in addition to the cash prizes, which totalled $15,750. There were 3,000 paintings of Nativity scenes, and the organiser " explained the high percentage of Nativity paintings by saying that the French were fundamentally less religious than Americans and that therefore they were less aware that it was a common subject for Christmas card art ". (The jury consisted of Jean Cassou, René Huyghe, Raymond Cogniat and Georges Huysman, all of France.)

POLITICAL
Christmas Cards

M O S T people to-day would consider it natural that Christmas cards should not express political opinion or comment even in times of heated political controversies. Such cards are, indeed, rather rare. Even those which can be classified as " political " represent an almost a-political, above-party attitude. They resemble the spirit of the cartoon in the *Hornet* of 1874, entitled " Britannia's Valentine ". In this Britannia is seen with Gladstone and Disraeli kneeling at her feet, both asking for her favour. The text explains that—

> " Neither of you is Choice of Mine ;
> Lord Derby is my Valentine."

Almost the same attitude is expressed in a Christmas card designed by Walter Crane in 1874. In this Lord Derby is replaced by Father Christmas as popular favourite instead of a party candidate. " Triumphant return of Mr. Christmas " shows him standing in an open carriage with, as its coats of arms, a plum pudding, fork and knife (Dust Jacket No. 35). Instead of horses, it is being pulled and pushed along by a crowd of voters from all walks of life. Mr. Christmas is seen in breeches and top-boots with a fur-lined overcoat, waving his top-hat and smiling broadly. Around his bald head is a wreath of holly, and the same decorates his waistcoat. The rejoicing crowd are carrying banners with such inscriptions as " Everyman's Candidate " and " Plum P for Christmas ".

Similarly, no controversy was voiced in the " political " cards which carried cartoons of prominent political figures of the 1880's drawn by Bryan. Gladstone is shown in an express train (" I soon shall be back into power "), Joseph Chamberlain as a young dandy standing on a small globe, under a smiling sun (" I mean to rule the earth, as he the sky," etc.) or Randolph Churchill, also a young man, sitting on a crescent moon high in the sky and playing a mandoline, and so on.

A card with an early suffragette flavour, though it is not quite clear whether supporting or opposing the great struggle, featured a lady of somewhat forbiddingly masculine aspect—especially in her dress. The text of the card reads :

> " Downtrodden woman now arise,
> No more let men thus tyrannise ;
> Let's push the tyrant from his throne,
> And have a Christmas of our own."

The famous demonstrations in London in the 1880's were also commemorated, but only slightly treated on contemporary English Christmas cards, in spite of the fact that some of the artists who were prominent in Christmas card designs were politically interested in them. A series of four cards with black-and-white wood-engravings appeared for Christmas, 1887, which were to have a " very large sale as Christmas cards ", partly " because of the intense interest and excitement aroused by the proceedings they depict ", and " on account of their novelty ". The proceedings were the charge opposite the National Gallery ; the police clearing Northumberland Avenue ; the arrival of the Guards ; and the fight at the bottom of Parliament Street. Each card was sold in big black envelopes with gold lettering on them. " Bloody Sunday " was commemorated also by a Christmas card produced without any artistry whatsoever. The regular police were supplemented by " specials " sworn in for these occasions and equipped with batons, one of which is shown in black silhouette as an initial letter on this very rare card (Fig. 18).

In the same year Christmas cards also celebrated a more harmonious national event in Britain, the fiftieth anniversary of the Queen's Accession to the Throne. Cards with her crowned portrait and small views of Windsor Castle, Kensington Palace, Balmoral Castle and Osborne House and the two dates, 1837-1887, were welcome everywhere, irrespective of party allegiance or any other divisions. Similarly, when the long Victorian reign ended, the new reign was loyally greeted by Christmas cards decorated with the photographs of King Edward VII and Queen Alexandra, and the beflagged greeting : " To wish you Every Happiness under the Old Flag and the New Reign."

Peaceful motifs are characteristic of some other Christmas cards which may vaguely be classified as political,[1] but in no sense partisan, such as the Cabinet Room at 10 Downing Street (its peacefulness increased by the total absence of the Cabinet!) or patriotic symbols and verses on American, particularly wartime, Christmas cards.

INSIGNIA OF OFFICE.
"WARRENTED.
·TO BE USED WITH GREAT CARE.
FOR EXTERNAL APPLICATION ONLY.

ODE TO THE
"SPECIALS."

In Trafalgar Bay where the Frenchmen lay,
A Hero was Nelson there!
But nothing was he tho' King of the Sea,
To the Kings of Trafalgar Square!
With Jack on the watch and with battened hatch,
There France in its pride was quashed,
Washed in the wave where they found a grave—
But they baton'd 'The Great Unwashed'!
Then surely the fame of Nelson's name
The 'Specials' have right to share:
"He won the day in Trafalgar Bay,
But They(?) in Trafalgar Square!"

With Best Wishes for a Specially Jolly Christmas

Fig. 18. An unusual and rare Christmas card issued by Angus Thomas, London, after the famous demonstrations in Trafalgar Square (1887).

An impressive 8-by-10-inch Christmas card was sent to their friends by the Maharaja Rana and the Maharani of Jhalawar in recent times (Christmas, 1930), commemorating the Indian Round Table Conference of that year. The cover of the folder bears the map of India and the Malay States. Inside a large, full-page photograph shows the great

[1] The card published in the 1860's in Richmond, Virginia, with the verses—

" Anathema on him who screws and hoards,
Who robs the poor of wheat, potatoes, bread ;
On all his gains may withering blights descend—
On body, bones, on intellect and head "

may have been sent to people thought to be suitable at Christmas, New Year or St. Valentine's Day, but cannot be considered a greeting card in the ordinary sense.

Conference in session. The central figures can be seen even before unfolding the card through a cut-out window in its cover. The sentiment is printed in gold :

> " The honour'd gods plant love among us,
> Fill our large temples with the shows of peace,
> And not our streets with war,"

a motto without direct reference to Christmas or politics, but truly in the spirit of both.

WARTIME
Christmas Cards

NOTHING is further from the traditional spirit of the Christmas card than war and " militarism ", and yet the recent devastating wars saw a great increase in the volume of Christmas cards. Families and friendships were forcibly broken up and dispersed. People often had to spend Christmas in circumstances which were in sharp contrast to all that was associated with this season in their memories of the past. The number of " absent friends " was greater than ever before, and the un-Christmaslike surroundings made people wish more than ever to grasp at little cheerful trivialities. Even in the grimmest years of the total struggle, the pictures and texts rarely carried on the fighting, but rather concentrated on the sentimental and peaceful recollections of Christmas meetings in the past, or looked forward to the same in the future. The enemy and the blood and sweat of the life-and-death struggle were tacitly ignored in the majority of wartime Christmas cards in much the same way as they were in the popular marching songs. If and when Christmas cards referred to the war directly, this was done in most cases lightly or pointing to the humorous and grotesque instead of its horrible aspects. A good example of this is the so-called " Hooverised Xmas Greeting ", a best-selling American card in 1918, the last year of the First World War. Published by the Campbell Art Company this card was produced very " poorly " (in the same mock, cheap manner as some Victorian cards entitled " Hard Times " used to be in the 70's and 80's) in red ink printed on cheap grey boards and tied up with ordinary string, described on the card as " camouflaged ribbon " (Plate 199). The words " This is holly " and " This is mistletoe " printed on the card point to two strictly rationed specimens of the respective evergreens, and underneath the " fowl " is described as " a Bluebird ". The sentiment inside the folder reads :

" I've Hooverised on Pork and Beans
And Butter, Cake and Bread,

I've cut out Auto-riding
And now I walk instead ;
I've Hooverised on Sugar,
On Coal and Light and Lard,
And here's my Xmas Greeting
On a Hoover Xmas Card.

" I wish you a very M.C. and H.N.Y."

Amongst wartime cards there are many more cartoons than on ordinary peacetime cards. They were usually designed on the fronts by often non-professional designers caricaturing camp scenes and anecdotes, self-irony, new elements of scenery and the " queer " appearance and behaviour of the " natives ". Wartime cards are too recent to justify detailed study in this book, but it is interesting to compare a few examples with older Christmas cards depicting military life in times of peace. The pictures on these relied mainly on the colour and grandeur of uniforms of the olden days, the impressive six-foot Grenadier or mounted Lifeguardsmen, the attraction of the busby and the military band or the extensive moustache of " the gallant soldier " of the American Civil War, or the comic aspects of the unprofessional appearance of the " carpet knights ", i.e. the Home Guards of the same period. Some romantic cards pictured the lonely lancer pensively dreaming of home with a " Bright and Merry Christmas " written in the snow at his feet, or, mounted, picking mistletoe with his lance (Plate 200). Actually, in some recent wartime cards the peacetime glory of colourful parade uniforms reappeared. Regimental cards often included two pictures side by side : one of a soldier some 100 years earlier, and the other a private of the regiment of that time in khaki. A humorous card of this type shows the sentry of the Royal Welsh Fusiliers in the battle-dress of 1917, when the card was published, talking to the ghost of a predecessor in the full-dress uniform of the Welsh Fusilier of 1742. The soldier of 1917 shouts out : " I say, mate, you'd better keep your lurid hat down ; also your blanketty meat-chopper ! " (Plate 197).

Tanks, aeroplanes, air raids and balloons, gas-masks and U-boats—in fact, all modern devices of war—often appear on wartime Christmas cards in this same spirit.[1]

Perhaps it is fitting to conclude this brief chapter with a card published by the youngest Service, the Royal Air Force, in 1942. This card, also from Queen Mary's collection, is a folder with the familiar " *Per Ardua ad Astra* " crest of the R.A.F. on its cover. Inside a photograph of a fighter plane is seen high in the sky. Opposite it appears a poem by John Gillespie Magee, Jr., who was killed in action on December 11th, 1941, aged nineteen. He was an American volunteer to the Royal Canadian Air Force, serving in England. His poem reads :

" Oh, I have slipped the surly bonds of earth
    And danced the skies on laughter-silvered wings ;
Sunward I've climbed, and joined the tumbling mirth
    On sun-split clouds—and done a hundred things
You have not dreamed of—wheeled and soared and swung.
    My eager craft through footless halls of air.
Up, up the long, delirious, burning blue,
    I've topped the wind-swept heights with easy grace
Where never lark or even eagle flew—
    And while with silent, lifting mind I've trod
The high, untrespassed sanctity of space,
    Put out my hand and touched the face of God."

[1] The majority of wartime cards in this volume are reproduced from Queen Mary's collection. Several large albums are entirely filled with these interesting wartime cards selected by her for preservation from the vast numbers she received during the last two wars from members of all Services on all fronts as a mark of their loyalty and affection. These Christmas cards were but one characteristic sign of " the new, direct relationship between the Throne and every individual and household in the realm ", as was truly said recently in a leading article,—a relationship established by King George V and Queen Mary by a " real warmth of heart and devotion to the welfare of their subjects ". Thus these cards are documents not only in the history of Christmas cards, but of a wider historial significance.

SENTIMENTS
and their Writers

T O a sophisticated minority, the sentiment, i.e. the verse or motto, of the Christmas card has always been of no importance—even during the reign of Queen Victoria. To those who sought the highest aesthetic standard of contemporary decorative art in the Christmas card, the often naïve poems and clumsy rhymes must have been superfluous, if not deterring. " It is obvious that for the sake of their literature no collection would be worth making ", wrote Gleeson White.

But to the far greater majority, who with minute care and utmost circumspection chose the " most appropriate " card—that is, the card with the most appropriate subject and illustration—and to whom the right card for the right person was of such importance, the sentiment cast, as it were, quite a decisive, if not the decisive vote. It may well be that one of the attractions of a Christmas card is its " impersonality ", expressing in an accepted form a conventional greeting, acceptable as such to a great many people who might be embarrassed by a more personal outburst of individual affection. The very fact that it is printed obviates the too personal element and enables the sender to choose within this limitation the appropriately affectionate card and sentiment without any inhibitions. This explains the care and thought put into the selection of Christmas cards and their sentiments by nearly all in the last century. Queen Victoria, who not only " gave her name to the age ", but was in most of her habits its " faultless embodiment ", frequently commented on a well-chosen Christmas card, and chose hers with deliberation, with attention fairly divided between subject, picture and sentiment. It would be wrong, however, to imagine that the emphasis on the sentiments has passed away with the Victorian Era. On the contrary, most of the biggest and most successful American publishing houses owe their initial popularity to their recognition of the fact that the general public reads and considers the sentiment of each card as much as anything else. The A. M. Davis Company, the

Gibson Art Company, Rust Craft, Buzza and Volland, as well as many others, began their careers at the beginning of the century by producing smaller or larger sets of cards which were at the beginning practically confined to text, in verse or prose, and seldom decorated except by a few leaves of holly or an ornamental border. Even to-day prominent men of the creative and advertising departments of these big American houses are unanimous in their opinion that " the sentiment on the card sells it ". E. D. Chase, for example, clearly states : " Ask any dealer what makes a card a success, and he will unhesitatingly say—' the wording '."[1]

Some attention, therefore, should be paid to Christmas card sentiments. They have the same interest as have many other popular rhymes and sayings which have been adopted and handed down by generations of men and women, who freely changed and adapted them and often still recite them to-day, though their authors have long since sunk into oblivion. The fact that a considerable percentage of the old and new Christmas card sentiments were written not by celebrated " professional " poets, not even by poetic failures (as is often thought to have been the case), but by honest to goodness amateurs, from a

[1] Most British and American Christmas card publishers assure us that they read every single sentiment received by them from members of the public. They must. Sometimes the best—that is, most popular—sentiment of the year arrives in the same inconspicuous envelope which contains others which are quite useless. " It's like hunting for gold ", says Mr. Chase. " Several batches may not reveal a single thing worth reading twice ; then, again, some evening one or more nuggets greet the eye ! " Mr. Fred Rust, the founder of the Rust Craft Publishers, Boston, wrote and printed an amusing set of rhymes to advise Yuletide poets " how to do it ", or, rather, " how not to do it " :

"Don't write so many verses to friends now ' far away ',
For many greeting cards are sent to those we see each day !
A word that's often overworked has just three letters, ' too ',
And another just as trite, I'm sure, is the little word ' anew ' !
The phrase ' my friend ' you use too much, the same is true of ' my dear '.
To everyone you can't wish ' health and wealth and a prosperous year ' !
And ' fond and true ', ' without alloy ', ' old pal ', ' your natal day ',
' This birthday is a milestone ' are decidedly *passé* !
Don't start a verse like this, ' I've tried to think of something new ',
Nor ' If I could only have my way, I know what I should do ' !
In fact, in writing greetings, just say the things you'd say
In writing notes to those you like to greet them on Christmas Day !
And don't be too poetical, be simple as can be,
For those who buy the greeting cards are just like you and me ! "

professional point of view, only adds to their interest in another aspect.

One of the most popular and prolific of the Victorian Christmas card sentiment writers, almost a professional in this particular brand of seasonal poetry, was a rather shy and reserved woman, Miss Helen Marion Burnside. A charming newspaper article claimed for her that which her public and old Christmas card publishers had granted to her, the " Poet Laureateship of Christmas cards ". Miss Burnside, who was born in 1843 at Bromley Hall, Middlesex, became totally deaf at the age of twelve following a severe attack of scarlet fever, and was educated privately. She is said to have written about 6,000 Christmas card sentiments and birthday verses for British and American publishers, besides stories for the *Girl's Own* and the *Woman's Magazine*, lyrics set to music and a volume of verses called *Driftweed*. As a regular " Sunday painter ", she used to exhibit at the Royal Academy and is said to have been a clever needlewoman. Her sentiments were usually signed either fully or by her initials, " H.M.B." Another early and popular sentiment writer for both British and American Christmas cards was Eliza Cook. She was a regular poetess of the *Daily Dispatch*, London, from 1836, signing her contributions, both for the paper and for Christmas cards, " E." or " E.C.", and later by her full name. Frances Ridley Havergal, whose expensively produced volumes of poetry entitled *Life Mosaics* and *Life Chords* were illustrated by that rather amateurish Christmas card artist, Helga von Cramm, wrote a great number of religious sentiments in the mid-Victorian manner. Judging from the number of cards with their sentiments preserved in surviving family albums, popular Victorian and Edwardian Christmas card poets were also Warwick Armstrong, E. H. Bickersteth, C. Bingham, Phillips Brooks, S. K. Cowan, F. Davis, H. Van Dyke, E. J. Ellis, J. and F. Goddard, E. E. Griffin, E. Hooper, E. Hardy, F. Langbridge, R. E. Lonsdale, S. C. Lowry, J. W. Meek, Charlotte Murray, James Whitcomb Riley, F. Rochat, Emily Sélinger, E. B. Snow, C. Thaxter, F. E. Weatherly, K. S. Wiggin and others.

But, of course, the great majority of the sentiments of old Christmas cards are anonymous in a full sense. The American experiment shows that the public really prefer them so. At the beginning, names or initials of the writers used to be printed under the verses, but, as E. D. Chase states, " this courtesy was soon discontinued at the request of the public, although this same public accepts a few authors whose names are well known ". This is a return to the original idea : the sentiments were seldom if ever signed by the name of their author in the 60's, and it was not before the late 70's, when publishers wanted to outbid each other with exclusive attractions of their cards, that the sentiment writer's signature became a regular feature on Christmas cards. This was the time when High Churchmen were asked to follow the example of the Bishop of Exeter, who wrote regularly for cards, and Tennyson was offered 1,000 guineas for a few stanzas which could be used on Christmas cards.

Some of the most successful sentiments were the results of combined efforts, and sometimes traditional carols or ballads were modified to suit the purpose of a Christmas card. Some sentiments are in no way related to the pictorial subject of the card ; others were, in fact, written for it. On one of Kate Greenaway's charming cards of a little girl, for example, the rhyme reads :

> " I send the sweetest maid
>   With letter unto thee
> Of Christmas greeting on the seal,
>   ' Remember me.'
> " So sweet is she, my friend,
>   I'm more than half afraid
> That you'll forget me and will think
>   But of the maid ! "

On another, showing a boy in green costume knocking on a door :

> " Don't think me bold
> But I've been told
> A Mistletoe is hanging here ;
> And not a miss
> " A Christmas kiss
> Would be to me dear ;
> So ope' the door and let me take
> And give a kiss for Christmas sake ! "

Quite a different kind of Christmas visitor was depicted on an American card, but apparently made for British consumption in the 80's. It featured a fat late-Victorian stockbroker dancing on the tips of his toes, and not only bewhiskered, but bewinged as an angel. With both hands pressed to his heart, he sings, according to the sentiment :

> " I hope you will not think it strange,
> If I fly from the Stock Exchange,
> To bring to you the news surprising,
> That all the New Year bonds are rising ! "

The following are typical Christmas card sentiments, though selected at random from British and American cards ranging from 1860 to 1930 :

> " A happy, happy Christmas,
> A merry, bright New Year,
> How sweet the kind old greeting,
> To every heart and ear."
>
> (From a Mansell card of 1860.)

> " Oh, yes, well do I remember
> Your joyful voice and heartfelt glee ;
> Accept, then, in this bleak December,
> A merry Christmas, dear, from me."
>
> (From a lacy, gold and white card with oval border for mirror or photograph, 1860-70.)

> " Though times and seasons ever change,
> And friends grow scarce and few ;
> May each succeeding Christmas bring
> Fresh hopes and joys to you."
>
> (From a valentine-type scented card, 1870's.)

> " Hark the word
> By Christmas spoken—
> Let the sword
> Of war be broken."

" Let the wrath
    Of battle cease—
Christmas hath
    No word but—Peace."
    (Sentiment by Eden Hooper on an Eyre
    and Spottiswoode card of the 1870's.)

" Though to the eye
    There seems no meeting,
Though to the ear
    No word is spoken,

" Yet heart to heart
    Will go in greeting,
And *this* shall be
    The silent token."

" *This* " refers to a red rose on one and a mistletoe scrap on another copy of the charming, valentine-type Christmas card of the early 70's. (According to the vocabulary of the language of flowers, a red rose means : " *I love* " and mistletoe " *To surmount all difficulties* . . . ".

" Peace and love and joy abide
    In your home this Christmas tide."
                                            (1880's.)

" A happy Christmas to my Friend,
    And countless Blessings, without end."
                                            (1878.)

" Ah ! to-day I'm vainly longing
    Just to clasp your hand in mine,
While I wish you ' merry Christmas ',
    As we've done so oft lang syne ;

" But my thoughts go out to greet you
    For no absence can divide
Hearts so warmly pledged for meeting
    'Neath the spell of Christmastide."
    (A sentiment by H. M. Whitlaw of the 1880's.)

" Notwithstanding we are parted,
    Yet my thoughts are oft with thee,
And I hope if God so wills it
    That I soon thy face may see.

" In the meantime I am asking
    That we each may trust His will ;
And that He in us may fully
    All His purposes fulfil ! "
    (Sentiment by Charlotte Murray of the 1880's.)

" Remember, remember !
Thus carols December,
    And do not forget Christmas
      Greetings to send ;

" Unlimited pleasure,
    And joy beyond measure,
      Is found in thus saying,
      ' Heaven bless you, my friend '."
        (Anonymous, 1876.)

" You will love old Christmas dearly
If he brings, of blessings, merely
Half, now wished by—yours sincerely."
      (S. K. Cowan, 1880's.)

" Some guide the brush, and some the pen,
    Some sing in chorus high ;
I beg a plume from every wing,
    But cannot learn to fly ;
Yet well I know my Christmas wish
    Is just as fond and true
As Art or Pen could e'er express,
    Because inspired by you."
      (Anonymous sentiment from an
      Australian card published in 1884.)

SENTIMENTS AND THEIR WRITERS

"A Happy Christmas!
To thee my wishes wing their eager flight
Swift as my messenger, and not less bright."

(U.S.A., 1877.)

"We wish Merry Christmas and Happy New Years
To friends near and far in Life's race.
May we find in most seasons much gladness, few tears,
As time travels onward aspace."

(Anonymous sentiment on a Louis Prang card of 1875.)

"Christmas comes! While you are sleeping,
In the holy Angels' keeping,
He around your bed is creeping,
And within the curtains peeping,
Leaving for all good girls and boys
Such merry games, and pretty toys."

(Prang, 1878.)

"We have waited
For thy coming,
Although brief must be
Thy reign,
Father Christmas,
Bright and Cheery,
Welcome, Welcome!
Once again!

"Merry Christmas!
Happy Christmas!
Blessed, holy,
Christmas-tide!
When the spirit
Of the Season,
Sitteth by
Each fireside!"

(American sentiment by A. H. Baldwin, 1880.)

" We seem too busy every day
To say the things we want to say ;
Our deepest thoughts we seem to hide
Until we reach the Christmas-tide.
'Tis then we send to friends again
In happy words the Old Refrain—
' A Very Merry Christmas '."

(U.S.A. sentiment, 1920's.)

" Never a Christmas morning,
Never the Old Year ends,
But somebody thinks of somebody,
Old days, old times, old friends ! "

(U.S.A. 1920's.)

" Everybody in our house wishes everybody in your house
A Merry Christmas."

(Sentiment by N. F. Bickford in 1912.)

" Only a simple greeting,
But it brings a wish sincere
For the happiest kind of a Christmas
And the finest sort of a year."

(1920's.)

" It's an old, old wish
On a tiny little card,
It's simply ' Merry Christmas ',
But I wish it awfully hard."

(1910's.)

Christmas card sentiments, however, were not necessarily written in verse. Perhaps " the biggest selling sentiment ever made " was a prose text printed with only a frame of holly leaves in black, green, red and gold. It was written by H. Van Dyke and was one of the first great successes of the A. M. Davis Co. I am quoting it as the conclusion of this chapter and book :

> " I am thinking of you to-day because it is Christmas, and I wish you Happiness. And to-morrow, because it will be the day after Christmas, I shall still wish you Happiness ; and so on clear through the year."

ALLEN FREUNDEN UND SAMMLERN
DEUTSCHER GRAPHIK UND BUCHKUNST
WÜNSCHT EIN GLÜCKLICHES u. ERTRAGREICHES
JAHR 1908
WALTER VON ZUR WESTEN

Fig. 19. W. von zur Westen, a distinguished German print-collector, sent this card to his collector friends for Christmas, 1907. (The charmingly "dated" drawing explains the collectors' wishes without a translation of the greeting text.)

A Short Bibliography*

" Christmas Cards and Their Chief Designers ", by Gleeson White. Extra Number of *Studio*, London, Christmas, 1894.

Vom Kunstgewand der Hoeflichkeit, by Walter von zur Westen. Otto von Holten, Berlin, 1921.

American Graphic Art, by F. Weitenkampf. New edition, revised and enlarged. The Macmillan Company, New York, 1924.

The Romance of Greeting Cards, by Ernest Dudley Chase. University Press, Cambridge, Mass., 1926.

The English Print, by Basil Gray. A. and C. Black, London, 1937.

The Victorian Sunset, by Esmé Wingfield-Stratford. George Routledge & Sons, London, 1932.

" The Paper Valentine ", and " More about the Paper Valentine ", by Mrs. Willoughby Hodgson, *Connoisseur,* Vol. LXXXIII, Nos. 329-30, London, 1929.

" Neujahrswünsche der Empire und Biedermeierzeit ", by G. E. Pazaurek. *Archiv für Buchgewerbe und Gebrauchsgraphik,* Vol. XLIII (1906).

English and Popular Traditional Art, by Enid Marx and Margaret Lambert. Collins, London, 1946.

Popular Art in Britain, by Noel Carrington. Penguin Books Ltd., London and New York, 1945.

" The First Christmas Cards ", by James Laver. *Strand Magazine,* London, 1938.

Taste and Fashion, by James Laver. Harrap, London, 1937.

Japanese Illustration, by Edward F. Strange. Connoisseur Series, G. Bell, London, 1897.

Britain's Post Office, by Howard Robinson, Cumberlege, Oxford University Press, London, New York, Toronto, 1953.

Royal Mail, The Story of the Posts in England, by F. George Kay. Rockliff, London, 1951.

A History of the Cries of London, by Charles Hindley. Second edition, Charles Hindley, the Younger. London [1885].

" Alte und moderne Neujahrswünsche und ihre künstlerische Wiedergeburt ", by R. Forrer. *Zeitschrift für Bücherfreunde,* 1899-900.

The Language of Flowers, by George Buday. G.B.'s Little Books, No. 8. Westminster Press, London, 1952.

---

* Other shorter articles and notes in Victorian and modern periodicals and newspapers, and occasional references in handbooks and dictionaries, unfortunately, cannot be listed here, but some are referred to in the footnotes. Books published in or after 1947, when this book was written, are included for the benefit of those who want to read more about the subject.

A SHORT BIBLIOGRAPHY

" Christmas Cards ", by W. Turner Berry and Michael Gifford. *Printing Review*, Vol. III, 1933.

" The Nineteenth-century Chromolithograph ", by Nicolette Gray. *Architectural Review*, Vol. LXXXIV, No. 503, October, 1938.

" A Christmas Card Museum ", by T. W. Wilkinson. *Cassell's Magazine*, London, 1910.

" Christmas Card Poets ", by W. J. Wintle. *Windsor Magazine*, London, 1896.

" A Chat with a Great Collector " and " Christmas Cards ", by V. C. Feesey. *Our Home*, London, 1910 and 1911.

Christmas Cards of Long Ago, by L. F. Strongitharm. *Bazaar*, Vol. CXV, London, 1926.

" The Story and Origin of Christmas Cards ", by G. H. S. *Illustrated London News*, Christmas Number, 1938.

Punch's History of Modern England, by Charles L. Graves. Cassell, London, 1921.

English Illustration : The Sixties, 1857–70, by Gleeson White. Archibald Constable & Co., London, 1897.

Children's Books in England, by F. J. Harvey Darton. University Press, Cambridge, 1932.

English Book Illustration, 1800–1900, by Philip James. Penguin Books, London and New York, 1947.

Compliments of the Season, by L. D. Ettlinger and R. G. Holloway. Penguin Books, London, 1947.

A History of Children's Books, by Percy Muir. Batsford, London, 1954.

A History of Valentines, by Ruth Webb Lee. *Studio* Publications, Inc., New York, 1952.

A Righte Merrie Christmasse !, by John Ashton. The Leadenhall Press, Ltd., London, and Charles Scribner's Sons, New York, 1886.

The Story of the Christmas Card, by George Buday. Odhams Press, 1951.

" The Geography of Christmas Cards " (*Geographical Magazine*, London, December, 1948), " The Story of the Christmas Card " (Christmas Number, *London Calling*, B.B.C., London, 1950), " My Christmas Card Collection ", *John o'London's*, London, November 23, 1951.

APPENDICES

THE following lists of artists, writers and publishers are the results of years of research and are included to help collectors and others. No enumeration of such extensive and essentially anonymous material can claim to be comprehensive, so the lists must be taken as representative but not exhaustive, i.e. based on the Christmas card collections to which I had access, including my own, possibly the largest single collection of old cards today. This should be noted particularly in respect of more recent cards, their artists, writers and publishers, whose production is really outside the scope of this book and mentioned only accidentally.

I have had also to exclude reproductions, Old Masters and quotations from the classics, although it would be interesting sometime to explore which of these were particularly preferred at times.

If and when dates are included after names, they refer to the years as far as I could trace during which Christmas cards were produced and *not* the lifetime of the firm or individual. "Modern" stands for 1930's-1950's, and of course does not necessarily indicate "contemporary" idiom. I have tried to avoid aesthetic evaluation and have concentrated on contemporary references whenever possible and my comments endeavour to assist the collector to identify the particular card, artist or publisher.

A List of
Artists and Designers

For full titles of publishers given in abbreviated forms—see pp. 262-282.

R. J. ABRAHAM (H.&F. Tuck, 1881), " The Recorders of the Past and Coming Year ", set of two folding cards, "admirable classic designs of figures", Fourth Prize winners Tuck 1880 Competition.

W. G. ADDISON (Nister; Griffith Farran, 1880). Landscapes, flowers, trees.

Daniel AIKMAN (1840's). Said to have engraved on copper an early Christmas card with a Scottish motto.

Mrs. C. S. AINSLIE (S. Hr., 1880's). Winner of a £20 Prize in 1881.

I. K. AÏVASOVSKY (1890-1900). Russian?

Cecil ALDIN (1915). Comic dog designs. Aldin was invited to do stage designs for the *Good Old Days* at the Gaiety Theatre in 1925.

Francesca ALEXANDER (1880's).

Andrew ALLAN, Glasgow (1896). Hon mention, *Studio* Competition.

T. Herbert ALLCHIN (H.&F., Tuck, 1880). £50 prize-winner at H.&F. competition with design of birds and wild roses, 1881; also second prize with butterflies, wild flowers and bird subjects at Tuck's Competition.

Helen ALLINGHAM (*née* Patterson), (1880-90).

Edith A. ANDERS (1910-20).

Alfred G. ANDERSON, (Buzza, U.S.A. 1915—). Head of Art and Design Section of the Buzza Co.

Stanley ANDERSON, R.A., R.E. (Modern, private).

Will ANDERSON (1880-90). Landscapes.

R. ANDRÉ (S.P.C.K., Castell, 1880's). Pigs riding bicycles, etc.

Edith ANDREWS (Tuck, 1930's). " . . . The Queen and the Princess Royal have chosen . . . garden pictures—both are by Edith Andrews " (*Daily Telegraph*, 1934).

Edward W. ANDREWS (H.&F., 1880's).

Ellen J. ANDREWS (H.&F., 1881). Winner of a smaller prize.

Henry ANELAY (S.Hr., 1881). A set of three religious cards.

Helen C. ANGELL (1880). Dead birds lying on their backs amongst autumn leaves, etc.

R. S. ANGELL (1890's). First Prize, *Studio* Competition : wintry landscape.

Fred. APPLEYARD (M.W., 1895). " A young South Kensington artist." Illustrated "Literary" Series of that year in red and black. " They are as dainty as can well be," wrote *The Artist* (December, 1895).

E. A. ARNOLD (1895).   Second Prize, *Studio* Competition.

Harry ARNOLD (E.&S., M.W., S.Hr., H.&F., 1880's).   £75, Third Prize at S.Hr. and a £25 prize at H.&F. competitions.—Snowballing, carol singers, boys and girls with holly branches, etc.

S. A. ASHWORTH (S.Hr., 1881).   Lichens, ferns.   (Winner of smaller prizes.)

E. Merton ATKINS (and his wife, G.G.A.) (Savory, etc., 1894-20's).   Hand-painted birds, flowers.

Emily A. ATTWELL (1896).   Hon. Mention, *Studio* Competition.

Mabel Lucie ATTWELL (1920's).   " Chubby-legged, round-eyed children " and " cuddlesome babies " (*Daily Sketch*, 1924).

AUBERT (De La Rue, 1870-80).   General decoration of De La Rue cards.

Georges AURIOL (French, 1900's).   Figures in colour lithography.

Paul AVRIL (Paris, 1890's)

A. W. B.   Biblical subjects.

C. B.   Wintry landscapes with figures.

E. B. (1885).   Seascape, moon.

F. B. (or E. B. ?).   Boy jockeys.

F. B. (Prang, U.S.A.), (Fidelia Bridges).

E. P. B. (S.H.&Co., 1886).   (E. P. Bucknall ?).   English cathedrals.

U. B. (M.W., 1870-80).   The shepherds, somewhat resembling Crane's and Stacy Marks's manners.

L. F. B. (Faudel Phillips, 1885).

W. G. B. (W. G. Baxter).

G. W. BADDELEY (Modern).

J. BADELEY (Modern).

B. P. (Lord Baden-Powell) (1930's).   Pen-and-ink.

E. A. BAILY (Tuck, 1881).   Studies of owls won Seventh Prize at Tuck Competition.

George BAIN (Modern).   Designer of Gaelic text and Celtic ornament cards.

Miss BALFOUR (Tuck, 1881).   Robins, owls, elves.

F. H. BALL (1896).   Hon. Mention, *Studio* Competition.

Wilfrid Williams BALL, R.E. (S.Hr.&Co., 1881-6).   Etchings, including " Up Stream ", " Below Bridge ", " Oxford ", " Cambridge ", etc., sets. In 1885 miniature sketch-book Christmas cards with facsimile water-colours and alternative text pages. Subjects: " Epping Forest ", " Burnham Beeches ", " Richmond ", " Hampton Wick ", " Windsor ", " Putney "; also similar facsimile water-colours as if on an easel. See pp. 72-3.

M. F. (or E. ?) BALLACHEY (H.&F., 1880's).   A smaller prize at 1881 Competition.

N. BALSTONE (Modern).

J. Edward BARCLAY (H.&F., 1880's). "The popular portrait-painter of New York " (G. W.). Floral subjects; also flowers and crosses. Winner of £50 Prize at H.&F. Competition in 1881, with rather badly drawn yellow roses, heartsease and vignetted landscape card.

S. BARHAM (C. W. Faulkner, 1920's).

E. (Emily) BARNARD (Tuck, 1880-90's). Sailor boy of " H.M.S. Britannia". In 1887 Tuck produced her " Lilian ", " Gladys ", " Eleanor " and " Florence " designs on porcelain.

Allan BARRAUD (H.&F., 1881). £50 Prize at 1881 Competition. In 1886 Tuck included four of his " choice sepia sketches " in the Mizpah series.

Adam BARTSCH (Vienna). Engraving of children and big dog, after Jordaens, made as a personal plate for the New Year, 1789, by the later famous author of the *Peintre Graveur.*

Hanns BASTANIER (Berlin, 1912-3). Delicate etchings.

Brainard BATES (Davis, U.S.A., 1915-30). " Head of Creative Department. This Department has to originate over 2,000 items each year " (Chase)

W. H. BATLEY (H.&F., 1880's). £50 Prize at 1881 Competition.

W. G. BAXTER (M. W. Gray, 1880-90). Cartoons, usually pen-and-ink.

A. W. BAYES (S.Hr., 1881). Winner of a £20 Prize.

F. BAYROS (Vienna, 1900's). Personal card.

J. T. BEADLE (J. Haworth, 1917). Designer of " Writing Home " card: soldiers in trenches at fronts in France during World War I (Plate 198).

K. L. BEARD (1895). Hon. Mention, *Studio* Competition, 1895.

Aubrey BEARDSLEY (1890's). " . . . . capped by the stately *Christmas Card* of the Madonna and Child, lifted the new magazine [*The Savoy*] into the rank of the books of the year " (A. Beardsley, The Man and his Work by Haldane Macfall, London, 1928).

PRINCESS BEATRICE (Private, 1902).

Marie von BECKENDORFF (Tuck, 1884-9).

J. Carroll BECKWITH (Prang, U.S.A., 1884).

Cuthbert BEDE (Rev. Edward Bradley). The author of " Verdant Green " 1853-6; " Funny Figures " 1868, etc., said to have designed a Christmas card in 1842 (?), which was issued by Messrs. Lambert, who did the lithographic work for him, for general sale in 1847.

Jean van BEERS (1890's). Elegant end-of-century designs of fashionable men and women, usually in evening dress; also some comic and " daring " designs of similar types (Colour Plate XIII b).

K. H. BELFORD (S.Hr., 1881).

R. Anning BELL (Bartlett, U.S.A., 1900's).

C. H. BENNETT (Goodall, 1860–70's). G. White reproduced in the *Studio* (1894) eight of Bennett's early designs. " None of these cards appears to have survived in the original ", says the *Illustrated London News*, Christmas Number, 1938, which is not quite correct. The author of this book possesses several of them, but they are certainly very rare. (See Colour Plate IV b.)

H. (Harriet) M. BENNETT (or BENNET). Winner of one of two £100 Prizes in S.Hr. 1881 Competition. According to Sir Adolph Tuck's recollections, won the firm's £50 prize at their first competition. Queen Victoria was very pleased with the card and sent for the address of the artist, and she wrote a congratulatory letter to her; " . . . Each year the Royal Lady insisted upon having Miss Bennet's work for her card. Indeed, that artist, who is still painting, has also found great favour with Queen Alexandra " (*Evening News*, November 28th, 1921).

Miss BENNETT (H.&F., 1886). " A tiny set of wee people " (G. W.).

C. M. BERESFORD (S.Hr., 1880's). A set of Neapolitan figures: girl with tambourine, boy with clarionette, child with fruit, won a smaller prize in 1881.

Frank E. BERESFORD (Modern).

Joseph BERGLER (Rome, Prague, 1806-28). See Plate 13.

G. BICKHAM (1700's). Engraver represented on *quodlibet*. See Plate 10.

R. J. BIDDLE (H.&F., 1881).

John R. BIGGS (Modern). See Fig. 12 and pp. 139-40.

P. J. BILLINGHURST (1890's). See Plate 28.

F. BINDLEY (M.W., 1890-1898). Designer also of the Marcus Ward Tennyson Calendar and Shakespeare Calendar for 1896.

A. BIRBECK (H.&F., 1880's).

E. H. BIRCH (Private, 1876). Designed some of the earliest personal cards.

S. J. Lamorna BIRCH, R.A. (Modern).

Ursula BIRNSTINGL (Favil, modern).

George BISHOP (S.Hr., 1881). Girl playing violin, boy painting, etc.

Edouard BISSON (1894). End-of-century women figures.

Sam. BLACK (Toronto, Canada). Modern.

Edwin Howland BLASHFIELD (Prang, U.S.A., 1884).

M. BLATCHFORD (S.Hr., H.&F., 1880's).

Robert F. BLOODGOOD (Prang, U.S.A., 1880's).

Walter BOTHAMS (or BOTHAM) (H.&F., Tuck, 1885-95). Landscapes with figures, including " The Mizpah " Series, etc.

G. H. BOUGHTON, A.R.A. (Tuck ?, 1880's ?).

F. Cecil BOULT (Hamilton, 1897). Hunting sketches.

Alfred BOWER (H.&F., 1886). Landscapes.

ARTISTS AND DESIGNERS

Albt. BOWERS (sometimes Albert Bower) (Tuck, Marx, 1890's). A great number of landscapes, wintry and other scenes.

Fanny BOWERS (Tuck, 1890's). Six Biblical illustrations, " The Mizpah " Series, etc.

Georgina BOWERS (M.W., 1869-80). Hunting sketches. " Altogether the intention is better than the execution " says the critic of the *Art Journal* 1869; but " a bold set of Hunting Sketches . . . not unlike Caldecott's ", comments G. W.

S. BOWERS (Tuck, 1886). Richmond Park, wintry scenes.

A. L. BOWLEY (Tuck, 1920's). Snowballing, skating, children.

Thomas Shotter BOYS (Early chromolithograph landscapes. Boys, " Printseller to the Royal Family " produced the famous *Picturesque Architecture* in 1839 printed with oil inks by Hullmandel.

E. BRADLEY. See Cuthbert Bede.

C. V. BRIDGEMAN (D.&S., 1860-70's).

Fidelia BRIDGES (Prang, U.S.A., 1880's).

W. F. BRIGGS (Regimental, 1914–18). Wartime cartoon cards, printed in Paris.

Henry (Harry) BRIGHT (M.W., H.&F., 1880's; Relig. Tract Soc., 1890). Designer, amongst others, of a " Silent Songsters " series of four " dead birds lying on the ground with natural backgrounds " (robin in snow, bullfinch, goldfinch, and blue-tit) cards, to quote a contemporary advertisement.

G. BRINSLEY (Le Fanu) (H.&F., 1881). Four seasons subjects, etc.

Ella BRISON (Volland, U.S.A., 1900-10). " Amongst the best in U.S.A." (Chase.)

H. M. BROCK (Private, 1895-1900).

C. E. BROCK (1890's).

Bill BROWN (Rust Craft, U.S.A., 1920—).

C. BROWN (1880's). Large floral cards.

Paul BROWN (U.S.A.). Modern, private.

Peter BROWN (Military, 1914–18).

Gordon BROWNE (D.L.R., 1880). Squirrels. " The Son of ' Phiz ' and an unduly neglected artist " according to Percy Muir.

[Alfred] BRYAN (H.&F., 1890). Political figures, such as Gladstone, Chamberlain and Randolph Churchill cartoons. See p. 191.

J. BUCKLAND-WRIGHT, A.R.E. (Modern).

GEORGE BUDAY, R.E. (Modern).

Mabel E. BUDD (1895). Hon. Mention, *Studio* Competition, 1895.

Ludwig BURGER (German, late 1850's). One of the early advertisement-combined with New Year greetings, made for Storch & Kramer, the lithographers, for 1858-9.

Sir Edward BURNE-JONES (Private, 1880's).

Joseph BURY (Tuck, 1887). Mountain and seascapes on "Gem Opal Panels with Stand-up back. A highly artistic line" according to advertisement.

A. BUSHBY (S.Hr., 1880's).

Robert William BUSS (1850's). Waits, the Yule log, etc.

M. E. BUTLER (1880-90). Flowers in vases. Probably Mrs. Butler, *née* Elizabeth Thompson, a pupil of R. Burchett at South Kensington.

Dudley BUXTON (C. W. Faulkner, 1912). Motorist designs.

W. Graham BUXTON (Washington Kell., 1897). Boats making for shore.

George BUZZA (Buzza, U.S.A., 1909—). In 1908 he and his partner, Rheem, produced posters, but after his friend's death in 1909, Buzza "drifted to the card business". His first twenty-four designs "may be classed as crude and amateurish to-day, but they were of such decided originality in design and colour that they were really innovations in the then young American card business" (E. D. Chase).

G. C. (1886, U.S.A.?) G. Clements.

H. W. C. (1880). Rather well drawn robin designs.

Randolph CALDECOTT (M.W., 1870's). See p. 137. A card drawn and sent by Caldecott to Lady Charnwood in the late 70's shows New Year in the form of a young man in dressing gown, cup of tea behind him, facing a chest of drawers on which the "topper" of peace and "a helmet of war" are exhibited. "New Year" is seen thinking hard which to wear ! (Reproduced in *Daily Mail*, December 27th, 1929.)

Isaac Henry CALIGA (Prang, U.S.A., 1884).

J. CALLOW (M.W. 1868–).

A. L. F. CARY (Military, modern).

A. M. CHAMBERS (S.Hr., 1881). Fourth prize at 1881 Competition.

Jay CHAMBERS (Bartlett, U.S.A., 1900-10).

F. T. CHAPMAN (U.S.A., 1920's). New York Public Library Exhibition of Christmas Card designs, 1922-3.

J. CHASE (Tuck, 1886). "Famous Country Churches", four designs.

Marian CHASE (S.Hr., 1881).

Jules CHÉRET (France, 1880-90). "No artist is more the object of the collector's anxious research at the present time than the Chéret of 400 *affiches*," wrote G. W. in 1894, adding that many of his cards were " curiously prophetic of his *Buttes Chaumont* posters ". Rimmel's Almanac for 1870 ", richly printed and a right good example of Art " was produced by Chéret. The subjects chosen for illustration were the heroines of the poets—Moore, Scott, Byron, Tennyson, Longfellow and Shakespeare. " The ladies are prettily drawn and coloured " *Art Journal*, December, 1869.

William CHODOWIECHI (Vienna). A copper plate engraving portraying the artist riding on an easel and blowing a trumpet, as a postman of the day.

The text, Prosit das neue Jahr, is written as a scroll coming out of the trumpet. It was made for the New Year, 1787.

Constance M. CHRISTIE (1896). Hon. Mention, *Studio* Competition, 1896.

J. S. CHURCHILL (Castell, 1880's). Floral designs. " The Peniel ", a set of silver-bevelled cards with sentiment by Canon Bell.

Sir Winston S. CHURCHILL (Modern). As it is well known, Sir Winston's favourite recreation is painting and several of his vivid landscape studies were reproduced as Christmas cards in recent years.

Charles CLARKE (Wyman & Sons, London, lithography, 1878).

W. CLAUDIUS (D.&S., 1880's).

A. M. CLAUSEN (Tuck, 1890). Triptych religious cards.

Sir George CLAUSEN, R.A. (Tuck, 1880; Nister, 1885; Griffith, 1885). Won seventh prize at Tuck Competition of 1880 with two pastoral designs.

B. CLAYTON (D.&S., 1869).

Naomi CLEMENT (Rust Craft, U.S.A., 1920's). " The coaches used so effectively on Christmas cards are made by Miss Clement " (E. D. Chase).

G. CLEMENTS (1886). Two sets of three cards each with special envelopes, entitled "Homes of English Poets ", i.e. Moore, Scott, Burns, Tennyson, etc. The cards include facsimile signatures of the poets. Publishers' name is carefully erased on all copies, but the line " No. 1419. Copyright, 1886 " indicates that the sets were published in the U.S.A.

A. G. CLIFFORD (D.&S., 1897). Drawings of children.

H. W. COLBY (Bartlett, U.S.A., 1900-10).

Charles Caryll COLEMAN (Prang, U.S.A., 1881). Winner of $500 third prize at Prang Competition of 1881.

Rebecca COLEMAN (D.L.R., 1879-83, Tuck, 1881). " Little Maidens ", " Sunbeams ", " Japanese Belles " (No. 466, 1882, see Plate 16), " Wild Flowers " (No. 503), " Elizabethan Studies " (No. 467, 1882), " Japanese Coquettes ", etc., nearly all of them heads of girls or children. The set of three " Angel Heads ", which " broke the record for popular success " (G. W.) was published by Tuck in 1881. " They are simply beautiful " wrote a contemporary critic. (Plate 191).

William Stephen COLEMAN (D.L.R., 1878-85). " Eastern Damsels " (No. 214, 1878), " Nymphs of the Grove " (No. 219, 1878), " Cupid's Gambols " (No. 174), " Youthful Graces " (No. 202), " Girlish Beauties" (No. 579), " Blowing Bubbles " of 1879?, " Harvest of Beauty " (No. 149), " Sylvan Sports " (No. 156), "At Rest " (No. 394), "By the Pool" (No. 395), "Jocund Youth" (No. 317), "Playmates" (?), " Boating ", " In the Shade " (1880), " Shell Gatherers ", " Girlish Delights ", " Dancing Girls " (No. 272), " The Bathers " (No. 468,

1882, see Plate 96), " Youthful Studies ", " Swimming Figures "
(including Nos. 132, 134, 141, 272, 306, 317, 394, 395, 414, 415,
468, 479, 514, 549, 506, 557, 567, and probably 699), etc., were the
titles of the sets, usually three designs in each. In the late 80's Nister
and Dutton jointly produced a large fan for Britain and America
respectively with Coleman's flowers, butterflies and tiny maidens,
printed in Bavaria. In the 90's Tuck produced " ' The Age of Innocence ' Portfolio . . . reproduced in Goupilgravure, direct from the
original drawings " and with the sentiment, "With kindlie Greetynges
and goode Wyshes from . . . . " printed on the cover of the " India
Proofs ". They also published three angel-heads in 1886 and postcards
with Coleman's " On Gossamer Wings " water colours in 1900.
Also two sets (four designs in each) of light, almost impressionist,
water colours of cottages in Kent and Surrey, etc., published as postcard-
size and smaller Christmas cards in 1887.

Mrs. H. COLEMAN-ANGELL (M.W., 1880's).

Franklin P. COLLIER (U.S.A., 1920). Humorous designs.

Lizbeth B. COMINS (Prang, 1887). Identical with Miss Lizbeth B.
Humphrey ?

Hugh CONCAN (Private, 1879). Humorous.

CONTINI (Tuck, 1890's). Cupid in snow.

Fred COOK (S.Hr., 1881).

A. Davis COOPER (H.&F., 1881). Winner of a smaller prize.

A. W. COOPER (H.&F., S.Hr., 1881), £50 prize at H.&F., and a smaller
prize at S.Hr. competitions in 1881.

Marjorie COOPER (Rust Craft, U.S.A., 1920's).

H. (?) CORBOULD (1850 ?).

Horatio H. COULDERY (H.&F., 1880's; S. Poulton & Sons, late 1890's).
" Orphans "—two puppies in basket with milk-bottles; kittens,
" Willoughby Pug and Pussy ". Kittens in a lady's hat design won
a £50 prize and another design a £75 prize in 1881, at the H.&F.
Competition. Geo. C. Whitney of New York co-operated with H.&F.
in publishing some of Couldery's cat designs as Christmas card booklets.

N. D. COULDERY (Tuck ?, 1890).

Frank E. COX (S.Hr., 1881), Fifth prize winner in 1881.

Hilda G. COWHAM (1896). Hon. Mention, *Studio* Competition, 1896.

Helga von CRAMM (Caswell, 1880-1900). Landscapes and flowers.

Gordon CRAIG (Bartlett, U.S.A., 1900-10).

Thomas CRANE (M.W., 1870-95). Many decorative flower and other
ornaments in what was called " semi-decorative treatment " at the end
of the century. Seldom signed, but easily recognisible cards.

Walter CRANE (M.W., 1870-95). " The Four Seasons ", 1872-3 (Plate
102); chiaroscuro Cupid designs, 1873-4; " The Return of Mr. Christ-

mas", 1875 (Dust Jacket, No. 35); kneeling Cupid and dandelion, etc., 1895, etc. See also Fig. 14 and Colour Plate VIII.

E. B. CRAPPER (C. W. Faulkner, 1920's).

Joseph CRAWHALL (Mason Swan & Morgan, Leadenhall Press, 1880-90's). Good woodcuts, revival of the chapbook style.

Marian CROFT (Tuck, 1881). Four designs of single figures of children with rich foliage for background and " the colouring, the lights and shades, are very peculiar ... indeed, we never saw sweeter cards " commented a critic in a contemporary trade paper. Seventh prize at 1880 Competition.

Alfred CROWQUILL (Goodall, 1850-72; D.&S., 1850-60's). Alfred Henry Forrester used this name jointly with his brother, Charles Robert, " one drawing, the other writing, until Charles died, when Alfred continued as an artist alone ". (Harvey Darton, p. 287.) According to Everitt " Most of the Christmas pantomimes of his time were indebted to him for clever designs, devices, and effects ". See Plate 42.

GEORGE CRUIKSHANK (Jun.) (A.S.Co., 1882; Tuck, 1886-7). Black-and-white, printed on satin, Plate 52; also four bevelled cards of coaches in snow, printed in bright colours and silver lettering, published by Tuck in the later 80's. " Turkey designs " and " Dwarfs removing Turkey " (two designs in each set) in 1886; four " Sketches of Barristers " and three " Boating incidents " in 1887.

CYNICUS (Cynicus Publishing Ltd., 1890-1910). Single cards as well as eight pages folders with often hand-coloured caricatures of surprisingly " modern " effect. " Cynicus " had his own " Limited Company " in Scotland with an office in London.

A. M. D. (1880-90). Round-shaped cards of comic frogs, etc.; also cards with owls singing, playing the violin, etc.

F. V. D. (H.&F., 1880's). Wintry landscapes with church towers, sheep, etc.

H. D. (Castell, 1880-90). Birth of Christ with angel above, distant view of Bethlehem, etc. The " Peniel " Series.

L. D (Hagelberg, 1880-90). (Lucien Davis, R.I. ?.) Landscape with cattle.

M. E. D. (H.&F., 1870-80's). Mrs. Duffield.

N. D. (H.&F., 1880-90). Imitation envelopes with flowers inside, instead of letters.

W. L. D. (H.&F., 1880's). William L. DUFFIELD.

Frank DADD (M.W , 1880's).

Sidney T. DADD (M.W., H.&F., 1884-90). Monkeys fighting parrots; dogs and squirrels; monkey and dog fighting on table, etc.

E. G. DANZIEL (1870's). Children.

F. O. C. DARLEY (U.S.A., 1860's). Possibly the designer of illustrations for Prang, see Frontispiece No. 16.

Louis DAVIS (Fitzroy, 1895). " The false naturalism that offends in most chromolithographs is here replaced by a convention that in its simplicity and dignified reticence is at least inoffensive, at its best distinctly beautiful " (*Studio*, 1895).

C. DAVISON (H.&F., 1880's). Boats.

Jane M. DEALY (D.L.R., 1876-8; H.&F., 1881-9). Mainly charming, lightly drawn, children compositions. Won two prizes at H.&F. Competition in 1881. A typical example of her cards on Plate 90 was entitled " Three Little Maids from School " (1886).

Edna Adeline DELL (Hills & Co., 1895). First prize, *Studio* Competition, 1895. (Reproduced in *Studio*, Vol. IV, No. 23.)

Thomas (Wilmer) DEWING (Prang, U.S.A., 1884).

C. DICKS (Modern). Etchings; architectural.

Herbert DICKSEE, R.E. (1890). Etchings.

Frederick DIELMAN (Prang, U.S.A., 1880's). Third prize winner, 1881, and Fourth prize winner, 1884, Prang Competitions.

Henri Patrice DILLON (France, 1890's). Women.

J. DIVEKY (Hungary, 1910's ; Switzerland, 1920's—). Pen-and-ink, and wood-engravings.

W. A. DOBSON. (Probably erroneous initials.)

W. C. T. DOBSON, R.A. (Tuck, 1881). A set of children decorating the home in the " Royal Academy " Series. Dobson was said to have drawn a card on a Bristol board and sent it to a friend in 1844. For some time it was claimed that this was " the first " Christmas card ever sent.

Catherine Sturgis DODGE (Volland, U.S.A., 1900-10).

Pauline von DOEMING (Tuck, 1884). Floral studies.

P. DOIG (C. W. Faulkner, 1920's).

(?) DOLLMAN, Jun. (Sulman, 1866). Comic pen-and-ink drawings.

A. E. S. DOUGLAS (Ackermann, 1880's). Hunting and other sporting subjects.

J. Nelson DRUMMOND (H.&F., 1886). Boats.

Paul DRURY, R.E. (Private, modern).

Victoria DUBOURG (Madame Dubourg) (H.&F., 1881). Several prizes at H.&F. Competition.

Robert DUDLEY (Goodall, 1870's?, D.L.R., 1879-85; Castell, 1886-90). Designs include a set of lovely DLR cards (No. 435, size $4\frac{7}{10}$ by $4\frac{8}{10}$ inches) of cupids sharpening arrows, etc.; figures representing " Air ", " Fire ", " Water " and " Earth " (D.L.R., 1881, size $6\frac{3}{8}$ by $4\frac{1}{8}$ inches); " Cupid's Studio " (D.L.R. 1882, No. 474, Cupids painting, drawing, taking photograph of children, while others are watching); " Garlands of the

Year ", D.L.R., 1883; Angels seated on clouds (Milton quotations on the back of cards), D.L.R., No. 628; " Processions of the Arts " (Painting, Music, Poetry), D.L.R., 1884, No. 663, size 6⅜ by 3⅞ (the same designs, as most of the other sets, also, were issued on thick gold bevelled and bronzed mounts, No. 1097, " to retail 1/6 each "); a similar set of cards of six children singers and musicians with motto " Nowell we sing, Gladness to bring " etc.; Half-figures of single, winged Archangels mounted on large, enamelled and gilt mounts (6¾ by 4¾ inches); A set of children in boat, also printed on satin (6⅛ by 4 inches) and a set of two designs : " A Sprite of the Ivy " and " A Pearl of the Mistletoe " (see Plate 35). Amongst Dudley's designs for Castell Brothers the following, well drawn comic robin and bird designs should be mentioned: Four designs (No. 501) of Chirstmas Waits, Noctes Ambrosianae, In Spring the Cuckoo, Now Boys; No. 502 of Jago, a Turkey, excites the jealousy of Othello, and illustrations in similar manner for Macbeth, Tempest and Hamlet; No. 503 Nursery Rhymes (a goose representing Little Red Riding Hood, a gallant fox the wolf, etc.); clever humanised-robin sets including No. 520 (Uncle Robin's Christmas Visit, The Kindly Robin, Robin the Mail, Friends of the Old School; No. 521 (Evenings at Home, A Winter's Tale, Nice Weather for young—Ducks); No. 522 (An Offering of Friendship, Timely Cheque, Love); No. 525: A Warm Greeting, Here's to the year that's awa, A Merry Go-Rounder; the Father Christmas sets of No. 504: "Greeting Time", "Present Time" (see Dust Jacket No. 7); etc.; No. 505: " The Temptations of Good St. Anthony-Noel ", " Old King Cole," " Robin Hood & Friar Tuck ", and " Apollo and Daphne" (see Dust Jacket No. 15). Dudley's early designs for Goodall cannot now be identified for certain, but the robin card reproduced on Plate 22 is probably his design.

Mrs. WILLIAM DUFFIELD, née Mary Elizabeth Rosenberg, usually signing as M. E. D. (S.Hr., H.&F., 1870-80's). " Well known as a water-colour painter of flowers, birds' nests, and fish " (Bryan's Dictionary of Painters and Engravers, 1893 ed.).

Wm. L. DUFFIELD (H.&F., 1881). Oblong cards with four young women skating in a row, boating, or in a deep forest, three on a swing, the fourth pushing them. (See Plate 77.)

H. BOYLSTON DUMMER (U.S.A., 1920's). Farmer types.

James DURDEN (1890's). Hon. Mention, *Studio* Competition, 1896.

Cel DÜSSER (S.Hr., 1880's). Winner of a smaller prize in 1881.

D. G. DUTTON (1890's).

Will A. DWIGGINS (Bartlett, U.S.A., 1900-10). See Fig. 7. " . . . Always direct, happy and sufficient " (Weitenkampf).

J. E. (Castell, 1890's).
K. E. (1920's).

M. E. E. (Mrs. M. E. Staples, *née* Miss M. Ellen Edwards).

L. S. E. Flowers.

Alfred EAST (Private, 1890's). Etchings.

M. Ellen EDWARDS (M. E. E.) (H.&F., 1880-90). " Maidens set in Rings and Hearts " (1881), Children figures (1882-3) ; children kneeling; at church; and " Guardian Angels " (1886), etc.

William Maw EGLEY (1848). For some time Egley's etching (see Plate 7) was thought to be " the first " real Christmas card. Photographic enlargement of the date (Plate 5) and the artist's own catalogue (p. 14) now prove that the etching was made in 1848, i.e. five years after the Cole-Horsley card.

A. ELLAM (Birn, 1880-90). Comic cards of negros skating and playing a mandoline, etc., entitled " A (n)ice Christmas Serenade ". Also " Cricket "—four " Gem Portfolios " published by Tuck in 1887.

Edwin J. ELLIS (M.W., 1870-80). A set of heads.

Frank ELLIS (Relig. Tract Soc., 1890). Booklet cards in the shape of a scallop shell.

Tristram ELLIS (Horrock, 1880-90). Etchings. See Plate 54.

Rosina EMMETT (later Mrs: Sherwood) (Prang, U.S.A., 1880-90). Winner of first prize at Prang's first Competition in 1880 and fourth prize at second Competition in 1881.

Mildred EMRA (1896). Hon. Mention, *Studio* Competition, 1896.

Marie ENDELL (Tuck, 1884). Flowers.

Edmund EVANS (1850-80's). Wood-engraver and colour-printer who engraved many of Kate Greenaway's designs for the Goodall cards, etc. See pp. 64 and 229.

Mrs. F. M. EVANS (H.&F., 1881).

A. F. (Appel, Paris, 1880's). Curious " Victorian surrealist " designs.

F. F. (H.&F., 1880's). Negro with concertina, etc.

R. W. F. (H.&F., 1880's). Seven pretty landscape vignettes.

EDWARD H. FAHEY (D.L.R., 1876-84). " Marionettes " (Series No. 162); " Divers " (No. 185); " Fruitful Branches "—unloading of a Christmas Tree in China (No. 187); " Friendly Waftings " (No. 192); " Fairy Bowers " (fairies and elves playing with flowers, No. 393); " The Magician " (No. 469); and " Finger Shadows "—remarkable sets of three varieties in each.

Robert FAULKNER (H.&F., 1890's). Children portraits.

FAUSTIN, i.e. Faustin Betbeder. Cartoons of political personalities, etc.

Frank FELLER (E.&S., 1880's). Sportsmen, sailors, policemen, soldiers.

Mrs. FELLOWES (H.&F., 1883). A set of still life " wherein a Japanese yellow ' sprinker ' vase figures prominently ". (G. W.)

Georges DE FEURE (French, 1890's). End of century women. See Plate 109.

J. FINNEMORE (Tuck, 1886-1900's). "The Gorgeous East", six designs in 1887; "The King's Card" in 1911.

Joseph FISCHER (Austria). Self portrait of the artist, head of the famous Esterházy Collections, in his studio; made as a personal New Year greeting for 1809.

Fred FITCH (1890's). Wintry landscape of "Near Battle, where William the Conqueror landed".

Martha FJETTERSTROIN (Sweden, 1890's). Hon. Mention, *Studio* Competition, 1896.

Sir W. Russell FLINT, R.A., P.R.W.A., R.E. (Modern).

Elizabeth FOLKHARD (H.&F., 1877-84). £50 prize winner at 1881 Competition.

FORRESTER. See CROWQUILL.

Birket FOSTER (B. F.) (H.&F., 1880's). "Going to Market" triptych card; a set of two cards of characteristic village children. Before 1859 when he was elected a member of the Old Water Colour Society and devoted himself exclusively to painting, Birket Foster illustrated "Christmas with the Poets", etc. for Vizetelly (see p. 63).

H. (or W. ?) Gilbert FOSTER (Wolff Davidson, 1890's). Wintry landscapes.

Marie FOUBERT (C. W. Faulkner, 1920's). Flowers.

Georgie Cave FRANCE (Leadenhall Press, 1890's). Later, Mrs. Arthur Gaskin.

F. A. FRASER (1870's).

G. C. FRASER (H.&F., 1880's). Landscapes with mills.

Alfred FREDERICKS (Prang, U.S.A., 1880's). Third prize in 1880 and Fourth in 1881 Competitions.

Barnett FREEDMAN (Modern). Lithographs.

Miss FREEMAN-KEMPSON (H.&F., 1881). Winner of a smaller prize at Competition.

Frederick W. FREER (Prang, U.S.A., 1884).

H. FRENCH (1870-80).

W. FRENCH (M.W.). Floral designs.

Catherine FRERE (S.Hr., 1881). Winner of a smaller prize at Competition.

Edouard FRÈRE (French, 1880's). " . . . whose pictures of children are of quite immortal beauty " wrote Ruskin in 1884.

F. G. FROGGATT (1890's). Hon. Mention, *Studio* Competition, 1896.

FRÖHLICH (1880-90). Children.

C. E. G. or E. C. G. (H.&F., 1886). Probably Edwin C. Gardner. Birds, cats, also " some capital landscapes with similar initials ". (G.W.)

A. R. G. (Early private, Leicester, 1870's). A. R. Goddard ?

E. G. (H.&F., 1887). Artist of four monochrome cards depicting Trafalgar Square riots, etc. See p. 192.

K. G. (Kate Greenaway).

Edwin C. GARDNER (S.Hr., 1881). Winner of two small prizes.

A. I. G. (Arthur J. Gaskin, A.R.E.) (1890-1910).

Georgie Cave GASKIN (Miss G. C. France, Mrs. Arthur Gaskin) (Leadenhall Press, M.W., 1890-1900). See Fig. 17.

Ignaz Marcel GAUGENGIGL (Prang, U.S.A., 1884).

Edith J. GEDGE (1890's). Hon. Mention, *Studio* Competition, 1895.

Charles M. GERE (Private, 1890's). Some of Gere's designs were engraved on wood by William Hooper.

Hector GIACOMELLI (Tuck, 1887-90). A great variety of bird designs. Giacomelli was well known for his illustrations to Michelet's " The Bird " of 1856. (L. F. Strongitharm.)

Robert GIBBINS (Modern). Wood engravings.

Edgar GIBERNE (S.Hr., 1881). Fourth prize winner in 1881.

Eric GILL (Modern). See Plate 195.

Ethel C. GILLESPY (1890's). Hon. Mention, *Studio* Competition, 1896.

L. J. GINNETT (1890's). Hon. Mention, *Studio* Competition, 1896.

A. GIRALDON (Paris, 1890's).

A. GLENDENNING, R.B.A. (H.&F., 1880's). Four small landscape designs won for him a £100 prize in 1881.

J. M. GLOVER (1890's). Hon. Mention, *Studio* Competition, 1896.

A. R. GODDARD (J.F.&Co., 1876). One of the first private card designers.

Christophine GODDARD (D.&S., 1880's). Kate Greenaway school.

John GOODACRE (Buzza, U.S.A., 1920's).

Maud GOODMAN—Mrs. A. E. Scanes (1890's). Children subjects.

Thomas GOODMAN (M.W., 1875-80). Four cards, " The Nativity ", probably by him.

C. D. van GORDER (Buzza, U.S.A., 1920's).

Fred GOUDY (Bartlett, U.S.A., 1900-10).

M. L. GOW (H.&F., 1886). Kneeling children.

C. J. GRANT (Kendrick's Almanacs for the hat or bonnet, etc., 1830's-1840's).

Alfred GRAY (Gray, 1880-1910). Mainly pen-and-ink caricatures. See Plate 108 and pp. 82, 151-2.

C. GREEN (1878 ?). " Little Jack Horner ", etc.

John GREENAWAY (1860-70's). Kate's father, a well-known wood-engraver who actually engraved his daughter's first designs on wood.

Kate GREENAWAY (K.G.) (M.W., Kronheim, Goodall, 1868-1900). Some of her unsigned cards are: Designs for " The Story of Little Red Riding-hoods " which, according to Jonathan King, " came in in 1868 " (M.W., size $2\frac{1}{2}$ by $3\frac{3}{4}$ inches each, see Plate 124 and pp. 154-6); other early cards include: a set of two designs of children sitting in meadow, talking to a snail and butterflies (M.W., size $3\frac{3}{4}$ by $5\frac{3}{16}$ inches); small blue-bordered cards of wounded robin and two wee-figures, etc. ; three designs of small red, red and green dressed figures in snowy scenes, issued in two sizes with somewhat different, three sides border designs of snowdrops, violets, holly, ivy, mistletoe, Christmas roses and narcissi, (sizes: $2\frac{7}{8}$ by $4\frac{1}{2}$, and $3\frac{1}{8}$ by $4\frac{11}{16}$ inches); " Forging the Ring " set (name assigned by C. A. Means)[1] four designs, two styles; a set of six designs identified as " Puck and Blossom " (after a book of fairy tales by Rosa Mulholland, published by M.W. in 1875, with the same designs as illustrations). Size including white, scallop-edges, $3\frac{1}{8}$ by $4\frac{5}{8}$ inches, but the oval medallions with boy and girl figures were issued also with larger borders including floral, fungi patterns and wee-people, for valentines. Six designs called by Means " Floral, Oval Vignette " set, known both in white embossed and scallop-edge (size $3\frac{7}{8}$ by $5\frac{3}{8}$) versions as well as stuck on $7\frac{1}{8}$ by $9\frac{1}{8}$ inches mounts. " Melcomb Manor " set of 6 designs. These are valentines and since two in my collection carry handwritten " February 14th, 1874 " on their reverses, they must have been published in that year or before. " Quiver of Love " set of four pages folder valentines, four designs, of, or before, 1876. (Size of pages $5\frac{1}{2}$ by $7\frac{1}{4}$ inches, including white scallop edges.) A set of four designs of young couples issued with two different wild-rose borders on three sides of the main panel.[2] Reproduced with original sketch between two finished versions on Plate 99. Two similar sets of 5 by $3\frac{1}{2}$ inches, with gold borders, with mostly single children and prominently placed verses. On one set, of three cards depicting the three ages of a little girl, the first letter of the poem is as if it was made of a blue or pink ribbon, on the other set the equally prominent initials are " composed " of tree branches, etc. Two sets (four designs in each) with—usually two—child figures, one of which is seen as incorporated in the design of initial letters beginning the accompanying verses. Sizes $5\frac{1}{8}$ by $3\frac{7}{8}$, but some of these designs, for example two girls dancing with each other, were published also without the poem on $3\frac{3}{4}$ by $4\frac{7}{8}$ inches cards. A set of girls dancing and playing in fields, pretty small, rosette bordered single cards of *c.* 4 by 3 inches. Four designs of children, boy and girl watching and feeding ducklings by a pond, three girls under a window, a boy looking out, slightly older girl and boy inspecting birds' nest which the

[1] In addition to the vague and contradictory references by contemporaries, the identification of Miss Greenaway's designs are further handicapped by the absence of serial numbers and titles on all Marcus Ward cards. The same pictures were also frequently issued with alternative wordings and sentiments suitable for Christmas, New Year, St. Valentine's Day or Birthday greetings. Thus, if and when an assigned name is established regarding a set of designs, it will be alluded to even when we are not in full agreement about dates and some other data.

[2] Means enlists this set as " Quiver of Love No. 2 ".

latter holds in his hand, and finally two lovers under floral garden-gate. G. White refers to this set as " Children by ponds ". The designs were issued singly as well as coupled (folders of twos, with verse on backs), with scallop-edge borders as well as on pretty white lace-paper mounts. I know them in three sizes: 2⅝ by 4¾, 3¼ by 5½ and 7 by 9 inches. The small version was used as their specially printed calendar for 1878 by Messrs. John Rose, tea dealers of 178-9 Shoreditch, thus it must have been published in or before 1877. " An oblong set, with processions of little people " mentioned by G. White I am now able to identify as " A Christmas Procession of Mirth and Good Cheer ", a set of four cards (one reproduced on Plate 127) described on p. 159. A somewhat similar oblong set " Robin Hood & the Black Bird, A Tale of a Christmas Dinner ", four designs, is described on pp. 158-9, and one example reproduced on Plate 130.[3] A set of gold edged, yellow cards of 3⅛ by 5 inches, with pale blue circular panel showing little girl swinging (and losing one of her shoes), etc., and another, somewhat similar set of 3 by 4⅝ inches of blue or mauve edged cards of single children with toys, butterfly, etc.— Two cards of full figures (page-boy in red holding his plumed hat in hands, and a girl holding a sealed letter) issued in sizes 3½ by 5⅛ inches and 2¾ by 4¼ inches, the latter reproduced on Colour Plate IX. Two designs issued with same blue and gold border, but with different borders, also, picturing three-quarter figures (boy in green coat making use of a door-knocker, girl wearing " Japanese " hat and muff) published in or before 1877. Single " Children in Ulsters " set of three, two girls and one boy designs, published in sizes: 3 by 5⅞ and 3⅞ by 5½ inches, with different backgrounds and margins. A set of Fairy children on flowers (pansy, peach blossoms, daffodil and primrose), surely an echo of the Dicky Doyle-Evans engravings for Allingham's In Fairyland. Four designs, two editions of 4 by 5½ (scallop-edged) and 3⅝ by 4¾ inches. A set of three hatted and muffed girls coming (front views), going (backs), and two sitting in garden chatting. Sizes of cards are 3½ by 3⅞, but the tiny pictures themselves are only 2 by 1½ inches. They were issued as calendars also for 1881, thus their date must be 1880 or earlier. Single figures of girls, one in blue with madonna-lilies behind her, another in pink with large feathered hat. Size 3 by 4¼ with white margins, the actual pictures are only 1½ by 2¾ inches. These were issued also as dance programmes, etc. Four charming designs of boy and girl representing the four seasons. In their original size (2¾ by 3¾ inches) they were issued, also, as a four-fold Calendar of the Seasons, for 1876, and, again, somewhat reduced and in the then fashionable vignetted manner, for 1882. The designs also appeared in Marcus Ward's language of flowers booklet, " Flowers and Fancies " in 1883, and the set is now usually referred to by this name. See one of the designs applied on a tab card, Plate 176. A set of four cards, somewhat unexpectedly badly reproduced, of two children on each. Published also as Calendar of the Seasons, 1877. A more ambitious,

---

[3] Sizes of these cards are given in List of Illustrations.

but again not well lithographed folder of four pages with two larger, figural and two smaller, scenery panels appeared probably in the same year.[4] Size of pages 4⅝ by 6⅜ inches. The folder contains " Bells across the snow " (on the left), and " Christmas Gifts for thee " (on the right) by Frances Ridley Havergal. These were considered the most successful sentiments of the period. G. White mentions " a set on circular panels on small cards published by Goodall ". These are, I believe, the children heads on circular (1¾ inches) and elongated panels (3 by 1¼ inches) which are also known from " Topo " by G. E. Brunefille (1874). Kate Greenaway's signed designs are, of course, easily recognised and thus it is sufficient only to mention a set of three single girl-figures, with grey-blue margins and backs (4¼ by 6 inches); the coachman waiting set c. 4¼ by 6 inches each (a girl on tiptoes throwing a kiss, boy waving a handkerchief, coachman-boy with hat and crop in hands), which with an additional design (girl throwing red roses) were also published in smaller form as Marcus Ward's Calendar for 1882; the set of two cards (6¼ by 3⅜ inches) of the garland of six slim girls with a chain of roses (1878?) the " Dainty Airs " issued both with Christmas and New Year wishes and music (6¼ by 4 inches); the pretty set of 3 square (3¾ inches) cards of children's heads on circular panels with various, lovely border designs, and " The Kate Greenaway series of Christmas Cards, No. 504 " published by Goodall in 1887 on thick gold-bevelled boards of 7⅝ by 3½ inches. These are garlands of long-frocked girls, dancing, and beautifully engraved on wood, and printed in colours, by Edmund Evans. There are 14 volumes of "Almanacks" published from 1883 to 1897 by Messrs. Geo. Routledge & Sons, and the hanging Calendars for 1884, but these do not directly concern us here.

A. GREENBANK (Washington Kell, 1897). " Sea Nymph ", fishes and an abundance of sea-weed.

Barbara GREG, R.E. (Modern).

Carl GREGORY (H.&F., 1880). Children.

Herbert GREGSON (Bartlett, U.S.A., 1908-10).

Bernard GRIBBLE (Tuck, modern). " Royal card " in 1934: Windsor Castle from the River.

Kate GRIFFITH (S.Hr., 1881). Winner of a smaller prize.

F. L. GRIGGS, R.A., R.E. (1930's).

Ernest GRISET (D.L.R., 1876-85; S. Hr., 1886-90). Characteristic of the great number of designs by this highly imaginative artist are " Pigmy Pantomimes ", D.L.R., No. 188; " Mice at Play ", D.L.R., No. 199; "Dainty Viands ", D.L.R., No. 190; each set consisting of three varieties.

[4] It was at this time that Kate Greenaway quarrelled with the publishers. Previously she used to give away drawings and rights, outright, and now she wanted to retain the copyrights and requested the return of the original drawings. These disagreements finally led to the break up of her association with the Marcus Ward firm, though it was mutually very beneficial, and prompted the new partnership with Edmund Evans and Messrs. Routledge. As it is well known the result was a long series of extremely successful books, mainly for children.

ARTISTS AND DESIGNERS

Johnny GRUELLE (Volland, U.S.A., 1910's).

S. GUNILA (Nordisk Konst, Stockholm, 1900).

E. H. (Tuck, 1886). Kate Greenaway imitations.

Philip HAGREEN (Modern). Religious.

Axel H. HAIG (1890's). Etchings.

George C. HAITÉ, R.B.A. (H.&F., Tuck, 1880-90). Landscapes.

Sydney HALL (Relig. Tract Soc., 1880's). Engravings.

Ada HANBURY (Sockl, 1880-90). Flowers.

Christoph HALLER (Nuremberg, Germany, 1813-6). See Fig. 6.

T. B. HAPGOOD (Bartlett, U.S.A., 1900's). Chiefly delightful lettering.

Emily J. HARDING (Tuck, 1880's). Four designs of heads of children (No. 2443-1886); Angel-heads with small wings (1887).

Florence HARDY (1920's). Children in fancy dresses.

Leo HARDY (Modern).

Louis K. HARLOW (Prang, U.S.A., 1890). " Voice of the Grass ", also " Haunts of Poets ", etc.

William St. John HARPER (Prang, U.S.A., 1884).

William HARRING (Prang, U.S.A.). " An Englishman and all round artist in lithography and a good colourist to boot " with whom Prang formed his lasting connection during his European trip in 1864 (E. Morrill, " Louis Prang—Lithographer ", *Hobbies*, August, 1940).

Miss HARRIS (Schipper, 1880-90). Comics; also cut out tea-table trick card.

E. H. HARRIS (Gibson, U.S.A., 1910-30).

Walt HARRIS (Bartlett, U.S.A., 1900—).

WILLIAM HARVEY (1829). Designer of the " Anniversarie " card reproduced on p. 13 (Fig. 1). Harvey was originally a wood-engraver as well as designer and a favourite pupil of Bewick in Newcastle. In 1817 he came to London and after 1824 confined himself to designing for copper and wood-engravers.

Joan HASSALL, R.E. (Modern).

John HASSALL (Tuck, 1910's). Postcard size cards in the style of his familiar posters.

Alice HAVERS (Mrs. Fred Morgan) (H. & F., 1880-91; Tuck, 1881-7; Schipper 1884). " A Dream of Patience " (H. & F., 1881-2, No. 493) " an idyll set in a forest with groups, painted with Leightonesque finesse, of lovely female forms; the backs of the cards, cloud studies worthy of Turner, of early dawn and the setting sun, and cumulo-cirro banks, silver-lined by a half hidden moon—this seems to me the gem of the collection ", wrote the art critic of *Society* (August 13, 1881) after the opening of the Exhibition of Competitive Designs at the Suffolk Street Galleries, and on August 20th it was announced that " The forecast in last week's notice

230

was correct." Another large card, dated 1881, shows a couple of children amongst trees, at a picnic party (size 9 by 5¼ inches). G. White mentions a set of Fairies in Mid-air (1883), but these I am unable to trace. A set of four attractive cards of nude child figures settled on holly, etc., branches feeding birds and insects (H.&F., 1884, No. 491, W., size 4 by 6½ inches). Characteristic period ladies at windows sending letters *via* birds (H.&F., No. 490, W., 1884). A three-fold card, " The Child Jesus " produced by J. F. Schipper in two sizes (4 7/16 by 5 7/16 and 7 by 8 7/16 inches, 1884), " a genuine Christmas card of high merit as a work of art, and especially admirable as to its Christian significance " of six gold or silver bordered compositions. H.&F., No. 661: A set of two designs of (single) dreamy little girls, with a dog or kittens (size 5⅝ by 9½ inches). Kneeling and praying nude children in bed, depicted on 4¼ inches square cards with circular panels in centre (H.&F., 98 C.). Set No. 80 W. (H.&F., 1886?) pictures happily sleeping children surrounded by sprays of ivy, etc. A Madonna and Child set, see Plate 193. In 1886 Tuck produced two cards of children sleeping on pillow and bolster with white winged Guardian Angels watching and praying behind them (Tuck No. 2700, size 6¼ by 9½ inches). They were re-issued in smaller versions (No. 414, size 4⅝ by 6⅝ inches) in 1887. Similarly " The Infant Saviour and Mary " (2 designs) produced both as a simpler (No. 2725) and silver bevelled, satin tablet card versions, were reissued in 1887 as No. 457. Large cards of a boy rather timidly playing with rabbits, and another of Miss Havers' dreamy little girls playing with a small lamb (No. 589, two designs, silver block lettering and gold mounts) were published by Tuck in 1887 (sizes *c.* 9½ by 5½ inches). In the same year Angels with Doves, and a set of Shepherds were published by H.&F., who also reprinted as Christmas cards in 1891 some Havers designs, illustrating Old Songs, which she made for one of their earlier books.

William HAVICAN (Ruft Craft, U.S.A., late 1910's). Lettering.

Frank D. HAWKES (1918). See Plate 138 and p. 166.

Lorenz L. HAYD (*c.* 1702-56). Designer of Wall Calendar for 1738 (Plate 10).

E. (Edwin ?) W. HAYES (1890's). Lake with boat and swans.

Sidney HEATH (1890's). Private cards in pen-and-ink.

Ralph HEDLEY (H.&F., 1881).

Thomas HENRY (1897). First prize, *Studio* competition.

J. R. HERBERT, R.A. (Tuck, 1881). " Angels with Harps " . . . . " for which silence is the only polite comment " wrote G. W.

Hubert HERKOMER, R.A. (1880-90). Pen-and-ink drawings, usually signed. " Mummers in *An Idyl* " (1889) reproduced in the *Bazaar*, November 27th, 1926, by Mrs. Strongitharm, while James Laver published his motor car card of 1903, which is now in the Victoria and Albert Museum. (See p. 133.)

Gertrude HERMES, R.E. (Modern).

C. E. HERN (1890's). Yachts at Gravesend.

Bruno HÉROUX (Leipzig, Germany, 1904-20's). Attractive etchings of young girls and old men representing the New and old years.

Fred HINES (H.&F., 1880's; Tuck, 1897). Landscape vignettes; The Seasons. Winner of a smaller prize at H.&F. competition in 1881. Some of his pleasant landscapes were published also by Dutton, New York, in the 90's.

A. HJERSING (1910's).

Harold HODGE (1900-12). Private cards.

William J. HODGSON (H.&F., 1881-89). A great number of well drawn comic cards, usually produced also in booklet form. For example, the following were published for Christmas, 1884: " Going to Cover ", " He's Away ", " The Right Sort to Follow ", " Confound weather " (No. 478); The Hat Trick (four designs, No. 479); Lawn Tennis (four designs, No. 480); A Butterfly Chase (four designs, No. 482); Keep the Pot A-Boiling (three designs, No. 483); Tally Ho ! (No. 484); A Day with the Harriers (No. 485); The Story of a Snowball (four designs, No. 486); Mr. Verdant Green's Adventures on the Ice (four designs, No. 487).

HÖPPNER (1870-80). Tiny girl sheltering under " outsize " snowdrops; another card with little fairy-girl reading to attentive nestlings under pretty wild roses.

John Calcott HORSLEY, R.A. (Summerly's, 1843; Tuck, 1881). Designer of the first Christmas card in 1843. See Plates 1 and 2; and pp. 6-11. In 1881 Horsley made a set for Tuck's " Royal Academy Series " of cards.

T. HOSEMANN (Berlin, 1843-6). Two lithographed personal New Year cards of rather rough humour (making fun of the artist's name).

William T. HORTON (1890-1900). " Inner Circle " and " The Outer Circle " cards, printed in black and red.

W. HOUGH (S.Hr., 1881). Winner of two smaller prizes in 1881.

A. B. HOUGHTON (1870's).

Ellen HOUGHTON (M.W., 1870-80's).

T. HOURY (1890's). Hon. Mention, *Studio* Competition, 1896.

Kate A. HOWES (1895).

W. HUGHES (Schipper, 1884). A set of six floral designs on gold panels.

Wyndham H. HUGHES (Mowbray, 1880). Religious. See p. 85.

W. F. HULK (S.Hr., 1881). Landscape with cattle, etc.

Lizbeth B. HUMPHREY (Prang, U.S.A., 1880-90). Second and Third prizes, Prang's second competition, 1881.

Alfred HUNT (D.L.R., 1876-80).

Wilmot HUNT (C. W. Faulkner, 1912). Two designs of gamins at cricket and football.

PLATE 159

Little angels ringing the Christmas bells. A very pretty trick card which can be folded flat fitting into an envelope or made to stand by itself in three dimensions. If placed with a light behind the window, the effect is enhanced.

PLATE 160 Purse cards were very popular, though rather expensive, in the 1870's and early 80's. This charming purse card in the lovely snow-white embossed envelope was sent to Princess May by her mother, Princess Mary Adelaide, for Christmas, 1874. Another purse, or, rather, small wallet, card which, as it is opened, brings forward an array of cheques, banknotes, gold and silver coins, is seen in the photograph below.

PLATE 161

PLATE 162 The first page of the first album of Queen Mary's Christmas card collection. The first card on the top left hand corner is an example of the old Marcus Ward cards (4¾ by 3¼ inches), with a sentiment by Francis Davis. Queen Mary received this card when she was five years old in 1872. The other three cards on this page are all animated.

PLATE 163 A spray of lilac is the inconspicuous disguise of this animated card. The photograph shows it in its second state, when the card is extended and reversed. Note the silk roses and the cracker-like appearance of the whole charming card.

PLATE 165 A pretty pink-edged white embossed card. A bunch of violets, its central scrap, disguises a fan, the handle of which seems to be, in its original state, the wrapping of the bouquet. The photograph shows the fan being partly extracted from its sheath.

PLATE 164 A bouquet Christmas card which, by the pulling of a silk string, becomes a fan of flowers.
(*Description on p. 173.*)

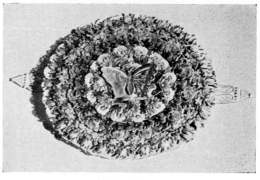

PLATE 167
The composite paper bouquet described
on page 174.

PLATE 166
(On the left)

This card before animation resembles a simple cardboard fan. Animation turns it into a three-dimensional, colourful combination of scraps, grasses and flowers.

PLATE 168 The same card when animated by drawing the two tabs together.
A very attractive and colourful animated card. The shadow gives an idea of its construction.

PLATE 169

A Nativity Christmas card when animated. It was probably manufactured in Germany and composed of chromolithograph scraps.

PLATE 170

A charming tableau of the Nativity. Note the scrap angels on the roof of the stable and the nine rows of connected and concertedly moving scraps.

PLATE 171

The front view of a stage-like animated card, showing a garden party when the card is opened by sideways movement of the hands.

PLATE 172

An "aerial view" of the same card, showing its structure and manipulation.

PLATE 173

A much simpler—and earlier—card with the same basic structure and theatrical effect.

PLATE 174 At first sight this card looks like a flat cardboard card which fits well into a 4¼ by 3¾ inches envelope. It is a rare animated card of the 1890's, with tiers of scrap angels heads, nicely "frosted" and appearing in charming contrast against the pale blue background. The animation is effected by simply lifting the top page of what seems to be an ordinary folded card.

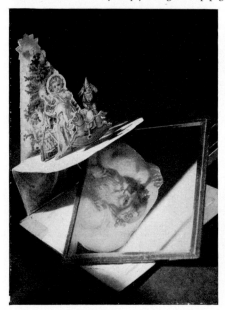

PLATE 175 This card again, when flat, is a realistic cardboard imitation of an almond slice, except for the silken tape attached to one strip of "angelica". When this is pulled, the cover lifts up and the card comes into animation as described on p. 179.

PLATE 176 A popular tab card, including in the centre a Kate Greenaway card of the "Flowers and Fancies" set. The single card is multiplied by pulling each tab outwardly. The photograph shows the card fully extended.

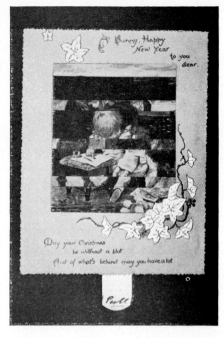

PLATE 177

Three photographs are needed to indicate the working of this dissolving-picture tab card, described on p. 180.

PLATE 178

The first illustration (*above on the left*) shows the original state, the second (*on the right*) the transition, and the third (*below on the left*) when the tab is fully pulled out.

PLATE 179

The complete change of the little picture mounted on the above card.

PLATE 180

Metal tabs enabled Christmas card makers to construct even more complicated scrap edifices on their cards. *Description on pp. 181-2.*

PLATE 181

An extending three dimensional tab-card of 1876, described on p. 180. When the tab is pulled downwards the flat card becomes three dimensional and through the oval opening layers of a scrap panorama can be seen.

PLATE 182

No photograph can do justice to this delicate and complex animated card of the 1870's. It is photographed in the third state of animation, but when the disc at the bottom of the card is slowly turned further tiny chromolithographs appear in the central oval opening.

PLATE 183   An example of a Christmas card made of thin "enamelled" cardboard, realistically imitating china plates and dishes. It was very difficult to preserve this type of card in albums, etc., hence the rather battered appearance of the few which have survived the past sixty or seventy years.

PLATE 184 A "daring" mechanical card of the late 1880's. By pulling the tab in and out, the pasteboard legs of the young lady on the card perform a frantic dance in a manner probably considered rather piquant even in pasteboard. Seen in action, the static upper and fast-moving lower parts of the figure certainly look rather—comic.

PLATE 185 At least three photographs would be required to show the simple working of this small late-Victorian trick card. The cover carries a floral decoration and the intriguing text : "May all Christmas pleasures be *fetching* and above board." The above illustration shows the card half-opened. A strip of paper forms the front of the skirt and the left leg of the young lady.

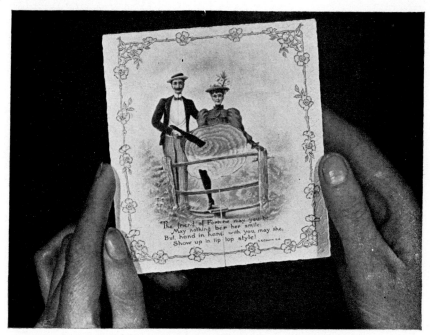

PLATE 186 Here the card is fully opened, showing all the frills which were so "fetching" in those days.

PLATE 187 Although its sentiment is very characteristic of its period (1885-90) this charming old mechanical card is very rare. The photograph was taken when the card is extended, to show the sleeping infant, but the card can be folded so that it fits into an envelope of about 5 by 4 inches.

PLATE 188 One of the early "private" cards, designed by J. Goddard of Leicester for 1876, lithographed in six colours, including gold and silver. White appraised it and others by the same artist as "in all respect typical and admirable examples of the ideal card."

PLATE 189 A lovely old religious card of fine, thick, gold-bevelled single black board. The panel is rich gold, and the reproduction of the angel is a fine piece of chromo-lithography.

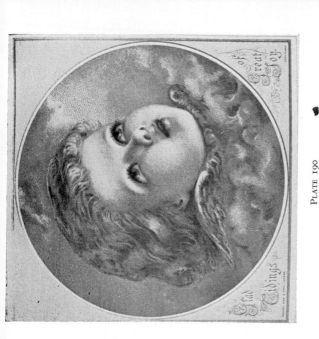

Glad Tidings of Great Joy.

PLATE 190

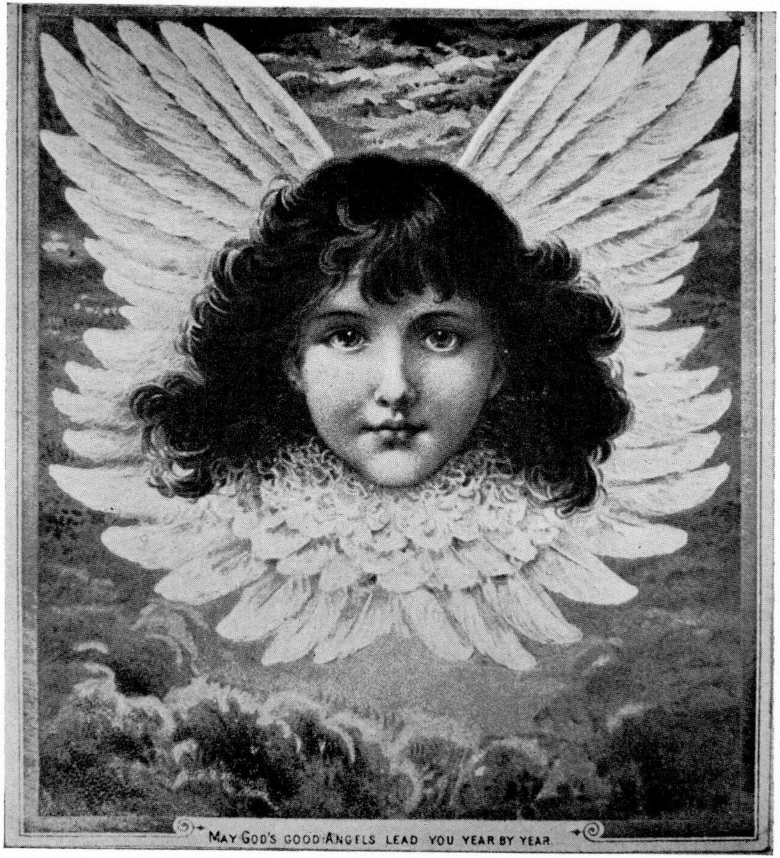

MAY GOD'S GOOD ANGELS LEAD YOU YEAR BY YEAR.

PLATE 191

Very popular Victorian angel-head Christmas cards, which were given prominent places in many old albums. The one on the right is by Rebecca Coleman and the other by J. Sant, R.A., and each belongs to a set of similar cards. In 1894 Gleeson White pointed out that the public admired Miss Coleman's designs more than those of the well-known Academician.

PLATE 192 A pretty early Goodall card of two angels. It is printed in pale colours against a fine gold background.

PLATE 193 A Madonna and Child Christmas card by Alice Havers, a celebrated woman artist, published by Hildesheimer and Faulkner.

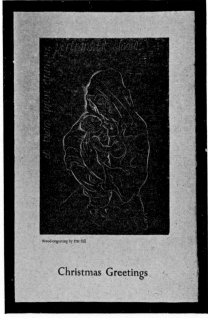

PLATE 194 One of the few—if not only— Beardsley Christmas card designs in the artist's characteristic manner (1890's).

PLATE 195 Wood-engraved Christmas card by Eric Gill, printed in dark red with black lettering. Published by Hague and Gill.

PLATE 197

PLATE 198

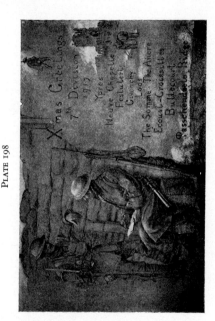

PLATE 199 A witty American wartime Christmas card published in 1918 by the Campbell Art Company. (See description on pp. 195-6.)

PLATE 198 (*lower centre*) Typical World War I card from the fronts. Monochrome drawing by J. T. Beadle.

PLATE 196 A French postcard size Christmas card published during the First World War by Le Rire Rouge. The design by Louis Vallet shows a French woman standing on a hat-box to light the pipe of a British officer. The lighter is her red heart.

PLATE 197 A Welsh fusilier of 1917 with the ghost of the fusilier of 1742. "I say, mate," the soldier of 1917 shouts out, "you'd better keep your lurid hat down; also your blanketty meat-chopper!"

PLATE 201 An airgraph letter Christmas card with a sketch of "the little town of Bethlehem" sent from the Holy Land almost exactly a century after the first card, reproduced on Plate I in this book, in 1943.

PLATE 200 A page of "old soldier Christmas cards" designed by Harry Payne and published in the late 80's.

Hal HURST (Artistic Supply, 1895).

Dorothy HUTTON (Holly Bush, 1920-30's). A great variety of chiefly floral cards.

HYNN (Hill & Co., 1888-90). Hunting scenes.

Selwyn IMAGE (A.W.G., 1909-10).

John E. INGLIS (Whiteman Litho. (?), 1890's). An overflowing punch bowl, with male and female figures.

H. S. J. (S.Hr., 1877. Little boy with " Jumping Jack " and girl, making ready for Sunday School Class party.

P. J. (Castell, 1880's). Holly leaves and floral decorations.

Frank G. JACKSON (Private, 1880-90).

Charlotte Isa JAMES (S.Hr., 1881). Winner of a smaller prize.

N. R. JAMIESON (Modern, military).

Norman JANES, R.E. (Modern).

Bertha E. JAQUES (U.S.A.). See List of Christmas Card Publishers, p. 272.

J. A. B. JAY (H.&F., 1881).

Payne JENNINGS (S.Hr. and W. A. Mansell, 1879-80's). Early photo-cards " photographed from Nature ". " Wood and Water "—a new series (S.Hr., No. 1813, in 1881) of " photographic gems " consisted of ten varieties and was apparently a great success. In 1882 "Views on the Thames " (No. 3600) were published.

C. M. JESSOP (E.&S., 1879-87).

E. M. JESSOP (E.&S., 1880's).

E. K. JOHNSON, R.W.S. (H.&F., 1880-5). " Winter Scenes " won Second prize at H.&F. Competition, 1881. Also Studies of Children (1880) and Heads (1884).

Louisa JOHNSON (S.Hr., 1881).

JONAS (" of Dresden ") (D.&S., 1884).

Reginald JONES (H.&F., 1880's). Landscapes.

JUNIOR (1910's). " The Blues " hand-coloured, comic cards.

Marion JUSTICE (Rust Craft, U.S.A., 1910-20). Children.

G. C. K. (G. C. Kilburne).

W. D. KEATING (Keating, U.S.A., 1906-7). Designed and engraved the first cards of his Company, but retired in 1907.

Felix KELLY (Modern).

T. R. KENNEDY (E.&S., 1878-87). Birds, wild roses.

Esther KENWORTHY (H. & F., 1881). Winner of a smaller prize at Competition.

Augustus KERSTING (S.Hr., 1881).

G. C. (or G. ?) KILBURNE (D.L.R., 1877-82; H.&F., 1880-5). " Liliputians . . . depicting diminutive doings " (D.L.R., No. 217, three designs, 1879); " Fairy Skiffs . . . children and fairies boating " (D.L.R., No. 220, three designs, 1879); " The Skaters " (D.L.R. No. 497, three designs, 1882) and many others. Probably also " Christmas reprisals " (D.L.R. No. 215, three designs, 1879-80) see Plate 51. " Twickenham Ferry " boating sketches on oval mounts (H.&F., No. 315, three designs, 1884), " Blind Man's Buff ", " Evening Party " and " Snowball Fight " (H.&F., No. 388, three designs, 1884-5), etc.

Agnes G. KING (Meissner and Buch, 1890).

E. M. KING (Military, modern).

Raphael KIRCHNER (Tuck, 1900-10). Pretty girls of the period driving early motor cars on monochrome cards. " Make use of Time, let not advantage slip " and similar mottoes.

Purvis KIRMOE (Modern).

Ernst KREIDOLF (Switzerland, 1899-1920).

A. L. (A. Ludovici) (H.&F., c. 1880).

A. L. (Susse, Paris, c. 1840-60).

A. F. L. Amusing " shaped " trick card of red Post Office pillar box. When opened kittens are seen reading and clearly enjoying the letters !

E. A. L. (Eliza Anne Lemann) (S.Hr., 1880's).

E. D. L. (1885's).

L. L. (Lizzie Lawson).

T. L. (1882's). " A Christmas Dream " and a New Year card of surprisingly " modern " designs.

V. L. (Dean, 1860's). Rather naive comic cards.

H. G. C. Marsh LAMBERT (C. W. Faulkner, 1920's).

Ebenezer LANDELLS (1840-60's). Wood-engraver of *Punch* fame, engraved many Crowquill, K. Meadows, etc., designs.

Walter LANGLEY, R.I. (Private, 1880's). Etchings.

Julius J. LANKES (U.S.A., modern). Woodcuts and engravings.

B. B. LAURENCE (H.&F., 1880's). Probably Lawrance, (Bringhurst, B.)

Bringhurst B. LAWRANCE (S.Hr., H.&F., 1880's). Monkeys in a row (1881) and many other comic animal pictures. Winner of smaller prizes at both S.Hr. and H.&F. Competitions in 1881.

L. E. LAWRANCE (S.Hr., 1882). Possibly Laurence ? " Four studies of figures . . . one of the most original sets for this, or indeed for any year . . . which in their unconventional composition recall Mr. Alma Tadema " says G. White, but I am unable to identify the set. No. 24, " Classical Female Figures " (three designs) or No. 30, " The Four Elements " (four designs), both of 1881, may be by Laurence.

J. LAWSON (D.L.R., 1881-5). Sets named " The Lovers' Creed " (1881), " Reposing " (1883), " Little Folks " (1884).

Lizzie LAWSON (Nister, Griffith Farran, 1885; H.&F., 1886). Charming heads of children on circular cards, gilt edge (H.&F., No. 155, in 1886; also single girls standing, framed by Japanese fan and floral designs.

Leon LEBÈGUE (Paris, 1890's).

LE FANU (G. Brinsley).

John LEECH. (See Plate 14.)

W. Heneage LEGGE (1896). *Studio* Competition in 1896.

E. Blair LEIGHTON (H.&F., M.W., 1881). " Memory and Hope " won £75 prize at H.&F. Competition in 1881. (Woman with candle, size of cards 4¾ by 6¼ inches).

Frederick LEIGHTON (1910's).

Henry LEIGHTON (1860's). Wood-engraver, engraved some of John Leighton's drawings on wood.

John LEIGHTON (" Luke Limner ") (1860-70's).

E. LEISTNER (Tuck, 1880's). Flowering branches.

Eliza Anne LEMANN (S.Hr., 1881-3). Third prize, i.e. £75, S.Hr. Competition, 1881. Three charming designs: 1. Children representing the twelve months; 2. Bringing home the Yule log; 3. Fruit gathering (Series No. 377, size 6¼ by 4¾ inches each). Also four " Figures of Children " (No. 56, size 4¾ by 3¼).

G. D. LESLIE, R.A. (Tuck, 1881). See pp. 149-50.

A. A. LEWIS (U.S.A., 1920's). New York Public Library Exhibition of Christmas Card Designs, 1922-3.

A. C. V. LILLY (Private, 1893).

" LUKE LIMNER ". John Leighton's *nom de plume* (cf. pp. 55, 61, 100-2, 105, etc.). Also Fig. 5, Plate 19, Colour Plates 1c and VI.

Sir Coutts LINDSAY (1880's).

Sir Frank LOCKWOOD (Private, 1896). See Fig. 11.

A. M. LOCKYER (M.W., H.&F., 1878-85). Remarkably well drawn comic animal subjects.

LOFTS (Military, modern).

Edgar LONGMAN (Airmail, modern).

The Marquis of LORNE (Relig. Tract Soc., 1884).

J. LOUDON (1840-50). Engraver on wood of " Some Christmas Faces ".

Will H. Low (Prang, U.S.A., 1880's). Second prize at Prang's fourth Competition, 1884. See p. 79. (Low and Blashfield painted the murals in the famous great ballroom of the Waldorf-Astoria Hotel.)

A. (Albert) LUDOVICI, R.B.A. (H.&F., Tuck, 1880-90's). Won a £25 prize at H.&F. Competition, 1881, for his set called " Young Albion ". Other sets by him include " The Ice Field " (H.&F., No. 430, 1884), a set of charming little crossing sweepers (Tuck, No. 1589), etc.

A. (Allan J.) LUDOVICI, Jun., R.B.A. (H.&F., Mawson Swan & Morgan, 1880-90's). Winner of two £25 prizes at H. & F. Competition, 1881, with sets " Athletic Sports " and the very popular " Quite too-too ! " caricaturing " those aethereal beings who can lunch on a lily, dine on a daffodil, enjoy a Barmicide feast at any hour on a sunflower, to whom fans are necessaries of life, and teapots teach a high moral lesson ", i.e. the aesthetes (*Society*, October 1, 1881 in their review of Ludovici's designs). In 1880 a Circus set of clowns and pierrette (four designs), pretty skating women with a child and in 1881 a set of " Street Arabs " and " Penny-farthing Cyclists " appeared. Also elegant dancing groups, and girls cycling in bloomers.

Miss Margaret (Marguerite) LUDOVICI (H.&F., 1881, Tuck, 1887). Winner of two £20 prizes at H.&F. Competition, 1881. A card of 1887, " The nicest Ball of the Season " pictures a clown settled on a big snow-ball under red umbrella—rather badly drawn.

Julius LUZ (Nister, 1885). A caged nightingale, pen-and-ink drawing.

A. F. LYDON (S.Hr., Misch & Stock, 1880-90's). A number of not very well drawn " shaped " cards (crescent moons, crosses, circular, etc.) picturing moon-lit churches and landscapes and Biblical scenes. (Lydon illustrated many books printed in colour by Fawcett by the Baxter process.)

E. M. (E. Manly) (H.&F.).

E. E. M. (Eleanor E. Manly). Girls' heads.

E. E. M. Floral cards.

M. v. M. (Rothe).

M. H. g. v. M. (G.O., Tuck).

R. J. M. (Schipper, 1886 ?). Daisy, forget-me-not, jasmine and snowdrop sprays decorating horse-shoe shaped silver Christmas cards (No. 1445).

B. W. M. (Davidson, 1880-90). Floral with vignetted landscapes.

R. F. Mc. (Tuck, 1890's ?). (McIntyre).

Robert Ellice MACK (Nister, Griffith, 1885). Landscapes, flowers.

A. D. McCORMICK (Tuck, 1934). " The Prince of Wales has commissioned cards on which are reproduced A. D. McCormick's painting of ' Queen Elizabeth giving audience to Shakespeare ' " (*Daily Telegraph*, October 5, 1934).

MacDUNCAN (M.W., 1860-70).

R. W. MACBETH, A.R.A., R.E. (Private, 1892).

Jessie MacGREGOR (M.W., 1880's).

Newton MACINTOSH (Prang, U.S.A., 1880's). " Lettered panels ... framed by a few, broadly designed flowers " (G. W.).

Peter McINTYRE (New Zealand). Modern, military.

R. F. McINTYRE (Tuck, 1886-90). Windmill, etc. in winter (1886); " Snow-flake Series " (1887).

Iain MACNAB, R.E. (Modern).

Percy MACQUOID (M.W., 1870-80's).

B. Jessopp MACKEI (Portheim, 1890's). " Monotints ".

Bertha MAGUIRE (E.&S., 1879-87; S.Hr., 1881; Tuck, 1886-90). A great number of mainly floral designs, " Penny baskets ".

Helena J. MAGUIRE (H.&F., 1880-1; S.Hr., 1881; Tuck, 1885-90). Two £20 prizes at H.&F. Competition, 1881. Numerous animal and bird cards.

E.   MANBY (H.&F., 1881). Erroneous spelling, see Manly.

MANDY (Roumania, 1900). Photographs.

Betty MANLEY (Rust Craft, 1920's). Figures of children.

Alice MANLY (S.Hr., 1880's). Winner of a £20 prize in 1881.

Eleanor E. MANLY (H.&F., 1881). Competition: two cards of " Old English Christmas " and " Seasons' Games " won smaller prizes. Her charming set of children heads (six designs) entitled " Helen's Babies " (Gold borders, No. 276; chocolate brown and gold borders, No. 277) and the four studies of children in fancy costumes, " Baby Bell " (No. 319) appeared in 1884.

J. H. S. MANN (H.&F., 1881). Little Miss Muffet and Little Boy Blue, etc. Winner of £20 prize at Competition, 1881.

Miss MANNING (H.&F., 1886). A set of figures.

MARIA, Princess Waldemar of Denmark (Giese Forlag, 1897). Flower designs on private cards.

George MARKS (H.&F., 1880's). In 1881 won one of the two £100 prizes with a three-fold card with a landscape in centre.

Henry Stacy MARKS, R.A. (M.W., 1870's). (See Plate 41.) The Publisher advertised this celebrated set in the *Illustrated London News* (December 19, 1874) thus: " H. Stacy Marks, A.R.A. Christmas Cards by this eminent Artist are ready. Four Designs, 6d. each, or the Set, in ornamental Cover, 2s.; by post, 1d. extra ". The first edition of the set was larger, 6 by 4¼ inches each (1873), but next year a smaller version followed (about 4 by 3 inches).

Mrs. Philippa MARSHALL (H.&F., 1880's).

Frank MARTIN (Modern).

Frans MASAREEL (Belgium) (Modern).

Fred MASON (Private, 1890). Wood-engraving.

H. P. MASTING (or MASHING ?) (Modern).

Fortunino MATANIA, R.I. (Sharpe, modern).

F. S. MATHER (Prang, U.S.A., 1880-90).

W. MATTHEWS (New Zealand, modern).

Margery MAY (H.&F., 1880's).

Phil MAY (1890's). Clown with sausages and goose.

Kenneth ("Kenny") MEADOWS (Goodall, D.&S., etc., 1840's-74). See Fig. 9 and p. 122.

Israel von MECKENEM. (See p. 20.)

Adolph MENZEL (L. Sachse & Co., Berlin, about 1834-40). According to Westen fifteen humorous designs. See p. 30.

Lee MERO (Buzza, U.S.A., 1915—).

Emily M. MERRICK (H.&F., 1880's).

Edna MERRITT (Buzza, U.S.A., 1920's).

Al METELL (Buzza, U.S.A., 1920's).

Johann MEYER (Zürich, 1703). See Plate 11, and p. 25. After Meyer's death in 1712, his pupil, J. M. Füssli made some New Year engravings for the Zurich Constaffler Association.

P. MEYERHEIM (German, 1860's). Comic animal subjects.

Walter MEYNER (U.S.A., 1920's). New York Public Library Exhibition of Christmas Card Designs, 1922-3.

F. MICHL (Austria, 1900's). Etchings in colours. A pretty Viennese lady greets the season with mistletoe "nach englischem Muster" (Westen).

W. MIDGLEY (Private, 1890's).

Frank MILES (W. A. Mansell, 1870-80). "Charming platinotypes" (G.W.).

Helen J. MILES (H.&F., 1883; Tuck, 1881-6; Sockl, 1886-7). Winner of £25 at Tuck Competition, 1881, with "Infancy", "Youth", "Middle Age", "Ripe Age"—circular panels of figures on square gold backgrounds. A great number of animal studies.

J. E. MILLAIS, P.R.A. (1878-80).

Agnes MILLER PARKER, R.E. (Modern).

Fred MILLER (M.W.).

J. H. MILLER (MacLellan, modern). Celtic motives.

J. MITCHELL (1897). Second prize, Studio Competition.

G. M. MITELLI (1634-1718). (See pp. 22-3 and Plate 8.)

E. Reynell MOHUN (Private, 1914-18).

Georges MONTBARD (H.&F., 1880's). Rivers, lakes in black and white; winner of £50 prize in 1881 Competition.

E. B. S. MONTEFIORE (S.Hr., 1881). Dogs; Fifth prize winner.

Boutet de MONVEL (Paris, 1880–90's).

MORA (Tuck, 1886). "Photographs of children from life" (No. 2476), three designs.

Leon MORAN (Prang, U.S.A., 1884).

Percy MORAN (Prang, U.S.A., 1884).

Thomas MORAN (Prang, U.S.A., 1884). Third prize at Prang's fourth Competition, 1884. The American landscape painter of "most sincere and passionate enthusiasm" (Ruskin).

Fred MORGAN (H.&F., 1883). Figures.

W. Morgan (M.W., 1880's).

F. Moro (Firenze) (1890-91).

Mrs. Frances Morris (H.&F., 1881).

Joan Morris, S.P. (Church Artists' Agency, modern).

Anna G. Morse (Prang, U.S.A., 1880's). Fourth prize, i.e. $200, Prang's first Competition, 1880, with a design of four kneeling boys holding holly and mistletoe branches.

J. M. Morse (Tuck). Little landscapes on circular mounts; also " Aesthetic maid playing violin, etc." (No. 2236-1886).

Marjorie W. Morse (Rust Craft, U.S.A., 1920's).

Mrs. Sydney Morse (S.Hr., 1881). Winner of two £20 prizes.

" Grandma " Moses (U.S.A., modern).

W. J. Muckley (H.&F., 1880-4). A virtuoso in flower painting who produced annually sets of cards with flowers in vases and blue jars. Series Nos. 285 (White flowers and pink May on gold panels) and 403 " Rich Flowers arranged in Costly Vases " (1884) are characteristic examples.

Sir Alfred J. Munnings, R.A. (Modern).

C. O. Murray (M.W., 1880's).

S. Myers (Tuck, 1886). Portfolios of etchings after Turner, Collins, Etty, Constable.

R. Morton Nance (1896). First prize winner, *Studio* Competition, 1896.

G. Napier (Heffer, modern).

Thomas Nast (U.S.A., 1866-70). See Dust Jacket No. 22.

Elizabeth S. Naughten (S.Hr., 1880's). Winner of a £20 prize, 1881.

Harold Nelson (Modern).

Margaret Nelson (Modern).

F. H. New (Private, 1889).

Ruth Newton (Rust Craft, U.S.A., 1920's). Children.

C. Noakes (Tuck, 1880-90). " Old London ", " Old Edinburgh ", etc. (four designs each).

Chas. G. Noakes (Portheim, 1890). Water colours.

Noël (H.&F., 1880's). Heavily frosted landscapes on cut out scrolls.

Orlando Norie (Ackermann-Prang, 1881). Military, naval and volunteer sets.

Val. Norman (Tuck, 1920).

W. Tasker Nugent (M.W., 1870-80). See pp. 174 and 121, also Plate 41 a, b.

Marie Nussbaum (S.Hr., 1880's). Winner of one £20 prize in 1881.

T. O. (J. S. & Co., 1850's). T. Onwhyn.

ARTISTS AND DESIGNERS

Henry R. ODDY (H.&F., 1880's). Won one of the £25 prizes in 1881.

J. OGDEN (Modern). Etchings.

OLGA, Grand Duchess (Private, 1927-39).

E. H. OLIVER (1896). Second prize, *Studio* Competition, 1896.

Käthe OLSHAUSEN-SCHÖNBERGER (Berlin, Germany, 1907). Designer of card reproduced on Fig. 19.

T. ONWHYN (Rock & Co., J. S. & Co., 1840-50's). Onwhyn drew the note-paper headings (published December 23, 1853) described on p. 54 and the " Heavy Fall " card (Plate 75). His initials, T.O. are sometimes made to look like a little human figure and two strokes (legs !) are added to O, the " body " (A Dream of Christmas, No. 46) or hidden as an inscription on a nearby boat (The Pier ! Llandudno, Rock & Co., 1857). A witty set "Cupid & Crinoline" (1858) tells the story of the ill effects on love, for man and dog, of a " Ladies' Expander " in twelve cartoons, with captions almost as brief as fashionable to-day.

OSTRANDER (Tuck, 1887). Vignetted scenery, tobogganing, etc. (No. 497). (Four designs.)

Malcolm OSBORNE, R.A., P.R.E. (Modern). Only one design, a military card, made in 1918 when serving in the Holy Land. Soldiers with Jerusalem in the background.

A. P. (Schipper, 1880; H.&F., 1882-3). Children in fancy dresses, Japanese fans, vignette landscapes.

C. A. P. (1890's). Monochrome female figures.

F. C. P. (F. Corbyn Price).

T. P. (M.W., 1880's). Figures representing the seasons, etc.

H. Maurice PAGE (H.&F., 1880's). £50 prize, 1881 Competition.

Ethel PARKINSON (Tuck, C. W. Faulkner, M. M. Vienne, 1890-1910). Mostly figures with strong outlines, characteristic of the period.

C. PATERSON (M.W., 1880's).

Caroline PATERSON (S.Hr., 1880's). Second prize, £100, S.Hr. Competition, 1881; Series Nos. 35 and 129. Designer of silkfringed card reproduced on Plate 86.

Arthur C. PAYNE (Tuck, 1880-90's). Mostly comic military subjects. Examples: " Humorous military experiences " (No. 421, four designs), " Black-eyed Susan " (No. 740, four designs) 1887.

Harry PAYNE (Nathan, Ackermann, Tuck, 1885-90). Military life, the gallant and sentimental version. For examples, see Plate 200.

M. S. PEACOCK (Modern). Popular art.

Shirley PEARCE (Modern).

Chas. PEARS (Modern). Naval.

R. M. PEARSON (U.S.A.). New York Public Library Exhibition of Christmas Card Designs, 1922-3.

Edward PENFIELD (Bartlett, U.S.A., 1910's).

Edwin A. PENLEY (S.Hr., Tuck, 1880's). Landscapes, often on palette, oval, etc. " shaped " cards.

Hall Ross PERRIGARD, A.R.C.A. (Canada, modern).

Kate PERUGINI (1880-90's). Children. (Mrs. Perugini was the younger daughter of Dickens.)

Rosa C. PETHERICK (1896).

Johann Andreas PFEFFEL (Vienna and later Augsburg). (See p. 23 and Plate 9.)

Florence A. PHILLIPS (1896). Mention, *Studio* Competition, 1896.

Pablo PICASSO (Hallmark, U.S.A., etc.). Modern.

H. Wintrop PIERCE (Prang, U.S.A., 1884).

Helen M. PIKE (Hills & Co., 1895).

Flora PILKINGTON (Tuck, modern). Mainly floral subjects, garden scenes.

Wilmot PILSBURY, A.R.W.S. (Tuck, 1890's). Harvest scenes, landscapes.

Erna PINNER (Modern).

G. J. PINWELL (M.W. ?, 1870-80).

Orovida PISSARRO (Ward Gallery, modern).

George Wolfe PLANK (Bartlett, U.S.A., 1910's). New York Public Library Exhibition of Christmas Card Designs, 1922-3.

POPLING (Canada, modern).

Mary POWELL (1896). *Studio* Competition, 1896.

E. J. POYNTER, R.A. (Tuck, 1881). (See Plate 104 and p. 149.)

N. PRESCOTT-DAVIS (Washington Kell., 1890's). Angels, Christ-mother, Child Christ, etc.

Alice PRICE (Tuck, Castell, 1880's). Religious cards.

F. PRINCE (Tuck, 1880's). " Angels floating in clouds with palms " (three designs, No. 433, 1887), etc.

F. Corbyn PRICE (H.&F., 1883-6; Tuck, 1890). Landscapes, churches.

W. H. PRIOR (S.Hr., 1881).

R. T. PRITCHARD (M.W., 1870-80's).

Dod PROCTOR, R.A. (1920's).

J. PROCTOR (E.&S., 1880's).

M. PYNE (Tuck, 1899). Monochrome landscapes.

T. PYNE (H.&F., 1886). Landscapes.

F. A. R. (Tuck, 1880's). Boys fighting in snow.

H. R. R. (1890 ?). Angel and shepherds, sheep.

P. R. (H.&F., 1880-90). Girls picking flowers (No. 720).

C. T. R. (or G. R. ?) (Castell, 1880's). Newspaper boys shouting, with " Special Edition "—" An Extra Specially Happy Christmas ".

Arthur RACKHAM, R.W.S. (Private, 1930).

Henrietta RAE (Mrs. Normand) (1890's). Women figures.

John RAE (Volland, U.S.A., 1910's).

J. McL. RALSTON (H.&F., 1881-3). Winner of a £25 prize at Competition, 1881. Shooting, skating, snowballing scenes.

William (?) RALSTON (H.&F., 1881).

Scott RANKIN (Tuck, 1890's). Comic.

Armand RASSENFOSSE (Modern).

W. RATHJEANS (H.&F., 1880's). £75 prize winner at H.&F. Competition, with designs of bouquets and flowers.

Gwendolen RAVERAT, R.E. (Modern).

Robert RAYMENTS (S.Hr., 1881). Winner of two £20 prizes.

Samuel READ (M.W., 1880's).

E. T. REED (M.W., 1895). Probably designer of " Beardsleyesque " card described as " audacious in the latest artistic phrase " (The Artist, December, 1895) reproduced on p. 151 (Fig. 15).

REES (Modern).

Augusta von REICHELT (Tuck, 1883-4). Floral studies.

Nan REID (Mrs. S. Green) (Modern).

Imre REINER (Hungary, later Switzerland). Modern, wood-engravings.

J. L. RHEAD (Hare & Co., Tuck, 1890's). " Mr. Rhead is not to be brushed aside as a mere disciple of the Bradley-Beardsley school ", wrote a critic in 1897.

Agnes RICHARDSON (Photochrom, C. W. Faulkner, 1910-20). Mainly children.

Frederick RICHARDSON (Volland, 1910's).

L. RICHETON (Tuck, 1886). " Satin tablet cards " with etchings.

Ludwig RICHTER (German, 1870-80's). Children. About his illustrations for the Lord's Prayer, Sunday and the Seasons, Ruskin wrote, " Perfect as types of easy line drawing, exquisite in ornamental composition, and refined to the utmost in ideal grace, they represent all that is simplest, purest, and happiest in human life, all that is most strengthening and comforting in nature and religion. They are enough in themselves, to show that whatever its errors, whatever its backslidings, this century of ours has in its heart understood and fostered, more than any former one, the joys of family affection, and of household piety . . . " " The Art of England " I. (1883).

Octavius RICKATSON (H.&F., 1881-3). £75 prize at H.&F. Competition, 1881. Landscapes, river scenes.

Charles RICKETTS (Private, 1890's).

A. RIMMER (Tuck, 1886). " Old Markets " (Boston, Peterborough, Chester, Winchester, Sherborne and Oakham) (Nos. 2340-2).

Paul E. RITTER (German, 1900's). Artist of the German Emperor's naval post card in 1901. See Plate 64 and description, p. 132.

Diego RIVERA (American Artists Group, 1930's).

Katherine M. ROBERTS (1896). Mention, *Studio* Competition, 1896.

Mrs. ROBERTS (Beatrice Wainwright).

Charles ROBERTSON, R.W.S., R.E. (H.&F., 1887-90). Several sets of cards (three designs each) of fishermen, etc., on decorated mounts.

Percy ROBERTSON (H.&F., 1884). " Lowtide ", " Barges ", etc. Etchings.

Charles ROBINSON (Modern).

Fred ROC (Modern).

A. ROESELER. Comic.

Bruce ROGERS (Bartlett, U.S.A., 1910's).

Nana Bickford ROLLINS (Rust Craft, 1920's).

" ROMEO " (1890's). Comic dog and cat designs.

ROMMLER (D.&S., 1884).

Henriette RONNER (H.&F., etc., 1869-82). Cats.

J. M. J. ROSE (W.B.&O., New York, U.S.A., 1880-90's). Flowers and landscapes.

Leonard ROSOMAN (Private, modern).

T. L. ROWBOTHAM (M.W., 1870-80's).

P. ROWE (Tuck, 1886). " A novel tamburine set with music on back ".

Sir Henry ROWLINSON (1916-18). Military.

L. A. ROWLINSON (Tuck, 1924).

Henry RYLAND (M.W., 1878-90; S.Hr., 1881; also private cards, 1895). A set of " Angels of the Nativity "; girls in the " Classical style ", etc. Winner of a £20 prize in S.Hr. Competition.

B. D. S. (H.&F., 1886). B. D. Sigmund.

E. S. (Private, 1894). Etchings.

J. P. S. (Prang, U.S.A., 1888). Girl with butterflies.

L. S. (1890's). Wintry landscapes, autumn leaves.

W. G. S. (1890's). Newly " evicted " chickens.

W. L. S. (Modern, wartime).

h. y. s. (H.&F., 1880's). Vignetted landscapes.

George SADLER (H.&F., 1880; S.Hr., 1881.) Figures. £20 prize, S.Hr. Competition.

Kate SADLER (H.&F., 1881; Tuck, 1881-5). With " very beautiful roses " and other flower designs, won one £75 and two £20 prizes at H.&F. Competitions.

E. SALAMAN (Tuck, 1880's). "Heroines of popular songs, heads". Four designs (No. 326, 1887).

Frank O. SALISBURY (Modern).

W. G. SANDERS (H.&F., 1881). "Decorative flowers for folding cards" won £50 prize.

Henry SANDHAM (Prang, U.S.A., 1887).

Alex SANDIER (Prang, U.S.A., H.&F., 1880's). His card of "The Child" clad with sheepskin won $500 second prize, Prang's first Competition, 1880), and two £20 prizes, H.&F. Competition, 1881.

H. SANDIER (Tuck, 1881).

James SANT, R.A. (Tuck, 1881). See Plate 190. Later another set of cards, small cherubs sitting on clouds.

F. SARGENT (Tuck, 1887). "The Squire's Daughter", "The Vicar's Daughter"—porcelain studies.

Charles SARKA (U.S.A., 1910-20's). New York Public Library Exhibition of Christmas Card Designs, 1922-3.

Walter SATTERLEE (Prang, U.S.A., 1881). His large design of carol-singers won Second Popular Prize, Prang's third Competition, 1881. Above the carol-singers winged angel-heads, behind a window, children, listen.

H. SAUNDERS (Tuck, 1887). "A Court Belle" and "My Queen".

Isabel SAUL (Modern).

Priscilla SAVAGE (Modern). One of the earliest "children artists" in 1930.

Edith SCANNELL (M.W., 1870-80's).

G. SCHACKINGER (Prang, U.S.A., 1890's).

(Johann) Gottfried SCHADOW (Berlin, 1795, 1828-32). Charming zincplate-prints made as personal New Year greetings. The artist's own visiting card, engraved in the 1790's, is reproduced on Plate 21. Schadow was a famous architect and head of the Royal Prussian Academy of Arts.

Adolph SCHRÖDTER (Berlin, later Düsseldorf, Germany, 1834). See p. 30.

H. SCHUBERT (1910's).

Randolphe SCHWABE (1910's).

Fanny C. SCOTT (S.Hr., 1880's). £20 prize, 1881 Competition.

Janet LAURA SCOTT (Volland, Buzza, U.S.A., 1900-20). "Among the best the country produced" (Chase).

Septimus E. SCOTT, R.I. (Modern).

Major T. S. SECCOMBE (D.L.R., 1878-82). Two sets: "In the Clouds" and "The Tournament" (1880). "... Whose illustrations of military life had a somewhat extended reputation". (G.W.)

Mark F. SEVERIN (Modern).

George L. SEYMOUR (Tuck, 1887). Military figures, porcelain on plush, etc. mounts.

Miss SHAVER (Buzza, U.S.A., 1915—).

Harry SHELDON (Modern, military).

J. A. SHEPHERD (Tuck, 1887). "The Fighting Dog" (Bull Terrier); "John Bull" (a Bulldog), "The Home Rule Dog" (Irish Terrier); also " A Funny Tale " (six monkeys enjoying themselves).

Ralph SHEPARD (U.S.A., 1920—).

Frederick SHIELDS (Bradshaw, etc., 1860's).

William Herbert SICKLES (Keating, U.S.A., 1912-16).

B. D. SIGMUND (H.&F., 1885-92). A great number of landscapes and sea-scapes characteristic of the period.

S. H. SIME (1890-1920). Humorous designs.

Richard SIMKIN (D.&S., 1897). Ships, girls, signal flags.

St. Clair SIMMONS (H.&F., 1882-91). Children playing with dolls.

Annie SIMPSON (Tuck, 1890's). Flowers, birds.

B. SIMPSON (1880's). Floral designs.

F. Markham SKIPWORTH (H.&F., 1882-6). Pleasant period pictures of young women on sofa; their daydreaming is accompanied by a playful, but less well drawn kitten (No. 137).

Edward SLOCOMBE, R.E. (1889-1907). Numerous etchings, mostly private cards.

R. I. SMART, R.E. (Modern). Etchings.

Moyr SMITH (M.W., 1875-8). Two sets " Christmasse in ye Olden Tyme". For examples, see Dust Jacket No. 9 card.

Noel SMITH (H.&F., 1886). Figures.

Pamela Coleman SMITH (Bartlett, U.S.A., 1900—).

Winifred SMITH (1890's).

George SOPER, R.E. (1930's). Horses, etc.

Catherine A. SPARKES (S.Hr., 1881). " The Story of Our Lives from Year to Year ". Six designs.

G. SPARROW (Modern, wartime).

Charlotte SPIERS (M.W., 1870-80's). "The well-known series of open envelope with flowers and a fan-fold ' Kakemono' screen ... flowers, birds and animals, all the animals being depicted in admirably decorative convention ". (G.W.)

Walter SPIERS (Private, 1876). " At least seven varieties ", one of the first private card designers.

Rose M. SPRAGUE (Prang, U.S.A., 1880).

Frederick SPURGIN (Avenue Series, 1900's). Comic postcard Christmas cards.

Alice SQUIRE (Tuck, 1881). £100 First prize, 1880 Competition. " Child-ren in landscapes—poppies are conspicuous in one of the cards ". (G.W.)

C. A. STANFIELD, R.A. Seapieces. " Private card " Series " In specially designed Tuck Box " (1887).

John C. STAPLES (H.&F., 1880's).

Mrs. M. Ellen STAPLES (*née* Miss M. E. Edwards—M.E.E.) (H.&F., 1881).

Arthur J. STARK (S.Hr., 1880's).

Henry Reynolds STEER (H.&F., 1880's). Fifth prize (£50) winner with four designs of musicians, Series No. 14, in 1881.

S. STEINBERG (U.S.A., modern). See Dust Jacket 37.

Emanuel STEINES (Basel).

J. STEPHENS (H.&F., 1882).

H. STERLING (S.Hr., 1881). Fifth prize winner.

W. K. STEVENS (H.&F., 1881). £25 prize winner.

Gunila STIERNGRANAT (Rust Craft, U.S.A., 1920's). Children.

H. J. STOCK (H.&F., 1889).

Marcus STONE, R.A. (Tuck, 1881-2). See Plate 106 and p. 149. Two of these designs were re-issued in 1887 on porcelain, entitled " Daydreams " and " Memories ".

Blanche STORY (S.Hr., H.&F., 1880's). £50 prize at H.&F., £20 prize at S.Hr. Competitions in 1881.

May (Mary) S. STORY (Tuck, S.Hr., 1880's). Fourth prize at Tuck, and £20 at S.Hr. Competitions. About the former designs—branches of beech trees, etc., with butterflies,—a contemporary critic wrote thus: "Natural is, perhaps, the highest praise we should accord them, but they are more; they show us nature in her most attractive mood. The subject is treated artistically throughout, the distances being kept very accurately . . ." *Stationer*, May 6, 1881.

George STUDDY (1920's). Comic dog sketches.

H. SUMNER (M.W., 1890's).

T. SULMAN (1870's).

Alice C. SWAN (S.Hr., 1881). Fourth prize in 1881.

Robert SWAN (Modern).

A. T. (T.B.&Co.). Highland dogs, robin and wren, etc.

Florence TABER (Prang, U.S.A., 1881). Fourth " popular award " prize, Prang's third Competition, 1881.

Margaret W. TARRANT (Medici, 1920's). Children, fairies.

Percy TARRANT (M.W., 1878; E.&S., H.&F., 1880's). £25 and £20 prizes, H.&F. Competition, 1881. Flowers, " exercises in the style of Japan " children, jester and other archaic characters, etc.

W. D. TEAGUE (U.S.A.). New York Public Library Exhibition of Christmas Card Designs, 1922-3.

Jane S. TEMPLAR (1895). (Third prize winner, *Studio* Competition, 1895).

Dorothy TENNANT (later Lady Stanley) (1880's). Children, dolls, street arabs.

K. TERRELL (Mrs. G. Koberwein-Terrell) (Tuck, 1880's). Three designs " after the style of Kate Greenaway " won Sixth prize (£25), Tuck's 1880 Competition. " Tolerably well done ", wrote a critic in 1881.

John THIRTLE (1896).

J. Gale THOMAS (Modern).

G. H. THOMPSON (Nister, Griffith Farran, 1880's). Female figures in windy landscapes, also " April Showers " (figures), 1885.

John THOMPSON (1829). Engraved on wood the " Anniversarie " card (see Fig. 1). He was a pupil of Robert Branston, the Bewick of what has been called the " London School " of wood-engraving at the end of the 18th and early 19th centuries. Thompson engraved many of Harvey's drawings after the latter came to London. " Among the very many excellent cuts which have been engraved in England within the last twenty years those executed by John Thompson rank foremost " stated Chatto and Jackson (History of Wood Engraving) in 1839.

S. (Stanley?) THOMPSON (Private, 1893). Pen and ink drawings.

Miss E. G. THOMSON (D.L.R., Ackermann, Prang, U.S.A., 1880's). " Fairy Land " series in 1881. Several sets of large cards: seahorses, shells, fishes and naked children.

J. K. THOMSON (S.Hr., 1881). £20 prize winner.

Archibald THORBURN (S.Hr., 1881). Fifth Prize winner. Floral subjects.

Charles THORNTON (Schipper, 1880's). Set of three gilt edge cards of Covent Gardens market (No. 1484), also Skating women (No. 1486), three cards of bell-ringers, carol-singers and waits (No. 1485).

Hall, THORPE (H.T. Studio, 1910-20's). Decorative flowers.

K. M. THORNTON (Modern).

C. TIGH (Modern).

Henri TILLEY (H.&F., 1881). £50 prize; " Adventures of Puss in Boots " and " The Marquis of Carabas amusingly depicted."

Patty TOWNSHEND (M.W., 1878-80 (cottages); H.&F., Tuck, 1881). Third prize for three cards with a crowd of quaint-looking children at Tuck competition, and £20 prize at H.&F.'s.

H. Tuck (S.Hr., 1881). Winner of a £20 prize.

W. H. (Harry) TUCK (Schipper, 1880's). Designer of " Our Pussy's Party " set of four cards, No. 797, two of which are reproduced on Plate 113. Other sets of four designs each include " The Feline Bicycle Club " (No. 1290) and a dogs' banquet with a cat as " The Uninvited Guest " (No. 1132).

Albert TUCKS (H.&F., 1880's). Smaller prize, 1881 Competition.

A. M. TURNER (Prang, U.S.A., 1884).

Arthur TWIDLE (1900-10).

May S. TYRER (1890's). Hon. Mention, Studio Competition, 1896.

E. M. U. (Hills, 1890's). "Illuminated" type of decoration.

Florence (and Bertha) UPTON (Nister, 1890's ?). Children, dolls.

A. V. (Marx, 1880's).

Louis VALLET (Paris, 1915-8). See Plate 196.

Elihu VEDDER (Prang, 1880-93). First prize ($1,000) Prang's Competition, 1880. (See Plate 105 and pp. 78, 150.) Another card, a folder, has " simply a glorious peacock feather " on the outside, while the inside is decorated by a large symbolic figure representing the title, " Aladdin's Lamp " (1884).

R. W. VERNON (A. Thomas, 1890's). Realistic spectacles with rosy glasses. The sentiment runs: " May everything this year Seem bright and rosy. This is my wish and I Firmly ' spec's ' it will ! "

Paul VINCZE (Modern).

A. VILIGIARDI (Modern). Italian " Anno Santo " card.

Henry VIZETELLY (1840-60). Engraved on wood many illustrations for Christmas books and subjects, including Birket Foster's " Christmas with the Poets " and " Christmas in the Olden Time ", Stanfield's " Poor Jack " by Marryat. Some of his blocks were used for Christmas cards.

Frederica VOGEL (Tuck, 1884). Flowers.

Douglas VOLK (Prang, U.S.A., 1884).

W. (1840-50). Two early cards of little girl feeding a robin, and boy in sailor's suit, Union Jack behind him, watching a robin.

A. W. (H.&F., 1880's). Birds.

C. W. (Tuck) (C. White).

E. W. (joined) (Emily Whymper).

I. W. (D.&S.) (Irwin Wood).

L.W. (joined) (Tuck) (Louisa, Marchioness of Waterford).

L. W. (not joined) (H.&F., and S.Hr.) (Linnie Watt).

W. J. W. (Tuck) (W. J. Wainwright or W. J. Webb ?).

Louis WAIN (Tuck, 1890-1900). Comic cat and dog drawings. Wain started at the age of 19 by making sketches for the *Sporting and Dramatic News* at agricultural shows, but his own " trained " cat, " Peter the Great ", made him more and more interested in " fanciful cat creations " as he called his designs. Sir W. Ingram published a double page of his " Cats " in the *Illustrated London News* and this established Wain's name as a house-hold word for a generation, though his designs—on cards and elsewhere—seem rather coarse to us to-day.

Henrietta G. WAINWRIGHT (1890's).

(S. ?) Beatrice WAINWRIGHT (Mrs. Roberts) (1890's).

W. J. WAINWRIGHT, A.R.W.S. (Private, 1890's). Etchings.

E. (Edward ?) WALKER (1880's).

Edith M. WALKER (Tuck, 1887). Palette shaped cards with moonlight seascapes, gold bevelled (four designs, No. 480), also in Mizpah series.

F. (Francis) S. WALKER, R.E. (D.L.R., 1882, Tuck, 1885 ?). Single female figures, for example a set of three designs " after the Leighton school, representing maidens dancing and playing on musical instruments " entitled " Queenly Beauties " (D.L.R., No. 541, 1882). " A Maid of Honour " and " A Leader of Fashion " (Tuck, " Artistic Series ").

M. (Marcella) WALKER (S.Hr., 1881, Tuck, 1887). £20 Prize, S.Hr. Competition. " Rosaline " (No. 870), " Juliet " (No. 871) and " Portia " (No. 872) vignetted crayon studies in black and white.

Marion WALKER (C. W. Faulkner, 1926).

Phyllis WALKER (C. W. Faulkner, 1920's). Figures.

Marjorie WALLINGFORD (Rust Craft, U.S.A., 1920's).

N. WALTER (?) (Tuck, 1887). Figures.

G. S. WALTERS, R.B.A. (S.Hr., 1881, C.W.F., 1900). £20 Prize winner. Boats. Plate 64.

Alfred WARD (M.W., 1878, H.&F., 1882). Female heads in monochrome.

A. H. WARREN (E.&S., 1880's).

Ellen WARRINGTON (Tuck, 1920's). Garden scenes. One of them showing an old sundial and " bearing most appropriately the nation's wish to Her Royal Highness [Princess Mary, the Princess Royal] on her betrothal, ' Upon the rounded dial of your life, Time's finger mark but bright and sunny hours ' " (1921).

Louisa, Marchioness of WATERFORD (Tuck, 1880's). A set of two designs, " Christmastide " (one of which is reproduced on Plate 93), the other shows a girl in white with orange and a holly branch in her hand and two pages holding her long white train. The popularity of the cards was probably due to the artist's name. It was reissued in various sizes in 1886, and again in Tuck's " Christmas Post Card Series " in the early 1900's.

Charles J. WATSON, R.E. (Private, 1892). Etchings.

Maud West WATSON (Tuck, 1920's). Dogs.

Linnie WATT (E.&S., 1879-85; H.&F., 1881; S.Hr., 1882-4 and Tuck, 1887). First prize (£150), and a £50 Fourth prize at S.Hr. Competition, and three prizes (£75, £50 and £20) at H.&F. Competition. Very charming children subjects. For an example see Plate 84.

G. F. WATTS, R.A. (1880's).

Clifford WEBB, R.E. (Heffer, modern).

W. J. WEBB (Tuck, 1887-8). Six designs illustrating the Parables of our Lord (Good Samaritan, Prodigal Son, etc.).

Thomas WEBSTER, R.A. (1840-50's).

A. W. WEEDON (H.&F., 1887). Boats.

Harrison WEIR (M.W., 1868-9, Ollendorff, 1870-80's). Animals, landscapes. Aesop set, 1881.

ulian Alden WEIR (Prang, U.S.A., 1884). Figures and landscapes.

C. D. (Charles Dater) WELDON (Prang, U.S.A., 1884). First prize, Prang's fourth Competition, 1884. Comics. Weldon was a popular cartoonist of the American *Daily Graphic*.

A. WEST (H.&F., 1890's). Birds on branches.

Dora WHEELER (Mrs. Keith) (Prang, U.S.A.). Second prize ($500), Prang's Competition, 1881, and the Artists' and Popular First Prizes, i.e. $2,000, in 1881. (See Colour Plate XIb and p. 150.)

W. H. WHEELER (Buzza, U.S.A., 1920's).

Rex WHISTLER (Modern).

C. WHITE (Mrs. Cheverton White) (Tuck, 1880-90's). "Famous Palaces" (four designs, scroll shaped cards, No. 2350, 1886), "Effective Country Views" (No. 2427, 1886), "Vignetted forest scenes" No. 234, 1887).

F. H. WHITE (H.&F., 1886). Landscapes.

Walter WHITEHEAD, F.S.A. New York Public Library Exhibition of Christmas Card Designs, 1922-3.

O. E. WHITNEY (U.S.A., 1870's). "The first ones, [i.e. Christmas cards], flower cards, were designed by Mrs. O. E. Whitney, who, it is said, based her idea on the decorated business card of Louis Prang, the lithographer, shown at the Vienna Exposition of 1873" (Weitenkampf, pp. 286-7). Gleeson White refers to these as "Charming flower studies by D. E. Whitney" (initials erroneous).

E. Herbert WHYDALE (1890's).

Annette WHYMPER (H.&F., 1880-6; E.&S., 1880's). Seascapes.

Edward WHYMPER (Relig. Tract Soc., 1884). Wood-engravings.

Emily (Mrs. J. W.) WHYMPER (S.Hr., 1880's). Two Fifth prizes in 1881 Competition ("Groups of Butterflies, with grasses and flowers and landscapes in circular panels", three designs, No. 49, issued also as Nos. 1249 and 3683, on different mounts); "Roses over the Garden Wall", four designs, issued as Nos. 98 and 37. She produced a great number of long, narrow cards with ferns and grasses which were surprisingly popular during the later 80's.

W. J. WIEGAND (M.W., 1870's; H.&F., 1880's; Tuck, 1887). £20 prize, H.&F. Competition, 1881. "Sir Roger de Coverley", four designs, Tuck, No. 741.

A. WILDE PARSONS (Tuck, Nister, Griffith Farran, 1885-90). Seascapes.

WILHELM, King of Württemberg (Private, 1902-6).

WILHELMINA, Queen of Holland (Private, 1943-6). (See Plate 36.)

Ellis WILKINSON (S.Hr., 1881). Fifth prize.

Norman WILKINSON (Modern).

Mrs. F. WILLIAMS (H.&F., 1881).

Sheldon WILLIAMS (Walker & Co., 1881). "Hunting" Series, No. 133.

Wilton WILLIAMS (Modern).

H. G. WILLINK (H.&F., 1880's).

Merton WILLMORE (Gibson, U.S.A.). Modern. "Largely responsible for many of their [Gibson's] clever ideas".

Ernest WILSON (H.&F., 1880-4). A number of attractive landscapes, floral vignettes, typical of the 80's and 90's.

T. Walter WILSON (M.W., 1878-80). Folding triptychs, "Japanese lacquer cabinet with folding doors" (G.W.).

E. M. WIMPERIS (M.W., 1869).

Rachel R. WINDHAM (Modern).

W. H. WINSRIDGE (Tuck, 1887). "Companions", "Under the Greenwood Tree" on porcelain.

C. WOLLETT (Tuck, 1887-90). "Ideal Heads from Tennyson" (four designs, No. 724), "Floral Designs" (crayon heads, four designs, No. 826), "Angels' Heads in Clouds" (two designs, No. 551).

Frank WOOD (1900's).

Irwin WOOD (D.&S., 1868-70).

Alice B. WOODWARD (1890's).

E. C. WOODWARD (1890's).

Stanley WOOLLETT (Savory, 1920's). Figures.

G. WOUGA (?) (Braun & Co., 1860's). Swiss mountain flowers.

Gilbert WRIGHT (Tuck, 1880-90.) Some reprinted in 1920's. Coaches.

W. L. WYLLIE (Private, 1892). Etchings.

Norman WYETH (U.S.A., 1920's).

D. W. WYNFIELD (H.&F., 1881-2). "Female figures illustrating the Seasons" won £50 at 1881 Competition.

W. F. YEAMES, R.A. (Tuck, 1881-2). Female figures for a set entitled "Caged Cupids". (See pp. 148-9 and Plate 103.)

Chiang YEE (Modern). Flowers, animals, English scenes painted in his Chinese manner.

The ZORACHS (U.S.A.). New York Public Library Exhibition of Christmas Designs, 1922-3.

J. B. ZWECKER (1870-80's). Birds.

A List of Old Christmas Card Sentiment Writers

L. N. A. (1880).

ADA (1870).

AIRD (H.&F., 1890).

Mrs. C. F. ALEXANDER (M.W., 1890's, including " Literary " Series of 1895).

Dean ALFORD (1880's).

W. R. ANDERSON (Volland, U.S.A., 1900).

Frances ANNANDALE (Meissner and Buch, 1890's).

Warwick ARMSTRONG (1870-80).

W. Blake ATKINSON (Goodall, Tuck, 1870-80).

A. AUSTIN (Hills & Co., 1908-10). " Empire " Series.

AUTHOR of *John Halifax, Gentleman*, i.e. Mrs. Craik (Miss D. M. Mulock).

C. B. (Nister, 1880).

G. B. (M.W., 1870—).

H. M. B. (Helen Marion Burnside).

J. B. (Meissner and Buch, 1890).

L. B. (1870-80).

N. S. B. (Tuck, 1880).

H. S. BAINBRIDGE (Relig. Tract. Soc., 1888-90).

Astley H. BALDWIN (U.S.A., 1880's). An example quoted on p. 205.

Julia A. BARKER (Nister, Dutton, U.S.A., 1890's).

May Geraldine BATEMAN (M. W., 1890's).

R. BATEMAN (Robert Bateman). Also on Kate Greenaway designs in *People's Magazine.*

Johnston BEALL (1880).

Canon BELL (Castell, 1880's).

Lucy A. BENNETT (" The Peniel " set, Castell Bros., 1880-90).

Dudley BERESFORD (Modern).

Edgar BERRIE (M.W., 1883).

E. H. BICKERSTETH, D.D., Bishop of Exeter (Tuck, 1880-90; also Relig. Tract Soc., 1884).

Nana French BICKFORD (U.S.A., 1910). For an example, see p. 206.

Clifton BINGHAM (1880-90).

Osburn BLACKBURN (1890).

BONAR (1880-90). (Horatius Bonar, D.D.).

Carrie Jacob BOND (Volland, U.S.A., 1910).

Edward BRADLEY (Cuthbert Bede) (1840's).

Ethel M. BRAINERD (U.S.A., 1910-20).

Mrs. Carey BROCK (M.W., 1880's).

C. BROOKE (Nister, Griffith Farran, 1880's).

Phillips BROOKS (U.S.A., 1890-1910). Famous " O little town of Bethlehem " and others often quoted, especially on American cards.

Evelyn Gage BROWN (U.S.A., 1920).

E. B. BROWNING (M.W., 1880-90).

(William C. ?) BRYANT (The American poet ?) (H.&F., 1870-80's).

Thornton W. BURGESS (U.S.A., 1910-20).

J. D. BURNS (Relig. Tract Soc., 1880's).

Helen Marion BURNSIDE (b. 1843). Many publishers, both in England and America; said to have written about 6,000 Christmas and other sentiments between 1874 and 1900. (See p. 200 and p. XXIV.)

A. T. C. (M.W., 1860-70).

E. H. C.

J. C. (or J. G. ?) (M.W., 1870-80, including Kate Greenaway cards).

M. C. (M.W., 1870).

N. C. (Prang, U.S.A., 1880).

S. K. C. (Major Samuel K. Cowan) (S.Hr., Tuck, etc., 1883-1898). N.B.— Sometimes cursive S.H.E. appears under sentiments on cards, but written so that the last two letters could very easily be taken as K and C. These were pirate cards, *not* by his usual publishers, and the pirating suggests the importance attached to a sentiment by a renowned specialist in the 1880's and 1890's !

CAMPBELL (1890).

Rosa Nouchette CAREY (1870-90).

Lewis CARROLL (C. L. Dodgson). N.B.—I only know one " card " by Lewis Carroll, a neatly printed folder " To All Child-Readers of Alice's Adventures in Wonderland " dated " Christmas, 1871 ".

Alice CARY (H.&F., 1880's). The American novelist.

M. CATHER (H.&F., 1880's).

Faith CHILTERN.

Eliza COOK (many publishers, 1860-90). See p. 200.

A. CONQUILL (1870).

CORE (Goodall, 1870).

Barry CORNWALL (i.e. Bryan W. PROCTER) (Goodall, 1870's).

Samuel K. COWAN (usually added: " M.A. ") (S.Hr., Tuck, M.&B., etc., 1883-98) Major Cowan wrote 1,005 verses in 1884 for eleven firms! See pp. 183, 204.

D. M. CRAIK (Tuck, 1880's).

Walter CRANE (M.W., 1870-95). Texts for his own designs.

CROWQUILL (Goodall, 1860). Alfred Henry Forrester and his brother, Charles Robert, used this pseudonym jointly. The latter wrote the rhymes, according to F. J. Harvey Darton. (See footnote, p. 121.)

J. CULVERWELL (M.W.).

G. E. D. (M.W.).

H. A. D. (M.W.).

C. D.

R. D.

S. D. (Sarah Doudney).

Coombes DAVIES (Davidson, 1880-90's).

Albert A. DAVIS (Davis, U.S.A., 1906).

Francis DAVIS (M.W., 1870-80).

Dorothy DE JAGERS (U.S.A., 1920).

A. Louise DENNISTON (U.S.A., 1910-20).

C. L. DODGSON (see Lewis Carroll).

Sarah DOUDNEY (M.W., Prang, U.S.A., 1890).

Constance A. DUBOIS (Davidson, 1890's).

E. Eliza Cook's early signature.

A. F. EARL (U.S.A., 1900).

EBA (1880).

Charles EDEN (M.W., including Kate Greenaway designs). Also in *People's Magazine.*

ELBETEE (L. B. T. ?) (Hagelberg, 1890).

C. ELLIOTT (1880's).

G. ELIOT (George Eliot, i.e. Marian Evans Lewes) (M.W., 1870-80).

E. J. ELLIS (M.W., including Kate Greenaway designs in *People's Magazine*).

" ERIN " (M.W.)

Evelyn EVERETT-GREEN (Nelson, 1870-80).

Julianna Horatia EWIG (S.P.C.K., 1880's).

F. (M.W., 1870's).

E. S. F. (Prang, U.S.A., 1880).

Frederick W. FABER (Hill & Co.). Religious poems.

Lady FALKLAND (1890's). Originator of the idea of Christmas cards (and Valentines) for the blind in Braille. (*Strand Magazine*, 1901).

C. A. FARMER (U.S.A., 1915-20).

Marianne FARNINGHAM.

H. FARRAND (Goodall, 1870's).

Canon [Frederick W.] FARRAR (sometimes Archdeacon Farrar) (Tuck, 1880-90; also for M.W. " Literary " Series in 1895).

Frank FERNDALE (1880).

G. A. FINLAYSON (Davidson, late 1890's).

Spencer M. FREE (U.S.A.). A surgeon by profession and man of letters by inclination, for many years Dr. Free used to send out " upwards 4,000 Christmas cards and in 1922 the number had increased to 4,900 ". (Chase.)

J. L. E. FREEMAN (E.&S., 1879).

Emily Shaw FORMAN (Prang, U.S.A., 1880-90's).

J. Hain FRISWELL (M.W., 1880's).

James (" Jim ") W. FOLEY (Buzza, Volland, U.S.A., 1910—).

Charles A. Fox (1880-90).

A. I. G. (M.W., 1860-70).

A. L. G. (M.W., 1860-80). Adam Lindsay Gordon, Australian poet ?

E. E. G. (E. E. Griffin). See p. 185.

E. M. G. (M.W.).

J. G. (Julia Goddard).

Norman GALE (M.W. " Literary " Series Christmas cards). " Admirable ", says the critic of the *Artist* in December, 1895.

Richard LE GALLIENNE (M.W., 1895). The " Literary " Series.

J. E. GALLIFORT (1880).

A. GASKELL (M.W., 1880).

Theo GIFT (?) (Nister, 1885-6).

W. S. GILBERT (H.&F., 1881).

A. GILL (S.Hr., 1880's).

Fannie GODDARD (Tuck, 1890).

Julia GODDARD (M.W., 1880-90).

"Meta GOING " (1880-90).

" Miss GOULD " (H.&F., 1880-90).

John Richard GREEN (M.W., 1870's, including K.G.). The historian ?

E. E. GRIFFIN (Hagelberg, 1882-90).

Ellen GUBBIN (Griffith, 1880's).

Edgar GUEST (Buzza, U.S.A., 1920-30. " The poet of the people ", well known for his " Just Folks " poems. In 1922 gave exclusive rights to his writing to this firm (Chase).

A. M. H. (1880).

A. R. H. (M.W., 1870).

F. E. E. H. (M.W., 1870).

F. G. H. (M.W.).

F. R. H. (Frances Ridley Havergal) (1870-90).

J. B. H. (M.W., 1870's).

M. H. (M.W., 1870).   Margaret Hamer ?

M. S. H. (G. W. Faulkner, 1888-1900).   Margaret Haycraft ?

S. C. H. (S. C. Hall).

W. H. (M.W., 1860-70).

Mary Estabrook HALE (U.S.A., 1920).

Molly A. HALEY (Volland, U.S.A., 1910).

Newman HALL (Tuck, 1887).

Samuel Carter HALL (Goodall, M.W., 1860-70).

Ada C. HANCROFT (1880's).

E. (Emma) HARDY (M.W.).

A. O. HARRIS (Tuck, 1890).

Clifford HARRISON (1900's).

Virginia Bioren HARRISON (Dutton, U.S.A.; Nister, 1890-1900).

W. H. HARPER (Portheim & Co., 1890).

Cecilia HAVERGAL (1890).

Frances Ridley HAVERGAL (M.W., and many publishers, 1870-90's).   (See p. 200.)

Margaret Scott HAYCRAFT (M.W., Relig. Tract Soc., 1885-90's).

M. S. HAYCRAFT (Tuck, 1880-90).

George HERBERT (Castell Bros., 1880's).

S. HERBERT (1880's).   Is it G. Herbert ?

M. E. HERITAGE(McKenzie, 1890).

Enis HERNE (M.W., 1870-80's).

M. HILL (M.W.).

Rowley HILL, Bishop of Sodor and Man (Tuck, 1880's).

J. G. HOLLAND (H.&F.).   Josiah Gilbert Holland, the American poet ?

A. M. HONE (1890).

(Tom) HOOD (H.&F.).   " Many men have written well, but Dickens wrote Weller ! ", etc.   His Prince Silverwings and Frank's visit to the Insect World may have contributed to the popularity of insects on Christmas card pictures in the latter 1870's.

Thomas HOOD (1860's-70's).   Father of " Tom ".

Eden HOOPER (M.W., Tuck, E.&S., 1880-90).   Example on p. 203.

I. St. A. HORTON (Ollendorff, 1880).

Agnes R. HOWELL.

M. J. J. (M.W.).

A. K. Harvey JAMES (1910-20).

Bertha E. JACQUES (U.S.A., 1900). See List of Publishers, p. 272.

M. R. JARVIS (1890's).

Sir W. JONES. " Asiatic Jones " of the late eighteenth century ?

E. K. (M.W., 1870-80). Also ballad on back of Kate Greenaway " Robin Hood " cards.

E. T. K. (M.W., 1896-7). " Evan T. Keane " (pseudonym).

Gus KAHN (Buzza, U.S.A., 1920-30).

" Evan T. KEANE ". Said to have been a clergyman holding a high public position in 1896.

Eliza (Annie ?) KEARY (M.W., 1880-90's).

KEBLE (the Rev. John Keble) (Griffith, 1880's).

Watson KIRKCONNELL (Canada, Modern).

Samuel E. KISER (Volland, U.S.A., 1910-20).

E. A. L. KNIGHT (sometimes E. A. Lampiere-Knight) (H.&F., 1890).

F. L. (M.W.). (F. Levien ?)

W. J. L. (M.W., 1880's).

The Rev. F. (Frederick) LANGBRIDGE (of St. John's, Limerick) (Tuck, 1870-86).

F. LEVIEN (M.W., 1870's).

R. E. LONSDALE (Goodall, 1870).

LORD (Davis, U.S.A., 1910).

The Marquis of LORNE (Tuck, 1880-90).

E. LOVE (1880).

The Rev. S. C. LOWRY (1880-90's).

B. M. (H.&F., 1880).

E. M. M. (H.&F., 1880-90).

E. N. M. (1860's).

G. P. M. (G. P. Meade).

J. M. (E.&S., 1880).

M. S. M. (1890).

Helen Lovejoy McCARTHY (Rust Craft, U.S.A., 1910-30). " Amongst the best sellers in America ".

George MACDONALD (Dr. G. Macdonald) (Tuck, 1880).

J. R. MACDUFF, the Rev. (M.W., 1880-93 ?).

Marguerite McGREGOR (U.S.A., 1920).

J. P. McEVOY (Volland, later Buzza, U.S.A., 1910-22, 1930).

C. (Charles) MACKAY (W. A. Mansell, 1880).

Joseph M'KAY (M.W., 1876).

M. MADDICK (1890).

John Gillespie MAGEE, Jr. (U.S.A., modern). His sentiment is reprinted on p. 197.

A. V. MAHAFFEY (U.S.A., 1920).

Edwin MARKHAM (Davis, U.S.A., 1910-20).

Janet MARSH (1890).

Averil C. MAYNARD (U.S.A., 1920).

G. P. MEADE (M.W., 1870-90, including many Kate Greenaway designs).

J. W. MEEK (U.S.A., 1920).

Alice MEYNELL (M.W., 1896-7).

J. S. B. MONSELL (1880's).

(James) MONTGOMERY (M.W., 1870).

MOORE (1860-90).

Clement Clark MOORE (U.S.A.). Author of " A Visit by St. Nicholas " frequently reprinted by American publishers. See Dust Jacket No. 16.

Sarah L. (Louisa) MOORE (U.S.A. ?) (H.&F., 1880's).

H. E. MORICE (1880-90).

Sir Lewis MORRIS (M.W., 1890's).

William MORRIS (1880-90's). See Plate 40.

M. F. MOSS (H.&F., A.Hr., 1880's).

Frank MOXON (U.S.A., 1920).

Dinah M. MULOCK (" The Author of *John Halifax, Gentleman* "), later Mrs. Craik (Tuck, 1870-80's).

Charlotte MURRAY (1880-90). For an example of her sentiments, see p. 204.

J. W. MYERS (H.&F., C. W. Faulkner, 1880-1900).

E. N. (1900).

Rev. Dr. NEALE, C.W.F., 1920's.

" E. NESBIT " (Mrs. Hubert Bland, afterwards Mrs. Bland-Tucker) (Griffith Farran, Nister, M.W., 1890's). The " Literary " Series. E. Nesbit, whose books were later sold in huge editions, had to undertake hand-colouring of Christmas cards in an effort to support himself and his family in former years.

Wilbur D. NESBIT (Volland, U.S.A., 1908-20, 1930).

Thomas (or Roden ?) NOEL (1860-70's).

Lewis NOVRA (1890).

R. I. O. (M.W.).

G. W. OLLETT (1900).

F. P. (1880-90).

Dollie M. PARKE (U.S.A., 1920).

Bernice PARKER (U.S.A., 1920).

Ella Randall PEARCE (Rust Craft, U.S.A., 1910-20).

Eva PEDEN (U.S.A., 1920).

Hannah Wheeler PINGREE (U.S.A., 1910-20). Six letter Christmas cards. (See p. 184.)

F. Ernest POWER (1880).

Kate PRICE (Tuck, 1880's).

Lawrence PRICE (early 1600's). Celebrated ballad-monger. Author of a pamphlet: *Make Room for Christmas*. (Reprinted by Professor Rollins in 1920.)

Edith PRINCE (Tuck, 1880's).

A. (Adelaide) PROCTER (Tuck, 1881).

" Roger QUIDDAM " (Ollendorff, etc., 1880's).

R. (M.W., including Kate Greenaway card).

H. R. R. (M.W., 1870-80).

M. E. R.

Mrs. Dollie Radford (M.W., 1896-7).

B. Montgomery RANKING (M.W., 1876-80).

Alice REED (Nister, 1890's).

Myrtle REED (Volland, U.S.A., 1910).

Percy W. REYNOLDS (U.S.A., 1920).

S. RICKARDS (M.W., 1870's).

James Whitcomb RILEY (U.S.A., 1910).

Sarah ROBERTS (Prang, U.S.A., 1890).

Fanny ROCHAT (many publishers, 1880-90).

Mary E. ROPES (Relig. Tract Soc., 1880-90's).

Christina G. ROSSETTI (on C. Gaskin designs (Fig. 17) and also on some Prang prize-winning cards, etc.).

James ROWE (U.S.A., 1920).

Fred RUST (Rust Craft, U.S.A., 1906). (See p. 199.)

Rt. Rev. J. C. RYLE, Bishop of Liverpool (Tuck, 1887).

A. S. (1880).

F. S. (1890).

G. E. S. (Mrs. Gertrude E. Shaw).

I. S. (H.&F., 1880).

S. L. S. (1890).

" SABINA " (1880-90).

Gladys SALISBURY (Buzza, U.S.A., 1920-30).

A. L. SALMON (H.&F., 1880).

E. SANGER (H.&F., 1890).

F. SCHUYLER MATHEWS (Prang, U.S.A., 1890).

W. H. SEAL (1880).

SEARS (M.W., 1890's, including " Literary " Series).

Emily SELINGER (U.S.A., 1910-20).

Richard SHANNE. An early 17th century Yorkshire commonplace book preserved an old, apparently Catholic, ballad " Bewailing the tyme of Christmas, so much decayed in Englande " of about 1624 (Rollins, Old English Ballads, Cambridge, 1920. pp. 372-5.)

Gertrude E. SHAW (M.W., 1892-7).

Henry SIMPSON (Modern).

A. (Alexander) SMITH (Dickes, H.&F., 1860-70). (See p. 116.)

Emma B. SNOW (U.S.A., 1900-10).

Marie L. SPADER (U.S.A., 1920's).

Robert N. STANNARD (U.S.A., 1920's).

Frank L. STANTON (Buzza, U.S.A., 1920-30).

Robert Louis STEVENSON (1880-1900's). See p. 162.

S. J. STONE (Relig. Tract Soc., 1880's).

Agnes STONEWER (M.W., 1870's).

Hesba Dora STRETTON (M.W., 1880's).

A. T. (Adolph Tuck). According to the recollection of his son, Sir Adolph Tuck was responsible for some of the sentiments on early Tuck cards from 1879 onwards. (*Evening Standard*, December 3, 1938.)

C. M. T. (M.W., 1870-80).

C. W. T. (M.W.).

E. I. T. (Emma J. Taylor).

J. T. (Yapp and Hawkins, 1857; Hawkins, 1880).

Y. E. T. (Caswell, 1878-80).

Emma J. TAYLOR (D.&S., 1884).

G. M. TAYLOR (Prang, U.S.A. ?, 1890).

Alfred, Lord TENNYSON (M.W., 1880's). " Christmas bells " and " Ring out, wild bells ". (See also p. 201.)

Celia THAXTER (Prang, U.S.A., 1880-93). Author of many prominently printed and signed sentiment verses on Prang's prize-winning cards. (See p. 150.)

Martha B. THOMAS (U.S.A., 1920's).

E. Constance THOMPSON (Meissner and Buch, 1890).

Clara THWAITES (1890-1900).

Mrs. Daniel TOMKINS (1886-7).

Thomas K. TULLY (M.W., 1880).

(Martin F.) TUPPER (1880-90).

V. Philip UNDERWOOD (1930's).

Henry VAN DYKE (Davis, U.S.A., 1900.). Writer of successful prose sentiment quoted on p. 207.

E. K. W. (M.W.).

F. D. W. (M.W., 1870-80). Sentiment set to music by B. H. Carroll, and published together as a folder card in the mid-70's.

J. L. W. (J. L. Watson) (M.W.).

Marion WALLACE (Davidson, 1897-8).

Ellis WALTON (Tuck, Nister, 1880-90's).

J. L. WATSON (M.W.).

F. E. WEATHERLY (M.W., Tuck, 1880-90).

W. Dutton WEGEFARTH (Volland, U.S.A., 1910-28).

The Rev. Charles WESLEY (M.W., Griffith, 1884).

J. L. WHERLAND (1880's).

Mrs. WHITCOMBE (D.&S., 1880's).

H. M. WHITLAW (1890). (See p. 203.)

Kate Douglas WIGGINS (U.S.A., 1880-1900).

R. WILTON (Walker, 1880-90's).

M. M. WINGRAVE (1890).

M. W. WOOD (1910's).

E. C. WRENFORD (1879-80).

Shirley WYNNE (H.&F., Ollendorff, 1880's).

Charlotte M. YONGE (M.W., Griffith, 1870-90's).

> " A tiny souvenir—but still
>   It proves affection and regard,
> For worlds of kindness and goodwill
>   Are carried by a Christmas card ! "
>
> *Anonymous sentiment on a long mono-chrome Christmas card from the 1890's.*

A List of
Christmas Card Publishers

A. S. Co. (Artistic Stationery Company, Ltd.).

S. PH. A., 1880's.

A. ABRAHAMS & SON, 1890. Mostly hand-painted cards.

Arthur ACKERMANN, London (191 Regent Street, W.), 1877-1900. Sole agent for L. Prang's American cards. (According to E. Morrill it was Ackermann's wife who "sent over in the 1870's the suggestion that on trade cards and announcements [then produced by Prang] the name and address of the firm be omitted and replaced by inserting words of greeting for such seasonal celebrations and occasions as Christmas and Easter".

ADAM & CO., Newcastle, 1870's.

ADAMS and SCANLAN, Southampton (Alhambra Studio, High Street), 1880's. (Photographic.)

Joseph ADDENBROOKE, London (101 Hatton Garden, E.C.), 1840—. (Valentine types.)

AMERICAN ARTISTS GROUP, New York, U.S.A., 1930's—.

F. ANGER, London (8 Newgate Street, E.C.), 1880's.

A. ANGERMANN, London (1 Old Jewry, E.C.), 1864-9. Sole agent for Hagelberg, Berlin.

William Collin ARCHER, London (4 Rose Street, E.C.), 1890's.

F. APPEL, Paris (12 Rue de Delta), 1870-80's.

ARS SACRA (H. Dubler Inc.), New York, U.S.A. Modern.

ARTISTIC LITHOGRAPHIC COMPANY (Obpacher Bros.), Munich and London (10 Bunhill Row, E.C.), 1890's.

ARTISTIC STATIONERY COMPANY, Ltd., originally founded in Glasgow and Leeds, later London (Plough Court, Fetter Lane, E.C.), 1879. Became Ltd. in 1882. Associated with Leadenhall Press.

AUBRY, Ed., Paris, 1870's. London distributor: Marion & Co. Delightful lace, silk and mother of pearl combination cards.

AUSTEN'S DRAPERY STORES—" For the Best Xmas Cards " (Advertisement on floral cards, 1880's).

B. & S., 1890's.

B. BROS. (Baddeley Bros.).

D. B., 1882.

E. B. & Co. (E. Bollans of Leamington).

J. B. B. & Co., 1880's. (Birds cards, including dead birds, by H. Bright, etc.)

O. B. SERIES. Represented by J. F. Schipper (Obpacher Bros.).

T. B. & Co. (1880's).

W. B. & O. (Wirths Bros. and Owen), New York, 1880's.

BADDELEY BROS., London (Fore Street, later Chapel Street and Moor Lane), 1865's—.

A. BAIRD & SON, Glasgow, 1890's. London agent: G. Stewart & Sons.

Samuel BARRETT, London (8 Shepherdess Walk), 1870's—.

(R. T.) BARRAS AND (J.) BLACKET, Sheffield and Rotherham, 1868—.

Alfred BARTLETT, Boston, U.S.A., 1900—. Publisher of famous " Cornhill Dodgers ", printed usually in two colours on bevelled boards. For an example, see Fig. 7.

George BAXTER, London (11, Great Distaff Lane, Cheapside, 1827-30 ; 29 King Square, Goswell Road, 1830-5 ; 3 Charterhouse Square, 1835-43 ; 11 Northampton Square, 1843-51 ; and 11 and 12 Northampton Square, 1851-60, when he retired). See pp. 37-8.

J. BEAGLES & Co., London, 1885. Small hand-coloured photographs.

" BENEATH THE APPLE TREE ". Gardenville (Orchard Avenue), New York, U.S.A., 1915-20. J. J. Lanke's early cards cut on apple wood.

J. F. BENNET, London (Queen Street, Cheapside, E.C.), 1880's. Introduced visiting card cases as Christmas cards, 1884.

John BENNETT, London (4 Carthusian Street, E.C.), 1870-90's.

BIRN BROS., London (27 Finsbury Street, E.C.), 1890's—. Large cards with floral decorations and Biblical texts.

G. BISHOP & Co., London (101 Houndsditch, N.E.), 1860's. " The cheapest house in the world " advertisement in *Stationer*, September 1, 1865.

J. BOGNARD, Jor. [*sic*], probably U.S.A., 1870's.

Edward BOLLANS & Co. (late H. GOODE & Co.), Leamington (Ranelagh Works; and Castle Court, St. Bride Street, London, E.C.), 1840's-1890. Perfume sachets, fan and other valentine type Christmas cards.

BOLLANS, FERRIMAN & Co. (E. Bollans & Co.).

BOLLEN AND TIDSWELL, London, 1880's.

BONASSE-LEBEL AND FILS AND MASSIN, Paris (29 Rue St. Sulpice), 1880-90's. Mainly religious cards.

BOOK SOCIETY, London, 1889-90. Large religious cards printed in Austria-Hungary.

BRACE, BRACE & Co., London (Red Lion Court, Fleet Street, E.C.), 1869. " Scented by Eugene Rimmel " cards.

BRADSHAW AND BLACKLOCK, Manchester (53 Boundary Street, W.), and London, 1850's-1860's. See pp. 39-40.

BRAINERD, Philadelphia, U.S.A., 1870's (?).

BRAUN & CO., Genève, Switzerland, 1860-70's. Mainly mountain flower subjects.

BRAUN & SCHNEIDER, Munich (Germany), 1890's (London distributors : H. Grevel and Co.). Movables and various animated cards.

Julius BRODHAG, London (90 Newgate Street, E.C.), 1870's. Taken over by H. W. Sanders in the summer of 1881.

W. BROOKE, 1860-70's. Notepaper headings, etc.

BROOKS, London (Vere Street, W.), 1876—. Pen-and-ink designs.

Charles S. BROWN, London (11 Castle Street, City Road), 1870's.

J. H. BUFFORD'S SONS, Boston, U.S.A., 1876. Little-known early American publishers. Some cards jointly marked with " J. Latham & Co."; others also claimed as " Bufford's Oil Chromos ", no doubt in competition with Prang's chromos, which " he coined with the intention of using it as a trade name ".

T. H. BURKE, London (12 Bull Head Court, Newgate), 1840's-1850's. Finely embossed cards; black swan, etc.

BURNS, OATES AND WASHBOURNE, Ltd., London, modern.

The BUZZA-RHEEM COMPANY, later The Buzza Company, Minneapolis, U.S.A. (Craft Acres). This firm commenced to produce Christmas cards— starting with twenty-four designs—in 1909. " The designs were more poster-like than other cards of that time " (E. D. Chase).

BYRNE & CO., Richmond (Hill Street), 1880's. Photo-compositions on 4¼ by 6¼ size mounts.

A. S. C. & Co., London, 1885.—Artistic Stationery Co.

J. C. & S. L., 1870-80's ?

CAMPBELL AND TUDHOPE, Glasgow, 1860's—. Religious cards, chiefly decorated with Biblical quotations. This firm's cards are sometimes also marked by Caswell. Opened London branch (45 St. Paul's Churchyard) in 1881.

CAMPBELL ART CO., U.S.A., 1910-20's. See Plate 199.

Robert CANTON, London (7 Dowgate Hill and 172 Aldersgate Street, E.C. in the 1860's; 22 and 23 Aldersgate Street, E.C., from 1869; and 2 Jewin Street, E.C., in 1884). Early publisher of valentine, visiting card and most other types of Christmas cards. See pp. 42, 62, Plates 31, 34 and Dust Jacket Nos. 5, 24.

CARFAX CARDS, LTD., modern.

CARR AND MASON, 1884.

CONRAD'S FINE ART PUBLISHING CO., London, modern.

CARTLER, London, Paris, New York, 1890's—and modern.

CASTELL BROS., London, 1870's-1900's. Cards, especially later, usually " Printed in Bavaria ".

Charles CASWELL, Birmingham (135, Broad Street), 1860-90. Chiefly religious cards.

CATHOLIC TRUTH SOCIETY, London (38 Eccleston Square), 1884—.

CATNACH PRESS, London (2 & 3 Monmouth Court, Seven Dials, Bloomsbury), 1813-41, James Catnach; 1841-5 J. (James) Paul & Co.; 1845-59, A. (Anne) Ryle & Co. ; and finally 1859-1880's, W. (William) S. Fortey. Song-sheets, Poetry Cards, Ballads and Hymns (broadsheets), Valentines, Scripture Sheets, Christmas Pieces, Twelfth Night Characters, Carols, etc., etc.

CAYER & CO., Paris, 1870-80's ?

CHAMPENOIS ET CIE, Paris, 1881—. Successors to Testu & Massin. (Their Christmas cards were stocked by Walmesley and Lewis, Islington, N.)

CHARLES, REYNOLDS & CO., 1870's.

J. CHENEY, Banbury (At the Unicorn) printed a delightful broadsheet for the local Bellmen, T. Harbert and B. James, in 1784. The broadsheet (size 16⅞ by 21¾ inches) contains verses " On Christmas Eve ", " On Christmas Day ", " On New Year's Day ", " On Twelfth Day " etc. (*John Cheney and his descendants*, 1936).

The SOCIETY FOR THE PROMOTION OF CHRISTIAN KNOWLEDGE (S.P.C.K.), London (13 Paternoster Row, E.C.), 1880's—.

The CHURCH ARTISTS' AGENCY, London (25 Ebury Street, S.W.1), 1940's.

CLEMENT, TOUNIER & CIE., Genéve, Switzerland, 1890-1900 ?

Wm. COLLINS, SONS & CO., Ltd., Glasgow (139 Stirling Road), Edinburgh (The Mound), London (Bridewell Place, E.C.), 1880's—.

William COLLYER & CO., London (42 Jewin Street, E.C.), 1868-70. Including chromos, lithographs imported from Paris.

F. Guy CORKE, Registered (?).

W. S. COWELL, Ipswich, 1873-4.

Joseph CUNDALL, London (12 Old Bond Street, W.). Cole's friend, printer and partner in Summerly's Home Treasury from 1841 to 49. (Later, in the 1850's, Cundall continued to edit, reprint or " superintend " many books illustrated by Harrison Weir, Birket Foster, John Absolon and others.)

CURRIER & IVES, New York, U.S.A., 1870-80's (?)

CYNICUS PUBLISHING CO., LTD., Taypart, Fife, 1905. Cards designed by the popular cartoonist, Cynicus.

D. & S., London (Dean and Son).

Duncan C. DALLAS, London, 1860's. Clowns rolling Christmas pudding of the size of a man, etc.

DARTON and CO., London (58 Holborn Hill), 1844-62. Illuminated cards.

DAVIDSON BROTHERS, Manchester and London (9 Jewin Street, E.C., and 27 Edmunds Buildings, E.C.), 1880's-90's. " Excellent taste and full of dainty inventions " (G. White, 1894).

Albert M. DAVIS (later THE A. M. Davis Company), Boston, U.S.A. Started in 1907 with eight postcard-size cards. Next year line increased to sixteen Christmas and eight New Year cards, chiefly text and very little ornamentation. To-day this firm is one of the biggest publishers, with a world-wide organisation.

A. M. DAVIS & CO., LTD., London, modern. Publishers of well known " Quality Cards ".

DAY & SON (or W. DAY & SON), London (Lincoln's Inn Fields), 1850—. (N.B.—William Day and Owen Jones produced the chromo-lithographs for the famous " Arabian Antiquities of Spain " (1842), one of the first books illustrated in colours in England.)

John B. DAY, London (Savoy Street, Strand), 1868—. In 1870 this firm produced attractive postcards, including realistic halfpenny stamps as well, with chiefly comic pictures and mottoes. These were probably withdrawn following an intervention by the P.M.G.

Thos. DE LA RUE & CO., London (Bunhill Row), 1874 (possibly 1873) to 1885. " [M. W. and] De La Rue stand out distinct, if not entirely alone, as the ' classical ' publishers ... " (G. White). From the late 70's their cards were usually equipped with serial numbers on the backs, which is a great help to the collector in identifying them.

DEAN & MUNDAY (formerly Dean and Bailey), London (35 Threadneedle Street). Published Christmas Broadsheets in the early 1830's. One of these entitled " Queen Elizabeth " and now in the Victoria and Albert Museum was an etching of 18¼ by 14⅝ inches in size. The pictures and text form a frame around the central space left blank for handwritten motto or greeting as seen on the broadsheet in the hands of a charity boy on Fig. 5.

(Thomas) DEAN & SON (formerly Dean & Munday), London (35 Threadneedle Street, later 160A Fleet Street), 1850's-1900. They produced a great number of early animated cards, both comic and sentimental. For Christmas, 1865, for example, 60 sorts of penny cards, 50 sorts of twopence cards and 30 sorts varying from 3d. to 1s. were published by them. These included " Coloured Ghost of the Season ". Four sorts (1. The Ghost we do not object to face, yet always cut from ; 2. The Ghost to cut and come again ; 3. The Ghost of the young man from the country ; 4. The Ghost ' done brown ') ; " Raised Robin and Holly, relief Christmas verse, in rose wreath, gold and tinted card, a very chaste device, 9d." ; " Christmas note-paper, 12 different relief designs, in wrapper, 1s." ; " Christmas envelopes, 12 different relief designs to take notepaper folded in three, 6d." ; " Father Christmas drinking your health, *arm and glass made to move*, Christmas verse in relief underneath " ; " Miss Christmas, *arm made to move* ... " etc. ; " Window made to open, showing young lady underneath, Christmas verse in relief, 2d." ; " Magic Christmas

Tree, and Robin in colour, Queen's lace, very suitable to send to children, 6d." and so on. The cards were offered to retailers at the prices quoted.

G. DELGADO, LTD., London (2 Tower Royal, E.C.), 1890, and modern.

DES ARTS STUDIOS, later Whiting and Cook, Holyoke, U.S.A., 1910-20's.

DEVAMBEZ, Paris (63 Passage des Panoramas), 1910-20's. Produced some British military cards.

W. (William) DICKES, London (4 Crescent Place, Blackfriars, in 1849; 5 Old Fish Street, Doctors' Common, in 1852; from the end of 1868, Farringdon Road, E.C., " the New Premises being now complete with ample Steam Machinery, and Presses of Various kinds "). Early Christmas card producer.

DIETRICH, London, 1860's (?). Early monochrome cards.

H. DOBBS & CO., London (8 New Bridge Street). Originally began to manufacture valentines in the first years of the nineteenth century. Dobbs, Baily & Co. (134 Fleet Street and 13 Soho Square) in the 1840's, and Dobbs, Kidd & Co. from the early 1850's up to the early 1890's produced chiefly embossed, lace-paper and valentine-type Christmas cards, comics.

DORENDORFF, London (Dowgate Hill; after 1897, 5 Worship Street).

M. H. DUPREY, Paris, 1869-70. Messrs. Barnard & Sons, of 115 Great Titchfield Street, London, apparently his agents, issued a circular through their solicitors to the effect that " certain badly executed copies from the original designs of M. H. Duprey, of Paris, are being offered for sale without consent ", cautioning all persons against dealing in pirated copies (*Stationer, P. and F. T. Register*, May 5th, 1869).

DUPREZ, Paris, 1870's. Pirated cards deliberately misspelling Duprez for Duprey ?

Th. (Theodore) DUPUY ET FILS., Paris and London (120 Newgate Street, E.C.; works at Paris), 1880's.

E. DUTTON & CO., New York, 1897-1900's. Valentines, but also Christmas cards.

E. & S. (Eyre and Spottiswoode).

F. EDWARDS & CO., London (23 Bonham Road, Brixton Hill, S.W.) and Chas. TAYLOR, London (23 Warwick Lane, E.C.), 1890's. Card usually " Printed in Bavaria ".

Thomas EGLEY, London (69 New Bond Street, W.), 1840-50. Bookshop and stationery owned by the uncle of W. M. Egley and William Gossling and later by the former by himself. The Egley card was probably sold, if not commissioned, by Thomas Egley, though so far I was unable to confirm this except by indirect evidence.

Paul ELDER & CO., San Francisco, U.S.A., 1901-1920's. " Impression Leaflets ", etc.: " although very few were published for actual use as greeting cards, many of them were used as greetings " (Chase).

ELLIOTT " of Buckle[r]sbury " (W. H. Elliot ?). A valentine maker who was said to have been the first who introduced foreign chromolithographs to replace hand colouring in 1850.

(W. H.) ELLIOT, London (Holywell Street; later, in the 1860's, 41 Kenton Street, Russell Square, W.C.).

ERDMANN and SCHANZ, London (4 Salcott Road, New Wandsworth, S.W.), 1890's.

ERHARDT, DRAMBURG & CO. (late H. Erhardt & Co.), London (2 Tower Royal, Cannon Street, and 49 Watling Street, E.C.), 1880's. Suppliers of fancy paper, embossed boards, lace-papers and borders, perfumed, sachet, etc., Christmas cards for the trade.

Max ETTLINGER & CO., LTD., London and New York, U.S.A., 1905-10. " Hands across the Sea " and other Christmas postcards, usually printed in Germany.

Frank O. EVANS, London (Parker House), late 1890's.

EYRE AND SPOTTISWOODE, London (Great New Street, Fetter Lane), later London, Edinburgh and New York (1880), 1877-87. Important firm, " Her Majesty's Printers " whose Christmas and birthday cards " have obtained a general and well-deserved reputation for artistic excellence ", to quote a contemporary critic in 1884. In 1880 they distributed big parcels of their Christmas cards to various London hospitals for the use of the patients, a generosity much applauded at the time.

B. F. & Co. (Bolland, Ferriman & Co.).

G. F. & S., 1890's (G. F. Faber ?). " Comic " with a bit of real straw attached to the card.

J. F. & Co., Leicester, 1870's ?

P. O. F., 1890-1900's. Curious photographic postcard Christmas cards of completely naked little girls sitting on flowering branches or talking to birds.

G. F. FABER (& S. ?), Nuremburg, 1880's. London agent: Leopold Fromm. " Real flower " cards in 1881.

Geo. C. FAIRSERVICE LTD., Glasgow, modern.

Ernest FALCK & CO., London (Crown Court, 64 Cheapside, " Under Bennett's clock "), late 1860's—. Agents for W. Hagelberg, Berlin.

George FALKNER & SONS, Manchester, 1880's. " Old style " cards. Etching in brown ink.

FARMER, LIVERMORE & CO., Providence, R.I., U.S.A., 1880's. Very fine wood, but mainly steel-plate, engravings, printed in monochrome on unusual shaped, tinted cards.

FAUDEL, PHILLIPS & SONS, London (36-40 Newgate Street, E.C.), 1870-90's. Sometimes also bearing the mark of Ackermann. Imported from America and elsewhere. Large selections for retailers. Produced a popular " Dancing Girl " card, probably the one reproduced on Plate 184.

C. W. FAULKNER & Co., London (28 City Road, E.C.) 1890's and modern. Elegant and fashionable cards during the Edwardian period and after. Successors of the earlier firm called Hildesheimer and Faulkner.

FAVILL PRESS, LTD., London, modern.

Benjamin FAWCETT Driffield (Middle Street), Yorkshire, 1831—; colour prints from c. 1855-85. Some churches, etc., used also for Christmas cards.

FIELD AND TUER, London (1870's-1890, from 1890 to 1900, " The Leadenhall Press ").

FINE ARTS PUBLISHING CO., LTD., London, modern.

J. Tayler FOOT, London (18 Poland Street, .W.), 1890's.

J. FRANCIS, London (4 Wilderness Row), 1860's. Cards and boxes " ornamented with various coloured shells. They are the neatest of the kind we have seen "—Fancy Trades Register, August, 1865.

The Gordon FRASER GALLERY, Bedford, modern.

A. W. G., Art Workers' Guild, London.

C. G. & S. (Charles Goodall & Son).

GALE AND POLDEN, LTD., Aldershot, modern.

I. GERSON, London (5 Rathbone Place, W.), 1862-90's. London depots of several early German photographic companies.

Andrew GEYER, New York (60 Duane Street), U.S.A. (1880-90's).

The GIBSON ART COMPANY, Cincinnati, Ohio, U.S.A., 1900's—. Founded by George Gibson, who arrived in America in the early 1850's. With the help of his French-made lithographic press, brought with him, Gibson set up a small family workshop in Cincinnati which gradually, first as Gibson & Co. in the 1880's, and finally as the Gibson Art Co. from 1895, built up probably the biggest sales organisation and greeting-card production in the world. First distributed Prang and European cards, but from 1907 or 1908 began to produce their own Christmas cards.

Karl GIESEN, Northampton, modern.

J. GILBERT, London (137 Cheapside), 1890's.

A. GIESE'S FORLAG, Copenhagen, 1890's.

Charles GOODALL & SON, London (Camden Works, N.W., and 17 St. Bride Street, E.C.), 1862 (or before) to 1885's. See pp. 55, 61, 100, etc., and Plates 19, 22, 23, 26, 42, etc., also Colour Plates I-c, III-b.

GOODE BROTHERS (established as Thomas Goode in 1830's), London (Clerkenwell Green), 1860-90's.

ALFRED GRAY, London. See p. 82, Plate 108.

GREETING CARD HOUSE, LTD., Sheffield, modern.

GRIFFITH, FARRAN & Co. (in 1884 Griffith, Farran, Okeden and Welsh), London (West Corner, St. Paul's Churchyard, E.C.), 1880-90's. In

June, 1897: Griffith, Farran, Browne & Co., Ltd., and moved to 35 Bow Street.

Walter GRUEN, Richmond, modern.

H.&F., i.e., Hildesheimer and Faulkner.

A. HR. (Albert Hildesheimer).

S.Hr., i.e. (S.) Hildesheimer & Co.

H. H. & Co., London, 1887-90's. " Unique " Series; also some with English and French greeting texts.

W. (Wolff) HAGELSBERG, Berlin, 1870-90's. London representative: A. Angermann in the early 1860's and E. Falck after 1869. Their cards include a number of expensive animated cards, both religious and comic varieties. Branch in London (12 Bunhill Row), from 1885; New York (36 and 38 East 12th Street) from 1889.

HAGUE & GILL, High Wycombe, Modern.

HALFORD Bros., E. Warwick, 1870 ? Small hand-painted cards.

HALLMARK GREETING CARD COMPANY, Kansas City, U.S.A., modern. See about their recent design competition on p. 190. This firm, known in the 1920's as a small house of Hall Brothers, by the 1950's became *the biggest*, and in many other ways also leading greeting card publishers of the present times.

HAMILTON. . . .One of those " whose speciality was to produce comparatively few cards, with clever sketches, or good ideas " (G. White).

HAMILTON, HILLS & CO., 1884-90.

HARDING, London, (Piccadilly), 1880's. See p. 84.

W. T. HARRIS, London (1 Queenhithe, E.C.). Early 1860's or earlier, visiting card size hand-coloured engravings of man at window and robin with greeting note in its beak, etc.

J. or J. E. HAWKINS, London (36 Baker Street, W.) (also James E. Hawkins, London (17 Paternoster Row, E.C.), 1880's. Chiefly religious cards, occasionally printed by W. Dickes; others printed by E. Kaufmann. Some of these cards carry the addresses, 70 Welbeck Street and 12 Paternoster Square, London.

James HAWORTH & BRO., London, 1917-20. Publishers of the first World War card reproduced on Plate 198.

J. T. HENDERSON, Montreal, Canada (printed by " Canada Bank Note Co., Lith., Montreal "), 1880's. " Montreal in Winter Garb ", etc.

Albert HILDESHEIMER, London, 1870-80's.

S. (Siegmund) HILDESHEIMER & Co., London (14, 15, 16 Silk Street, E.C.), Manchester, New York, 1876-90's. Started with two designs of their own, but from 1877 this firm became one of the important Christmas card publishers. They introduced the " Penny Basket " in 1879. Design competition and exhibition at St. James's Hall, London, in 1881; W. Ball's etching sets (and " sketch-book ") cards first in 1881. Later more and more flower cards. The critic of the *Stationer, Printer*, etc., reviews their output in 1884 as follows: " . . . Flowers are, as usual, the chief adornment; and, undoubtedly, all persons love these charming gifts of Nature, and thus there is little risk in the offer, if only the flowers be as truly rendered as they are in the cards under notice"—a popular version of Oscar Wilde's nature imitating the arts idea !

HILDESHEIMER AND FAULKNER, London (41 Jewin Street, E.C.), 1877—1890's. In 1881 and 1882 big design competitions and exhibitions of designs; in 1892 introduced photogravure cards; other technical innovations include mixing silver with the colours so that " in winter scenes the glistening of the snow may be more faithfully rendered ". The firm still flourishes to-day as C. W. Faulkner & Co.

(David) HILL & CO., London (Fore Street), 1885-97.

HILLS & CO., London, 1890's. " For the Empire " and " Unique " Series.

HILLS AND SAUNDERS, Eton in 1860's, London (Porchester Terrace).

HIORNE AND MILLER, Devonport, modern.

O. HODGSON, London (10 Cloth Fair). Published Christmas broadsheets in 1830's. One of these, " The Tower of Babel " (November, 1833) is in the Victoria and Albert Musem, London.

HORROCK AND HETHERINGTON (Artistic Stationery Co.), London, 1879. Tristram Ellis etchings and other largish cards, often printed on silk or satin. N.B.—Mr. Horrock, formerly connected with the Artistic Stationery Co., decided to settle in Sydney, New South Wales, in 1869, and to act as agent for many prominent English firms.

" HOLLY BUSH " PUBLICATIONS, London, 1920's, and modern.

A. HORWITZ, New York, 1910's. Postcard-type cards, printed in Dresden, Germany.

R. HOVENDEN & SONS, London (City Road, Finsbury Square, E.C.), 1897. Humorous cards.

J. HUGHES, LTD., Nottingham, modern.

Hugh Griffith HUGHES, Holyhead (29 Market Street), 1880 (later John Griffith Hughes, 8 and 10 Market Street).

Charles Joseph HULLMANDEL, London (Great Marlborough Street). So far no Christmas card is identified as the production of Hullmandel who began his experiments in lithography in 1818. Some early cards, however, which suggest his method of producing highlights by overprinting the black key impression with tints (which lead him to print in colours from several lithographic stones in the mid-1830's) may be his work.

HUTSON BROS., Croydon, modern.

INTERNATIONAL ART PUBLISHING CO. (I. A. P. Co.), New York and Berlin, 1890-1900's. Postcard-size cards.

C. T. J. (Chas T. Jefferies) & SONS, Bristol (Canynge Buildings), 1860's.

Bertha E. JAQUES, Chicago, Ill., U.S.A., 1900. A one-man, or, rather, "one-woman", enterprise. She wrote a sentiment and drew some holly leaves as ornament. "It was printed and a few put in gift-shops, which up to that time had no such cards for sale". It has been claimed that this card of 1901 originated the Christmas card custom (B. E. Jaques, "Holiday Greetings", Chicago, Ill., U.S.A., 1926) which is, of course, a mistake.

JARROLD & SONS, London, 1880's.

M. L. JONAS & CO., London (2 Gutter Lane, E.C.), in 1860's; in the 1880's Barbican, E.C.). Agents for Testu and Massin of Paris.

W. JONES, London (246 High Holborn), late 1860's.

JORDAN & SONS, London, modern.

KARDONIA LTD., London, modern.

The KEATING COMPANY, Philadelphia, U.S.A., 1906—. Started with a simple, holly-decorated, engraved card. "Keating cards have always been the last word in engraved style cards" (Chase).

J. KENDRICK, London (54 Leicester Square), 1833-5. Publications include amusing "Almanac for the hat or bonnet to be pasted inside or on top, for 1835".

KERSHAW & SON (or G. KERSHAW), London (17 Wilderness Row), 1840-60. Early valentine-type Christmas cards.

Chas. F. KIMBLE & SONS, London, modern.

Jonathan KING (or J. KING), London (Chapel Street, Somers Town, in 1850's; 56 Seymour Street, Euston Square, in 1860's, 304 Essex Road, Islington, from 1872 to 1912). Said to have introduced Christmas card "frosting" in 1867.

KINZE BROS., London (Tower Hill in 1865; later Bartholomew Close, and in the 1880's Aldersgate Street, E.C.), 1865-80's. Satin-faced reliefs and embossed figures a speciality. Agents for several firms in Europe.

Max KRACKE & CO., LTD., London, modern.

J.M. KRONHEIM & CO., London (Paternoster Row, later Shoe Lane), 1850-70. The delicate early cards produced by Kronheim who "has discovered a new method of printing in oil by means of lithography, which presents a manifest improvement over all previous attempts to imitate, by means of the press, the effect of a picture" (Art Journal, 1852) were probably produced for various publishers or distributors and thus not signed by him, but they are recognisable if compared with signed prints and book illustrations made for the Relig. Tract Society, the S.P.C.K., etc., apart from his better known prints by the Baxter process (some of which, including plates originally made for Cassell's Book of Birds, and many smaller ones were also used on Christmas cards). It will be remembered that in 1870-1

Kate Greenaway also worked for Kronheim's, but her cards are not yet identified.

Alexander LAIDLAW, London (3 Bury Court, St. Mary Axe, E.C.), 1863—. "Importer of, Dealer in, and Publisher of Prints and Scraps, Embossed and Cut out Flowers, etc. Printed in Colours ; Embossed and Perforated Cards, Lace Papers, Gelatined and Varnished Prints " . . . " expressly arranged and produced by him to suit the English Taste "—according to his card of 1864. At the same time he advertised that " Mr. Laidlaw will give £10 Reward to any Person informing him of the Infringement of his Copyrights ". (As a result in 1865 and 6 " Infringement of Copyright " notices appeared in *The Times* and other London newspapers announcing settlements between Thierry and Laidlaw.) This, now little known firm, not known by Gleeson White or other writers, introduced in 1865 " In place of the common flower bouquet ornaments which have been used so much of late " . . . " a variety of exceedingly pretty coloured chromo-lithograph trees, amongst the rest, *the now almost national Christmas tree*, the orange tree, and a variety of others " . . . " and it is satisfactory to find that they have been produced with greater regard to artistic care and skill, than it has been the custom in these matters " (The *Stationer, etc., Register*, September, 1865). Amongst his comic novelties six varieties of " Surprise Sachets " issued in the same year, one representing " a very elegant miniature fusee case " [a particular match-box] was recorded, which on examination " turns out to be a much more s(e)entimental matter ", and also " a cake of the best brown Windsor soap, which can only be said in many senses to resemble that article on the same ground as it is applied to a certain Bishop, who is very much admired by the ladies for his soapy sentimentality ",—according to the contemporary critic. (See also pp. 42 and 171.)

LAMBERT, Newcastle, 1840's. Said to have lithographed Cuthbert Bede's Christmas card and later, in 1847, issued it for general sale. (C. Carter, *Bazaar*, December 16, 1936). The only Lambert card I know, a very pleasant, symmetrical design of holly, ivy and mistletoe, with a dotted line to be filled in by hand, and the text " Wyshinge you the Compliments of The Season " certainly suggests the mid-1840's. Its size is 3¾ by 2½ inches, and it is delicately lithographed in three (possibly four) colours.

LAWRENCE BROS., London (Viaduct Works, Farringdon Road; later, from 1881, 48 Farringdon Street, E.C.). Sole agents for J. A. Lowell & Co.'s Christmas and menu cards. In 1890, P. Lawrence, 12 and 13 Barbican.

C. (Charles) and E. (Edwin) LAYTON, London (150 Fleet Street and 12 Gough Square, E.C.), 1850's and 1860's. Early attractively embossed and die-stamped cards.

The LEADENHALL PRESS, London (50 Leadenhall Street, E.C.).

Le BLOND & Co., London, 1850-60's. In 1842, 24 Budge Row, Cheapside, but by the 1850's they had about twenty hand-presses in their workshop at 4 Walbrook, off Budge Row, while about six lithographic and some copper plate presses continued at No. 24. About 1860 moved to Kingston-on-Thames. One of the principal Baxter licensees. Produced some attractive colour prints for Rimmel, etc., cards (see p. 40).

Chas. LEE & CO., 1880's. In 1884 introduced perforated cards so that the names of sender and addressee " may be worked in " with silk or other materials.

LEIGHTON, BROS., London, (first in 1847 or 8 at 19 Lamb's Conduit Street, later, in the 1860's Milford House, Strand), 1950's or before. See pp. 62-3. George C. Leighton claimed in 1851 that his was " just the reverse of Baxter's process ".

W. H. LEVER, London (46 Aldersgate Street, E.C.), in the 1890's advertised as " Wholesale Agent for the *Mildmay Series* ".

Bartholomew F. LLOYD & Co., Edinburgh, 1840's and 1850's.

John A. LOWELL & CO., Boston, U.S.A., 1880's (see also Lawrence). Very fine steel engravings, sometimes hand-coloured. For the latter type see Colour Plate XI-d.

William LUKS, London (14 Bedford Street, Covent Garden, W.C.), 1880's—. Photographic cards, hand-coloured. Mostly floral subjects, but also Irving, Ellen Terry, Mary Anderson, Sir Moses Montefiore (the Centenarian), " Children Statuary ", etc. (1884).

T. E. M. (Floral.)

R. J. M. (R. J. Mackay).

W. MACK, London, 1890's. Biblical text cards with floral decorations. In the early 1920's W. E. Mack in association with J. Salmon produced postcards.

T. McGANN, Gortaclare, Burren, Co. Clare, 1884-6. Introduced " . . . what he terms a novelty in Christmas, etc., cards, on which are mounted seaweeds, collected on the coasts of the localities referred to . . . The specimens have certainly a very fresh and bewitching appearance . . . they appeal directly for a hearty reception to persons of refined and cultivated tastes . . . " (critic in *Stationer, Printer*, etc., September 6th, 1884.)

R. J. MACKAY, 1880's. Cut-out " silver " horseshoes, floral decorations. Possibly connected with Sockl, but probably American firm or printed in America.

W. McKENZIE & CO., London, 1890's—. In the 90's Victorian rococo folders, often with tiny real photographs superimposed on the old cards of this firm.

William MacLELLAN, LTD., Glasgow, modern. Specialising in Celtic motifs and Gaelic as well as English texts.

Josiah R. MALLETT, 1880's. Three sets of ships, birds and roses in 1884.

A. Vivian MANSELL & CO., LTD., Croydon, modern.

Joseph MANSELL, London (35 Red Lion Square), 1850-80's. Early publisher with both valentine- and visiting-card type Christmas cards. See pp. 39, 61-2, 107 and Plate 72, Dust Jacket No. 26.

W. A. MANSELL, London (Percy Street, W., and in the 80's, 316 and 317 Oxford Street), 1870-90's. This firm should not be confused with Joseph Mansell's of Red Lion Square. W. A. Mansell produced silhouette cards; also many unusual religious cards with photographs stuck on to the boards.

MARION IMP., Paris, or Marion & Co., London (Soho Square, W.), 1860-90's. In 1868 and 1869 introduced cards with lace borders and rice-paper centres, "on which appear silk flowers, the stalks, petals, etc., being drawn with water-colours". Later introduced mother-of-pearl and opal cards. See also Aubry, Paris.

Albert MARKS (or MARX), London (22 Jewin Street, E.C.), 1870-90. Valentine-type, often comic, cards.

J. L. MARKS, London (23 Russell Court, Covent Garden), 1860-70's (?).

MARLBOROUGH, GOULD & CO., London (52 Old Bailey, E.C.), 1884. Distributors of the "Mildmay" Series of cards?

A. MASON & CO., LTD., Croydon (St. James' Road) 1910-20, and modern.

MAWSON, SWAN AND MORGAN, Newcastle-upon-Tyne (Grey Street), late 1870's and 1880's. Elongated feather and flower cards; also imitation "children's drawing" Christmas cards.

R. A. MAYNARD, LTD., London, modern.

MEAD AND DEVERELL, London, 1880's. Chiefly hand-painted cards on thick bevelled and gilt-edged boards.

The MEDICI SOCIETY, LTD., London (also New York, U.S.A.), modern.

Geo. MEEK (later Meek & Son), London (2 Crane Court, Fleet Street, E.C.), 1840's-1883, when the firm was liquidated. Usually very fine embossed, lace-paper cards of the valentine type.

(Lothar) MEGGENDORFER, Munich, Germany, 1880's and 1890's. Produced "Dissolving Views" type of cards, similar to those described on pp. 180-1.

MEISSNER AND BUCH, London (121 Bunhill Row, E.C.) and Leipzig, 1880's-90's. From 1884 this firm was represented in London by W. G. Wallis. "In the cards issued by this firm the High Church and Roman Catholicism are not forgotten, as is too often the case, but are offered really high class and appropriate designs", says the *Stationer*, 1884.

MILDMAY SERIES, 1870's-80's. See W. H. Lever. Religious cards.

MILLAR AND LANG, LTD., Glasgow, modern.

M. MILLER & CO., LTD., Blackpool, modern.

MIRA-CARRETAS, Madrid, Spain, 1900's.

MISCH AND STOCK, London (Cripplegate Street, Golden Lane), 1890's. Many celluloid, coloured gelatine and animated cards.

Sidney H. MITCHELL, LTD., Nottingham, modern.

E. B. MOMS & SON, 1884.

MORISON BROS., Glasgow (99 Buchanan Street), 1883—.

David MOSSMAN, London (Islington), 1840-60's. Embossed, valentine-type early cards; probably lace-paper blanks converted into Christmas cards. In 1865 the *Fancy Trades' Register* gives the name and address as " Mrs. Mossman, Lace-paper Manufacturers, Makers of leaves and ornaments for Valentines, 1A Stoke Newington Green ".

MOWBRAY & CO., Oxford, later London, 1880—. Started 1880 with printing about 2,000 copies of " The Nativity of Our Lord " Christmas card, a design by Wyndham H. Hughes, and produce chiefly religious cards.

MULLORD BROS., London (1 and 2 Penn Street, N.1), 1840-50's, but also later even in the 1870's. Nicely embossed lace-paper cards, scented, valentine types. According to one of their notices, they were for " Twelve years the only Die-sinkers to the Late Firm of Windsor & Sons " (1865).

N. & S. B. C., Chester (1 Egerton Terrace), (1880's ?). Lithographed text cards.

Joseph NATHAN (a partner in Messrs. M. H. Nathan & Co., ?), London (48 Barbican, E.C.), 1880's. In May, 1881, when some of the biggest Christmas card firms were busily organising competitions and exhibitions both in Britain and in America, an ingenious advertisement appeared in which " Joseph Nathan begs to intimate that he has been enabled to secure the services of the leading artists who recently exhibited at the Dudley Gallery " and that he " wishes emphatically to point out that, though by his enterprize and good fortune he has obtained the best work of the most eminent artists, yet he has not followed the example of other Houses, nor been compelled to expend thousands of Pounds in Prizes and other induce- ments (which must add to the cost of production), and is thus enabled to offer the advantage to the trade, by selling at much lower prices . . . "

M. (Michael) H. (Henry) NATHAN & Co., London (24 Australian Avenue, E.C.), 1880's. Imitation photo cards; also brought out in 1884 two " splendid mechanicals ", a " Brunette " and a " Blonde ", young ladies carrying fans, as well as a great number of all other sort fashionable at the period.

NELSON & SONS, Edinburgh, London and later New York, 1860-80's. Some- times Thomas Nelson & Co. Chiefly religious texts and motifs, but also landscapes. This firm produced some lovely early colour-printing.

NEWMAN & CO., London (48 Watling Street), late 1870's.

Ernest NISTER & CO., London (24 St. Bride Street, E.C.), 1880's and 1890's. Sometimes this firm is referred to as " Nister of Nuremburg " on account of their lithographic establishments, which were perhaps the largest in Germany in the 1890's. (In 1897 they entered a new field, " Keramic printing " in colours and turned out hundreds of thousands of plates with the portrait of Queen Victoria.)

F. O., 1860's. Fine early cards, embossed, with flower garlands.

G. O., 1880's. With English as well as sometimes German greeting texts.

O. B. (OBPACHER BROTHERS), Munich, before 1890. Later, Artistic Lithographic Company.

The ODD FELLOW, London (Printed and published by H. Hetherington, 13-14 Wine Office Court, Fleet Street) produced two " New Comic Scrap Sheets " of " 24 highly amusing Wood Engravings by first-rate Artists " for Christmas, 1841.

Bernard OLLENDORFF, Berlin, 1870-90's. Finely produced chromolithographs.

J. O'NEILL, London (5 Falcon Street, E.C.), 1880's.

Frederick OUGH, London (Albion Hall, London Wall, E.C., in 1881, 9 King Edward Street, E.C., 1869-80's). Probably chiefly imported chromos and paper ornaments. Ough was previously associated with Augustin Thierry & Co., one of the oldest importers of scraps, etc.

PALLAS Gallery, London, modern. (Modern French, etc., Masters).

PARKER. "Who painted the linen bands for the Irish trade, is said to have been the first to use ' jewels ' on Christmas cards ". (G.W.).

George PARKER, of Aldermanbury, 1881.

PARKINS AND GOTTO, London (Oxford Street), 1890's. Mainly private cards. Folders decorated with monogram, 28s. 6d. per 50 copies, " Monogram Die and Illuminating extra " (1892).

PEARSON, Bath (Milsom Street), 1880's. Religious.

L. F. PEASE, Buffalo, N.Y., U.S.A. (257 Laurel Street), 1900's. Christmas postcards with holly and bird decorations with mottoes, such as " The Snow Birds' Plum Pudding ", etc.

R. H. PEASE, Albany, New York, U.S.A., 1850-2 (?). I am indebted to Mr. E. D. Chase who sent me a reproduction of the " first American Christmas card " when my book was already in page proof and these notes are based on this copy and information supplied by him. The only known copy of the card is in the possession of the Rust Craft Company who secured it from a New York antique dealer a few years ago. No date appears on the lithograph itself, but as a result of some considerable research Mr. Chase satisfactorily established that it must be either 1850, 1 or 2, since it was only these three years that Mr. Pease occupied the building which is pictured prominently on the card. Above the holly decorated curved display line, carrying Pease's advertisement (see p. 80), the design includes the features of a small, rather elf-type Santa Claus with fur-trimmed cap, sleigh and reindeer. A ball-room with dancers, the building marked " Temple of Fancy ", an array of Christmas presents and Christmas dishes and drinks decorate the four corners of the card, while in the centre we see a young couple with three children visibly delighted with their presents ; behind the family group a black servant is laying the table for the Christmas dinner. In addition to the central " A Merry Christmas

And A Happy New Year " the ornamented lettering includes " To : " and " From : " with spaces to be filled by the sender.

PETTER AND GALPIN, London (Ludgate Hill, E.C.), 1851-9. See p. 43 and Colour Plate I-a.

PHILIPP BROS., London (4 and 5 Silk Street, E.C.), 1880's.

The PHOTOCHROM CO., LTD., London (61 and 63 Ludgate Hill, E.C.). (Before 1896 The Photograph Co. of Zürich and Orell Füssli Art Institute, 17 Knightrider Street, E.C.; now Tunbridge Wells). (Still flourishing.) 1896—.

PINCHES & CO., 1860's (?). Embossed cards.

J. PITTS, London (14 Great Street, Andrew Street, Seven Dials), 1840-50's. " A Pastoral Ode for Christmas Day ", the words by T. Poynton. Songsheet.

PORTBURY & CO., London (7 Westbourne Grove, Bayswater, W.). Small photographic compositions.

von PORTHEIM & CO., London (Lovell's Court, E.C.) and Leipzig, 1890's.

S. POULTON, London (Paragon, New Kent Road; from January, 1869, 9 and 10 St. Bride's Avenue, Fleet Street). Photographic cards of man and woman holding hands, etc. In the late 90's Poulton & Son, Leé.

LOUIS PRANG & CO., Boston and Roxbury, Mass., U.S.A., 1874-95. Called " The Father of the American Christmas card ". See pp. 74-80, Colour Plates XI (b and c), Dust Jacket 16 and Plate 114.

M. PRIESTER'S CONTINENTAL PRINTING COMPANY, U.S.A. (?), 1870's. Silk embossed cards, monochromes, sporting, etc., subjects.

J. V. QUICK, London (36 Bowling Green Lane, Clerkenwell). Printed and sold " Copy of Verses " broadsheets for bellmen for Christmas and New Year, 1830-1.

D. L. R.—De La Rue.

H. R. Floral cards.

RAYMENT, HOLLAND AND PAYTON, LTD., London, modern.

The REGENT PUBLISHING CO., LTD., Barnes, modern.

RELIGIOUS TRACT SOCIETY, London (56 Paternoster Row), 1860-80's. See p. 85 and elsewhere.

RIDDLE AND COUCHMAN, London (" Sumner " Printing Works, 22 Southwark Bridge Road), 1860's. Lithographs for Relig. Tract Soc. cards, etc.

Eugene RIMMEL, London (96 Strand, 128 Regent Street, 24 Cornhill), 1860-90's. See p. 169 and Plate 148. In 1884 Rimmel's " Artistic Perfumed " Christmas Cards were sold from 1s. per dozen to 10s. 6d. each, Christmas Sachets from 6d. to 10s. 6d. each to retailers. Previously he produced " The Guinea Musical " and " The Guinea Watteau, from One to Five Guineas " (1869).

Wm. RITCHIE & SONS, LTD., Edinburgh, modern.

RIXON AND ARNOLD, London (Poultry), 1860-70's.

F. J. ROBERTS, London (Little Britain), 1884.

ROBERTSON & CO., London (Islington), 1880's.

E. S. & A. ROBINSON, Bristol (2 Redcliffe Street), 1844—. (Still flourishing.)

J. ROBINSON, Glasgow, 1850's or earlier. Engraved cards.

ROCK BROS., London (11 Walbrook, E.C., 1840's and later but moved to Paul Street, Finsbury, in 1895). "Illustrated" notepapers, headings, "Compliment paper and cards", etc. See p. 54.

ROCKCLIFF, (Old Gravel Lane, Radcliff Highway) 1820's?, Broadsheets.

ROLPH, SMITH & CO., Toronto, Canada, 1881—. Publishers of rather large "Canadian Christmas cards". See p. 85.

ROTARY PHOTOGRAPHIC CO., West Drayton, modern.

H. (Herman) ROTHE, London (11 King Street, Covent Garden, W.C.), 1874-90's.

W. RUSSEL, Birmingham, modern.

RUST CRAFT PUBLISHERS, Kansas City, later Boston, U.S.A. Started with Christmas folders, called "letters", in 1906. These were mainly text cards, and only a red initial letter embellished them. From this small beginning the present huge organisation developed in less than fifty years.

A. S. CO. (Artistic Stationery Co.).

E. A. S. (E. A. Schwerdtfeger).

G. S., London and Paris, 1879.

J. F. S. or J. F. S. & Co. (Schipper & Co.).

J. S. & CO., 1840-50's. Notepaper headings, and also satirical cards of "A Heavy Fall", etc. See Plate 75.

S. J. S. & CO. (Saunders). Early flower- and ribbon-decorated cards.

L. SACHSE & CO., Berlin, Germany. Menzel lithographs of 1834-5.

J. SALMON, LTD., Sevenoaks, 1910—. Postcards.

SAMFORTH & CO., "England and New York" (probably American), 1900-10's. Comic, postcards.

M. SAMUEL & CO., London (Aldersgate Street. In 1890 also a branch at 77 Wood Street, Cheapside), 1884. "Draper, stationer and ticket writer".

SAUNDERS BROTHERS, London (104 London Wall, E.C.), 1860's.

SAUNDERS, McBEATH & CO., Dunedin, N.Z. (Princes Street), 1882—. See p. 85.

Sydney J. SAUNDERS & CO., London (St. Mary Axe), 1880-90. "Export only" cards; over 3,000 new designs for 1884-5.

E. W. SAVORY, LTD., Bristol, 1890's and modern.

G. SBORGI, Firenze, 1907. Italian Christmas and New Year cards.

SCHIPPER or J. F. SCHIPPER & CO., London (10 and 11 King Street, Covent Garden, W.C.), 1880's. This is probably the firm referred to by Gleeson White as SCHEFFER or SCHEIPER.

E. A. SCHWERDTFEGER & CO., London, 1900's. Usually " Printed in Berlin ".

GIBB SHALLARD & CO., Australia (?).

SHARP WALKER & CO., London (259 High Holborn), 1899. " Personal cards from 2/- per dozen ".

W. N. SHARPE, LTD., Bradford, modern.

SHMITH, London, 1880's. Imitation cheques, etc. See p. 85.

SIMPSON AND BROOKE, Birmingham (Upper Hockley Street), 1870-80's.

SOCKL AND NATHAN, London (32 Jewin Street), 1880's-1890. See p. 85.

SOHO GALLERY, London, modern.

F. C. SOUTHWOOD, London, 1900's. See Plate 66 and p. 135.

Geo. R. SOUTHWORTH, Milford, Conn., U.S.A., 1905-15 (?). Die-stamped cards.

Edward STANGE, Berlin, 1860-80's. Kinze Bros. in London.

STANNARD & SON. Chiefly hand-painted flowers, etc.

Thomas STEVENS, Coventry (Stevengraph Works), London (114 Newgate Street), and New York (4th Avenue) 1880's. See pp. 85, 95.

Wm. STRAIN & SONS, Belfast. In 1880's introduced ivorine and porcelain Christmas cards.

Thomas STURROCK, Leith, Scotland, 1840's. Said to have published, in the company of his friend, Charles Drummond, a Christmas card with a Scottish greeting text and an engraving of a laughing face one or two years before 1846. See p. 11 and Plate 3.

Benjamin SULMAN, London (177 Upper Thames Street, E.C., in the early 60's; later 40 City Road and 25 Warwick Lane), 1860's. Mostly small, delightfully engraved, embossed and die-stamped cards. Also sachet, and bouquet-cards; notepaper, envelopes in great numbers in 1864 and onwards. See pp. 44, 62, etc., and Dust Jacket No. 39.

Felix SUMMERLY'S HOME TREASURY OFFICE, London (12 Old Bond Street, W.). In 1843 published the first Christmas card. See pp. 6-11 and Plates 1 and 2.

SUSSE FRÈRES, Paris (Place de la Bourse 81), 1850-60's. Pretty, small chromolithographs of children, cards and scraps, small ovals.

SYMONDS & CO., Portsmouth, 1890's. Large bronzed, jewelled yachting cards with mounted photographs, including " Maid Marion ".

TAYLOR BROS., Leeds (Steam Colour Printing Works), 1884.

TERRY, STONEMAN & CO., London (82 Hatton Garden, E.C.), 1860-70. Notepaper headings, small cards: some printed at W. Dickes's workshop.

Augustus THIERRY, London (77 Newgate Street, E.C.), 1860-70. " Keeps the largest stock of foreign goods for valentine makers, etc." (Advertisement in 1865). In 1890's: Charles E. Thierry, 13A Finsbury Square, E.C.

Angus THOMAS, London (48A Jewin Street, E.C., in 1885, and 9 Silk Street, E.C., in the 1890's), 1885-1900's. Publishers of comic, imitation document and puzzle cards. See pp. 82-3, 166, Plates 139, 140, Fig. 18.

Norman THOMAS, London (Well Street, E.C.), 1885.

THOMPSON-SMITH COMPANY, New York, 1910's—. Manufacturers and distributors of chiefly engraved cards.

Raphael THOMSON & Co., London, 1860-70's.

Hall THORPE STUDIO, London (36 Redcliffe Square), 1920's.

TRUE & Co., Augusta, Maine, U.S.A., 1880's. Large flower vases, and similar fashionable subject cards in the end-of-the-century manner.

Raphael TUCK & SONS (before January, 1881, Raphael Tuck and Co.), London (72-73, Coleman Street, now Appold Street), 1870's—. Prize competitions in 1880; " Royal Academy " Series in 1882; Royal Warrant from Queen Victoria in 1893. As this is included in the trade mark, the date will help collectors in grouping their cards. Also " Artistic " Series, noted on the palette on the trade mark of the firm, was first produced for Christmas, 1883. Previous to January, 1881, Raphael Tuck & Co. New York branch (298 Broadway), established in 1885.

James VALENTINE & SONS, LTD., Dundee, Scotland, 1880's—. Particularly interesting for picture postcards, which were a speciality of this firm.

VALLET, MINOT & Co., Paris, 1870's-80's. See Plate 83.

Paul F. VOLLAND COMPANY, Chicago, Ill., U.S.A. Began producing Christmas cards in 1909. Introduced mottled cardboards, and probably the first firm to use offset printing for Christmas cards. In 1925 the firm was incorporated into the Gerlach-Barklow Company, Joliet, Ill., U.S.A.

W. & Co.

M. W. (Marcus Ward).

V. O. W., late 1870's. Resembling the Prang cards, probably American.

John WALKER & Co., late 1880's and 90's. Illuminated, etched and hand-painted cards.

WALMESLEY AND LEWIS, London (17 and 19, Park Street, Islington, N.), 1877-81.

WASHINGTON, KELL & Co., London (19 Farringdon Avenue, E.C.), 1890's.

Marcus WARD & Co., Belfast (Royal Ulster Works); later London and Belfast; London and New York, 1866-98. (London address, 67 Chandos Street, W.C., but in August, 1884, moved to Oriel House, Farringdon Street, E.C., the house having been designed by Thomas Crane, the Art Director of the firm.) Competition for Christmas card verses in 1894, " Literary " Series published in 1895. (See pp. 66-7, etc., etc.)

CHRISTMAS CARD PUBLISHERS

WARD GALLERY, London and Brighton, modern.

WATT AND RAYMENT, London (Guildhall Chambers, Basinghall Street), 1880's.

W. WELLING, London (33 and 35, Hanway Street, W.), 1860's. Notepaper with Scriptural texts printed in colours as an ornamental headline to each sheet.

W. WHEELER, Jun., Cork, possibly 1880's. Large cards.

WHEELER BROS., London (88 Mildmay Park, N.), 1888. Religious cards. Some connection with " Mildmay " Series ?

Geo. C. WHITNEY, New York. Previously Whitney Bros., and Whitney Manufacturing Co., Worcester, Mass., U.S.A., an old American valentine manufacturing firm. They gradually incorporated several other, similar firms, such as Esther Howland's, Jotham Taft's, Bullard's, etc., and in the late 1870's began to deal with Christmas and other greeting cards also. In the 1880's the Whitney company was associated with Hildesheimer and Faulkner in London, and some publications were jointly signed. Liquidated in 1942.

WILDT AND KRAY, London, 1900's. Postcard Christmas cards.

WILSON BROS., London, modern.

Chas. WILSON & Co., London (21 Thorburn Square, S.E.), 1880's. Chiefly photographic Christmas cards. In 1884 the company stated that they " have gone to much expense in engaging the services of artists' models, actresses, and others, in order to obtain photographs from the life " for their cards. Also produced " instantaneous photos " of birds, etc.

John WINDSOR & SONS, London (Vineyard Walk; later 2 Meredith Street, Clerkenwell), 1840-50. Attractive embossed cards.

WIRTHS BROS. AND OWEN (W. B. & O.), New York (12 Bond Street), San Francisco (Phelan Buildings), London (from April, 1884, 15 Long Lane, E.C.), 1880's.

WOLSEY, London, 1920's.

J. T. WOOD & Co., London (278, 279 and 280 Strand, W.C.; sometimes 33 Holywell Street, Strand), 1840-70's. Early embossed, lace-paper, valentine-type cards. (In 1893: 8 Plumtree Court, E.C.)

T. M. WOODHEAD'S SUCCRS., LTD., Bradford, modern.

WOOLLEY & Co., London (210 High Holborn), 1881.

F. W. WOOLWORTH LTD., about 1919. Christmas postcards.

WYMAN & SON, London (Gt. Queen Street, W.C.), 1877-8.

YAPP AND HAWKINS, London (70 Welbeck Street, W., and 12 Paternoster Square), 1870's. Mostly religious text cards.

YATES, Nottingham (?)

YORKSHIRE JOINT-STOCK PUBLISHING AND STATIONERY CO., LTD., Otley, Yorkshire, 1860's.

INDEX

NOTE : More details, subjects and names, will be found in the alphabetical Lists, pp. 211–282. Italic numerals indicate plate numbers.

A

A.N.F.F., Anno novo faustum felix tibi sit, 18–9
A.B., British, 133, *63*
ABRAHAM, R. J., 71, 213
absent friends, 10, 124, 195
Academy of Arts, Prague, 28, Royal Prussian, 244
accession, Queen Victoria's, 192
accumulation, of beauty, 92, of styles, 78
ACKERMANN, A., 83, 262
acrostics, 89, 156, *128, 129*
actresses, as models for cards, 282
ADAM & Co., 83, 262
Adam's Sacred Allegories, 11
address card, gentleman's, 43
Admiralty, British, 132
Adoration of the Magi, 12–3
adventures, bicycle, 131
advertisement, Christmas cards, *153*, 169, 172, of manufacturers, 92, ideas, 25
aerial view, *172*
aerophane, 184
aeroplanes, 125, 134–6
aesthetes, *28*, 30, 74, 108, 145, 149, 150–1
aesthetic criticism, 93
affection, 197, for members of opposite sex, 117, for flowers, 141
After the Opera, 113
Age of Innocence, The, 146
AIKMAN, D., 11, 213
air-raids, 196
airgraph letter cards, *68*, 136, *201*
airman, *68*
airship, *66–7*, 88, 133
alarm bell, 133
ALBERT, Prince (later King George VI), *131*
albums, old Christmas card, 87–8, 98, 102, 160–1, *172, 183*, 200, *190*
alcoves, 149
ALEXANDRA, Queen, 192
Alexandria, 21–2
ALLCHIN, T. H., 71, 213
allegorical figures, 22, on visiting cards, 43, *21*, 148
almond slice, imitation, *175*, 179
Alps, 127
altar, 182
aluminium frosting, 95, 184
amateurs, 199
American, Christmas cards, etc., 34, 64, 79–80, 86, 95–6, 150, 115, 124–5, 137, 165, 184–5, 190, 193, 195–7, 199, 202, *XI a, b, c, d, 82, 105, 114, 121, 198*,
Antiquarian Society, Worcester, Mass.,

V., 79, Art Galleries, New York, 76, editions, 165, export of cards, 58, father of the Christmas card, 74, the " First—Christmas card ", 80, 277, *American Graphic Art*, 80, G.I., 166, *138*, market, 80,—sentiments (quoted), 205, 206, 207, uniform postal rates, introduction of, 53, valentines, 75, volunteer, 197 (see also United States, etc.)
amusement of children, cards for the, 153–60
anathema, 193
anecdotical contents, 98
angelica, strips of, *175*, 179
angel, *Ia, V*, 22, 84, *159*, 169, *170, 169, 153*, 170, *159*, 175, 178–9, *174, 175*, 182, 187, *189, 190, 191, 192*, 224, 230, 231, 241, 243, 250–1, (v. also Guardian angels), 202, 205
angler, 181
Anglo-Norman carol singers, 63
animal subjects, 66, 88, *113–21*, 121, *123*, 153–5, 235, their association with Nativity legends, 154
animated cards, 66, 68, 98, *XV, 162*, 167–9
ANNA, the Cruel, 24, *9*
Anniversary card, 12–3, 230
anniversary, of Queen Victoria' accession to the Throne, 192
Anno novo faustum felix tibi sit, 18
anonymous, 200
antiquities, 105
apples, 128, apple trees, 111
apprentices, 25
Archaeological Society, London, 105
archaic cards, 109, 122
archers, 158
" architecturally " designed cards, *33*, 68, 93, 94, 96, 113
arms, national, 22
ARMSTRONG, W., 200, 252
ARNOLD, H., 66, 81, 214
arrangement of Christmas card collections, 98
art, bringing it into the life of the masses, 76, education, 75, its application to everyday life, 80
Art Journal, 7, 61, 100, 145, 169, 217–8, 272, " Art Nouveau ", *107*, *Art of England* by Ruskin, 144, " of Secret Writing " (1870), 57, teachers, 169, Art Workers' Guild, *102*, *Artist, The*, 213, 242, 255
ART PUBLISHING Co., International, 84, 271
Artemidorus, dreambook of, 118
artificial innocence, 146

INDEX

BIGGS, J. R., 140, 216
BILLINGHURST, P. J., *28*, 216
bills, *12*, 128
BINGHAM, C., 200, 252
biographers of K. Greenaway, 143
biplane, 135–6
" Birch, Susan ", 42
Bird in Hand, 25
birds, as subjects of designs, 22, 76–7, 88,
99, 100, 148, 158, 172, I*c*, *VI, 19, 22,
23, 24, 25, 26, 27, 28, 29, 30, 31,* made
of real feathers, 98, of velvet, 98, dead,
30, 117, 213, bird-killing, 109, 120,
percentage of bird cards, 188
Birmingham, 83
BIRN Bros., 83, 263
birthday card, 9, 62
black-and-gold design, 151, *108*
black-and-white, 38, 151, 192
black-background cards, 35, 77, *82, 88,*
121, fashionable black visiting cards,
172
black beetles, 164, -bird, 159, -stockings,
94
blankets, slices of, 164
blanks, embossed paper, 45, 48
BLASHFIELD, E. H., 79, 216, 235
blessings, 203
blind man buff, *14, 55,* 168, 234
blockmaker, effects of craftsmanship of,
38–9
block-making, 97
blood of Christ, 110
BLOODGOOD, R. F., 79, 216
" Bloody Sunday ", 192
bloomers, *XIIIc,* 131
BLOT, Paris, 86
blue, and white damozel, 152, *108,* china,
31, -birds, 162, 165, -cloak, *155,*
-decorated sachets, 90, -lovers' knot,
17, sky, 146, -streamer with inscriptions, 114, -tit, 217
boar's head, 17, *43, 63,* 121, 122
boasting of mechanisation, 112
boat houses, Putney, 73
boats, sailing, 133, *69,* 221–2, 234, 243
BOERNER, J. A., *59,* 127
BOGNARD, J., Junior, 83, 263
BOGUE, D., 65
Bohemia, 125
" Bohen, Miss ", 42
bold outlines and flat colours, style of, 33
BONASSE-LEBEL & Fils and Massin, 86,
263
bonnets, 106, 130, 272
BOOK SOCIETY, 83, 263
bookbinding, embossing methods of, 68
booklets, 85, *101, 124,* 148, 155, 224
books and magazines for children, 159
booksellers, 72
" Miss Bookworm ", 42
border ornaments, 199
Boston, Mass., 74–5, 80–1, 83, 199, *XId*
botanical works, 145–6
bottles, of wine, 120, imitation, 169,
153
bough, kissing, 128, of mistletoe, 148

BOUGHTON, G. H., 69, 71, 216
" Bouncing Billy ", 42
bouquets, 88, 119, *167,* 170, 172, 174,
175
bow, 158, silk, 95–6
bowl, wassail, 63
BOWER, Alfred, 73, 216
boxed cards, 171, *157–8,* 273
" Boxer, Madam ", 42
Boxing, *115,* 153, -Day activity, 26
boy, *V.,*—meets girl, *XIa, XII,* little boys,
57, 82–3, 60, 87, 125, 126, 131, 136,
147, 170, 174, 201, 205, the boy Jesus
playing with bird, 20, -scouts, 155
bracken, fronds of, 112
BRADLEY, E., 11, 215, 217, 273
BRADSHAW & BLACKLOCK, 39, 61, 245,
263
braid, red, 104
Branches, " All over the World ", Bank
of Providence, 85, of laurel or olive,
17, lettering composed of, *XII,* 227
brass card, 184
brawn, Christmas, 120
braziers, 122, *193*
bread, 193, 195
breakfast, Christmas, 106
BREWS, Dame Elizabeth, 46
BRIDGES, F., 79, 214, 217
BRINDLEY, I., 81
bringing in the yule log, 168
Britain, 86, Britannia's Valentine, 191
British, 110, art dealers' use of *quodlibet,*
24, Dominions, 74, folklore, 103–4,
officer, *196,* print, 105, publishers, 199,
Royal Family, three generations of,
78, tradition in art, 98, Tommy, 166
British Museum, 2, 7, 9, 12, 14, 21, *83,*
97, 110, 116, 143, 144
broadcast speech, Her Majesty's first, 70
broadsides or broadsheets, 3, 265, Christmas, 28, 278, left at door, 26–7, -seller,
27, printers, 265, 266, 271, 278,
279
Bromley Hall, 200
BROOKS, 83, 264
BROOKS, P., 200, 253
BROWNE, G., 68, 217
brushes, 152, 204
BRYAN, A., 73, 191, 217
bric-a-brac, 72, *108,* 152
bricks, 141
bridge, hump-backed, *162,* 176
bubbles, soap, *87*
BUCH, Meissner & —, 84, 275
Budapest, 149
Buddhist scriptures, 32
buds, 172
BUFFORD's H. Son, 83, 264
bulldogs, 153, boxing, *115*
bullfinch, 217
bumper, Christmas, 121
bunch, of mistletoe, *34,* of violet scraps,
165
Bungay, inhabitants of, 26
burgher, *12*
BURKE, T. H., 83, 264

285

INDEX

N

INDEX

purse cards, *160*, 171–2
Putney, 73
PYE, J., watchman, 26
PYNE, T., 74, 241

Q

quack (doctor), 154
Quebec, *27*, 108
quill pen, 106
Quiver of Love, The, 48, 227
quodlibet, 10, 24–5, 217, modern, *37*, 116

R

R.,D.L. (see De La Rue)
R., M. E.,
rabbit, *45*
racing car, early, *69*
radio, *70*
RAGG, Isaac, Bellman, 26
railway, *1d*, *60*, *61*, 125, 131, 166
rain, *29*
RALSTON, J. Mc. L., 74, 242
RANA, Maharaja, 193
RAPHAEL, 97, 143
rationing, 195
rattles, 141
rats, 154
razors, 164
Recorders, of the Past and Coming Year, The, 213
records, gramophone, 184
red, background, *XIc*, 77, 114–5, berries, 110, 171, cloth as fire symbol, 104, double pink, 119, flag on roads, 133, heart, *196*, ink, 195, nose, *143*, 165, rose, *153*, 169, rose bud, 119
Red Cross, British, *112*, 152
REDFERN GALLERY, 97
REDGRAVE, R., 7
reduction in taxation on account of Christmas cards, 60
reform, of social evils, 137, Reformation, 20, 22
Regent's Park, 100
regimental, *27*, 107–8
religious, *80*, *81*, 83, 84, 85, 110, 138–9, *169–170*, 175, 185–90, 187–95, 200, 276, 282
RELIGIOUS TRACT SOCIETY, 85, 187, 278
reprints of the first Christmas card, 15
retail, market, 28
Return from Bathing, 54
reunions, family, 138
reverse, decorations, 77, of transparency card, *152*, 170
reward cards, 40, 62, 188
Reynard the Fox, 7
ribbons, 153, 172, 227
RIBEISEN, 20
Richmond, 73, 83, Virginia, U.S.A., 193
RICKATSON, O., 74, 242
RILEY, J. W., 200, 259

RIMMEL, E., 40, 169, 218, 263, 278
RITTER, P. E., *62*, 132, 243
river, of milk and honey, *8*
RIVIERE, B., 84
roads, 130, 133, 189
Roast, Beef, 121, mice, *113*, turkey, 107
ROBERTSON, P., 74, 243
robin, *Ic*, *18*, *22*, *24*, *25*, *26*, *30*, *31*, 39, 43, 45, 77, 88, 98–107, 156, 168, 171, 221–2
Robin Hood & the Blackbird, set, *130*, 158–9, 228, 257
Robinson Crusoe, 147
ROCHAT, F., 200, 259
ROCK Bros., 54, 279
rocking horse, *175*, 179
rocks, 149
rococo, Victorian, 93, 96
ROLPH, SMITH & Co., 85, 279
Roman, mythology, 30, origins of the language of flowers, 118, scenery, *20* 43, wall decoration, 77
romantic, 128
Rome, 17, *20*, 43, 216
RONNER, H., 74, 243
rose, *17*, *28*, *114*, 118, *163*, 166, *167*, 173–4, 176, 180, 203, 228–9
rosemary, *43*, 122
ROSSETTI, D. G., 11, 31, 108
ROTHE, H., 85, 279
Round Tower, Windsor Castle, *131*, 161
rounded edges card, *189*
rowing boats, *62*, 131–2
ROWLINSON, Sir H., 71, 243
Roxbury, 74
Royal Academy, (R.A.), 15, 69, 70, 84, 149, *190*, 200, — series, 70, 71, 76, *103*, 222, 232, 281
Royal Air Force (R.A.F.), 136, 197, — Canadian Air Force, 197, 258
Royal Family, British, cards for the, 70, 213, 216, 225, 229, 236, 249, cards made by members of the — when they were children, 131–5, 160–2
Royal Society of British Artists (R.B.A.), Suffolk St. Galleries, 73
Royal Society of Painter Etchers and Engravers (R.E.), 68
RUBENS, 25
ruined columns, 171
RUSKIN, J., 74, 92, 143–4, 225, 238, 242
Russia, 24, 105, 125, Russian, 213
RUST CRAFT Co., 5, 166, 199, 279
RUST, F., 199, 259
rustic trellis, *1*, *2*, *6*, *7*, 10, 13
RYLAND, H., 67, 243

S

S., B.D. (B. D. Sigmund), 74, 243, 245
S., J. F. & Co. (Schipper & Co.), 85, 263, 279, 280
Sabine, goddess, 17
sachet cards, 90, 169, " surprise sachets ", 273

299

T

INDEX

V

VALENTINE, J. & Sons, Ltd., 281
valentine, 16, *17–8*, 29, 30, 41, 45–52,, 62, 67, 69, 74–5, 78–9, 85, 89, *99*, 101, *102*, 105, 107, 122, 143–4, 148, *159*, 163, 165, 168, 170, 177, 191, 202–3
VALLET, L., 196
VALLET, MINOT & Co., *83*, 86, 281
VAN DYKE, H., 200, 206–7, 259
VAN WINKLE, Rip, 137
Varden, Dolly, *101*, 148
vases of flowers, 189
VEDDER, E., 78, *105*, 150, 248
velvet, figures, *Jacket*, *19*, 88, birds, 98, 184
veneer, 184
Verdant Green, 11, 232
vestas, 91
VICTORIA, Queen, 27, *40*, 62, *150*, 169, 192, 198, 276, 281, cards, chosen by her, 70–1, 216, sent and inscribed by her, *40*, *149–52*, *154–5*
Victoria, winged figure of, 18–9
Victoria and Albert Museum, *5*, *6*, *7*, 14, 173, 182, *183*
Victorian Era, exhibition (1897), 67
Vienna, Viennese, 26, 28, 218, 238, 241
vine leaves, *1*, *2*, 13
violets, 173
Virgin Mary, *169*, *170* (see also Madonna, Mother, etc.)
visiting cards, *20*, *21*, 39, 43, size Christmas cards, *43*, *53*, 62, 67, 89, 96, 166
visiting, at Christmas, 12, 59, 127, season for, 124
VIZETELLY, H., 62–3, 122, 225
vocabulary of the Language of Flowers, 203
" voiced " cards (of 1878), *26*, 106
volcano, 181
VOLK, D., 79, 248
VOLLAND, P. F. Company, 199, 281
Von Zur WESTEN, 22, 207–8
vulgarisation of Christmas cards, 112

W

W.L. (L. Waterford), 71, *93*, 248–9
W., L., (L. Watt), 74, 82, *84*, 248–9
WAIN, L., 153, 248
WAINWRIGHT, W. J., 71, 249
waits, 127, 218, 223
Waldorf-Astoria Hotel, 235
WALKER, E., *66*, 135, 249
WALKER, F. S., 68, 249
WALKER, J. & Co., 85, 281
wall, calendars, *9*, 22, flowers, 66
wallet, 171
WALTERS, G. S., *64*, 132, 249
WARD, A., 74, 249
WARD GALLERY, 97, 281
WARD, J., 188

WARD, M., *VI*, *24*, *29*, 32, 34, *37–8*, *41*, 58, 64, 66–9, 76, 78, 89, 90, 93, 95, 97, *99*, 112–3, 116, *116–7*, *124*, 125, *127*, 144, 157–9, *162*, 174, 281
WARD, W. H., 66
wartime cards, 195–7, 217
Warwickshire, 103
Washington, D.C., 78
wassail, bowl, 63, -ing of fruit-trees, 17, 63
watchmen's bills, 128
water-colours, *IIIa*, *b*, 72, *96*, 132, *132*, 137, 161–2
Water Colour Society, old, 225
waterfall, 181
WATERFORD, LOUISA, Marchioness of, 71 *93*, 248–9
watering places, 53
water poet, 128
WATT, L., 74, 82, *84*, 248–9
WATTS, G. F., *93*, 249
Wayside Caterers, 122, *193*
WEATHERLY, F. E., 200, 261
WEBSTER, T., 7, 10, 249
WEEDON, A. W., 74, 249
WEIR, J. A., 79, 250
WEITENKAMPF, F., *V*, 80, 208, 223, 250
WELDON, C. D., 79, 250
Welsh, 196, *197*
Wenceslaus, Good King, 125
WESTALL, R., 67
WESTEN, Von Zur, *XII–III*, *XXII*, 22, 207, 208
WHEELER Brothers, 85, 282
WHEELER, D., *XIb*, 78, 150, 250
WHEELER, W. Jun., 85, 282
wheels, 104
whiskers, 65, 202
WHISTLER, J. McNeill, 8, 73
White Christmas, *46*, *53*, 122
WHITE, G., 4–6, 8, 11–2, 36, 61, 66–70, 72–3, 79, 84, 93, 99–100, 112–4, 164, *188*, *190*, 198, 216, 228–9
WHITLAW, H. M., 203, 261
WHITNEY, G. C. & Co., 45, 49, 75, 85, 220, 282
WHITNEY, O. E., 78, 250
WHYMPER, A., 82, 250
wicket basket, *66*, 135
WIGGINS, K. D., 200, 261
wild animals, 155
wild ducks, 108–9
WILENSKI, R. H., 143–4
WILHELM, II of Germany, see William II *64*, 132
WILHELMINA, Queen of Holland, *36*, 250
WILLIAM II, *64*, 132
WILLIAM, the Conqueror, 225
WILMORE, M., 5, 251
WILSON, E., 74, 251
WILSON, T. W., 34, 67, 251
WILLOUGHBY HODGSON, Mrs., 47, 208
windows lighted to show the way to the Child, 128
WINDSOR, 70, 73, 128, *131*, 161, 192, 229
WINDSOR, The Duke of, 4, 236
WINDSOR, J., & Sons, 182, 276
Windsor Magazine, The, 69

303

INDEX

Windsor Street, Putney, 73
wine-bottle, *45*, legs, 65
WINGFIELD-STRATFORD, E., 146, 208
Winter Cherries, 149
Winter, Solstice, 20, 110, 116, sports, 137
wintry scenes, *Id*, *37*, 84, 88, 147, 167, 215–6
WIRTHS BROTHERS & OWEN, 85, 263, 282
Wit and Humour, etc. (by C. H. Bennett), 64
witches, 110
Witley, Surrey, 64
wolves, 158, 223
women, *4*, *XIb*, *XIIIc*, 65, 68, 79, *84*, *106*, 108, 121, 123, *123*, 131, 146, 148–52, 154, 184, 189, 192, 196, 199, 200, 207, 242
Woman's Magazine, 200
Wonderland, 168, 253
wood-block, 20, 38, 97, -cut, 21, 26, 28, 32–3, 50, 78, 97, 139, -engraving, 57, 123, 192, 195
wooden crosses later replaced by gold and silver, 113
Worcester, Mass., U.S.A., 79, 85, V
WORDSWORTH, W., 53, 173
World War, I, 124, 195–6, *196*, *197*, II, 190, *201*
wren, 103–5, 108

X

" Xmas ", 188
" Mrs. " Xmas, *54*, 126

Y

yacht, *149*, 170, 232, 280, Royal — Britannia, 65
YATES, 85, 282
Ye Olde Christmasse, 116
YEAMES, W. F., 71, *103*, 148, 251
" yellery-greenery ", 82
Yorkshire, 129
Young Man's Valentine Writer, The, 48
Youthful Graces, set, 146
yule, log, 17, 63, 218, 235, -tide poets, 199

Z

zinc plate, 38, 75
Zurich, *11*, 25

304